★ ★

WHEN GOVERNMENTS COME TO WASHINGTON

★ ★

WHEN GOVERNMENTS COME TO WASHINGTON

GOVERNORS ★ MAYORS ★ AND
INTERGOVERNMENTAL LOBBYING

by DONALD H. HAIDER

★ ★

[FP] THE FREE PRESS ☆ ☆ ☆ ☆ ☆ ☆ ☆ ☆
A Division of Macmillan Publishing Co., Inc. ☆ ☆ ☆ ☆ ☆ ☆ ☆ ☆ ☆
New York ☆ ☆ ☆ ☆ ☆ ☆ ☆ ☆ ☆ ☆ ☆ ☆ ☆ ☆ ☆ ☆ ☆ ☆ ☆
Collier Macmillan Publishers ☆ ☆ ☆ ☆ ☆ ☆ ☆ ☆ ☆ ☆ ☆ ☆ ☆ ☆ ☆
London ☆

★ ★

The Free Press
A Division of Macmillan Publishing Co., Inc.
866 Third Avenue, New York, N.Y. 10022

Collier-Macmillan Canada Ltd.

Library of Congress Catalog Card Number: 73–17643

Printed in the United States of America

printing number
1 2 3 4 5 6 7 8 9 10

Library of Congress Cataloging in Publication Data

Haider, Donald H
    When governments come to Washington: governors,
mayors, and intergovernmental lobbying.

    Bibliography: p.
    1. Federal government--United States. 2. Governors
--United States. 3. Mayors--United States. 4. County
officials and employees--United States. 5. Lobbying.
I. Title.
JK325.H24   353.9'29   73-17643
ISBN 0-02-913370-X

CONTENTS

LIST OF
TABLES AND FIGURES

★ ★ ★

LIST OF ABBREVIATIONS

A-85	Bureau of the Budget Circular Number A-85
A-95	Bureau of the Budget Circular Number A-95
AASHO	American Association of State Highway Officials
ACIR	Advisory Commission on Intergovernmental Relations
AFL–CIO	American Federation of Labor–Congress of Industrial Organizations
AMA	American Municipal Association (changed to NLC)
BCA	Better Communities Act
BOB	Bureau of the Budget (changed to OMB)
CAA	Community Action Agency
CAP	Community Action Program
CEA	Council of Economic Advisors
CED	Committee for Economic Development
CERC	Chief Executive Review and Comment
COGS	Councils of Government
COSGO	Council of State Governments
DOT	Department of Transportation
DSG	Democratic Study Group
FHA	Federal Housing Administration
FHW	Federal Highway Administration
FRC	Federal Regional Councils
FY	Fiscal Year
GNP	Gross National Product
HEW	Department of Health, Education, and Welfare
HTF	Highway Trust Fund
HUD	Department of Housing and Urban Development
IBA	Investment Bankers Association of America
ICA	Intergovernmental Cooperation Act
ICMA	International City Managers Association
IDB	Industrial Development Bonds
IRS	Internal Revenue Service
LEAA	Law Enforcement Assistance Administration
NACO	National Association of Counties
NAHRO	National Association of Housing and Redevelopment Officials
NASBO	National Association of State Budget Officials
NGC	National Governors Conference
NHC	National Housing Conference
NLC	National League of Cities
NSF	National Science Foundation
OEO	Office of Economic Opportunity

OEP	Office of Emergency Planning
PACH	Public Administration Clearing House
PIGS	Public Interest Groups
POAC	Public Officials Advisory Council
PORGS	Public Official Organizations
RGA	Republican Governors Association
SEC	Securities and Exchange Commission
SMSA	Standard Metropolitan Statistical Area
SUR	State, Urban, Rural Highway Programs
TOPICS	Traffic Operations Program To Increase Capacity and Safety
UMTA	Urban Mass Transit Act (Administration)
USCM	United States Conference of Mayors

PREFACE

This study is about government interest groups operating at the national level. Its principal focus is upon various national associations of chief executives such as governors, mayors, and county officials. These officials are the principal heads of nonfederal government units and most belong to organizations formed around their office and government level: the National League of Cities (NLC), the United States Conference of Mayors (USCM), the National Governors' Conference (NGC), the National Association of Counties (NACO), and the Council of State Governments (COSGO). These organizations are referred to as the government interest groups rather than as their more familiar Washington acronym—PIGS—which stands for Public Interest Groups (and is appropriately associated, by some, with the four-legged animal because of the groups' insatiable appetite for federal funds).

The study dates essentially from 1966, the period when these officials were organized sufficiently to mobilize sustained pressure activities and demands upon the national government. Case studies with the exception of revenue sharing are drawn from the period 1965–1969, although events and supportive examples relating to the cases extending into the 1970s are included.

The purpose of this research involves several distinctive but related aims. It is a narrative of the history and activities of the government interest groups through various stages of development. It will investigate the collective behavior among governors, mayors, and county officials as manifested in the national interest groups to which they belong as well as the cooperative and competitive behavior between the groups. It will examine the roles and functions that government interest groups perform, the demands they articulate, their influence on federal policy, and their external strategies as means of implementing national policies favorable to their members.

A study of these groups has particular relevance to research about elected executives by providing deeper insight into the multiple roles assumed, audiences appealed to, targets of their influence strategies, and channels through which they work at the national level. It also provides insight into the basic differences among chief executives from the same government level as well as the broad range of competition between them, individually and collectively, in dealing with their federal constituency.

The evolutionary development of American federalism is not the principal focus of this study. However, to the extent that aggregate trends and activities on all government levels help structure many of the demands, pressures, and influences upon subnational chief executives, it will be dealt with. In focusing upon governors, mayors, and county officials in their relations with higher governmental levels, one must deal with the complexities of the federal system. Thus the study has relevance as well for students of the American federal system, a dynamic system undergoing constant change and requiring new insights. Indeed, the task of describing and analyzing the American federalist structure is a never-ending challenge. New methods of observation supply new data and new findings. New actors and emergent forces produce new processes and alter outcomes among these actors.

The absence of significant research on elected chief executives' behavior, activities, and roles has been comparable, until recently, to the marked lack of interest in state and—to a degree—local government. Rather than being a lost world or "Dullsville," as it once was considered, the study of state and urban political systems now has moved to center stage of political research.

In spite of this renewed interest, the comparative study of governors, mayors, and county officials—statehouses, courthouses, and city halls— in the execution of their multiple responsibilities as chief executive officers of general-purpose units of government remains one of the least explored areas of political inquiry. Moreover, research on American intergovernmental relations (federal, state, local), according to some knowledgeable observers, has not yet entered the mainstream of the political science discipline. Combining the comparative study of chief executives and the relation of these elected public officials to the federal government, one finds little in the way of current information or systematic research. This seems particularly disturbing at a time when state and local governments are experiencing severe fiscal problems, enormous growth and reform, and increased dependency upon higher government levels for programmatic and fiscal direction. Thus this study involves a focus upon both chief executives and intergovernmental relations, and it thereby may fill a void in research and inquiry on public officials and the federal system.

The preliminary emphasis, then, is these interest groups' internal characteristics: their transformation through various stages of development from ad hoc groups manifesting little membership interaction and narrow focuses of attention to well-organized and highly vocal pressure groups operating to effect a broad range of federal policies. More importantly, attention will be given to the groups' external behavior and the scope of the activities, including the acquisition of federal funds and greater executive control of federally assisted programs operating in their jurisdictions. The study endeavors to relate internal and external group pressures, particularly those exerted by the changing forces of federalism in the 1960s and 1970s, to group cleavages that affect the relations among government levels as well as among elected officeholders.

In raising these issues, one confronts the relationships between the national government and subnational governments, especially the federal grant-in-aid system which has made federalism ever more into a vast marble cake of shared functions and responsibilities among government levels. This system also has increasingly made state and local governments into clients of the federal government and their chief executives into lobbyists. The cooperative model of the American federal system, widely adhered to, holds that all levels of government significantly participate in all activities; that in theory and practice, a partnership exists among government levels—through distributed powers and shared functions—which necessitates cooperation with one another to achieve common goals; and that in the formulation, enactment, and implementation of major domestic programs, a significant influence is exercised by public officials on all government levels.

In spite of cyclical trends in American federalism between centralization and decentralization, it is further held that the system inherently strives toward balance between central national dominance and the countervailing forces of subnational flexibility and discretion. It assumes that the advantages of the American noncentralized, nondisciplined party structure and prolific interest-group activity are the protection of state and local interests which operate upon and are reflected at the federal level. Yet one must ask: To what extent does the history of public policy development at the federal level during the past decade offer credence to this theory? Does this explanation hold for governors, mayors, and county officials, who, after all, are the embodiment of these subnational units?

The federal grant system, with its more than five hundred separate programs, helps finance specific activities that cut across government levels. It offers little support directly to general-purpose governments to determine their own mix of services and priorities. It is generally acknowledged that this system has left little discretion to state-local elected officials to exercise decision making and gain control over the management and administration of these programs. The functional ties surrounding federal grants which link Congress, executive agencies and their state-local counterparts, and grant support groups together have created a system rife with conflict and tensions between these interests and those of state-local executives. Thus a major concern of this study is the federal grant system and the reaction to it by governors, mayors, and county officials. This involves the competition and interplay between the functional interests of Congress and the federal bureaucracy on the one hand with the spatial or geopolitical concerns of chief executives on the other. These tensions and conflicts have neither been approached from the perspective of subnational chief executives nor been included in a view of intergovernmental policy making.

This study will emphasize attempts by the government groups to affect national policy making and the extent to which they have been successful. Much more needs to be known about heads of state and local governments and their relations with their federal constituency. These officials are one set among many government and nongovernment claimants of subnational origin making substantial inputs into policies. They are one among many governmental interest groups and professional associations seeking to enhance their power, autonomy, and claims at the national level. What is important, however, is to determine the extent and the reasons for their efforts. What have state and local government chief executives done to strengthen their relations with the Washington community and what impact has this had? In practice, to what extent have mayors, governors, and county officials, responsible and accountable for the execution of public policies, become active participants in national decision making? To what extent are their demands frustrated by would-be or actual competitors for influence, including Congress and the bureaucracy, which hold many of the resources these groups seek? What are their relations with the White House and to what extent has the President become an ally of his fellow chief executives in dealing with Congress and the bureaucracy?

This research may shed some light on these and other questions. It also might provide better understanding of how political parties and elected officeholders maintain the federal system and preserve the role, access, and bargaining position among officials on different government levels. While the decentralized party system and structure may provide governors, mayors, and country officials, who are also key party leaders, resources with which to bargain in pursuit of their demands, it may not automatically confer other benefits which are perhaps more important in effecting policy. Thus one may ask: To what extent do specialized skills, expertise, information, knowledge of the political process, leadership, and other political resources affect the fortunes of the government groups at the federal level? To what extent does government or the official status of these groups aid their cause in competition with other groups? And to what degree might the activity of government groups resemble that of other public and private lobbying organizations?

Also, this study will explore the channels, tactics, and resources that government groups use to influence government decision making. Interest groups generally seek to affect government decisions through a multitude of coercive and persuasive techniques, of which lobbying is the most frequently although not the only tactic employed. Lobbying, therefore, will receive particular attention. To what degree is it a new activity by subnational chief executives, and how has it changed over the past decade? In what individuals, groups, institutions, and at what times does each of the groups invest its resources in lobbying, and how do they do it? While it is assumed that officials themselves frequently bring pressure upon each other and private interests, the nature of lobbying with officialdom has not been fully explored or its significance widely affirmed.

Finally, this study is concerned with public policies. It does not begin with the assumption that urban, state or county problems or demands can be considered a distinct field of public policy at the federal level, with an identifiable structure, a predictable set of participants, and characteristic patterns of legislative and executive behavior. On the contrary, it is assumed that American government has no single process that produces all policies but several different policies. Similarly, with Congress and the executive organized largely on the basis of government functions that cut across geopolitical boundaries, most government policies incorporate several levels of government in their design and implementation. Therefore this study is concerned both with policy and process and the interrelationship between them as they bear upon the articulation and resolution of demands by aggregates of state-local chief executives at the federal level.

To be sure, the study of government interest groups is not entirely new. Louis Brownlow paved the way years ago through his personal testimony to their origin and purposes. Later writers on the subject, however, tended to focus upon one particular group in its intergovernmental dimensions— the mayors, the governors, or the country officials—to the exclusion of the others. Each of these volumes is a valuable resource. But they are generally dated, incomplete, and, notably, inattentive to the collaboration and competition among subnational chief executives and the groups to which they belong. Even this work does not fully account for the constantly changing arena of intergovernmental lobbying. Both the International City Managers' Association (ICMA) and the National Legislative Conference were initially excluded because they had not yet emerged as a sustained Washington lobby. But by the early 1970s they had become recognized PIG members, bringing up the number from five to seven.

Recent events between completion of the manuscript and publication require a brief updating. The USCM-NLC's growth has slowed while its policies and committee structures have become more integrated. Intergroup collaboration begun under the State, County, and City Service Center has been continued in other forms, especially the New Coalition of State, County, and City Officials. Democratic governors and mayors have joined forces in working for a "veto proof" 94th Congress in 1975, one in which Democrats have sufficient votes to override presidential vetoes. New Federalism is alive but floundering. With his deepening involvement in the Watergate affair, President Nixon is encumbered by a personal survival strategy while his administration struggles with rising inflation and unemployment. The President's $304 billion budget proposed for FY 1975 provides for a 7 percent increase in aid to state and local government over FY 1974, an amount deficient from the recipients' perspective in accounting for inflation and for new responsibilities required by New Federalism.

Manpower revenue sharing became the first of Mr. Nixon's special revenue-sharing proposals to pass Congress. However, some view it as being a bloc grant; to others, it constitutes old wine in new bottles. Vast changes are under way in Congress, propelled by younger, more aggressive members who are quickly replacing their seniors. Reorganization of the congressional committee structure will likely produce further transformation of the grant-in-aid system. OMB continues to bear much of the burden for implementing New Federalism. Its Field Activities Division has relied on multiple strategies to simplify, consolidate, and otherwise rationalize the grant system as well as coordinate interagency activities. It has recorded some success in representing the views of state-local officials at all policy levels to the executive. These developments all the more suggest that the government groups and their relations with Washington will continue to undergo vast changes in the years ahead.

This work is the product of nearly four years of research on the subject. It never would have been completed without the assistance of colleagues in academia, the cooperation of practitioners, and the continual encouragement of my wife, Jean. My associates at Columbia University who commented upon several drafts of this work deserve a special word of appreciation: Professors Harvey C. Mansfield, Sr., Bruce L. R. Smith, Robert H. Connery, and the late Wallace S. Sayre. Professor Alan K. Campbell, Dean of the Maxwell School of Syracuse University, and David Walker of the Advisory Commission on Intergovernmental Relations also assisted me at various stages of completion. The Congressional Fellowship Program of the American Political Science Association, which afforded me a first-hand experience of Congress, deepened my understanding and appreciation of the political process. I wish to acknowledge my gratitude to Senator Edward M. Kennedy and his staff, in whose offices I served in 1967–1968, and to The Brookings Institution where, as a guest scholar, I pursued the greater part of this research. To the more than one hundred persons who were interviewed, too numerous to mention, I hope that the final product justifies their generous giving of time and sharing of insights. In particular, I wish to thank the executive directors of the government interest groups for their assistance and cooperation: Messrs. Patrick Healy and his successor at the National League of Cities, Allen Pritchard, John

Gunther of the United States Conference of Mayors, NACO's Bernie Hillenbrand, and Charles Byrley of the National Governors' Conference.

Finally, I cannot help but single out two persons whose support and efforts brought this work to fruition. I wish to acknowledge the personal contribution of my late father, who remains my first and finest teacher of politics. His profound convictions that public office is a public trust and that the nation's political leadership—its chief executives—must be strengthened if our political system is to work, have been the guiding force throughout this study. Also my wife, Jean, has had to bear the burdens of evenings and weekends with a husband preoccupied by his writing. Without her patience and editorial assistance, this book would never have materialized.

Donald Haider
Evanston, Illinois
April 1974

1
THE GOVERNMENT
INTEREST GROUPS
★ ★ ★

It is possible to trace federal-city relations back to the pre-New Deal period and also to establish patterns in cooperation among the nation's mayors.[1] However, for those interested in the collective activities and influence of mayors in the nation's capital, history begins with the Presidency of Franklin D. Roosevelt and his close relations with the United States Conference of Mayors.

The national elections of 1928 and 1932 had a formidable impact on the Democratic party's composition and direction. They created abiding loyalties among major portions of city dwellers, who became the underpinning and majority constituency within the party. Mindful of his growing urban constituency, President Roosevelt wove together a national coalition comprising urban ethnic groups, organized labor and workers, and the nation's large-city mayors. Some of these mayors would fall from the President's good graces for unpardonable indiscretions and disloyalty, but the great majority remained his most loyal and persistent allies. They became the political and vital administrative links between the federal government and the crippled urban centers.

"The states would not govern the cities, nor permit the cities to govern themselves." Thus the late Charles Merriam summarized the condition plaguing the cities in that period. Unresponsive, often incapacitated state governments and uncooperative, anti-New Deal governors in time reinforced President Roosevelt's own pragmatic instincts to forge flexible political machinery to cope with the national economic crisis during the Depression years. Federal-city relations grew out of political necessity for bypassing, wherever possible, recalcitrant state officials and bureaucracies

[1] See Daniel J. Elazar, "Urban Problems and the Federal Government," *Political Science Quarterly,* 82:520-525, December 1967.

in order to deal expeditiously with the "creatures of the states," the needful cities and their inhabitants.

Indeed, much of Roosevelt's domestic program, supported by the mayors and their allies, was directed at major populated areas as a strategy to maximize the impact of public works and relief programs and to minimize the time required for implementation.[2] Consequently, new municipal instrumentalities and machinery were established practically overnight from 1932 on, as federal funds and programs became the lifeline from Washington for millions of people. To deal with massive unemployment, the public and private welfare collapse, and the widespread economic paralysis so pervasive in urban areas, the President made unprecedented use of federal spending and regulatory powers to establish direct federal-city ties. Prevailing constitutional norms and existing traditions were virtually abandoned. A new phase in American federalism emerged during the Depression years whereby the cities were elevated to partners with the states and became their rivals as well.[3] The enlarged federal system readily sustained these new structures, links, and support groups connecting Washington and the cities. These prospered and multiplied in time, diminishing only slightly for a brief period during the postwar recovery.

THE MAYORS

The key political group linking the President to his urban constituency, supportive of greater federal-urban ties, long on votes and long on programs at the time, was the United States Conference of Mayors (USCM). Formally established in Washington, D.C., with Roosevelt's active involvement, the USCM became the first urban lobby of elected public officials to base itself in the nation's capital.

Initially comprising mayors from the 100 largest cities, the USCM convened for the first time shortly before FDR's inauguration to adopt a constitution and elect officers. Mayor Frank Murphy of Detroit became the organization's president and the mayors of Boston, Minneapolis, and Chicago were elected as officers. The chief purpose of the newly formed organization, as stated in its constitution, was "safeguarding the interests of cities as they may be affected by national legislation." The Conference also set as its aims the effective interchange of information and experience between major cities and the fostering of "proper and adequate relations" between the federal government and the cities.[4] In effect, the USCM rose

[2] Roscoe C. Martin, "Washington and the Cities," in the *Federal Government and the Cities*, George Washington University, Washington, D.C., 1961, p. 10.

[3] Roscoe C. Martin, *The Cities and the Federal System*, Atherton, New York, 1965.

[4] Robert H. Connery and Richard H. Leach, *The Federal Government and Metropolitan Areas*, Harvard University Press, Cambridge, 1960, pp. 74–75.

out of crisis conditions, with members strongly bound in the common goal of assisting the President and federal agencies in their urban relief efforts.

The Conference's specific goals as developed in the 1930s remain largely intact today: to expand direct federal-city programs, increase federal fiscal support for these programs, gain federal assumption of specific programs like public assistance, establish federal intrumentalities and safeguards for maintaining urban fiscal solvency—like tax-exemption on municipal bonds—and enhance the autonomy of cities as general-purpose units of government.

The USCM developed as a scion of another municipal group, the American Municipal Association (AMA), which had been officially formed in 1924 under John Stutz. It was founded by the ten existing state associations of municipalities and had operated out of Chicago since the 1930s. The AMA assisted the Conference in its infancy, lending the services of its staff and Paul Betters, its executive director. This cooperative venture was initiated out of the mutual expectation that integrative activities between the two associations might develop and flourish.[5]

But this was not to be the case. The AMA dismissed Betters after it was decided that he was devoting too much time to the Conference and not maintaining separate accounting for both organizations. The AMA's loss was the Conference's gain. USCM President Fiorello LaGuardia reinstated Betters as the Conference's executive director in 1935. This, indeed, ended for many years cooperation between the two mayors' organizations.

The USCM established offices on Jackson Place, across the street from the White House, where Betters and LaGuardia enjoyed considerable access to the Roosevelt administration on policies affecting the cities. The LaGuardia-Roosevelt friendship was a highly amicable one that lasted for a decade, joining the new organization of mayors to the highest policy-making circles within the national government. For at least its first decade of operation, the Conference was closely identified with LaGuardia, the New York City anti-Tammany fusion mayor and former congressman. It was a highly personal organization, with LaGuardia calling the shots and Betters conducting most of the lobbying. Former New York City Mayor Robert Wagner said of LaGuardia and the Conference, "The Little Flower liked being President of the Conference almost as much as he liked being mayor of New York."[6] For eight of the ten years that the fiery LaGuardia headed the USCM, annual meetings were held in his own city and not Washington.

[5] For a general background history of the two organizations, see National League of Cities, "The National League of Cities and the U.S. Conference of Mayors: An NLC Staff Paper," Washington, D.C., 1967 (mimeographed).

[6] U.S. Conference of Mayors, Proceedings of the Thirty-Second Annual Meeting, Washington, D.C., 1965, pp. 4–5. For Roosevelt's dealings with La Guardia and Tammany leaders, see Edward J. Flynn, You're The Boss, Viking, New York, 1947.

The Conference attained a temporary preeminence among governmental interest groups during those formative years. This resulted from the mayors' solidarity, the breakdown in traditional governmental structures, and the multiple functions that the Conference was capable of performing. The mayors formed a ready-made support group and constituency for the ad hoc, often multiagency relief programs instituted under Roosevelt. With the assistance of Louis Brownlow's Public Administration Clearing House in Chicago, the Conference aided federal officials in gathering information about the magnitude of urban economic and social problems. The USCM also participated fully in the planning and implementation of hastily assembled federal public works and relief programs. It served as a conduit for information between mayors and Washington, facilitating city participation in the Federal Emergency Relief Administration, Civil Works Administration, and Works Progress Administration programs. By ensuring that the mayors and their cities made full use of federal relief funds, the Conference, led by Betters and LaGuardia, lobbied Congress successfully for the above's expansion and increased funding.[7]

The importance of the Conference's electoral and programmatic support for the President and the New Deal cannot be underestimated. It had long-term consequences for the organization both in its executive orientation and its activities. The substantial success which the USCM achieved in these earlier years has been amply attested to by Connery and Leach. "Perhaps no organization has ever started off with such initial success," they concluded. "The USCM had the advantage of offering municipal solidarity at a time of crisis and was directed from the first to securing and facilitating federal action."[8]

But success was short-lived, particularly in the politics of the postwar period. Once "Doctor Win-the-War" replaced "Doctor New Deal," President Roosevelt's concern for domestic recovery was subordinated to near complete preoccupation with his commander-in-chief duties. New Deal programs faded, many terminated, others collapsed into more modest efforts. The immediate postwar environment was highlighted by intense congressional debates over the federal government's involvement in the private sector as well as in areas reserved for traditional state and local activity.

From the 1940s through the early 1960s, for example, USCM activities centered primarily around support for public housing, slum clearance, and urban renewal programs. These housing programs, in effect, constituted the real core of federal-city relations in that they received more than half of all federal funds that flowed directly to the cities during this period.

---

[7] See generally Suzanne Farkas, *Urban Lobbying,* New York University Press, New York, 1970, Chap. 4.

[8] Connery and Leach, *The Federal Government . . .,* p. 76.

Housing legislation increasingly reflected an omnibus composition, embodying often incompatible constituencies. A panoply of interests and widely divergent groups developed, requiring a nexus of complicated and often shifting alliances for the successful articulation of their views. Large and small cities, mortgage bankers, savings and loan associations, real estate groups, contractors, veterans, farm groups, labor unions, and others all had tangible stakes in specific housing programs, methods of financing, and types of federal subsidies. The USCM had to cope not only with an expanded arena of competing actors but also with a hostile alliance led by Republicans during the 1950s—an alliance bent on phasing out all public housing and renewal programs. For the greater part of the Eisenhower administration, in fact, large-city mayors, mostly Democrats, were on the defensive, while the USCM was on a survival rather than expansion course.

In the fifties the USCM fell on bad times. Bereft of recognizable leadership as experienced under LaGuardia and with special White House access terminated, the organization was run largely as a one-man show by the then incapacitated Paul Betters. At this time the AMA reemerged as the more diversified, fiscally solvent, and more effective urban lobby. With forty state leagues of cities and several thousand members nationally, the Association underwent sweeping structural reforms in 1954, encompassing membership, activities, and overall goals. It relocated its Chicago headquarters in Washington, D.C., reflecting a policy shift away from state activities exclusively to a national orientation. It also changed its membership qualifications, permitting, for the first time, individual-city membership. In so doing the AMA not only entered into direct competition with the Conference for city membership but also became a rival as spokesman for city interests in the Washington community. The Association waxed while the Conference waned, particularly as the more bipartisan Association with its many Republican small- and medium-sized city mayors were accorded considerably more attention from a Republican administration than the large-city Democratic mayor group, the USCM.[9]

Resuscitation of the nearly moribund Conference began in the late 1950s. Paul Betters died in 1955, to be replaced by his brother Harry, who passed away three years later. Leadership fell to John Gunther, USCM's general counsel, who as a skilled Washington attorney with much experience on Capitol Hill began rebuilding the organization. Elections proved helpful to Gunther and large-city mayors. In Congress, the Democrats won a near landslide midterm victory in 1958, bringing into the Senate especially a handful of Democratic liberals with largely urban constituencies. The return of the Democrats to the White House in 1961 also provided a substantial boost to the organization. Several of President Kennedy's earliest supporters—like Daley (Chicago), Lee (New Haven),

9 Ibid., pp. 62–74.

Lawrence (Pittsburgh), and Celebrezze (Cleveland)—were or had been officers in the USCM, which carried the Conference back into prominence as a major spokesman for urban interests.

Consolidation

In spite of the basic differences between the two mayors' groups, a function not only of the size of their members' constituencies but more often philosophical cleavages on issues, similarities in their Washington activities came to outweigh dissimilarities. Overlapping leadership and membership, developing into an interlocking directorate between the two groups, provided considerable impetus to extensive policy collaboration and joint lobbying strategies. Interchange of staff, services, and information further propelled the two toward merger discussions. Both organizations came increasingly to solicit membership directly from the same cities, with virtually all Conference cities being directly or ·indirectly members of the Association (but not vice versa).

Between 1947 and 1973, the Association expanded its direct membership cities from 38 to more than 400. The AMA, or National League of Cities as it was to be called after changing its name in 1964, first extended membership to cities over 100,000 in population. Eligibility for direct membership was broadened in 1955 to state capitals, the ten largest cities in each state, and cities of 50,000 or more. In 1969 the National League of Cities (NLC) set minimum direct membership size at cities with 30,000 in population, as did the USCM. Nearly three-quarters of the nation's 700 or so cities whose population exceeds 30,000 belong to either the League, the Conference, or both. Thus the membership of the League is broad-based and includes nearly 15,000 municipalities that are members of the fifty state leagues in addition to more than 400 direct members who also belong to state leagues. Table 1 indicates the enormous growth in the two organizations over the past few years.

Resolving the matter of partnership between the two remained an issue of long-standing dispute. The Conference unsuccessfully advocated for some time that the two organizations restrict their activities to spheres of operation. The League, it said, should revert to its earlier role as a federation of state leagues of municipalities exclusively, concentrating its services on building strong state leagues and lobbying state legislatures. The USCM, on the other hand, would operate at the national level, speaking for all mayors on national issues. But the League was in Washington to stay, resolved to carry on its services and activities with or without the Conference's cooperation.[10] As a result, relations between them during the

10 "NLC Staff Paper," pp. 5–9; American Municipal Association, *Proceedings of the Thirty-eighth Annual Congress,* Washington, D.C., 1962, p. 7.

T-1 Direct City Member-
ship in the USCM and NLC,
1933–1970

Year	USCM	NLC
1933	101	—
1945	239	—
1955	290	52
1966	405	344
1970	473	410

Source: USCM-NLC.

1950s remained strained as they competed with one another over members, recognition, and policies.

Yet both came to recognize that the problems of cities could not be neatly categorized or divided between those concerns involving states and municipalities and those involving the federal government alone. The problems of cities locally and at the state level were the problems of cities nationally. The League had effectively demonstrated during the Eisenhower administration that a broad-based urban lobby comprising large and small cities alike, Democrats and Republicans, could be more effective than an organization comprising large-city mayors. The USCM reluctantly conceded that it needed the League in building legislative support inside and outside Congress.

Prior to 1968, the mayors' groups entered into merger negotiations on at least four occasions: in the Conference's formative period in the early 1930s; in the mid-1950s when Betters proposed disbanding the USCM to combine it with the League; when USCM President Richardson Dilworth and League President Don Hummel unsuccessfully submitted merger proposals to their respective boards in 1960; and in 1966 when Detroit Mayor Jerry Cavanagh headed both organizations simultaneously. Early merger attempts were thwarted essentially by what some considered to be the League's jealousy of the Conference. Similarly, post-1960 efforts were discouraged by the antipathy some large-city mayors held toward "small-town" mayors and the general feeling that their own political effectiveness would be compromised by joining forces with them.

But rising competition over mayors' allegiances and services between the two tended to minimize the potential effectiveness of both as lobbyists. "It often developed," recalled USCM's Gunther, "that we needlessly contacted the same mayors, same congressmen and their staffs on pending legislation rather than dividing the labor and coordinating our efforts."[11] The League traditionally saw itself as the "long-term strategist" for the cities in contrast to the USCM's more acquisitive, short-term activism, which was summed up by one member as being "Get what you can from the 'feds' for the cities and worry about the consequences later." The League's highly developed research and service operations enabled it to keep members informed on nationwide activities affecting municipalities. In contrast to the Conference's rather nominal services in these areas, the League offered timely bulletins on federal aid programs, ran a city inquiry service, published a monthly magazine since 1963 called *Nation's Cities*—with more than 50,000 subscribers, and provided in-depth coverage on major urban problems and developments. Competition with the NLC in such services, as the Conference acknowledged, would be costly and strategically unwise, while joint activities would likely be financially and programmatically rewarding.

Between 1965 and 1968 the USCM and NLC were brought closer together by both successful lobbying activities and collaborative service ventures which included housing and pollution-control legislation, a Joint Council on Urban Development for subscribing cities, and the creation of a federal aid coordinator outlet. However, no single intergovernmental development had greater consequences for the mayors' organizations than the establishment of the Federal Department of Housing and Urban Development (HUD) in 1965. The mayors had lobbied for a cabinet office for the cities since the late 1950s; but once having achieved such a department, they faced mounting pressure to begin speaking with a unified voice on federal policies affecting the cities. HUD was certainly sympathetic to their needs, but it was also wedded to other constituencies. This fact required all the more that the two mayors' groups settle their outstanding differences. The Banking and Currency Committees in Congress, which oversaw a considerable amount of urban-oriented legislation in housing and transportation, also demanded of the mayors greater unanimity in presenting their views before Congress. The mayors learned from the 1966 Model Cities legislation, which almost faltered due to their lack of complete support, that they would not only have to work much closer on policy matters but also collaborate with a broader spectrum of coalitions and interests than previously had been the case.

Thus consolidation was given its ultimate push by outside forces. In addition to HUD's creation, the outcome of mayoralty elections in 1968–1969 and the election of a Republican President had major importance. The flight from city hall through retirement and defeat decimated the Conference's leadership ranks, notably Lee of New Haven, Allen of Atlanta,

[11] John Gunther, private interview held at the USCM's office, Washington, D.C., January 3, 1969.

and Cavanagh of Detroit.[12] Both mayors' associations traditionally had to contend with a 10 to 15 percent turnover in mayors annually, but the late 1960s found an entire generation of more tenured national urban leaders departing from city hall. This left the USCM in direct competition with the League over the allegiance of the Lindsays, Stokeses, and a handful of virtual unknowns who had ascended to large-city leadership.

Both organizations responded to new social and political conditions in the late 1960s, especially national population shifts away from older central cities and from the Northeastern United States by drawing into their leadership ranks representatives from growing population regions and expanding urban centers in the South, Southwest, and West. The age, background, and partisan characteristics of the large-city mayors changed as well. Forty of the nation's fifty largest cities elected new mayors between 1965 and 1971, and these new leaders were not only younger than their predecessors but more articulate and aggressive in their assertiveness on behalf of cities. They tended to be less wedded to local party structures and less enamored of the brick-and-mortar programs that were provided by the federal government to rebuild cities. Several new varieties of mayors emerged as well: the law-and-order type who often followed in the wake of backlash appeals; black mayors in cities of large concentrations of minorities; and chief executives academically trained in urban affairs.

Nationally, the election of Richard Nixon to the Presidency in 1968, the succession of five former governors to cabinet and subcabinet posts, and an administration dedicated to New Federalism did not augur well for the cities and their mayors. The mayors openly expressed fears that the new President would be highly partisan and anticity, mobilizing growing suburban constituencies, the states, and the more conservative South against Democratic urban strongholds. Mr. Nixon's election also ended whatever favored status the Conference had enjoyed under the Democratic administration. The more bipartisan League with its large constituency of GOP mayors immediately gained a more conspicuous position, being consulted on new appointments and accorded representation on various White House task forces. The cyclical relations between the two mayors' groups had turned once again.

By 1969 the leaders of the USCM and NLC reached agreement upon unification of the two most prominent associations of municipal government. The reorganization was formally constituted in December by the NLC's executive committee, and in January 1970 by the Conference's executive committee. The staff merger left each organization with its own executive

12 See Fred Powledge, "The Flight From City Hall," *Harper's Magazine,* November, 1969, pp. 69–86.

committee, staff director, and publication division as well as some separate membership services. "We sold the operation," observed Patrick Healy, the League's executive director, "as a consolidation but not a merger, as a balance between joint service operations necessary for efficiency and political strategy and organizational independence."[13] Allen Pritchard, then deputy executive vice president of the NLC and the person responsible for managing the union of the two staffs, perhaps best summarized the basis for consolidation:[14]

> *The League and the Conference need each other. On one hand, the Conference can mobilize political clout more quickly and efficiently than the League because the Conference has a smaller membership and concentrates on shortrun objectives for political reasons. The League, on the other hand, has a broader political base and greater continuity of resources and of programs.*

Consolidation was not a radical departure from the two organizations' preexisting arrangements as they were emerging in the sixties. It merely formalized them. Where the USCM traditionally relied upon ad hoc experts in policy fields—such as housing and transportation—for reviewing policy, the League divided policy analysis and lobbying operations among a permanent in-house staff. These two separate activities, policy analysis and lobbying, were merged initially into a division for program implementation in 1969 and one year later brought under a director of congressional relations.

Each of the groups derives more than $1 million annually from dues, publications, and conventions. USCM-NLC, Inc., in which each has a 50 percent interest, grossed more than $7 million in 1972 alone, much of which was passed on through subcontract or in direct payments to cities, state municipal leagues, and other associations. Contracts for educational and technical services come from at least six federal departments as well as the Office of Management and Budget (OMB), National Science Foundation (NSF), Office of Economic Opportunity (OEO), U. S. Civil Service Commission, and the Ford Foundation. The Office of Urban Services functions as the grant-acquisition arm of the NLC, conducting service programs that enhance appreciably the effectiveness of the organization, individual member cities, and state leagues. A dozen or so individual service and training projects are conducted by the office—several with the Conference—including a Model Cities service center, urban observatories, a municipal information system, a community development project, and

---

[13] "Editorial," *Nation's Cities,* June 1969, p. 21.

[14] "NLC-USCM," *National Journal,* May 23, 1970, p. 12.

various manpower training programs. The Office of Federal Affairs, clearly one of the most important services, provides clients with a constant flow of information on federal programs affecting cities. These data include federal aid manuals, bulletins on proposed or actual federal program guidelines, and information on the anticipated impact of federal programs on cities.[15]

In addition, the USCM-NLC cosponsor a Man-in-Washington Service, a career training program established under the Intergovernmental Personnel Act, a National Urban Fellows Program, and a Labor-Management Relations Service. The two organizations have created a joint Office of Congressional Relations where legislative associates maintain contact with representatives and their staffs, monitor legislation, draft bills and amendments, and schedule witnesses for congressional testimony. When Congress is in session, this office also publishes a weekly "Congressional Report" on major bills, and it follows congressional authorizations and appropriations closely. The NLC's Office of Policy Analysis functions as its policy study and research arm, providing information to the organization's standing committees, board of directors, and congressional relations staff. Besides maintaining an extensive publications and public affairs division, the Office of Organizational Development plans and executes NLC activities. This list by no means exhausts the scope and range of activities both groups engage in but merely suggests the enormous growth and structural changes which have overtaken the mayors' Washington operations during the past five years.

Besides Pritchard and Gunther, the USCM-NLC employ at least seven full-time lobbyists and periodic part-time consultants who also function as lobbyists. Each lobbyist is assigned a specific subject matter area or policy concern. The combined USCM-NLC staff consists of some 160 employees, roughly half of whom are professionals. Those not concerned with lobbying activities work in the Office of Urban Services and on special projects, policy analysis, and public affairs matters. The mayors have built up their own in-house expertise, employing economists, tax specialists, and persons versed on specific government programs and policies in housing, transportation, human resources, law enforcement, and labor-management problems. Since coming to Wasington, the two organizations have been located near the White House and the downtown center of federal agencies. Since merger, the USCM-NLC has moved from the City Building at 1612 K Street, N.W. to 1620 I Street, N.W., two blocks from the White House, as its continually expanding operations have required additional space.

---

[15] See National League of Cities—U.S. Conference of Mayors, *This Is NLC/USCM*, Washington, D.C., 1969)—and *Nation's Cities*, June 1969, pp. 20–21. For a more recent organizational chart, see "The NLC's: To Safeguard and Improve City Government," *Nation's Cities*, March, 1972, pp. 17–34.

Internal Structure

An understanding of the Conference and League in the lobbying arena would not be complete without a brief examination of their internal workings. The two manifest many characteristics endemic to large interest groups: notably elitist patterns, control by an active minority, strong integrative mechanisms and socializing norms, rewards for participation and sustaining membership interest, a hierarchy of positions and roles, and numerous procedures for building consensus and reducing open conflict among members.

Their constitutions reflect more an elaborate statement of principles and purposes than detailed prescriptions governing day-to-day activities. "We have no specific goals except for better cities," states Gunther. "Generally we don't have goals because they would change each year." NLC's Healy states that "the whole mission of the League is to develop our National Municipal Policy and to try to implement that policy."[16] In practice membership differences underlie much of the internal dynamics inherent in their operations. The USCM has moved away somewhat from its large-city mayor domination. Nevertheless, it still functions on a consensual basis as a club which executive director Gunther runs on a personal basis. "I operate with key activist mayors which, until recently, have persisted over the long haul." While the Conference concentrates its power in its leadership, the League has devolved considerable policy discretion from its executive leadership to large committees, placing more emphasis on policy agreement than direct political action by a select few.

Both organizations derive leadership from their executive committees. These consist of twenty-plus members selected by the organization's president, executive director, and staff, with consideration given to availability, expectation of service, party affiliation, size of city representation, and regional balance. Each has developed institutional patterns for promoting members, rewarding service, and coopting dissidents. The Conference follows successional lines to leadership positions: from trustees to advisory boards to chairman of the advisory boards, and from there to vice president and then president of the executive committee. The League adheres to comparable patterns, with past presidents serving one year on the executive committee and then moving to an advisory council. The League, however, has invested considerable authority in its committees and seeks to move former committee chairmen to higher positions. In both organizations, trustees, advisory councils, and advisory boards extend little advice, rarely meet, function as honorific posts, and serve as "waiting lists" for future executive committee positions when vacancies occur.

While the League rotates its executive committee every year, the Conference has no limitation on terms of service. The USCM relies more on

---

[16] "The Urban Voice in Washington," *Public Management*, July 1968, p. 173.

politically powerful and prestigious large-city mayors. It kept past presidents like Barr, Daley, Lee, and Cavanagh on this committee from 1963 to 1968. Prospective USCM presidents are acclaimed at least two years in advance of actual investiture, while in the case of the NLC it is only one year. No serious challenge to succession has developed in either organization, elevation being automatic, except at the NLC's forty-sixth annual convention in 1969. Then, for the first time, the nomination committee's choice of New York's John Lindsay as vice president was overthrown by an incipient floor revolt led by city officials from small towns and suburbs who protested the increased control of the League by big-city mayors like Lindsay. Elected instead was Richard Lugar, the young GOP mayor of Indianapolis, a city official considered to be on more favorable terms with the Nixon administration than Lindsay.

With its more heterogeneous membership, the NLC balances executive committee composition evenly among state leagues, cities of more than 100,000 in population, and smaller cities. Promotion to leadership in both is tied to forces outside the organization, notably success at elections and at least one term in office. Thus leaders are acclimated to group norms and procedures before assuming higher positions.

Leadership in policy, strategy, and tactics flows largely from the executive committees, which are empowered to change membership and structures, establish committees, and appoint members. They also hire the executive directors, determine time and place of annual meetings, influence resolutions and nominations, disperse rewards, and conduct affairs of the organization between annual meetings. The USCM's executive committee—consisting of trustees and principal officers—wields considerable power. The League, on the other hand, with its emphasis upon policy development (regularly reaffirmed or amended at annual meetings), has considerable difficulty at times in disengaging itself from an established policy and thus has somewhat less policy flexibility than the Conference.

Both organizations delegate discretionary powers directly to their respective executive directors. Patrick Healy, a prominent state league organizer and NLC member in the 1930s, succeeded Carl Chatters as NLC director in 1954, when the then AMA (and later NLC) moved from Chicago to Washington. The soft-spoken Healy served as the NLC director until he retired in June 1972. His successor, Allen E. Pritchard, Jr., like Healy, came to the NLC with vast executive service as a state municipal league organizer and officer. After brief Washington service, both legislative and executive, Pritchard joined the League in 1965, became assistant director and head of its congressional relations activities in 1966, and moved to deputy director in 1970.[17] Both Healy and Pritchard are identified as Republicans.

---

[17] For biographies on Healy and Pritchard, see *Nation's Cities*, June 1972, pp. 24–26.

John Gunther, despite legislative service with a Republican senator for many years, is identified as a Democrat. His organization's membership is primarily composed of Democrats, though the USCM has attempted to attract smaller cities and gain Republican members. Between Gunther's 14 years as USCM head, Healy's 18 years as NLC head, and Pritchard's 23 years with the League and its state associations, both organizations have had continuity in leadership from men who have enjoyed overwhelming support from rank and file members.

Selection for leadership posts is determined largely by officers and staff. It is governed by the general expectation that designated mayors will work for the organizations, contribute time and often staff of their own, testify before Congress, serve on task forces, and mobilize key congressmen behind legislation supported by the cities. Permanent staff members help identify "comers" by recruiting those who are willing to serve. Staff and organization leaders also try to satisfy the needs of solicitous members pursuing favorable press attention, and they identify which mayors may have a special leverage on elected or appointed federal officials. Generalizations notwithstanding, the USCM draws its leadership from the mayors of New York, Chicago, Pittsburgh, Boston, Detroit, Philadelphia, Los Angeles, St. Louis, Milwaukee, and Houston. The NLC has recruited largely from the second ten large cities, including Denver, Nashville, New Orleans, Indianapolis, San Diego, Phoenix, and—at times—Philadelphia, Cleveland, Atlanta, Milwaukee, Los Angeles, and Detroit. The Conference used to have a monopoly on the mayors more active nationally, like Daley, Naftalin, Lee, Barr, and Lindsay, but this has changed somewhat with the reduction in group competition. The USCM can rely on large-city mayors' participation at annual meetings, while the league cannot. Some two hundred to three hundred mayors have attended the USCM's annual gatherings in recent years—besides hundreds of other urban officials, while roughly two thousand to three thousand urban officials particpate in NLC meetings. Since anywhere from one-quarter to one-half of the NLC's executive and advisory committee members have been or are members of the Conference's leadership committees, overlapping leadership contributes to the determination of policy and the maintenance of continuity between the two organizations. Policy adopted by one typically is introduced and ratified by the other. Recently, both have attempted to build joint policies so that they might present a single position before congressional committees and federal agencies.

Participation is not without its rewards for mayors and cities, individually and collectively. All members benefit generally from federal programs or appropriations favorable to cities. While the NLC provides more comprehensive and continuous information services to direct and indirect members, the USCM offers specialized services and individual amenities for mayors visiting Washington. Such services are increasingly important to city officials who are often bewildered by the magnitude of pending legislation affecting cities and the avalanche of administrative rule changes and regulations governing federal programs. These officials often need assistance in finding their way through the federal bureaucracy. Large-city mayors, however, are not as dependent on these services as NLC members, usually obtaining them directly from other channels and more recently through individual lobbying offices.

Individual rewards and benefits, both tangible and intangible, are selective. They include publicity gained by the organizational office, congressional testimony, membership on government task forces and commissions, and appointment to federal office. The mayors, like other interest groups, seek to place their people or persons favorable to their interests in key federal policy-making positions. Organization members are aware of these rewards. They are inducements for participation and they further strengthen the organization leadership that controls the dispersal of these various perquisites.

Cleavages persist within both groups. They stem from differences in party, regional, ideological, and constituency size as well as other factors. To combat these internal cleavages and factions, operating procedures strengthen control of the active minority and aid in building consensus among members. Both have oligarchic tendencies which are reflected in the formation of policy, succession to leadership positions, and control over the information flow through the organization. The active minority maintains legitimacy largely as a perceived need for delegating authority. Members also recognize that planning, determination of strategies, and overall efficacy require action by a few to achieve organizational goals.

Policy Determination

Internal consensus on policy matters entails an elaborate process which suggests how cleavages are muted and dissension is blunted. Since 1948 the NLC has centered its activities around a National Municipal Policy developed at annual sessions of the association. Initially policy statements reflected a rather incomprehensible laundry list of individual resolutions passed by various mayors through logrolling methods. Each interested mayor normally returned home, if he wished, with League endorsement for his own pet resolution. The mayor could then use this endorsement for internal consumption or merely as a justification for his city's paying dues in support of the organization. NLC reorganization subsequently changed internal policy making to strengthen the mayors' declarations.

Beginning in 1966, the League moved to nine well-staffed standing committees, each with jurisdictional responsibility for policy in such areas as transportation, municipal revenue and finance, and so on. Committees contain 100 members on the average, with chairman, vice chairman, and several members selected by the NLC president. Each state league is allotted two to three members per committee, which accounts for their large size. In practice the committees are run by a small steering group which meets several times a year to review and revise policy. On the basis of pending federal legislation and consultation with federal officials and other interest groups, steering committees draft proposed changes in NLC policy for the full committees. Once full committees meet to review and approve steering groups' drafts, proposals are translated into policy resolutions. The reports of each NLC policy committee are presented to the Resolutions Committee which reviews these reports, revises and relates them to each other, and presents a final report for action by the voting delegates at the annual business session of the Congress of Cities. Following adoption as the National Municipal Policy for the coming year, the policy becomes "the foundation around which municipal officials, acting through their state leagues and the NLC, build their legislative action programs in city councils, state legislatures, and the national Congress."[18] The more difficult policy implementation process follows the earlier policy initiation and ratification stages. This involves the introduction of legislation in the Congress, continual updating of policy in light of specific legislation, and lobbying strategies aimed at gaining congressional approval. Once legislation is passed, League representatives meet with federal officials and other interest groups to help formulate administrative regulations governing its implementation. The policy process then begins anew.

The League's Committee process, the most elaborate policy-making structure among the government groups, is designed to promote broad municipal participation in policy formation. More than one thousand city officials participate actively through the NLC's nine standing committees, while the USCM relies upon some fifty or so mayors for its committees. This difference, again, is a function of the League's large membership, innumerable cleavages, and the importance attached to participation, even if tokenly, in policy determination. Figure 1 illustrates the NLC's National Policy through a step-by-step process.

In contrast to the League's lengthy process, the USCM's operation is more informal. Potentially conflictual issues and acrimonious debate generally are avoided at the annual sessions of the Conference of Mayors. The passing of resolutions, though the principal official business carried on during the final session at the June meetings, generally assumes secondary importance to discussions among mayors and between federal officials and other interest groups. Voting rules are flexible, tailored to the USCM's loosely knit operation. Voting is done without roll calls—most

---

[18] National League of Cities, *Proceedings of the Forty-fourth Annual Congress*, Washington, D.C., 1968, p. ii.

F-1 The NLC's National Municipal Policy, Step by Step

1 Steering committee meets, drafts new policy for presentation to . . .

2 The full committee, which reviews and revises steering committee draft and reports to . . .

3 The Resolutions Committee, which reviews reports of all policy committees, revises them, and presents policy to . . .

4 NLC Voting delegates at Annual Congress of Cities where they review and approve the National Municipal Policy for the coming year.

5 NLC representatives meet senators, congressmen, and staffs; other interest groups; and federal officials to build support for NLC positions.

6 Legislation to implement National Municipal Policy is introduced in Congress.

7 City officials meet at NLC's annual Congressional City Conference to review legislation relating to the Municipal Policy and to meet with congressmen.

8 Steering Committee meets to detail policy positions in light of specific legislation.

9 NLC testifies on legislation.

10 City officials and state leagues receive NLC bulletins explaining NLC position on pending legislation.

11 City officials, state league members, and NLC staff contact congressmen urging support for NLC position.

12 Legislation passes Congress.

13 NLC members meet with federal officials and other interest groups to formulate regulations for implementing new legislation.

14 Steering Committee meets to develop new policies to present to the next Congress of Cities.

Source: The National League of Cities (October 1973).

often by voice, standing vote, or show of delegate cards. From 1957 to 1969 an average of twenty-six resolutions was passed per conference on a range of subjects from apportionment to Vietnam.

Almost all resolutions are beamed toward Washington, advocating stronger federal-city relations, a larger federal contribution to specific programs, more consultation between federal officials and mayors in policy decisions affecting urban programs, and protection of the tax-exempt status of municipal bonds. Since 1969 both organizations have spoken out in favor of reordering national priorities. To most mayors, this means spending more federal money in urban areas and less in other places.

Cleavages between large and small cities emerge on issues like urban renewal, support for mass transit, and rent supplements. But civil rights perhaps has been the most divisive issue to date, followed in later years by busing, gun control, and Vietnam. President Kennedy and Justice Department officials attended the 1963 USCM convention to enlist the mayors' support for a strong civil rights resolution. One was adopted over considerable opposition when Conference President Richard Lee successfully moved that all resolutions including a civil rights plank be adopted by a single motion. Since 1963 cleavages have opened on new government programs in housing, Model Cities, transportation, and other policies. Generally stakes in policy resolutions are considered small except when

fanned by the media and where they assume a strict partisan nature—
for example, reordering national priorities and foreign policy. At the
USCM's 1971 meeting in Philadelphia, the mayors for the first time passed
a Vietnam resolution calling for complete withdrawal by the end of the
year. Most mayors deem foreign policy resolutions outside their area of
concern, and thus the debates turn on whether the mayors should become
involved. With administration loyalists conspicuous in their presence, the
mayors rescinded their earlier stand at the 1972 New Orleans meeting,
offering instead terms for withdrawal in the President's own language.
At this session, the mayors also adopted their first strong resolution on
national gun control and registration of firearms, an issue which had
divided Northern mayors from the rest and large-city mayors from small-
city mayors for a decade.

Mayors' interests are more in action than rhetoric. They acknowledge
that strategical and tactical choices are necessarily invested in their
executive committee and the permanent staff who are empowered to take
policy positions and actions provided that these are not inconsistent with
previous policy.

The USCM, like the other government interest groups, operates with
five committees: human resources, community development, urban renewal, transportation, environmental quality. Each has fourteen members
selected by the Conference president and Mr. Gunther. Each is staffed
by the individual mayor's assistants and meets six to eight times a year.
Mayors often delegate a large part of the committee work to a member of
their personal staff who is usually a policy expert in that area. The Conference thus benefits from outside expertise in housing, municipal finance,
and so on, reducing organizational costs and developing continuous liaison
to committee members. USCM-NLC staff maintain a low profile in lobbying, serving primarily as a brokerage operation for members that tells them
when, where, and how to turn the pressure on. Committee leaders perform
generalist lobbying functions through congressional testimony, while they
and others engage in specific functions as well. In addition to loaned
staff and specific consultants hired for their expertise, committees frequently operate with representatives from other major urban interest
groups—like the National Association of Housing and Redevelopment
Officials—touching base with federal officials, congressional staff members, urban task forces, and a spectrum of urban interests. With consolidation of the mayors' groups, the USCM gains from the League's research and
policy analysis staffs where previously it had largely relied on an individual
mayor's staff and allied associations for help.

Thus committees are able to build a working policy consensus from
within and without prior to formal deliberation on policy resolutions at
annual meetings. This policy process relieves USCM leaders of many
time-consuming activities and weds the organization to a nexus of over-

lapping urban interest groups. It also reduces intergroup conflict considerably, as final policy becomes the product of many individuals and groups rather than that of an individual mayor, a select group, or the Conference staff. To bolster public support for its policies, the USCM instituted its Legislative Action Committee in late 1970 headed by John Lindsay. The predecessor to this venture was Mayor Joseph Alioto's full-funding drives in Congress on behalf of urban renewal, public housing, and mass transit. As head of the USCM's Urban Renewal Committee, the San Francisco Mayor led his mayoral cohorts in gaining a 35 percent increase in urban renewal funds above what President Nixon had requested in fiscal 1970. Alioto also led the drive to get the Nixon administration to release more than $800 million in impounded funds for urban projects by filing suits in federal district court. Alioto's activities paved the way for a more institutionalized device for implementing the Conference's policies.

The Legislation Action Committee—comprising seventeen mayors— traveled all over the country in 1971–1972, publicizing the fiscal plight of the nation's cities. The committee presses for enactment of Conference resolutions, especially congressional appropriations. Three Republican and two black mayors serve on this basically young, articulate USCM legislative arm which has received considerable publicity for the mayors and their causes nationally. The committee overlaps with the USCM's executive committee, and, in effect, frequently operates as an internal lobby within the organization, staking out new policy positions in advance of rank and file members.

Since 1967 the NLC has sponsored its annual Congressional City Conference conducted in Washington in late winter or early spring. Such sessions allow committees and directors the opportunity to accommodate NLC policies to legislative work. The annual conferences provide an exchange of views between city officials and congressional and administration leaders. The USCM may join with the NLC at these sessions as occurred in 1971–1972, where both mounted a congresswide campaign on behalf of federal revenue sharing. Based on the feedback from these additional annual meetings, the mayors are better able to adjust their policies and priorities to the specifics of the congressional agenda.

Finally, the policy process and consensus-building mechanisms of the two groups point to essential differences between them. With its more unwieldy membership, visible cleavages, and multiple service operations, the League allocates extensive resources merely to building internal policy consensus within the organization. The Conference, on the other hand, with its more homogeneous membership and activist role, seeks policy accommodation with government and interest-group allies simultaneously while building internal consensus. The groups' policy differences, however, have narrowed since the consolidation of activities and merger of many operations. Increasingly the two join together on congressional testimony, collaborate on their dealings with HUD and other federal agencies, and share in planning overall strategies. They have come a long way in the past two decades from a rather inconspicuous status in the Washington interest-group complex to a prominent position in national policy making. One indication of this may be taken from growth in size, budget, and staff alone: from fewer than 15 employees, a $200,000 budget, and 300 member cities between them in 1954 to nearly 200 employees, a $7 million budget, and nearly 600 member cities in 1973.

THE GOVERNORS

The history of the National Governors' Conference (NGC) reflects the emergence of an organized group of state chief executives collectively searching for a national role and identity. As stated in the Conference's articles of organization, the association's functions are[19]

> To provide a medium for the exchange of views and experiences on subjects of general importance to the people of the several states; to foster interstate cooperation; to promote greater uniformity of state laws; to attain greater efficiency in state administration; and to facilitate and improve state-local and state-federal relationships.

President Theodore Roosevelt initiated the annual Governors' Conference (later National Governors' Conference) in 1908, when thirty-four governors convened at the White House for the purpose of pressuring Congress for the enactment of natural resource legislation which Roosevelt advocated. The governors were sufficiently convinced of the usefulness of such gatherings to convene their own sessions without White House sponsorship thereafter. From 1910 on, the governors met annually — although attendance rarely exceeded half their membership until after World War II.

From the outset the governors found themselves divided over organizational purposes. Progressive governors like Woodrow Wilson foresaw an institutional role for an organization set up outside Congress in order to influence federal action. But, by setting the tone and direction for the Conference, the conservatives opposed national activities and a federal orientation. They successfully defended the dominant constitutional position of the day — that state and federal responsibilities, both their spheres of

[19] Articles of Organization, The Governors' Conference. To avoid confusion with its regional and party affiliates, the Governors' Conference changed its name in 1966 to the National Governors' Conference. Hence the abbreviation NGC, used throughout this work, indicates the organization's later name.

operations and activities, were clearly separable if not mutually exclusive. "Dual federalism," as this doctrine was called, became operative in theory and practice in the organization's formative years. This largely precluded a national focus during the Conference's first fifty years, which were interrupted on occasion by sporadic attention to the Washington scene.

Persisting in the belief that the Conference's business should be restricted to state issues, governors and state governments were dealt a shattering blow by the Depression of the 1930s. "In the face of Roosevelt's aggressive policies," observed Glenn Brooks in his 1960 study of the governors, "the Conference was transformed from a staid social club into a forum for heated discussion of national programs and federal-state relations."[20] Brook's exuberance over the governors' apparent revival was a bit premature in light of later developments. Nevertheless, the Depression did produce a significant shift in the governors' agenda and focus of attention. The great issues of the 1920s—such as agriculture, prohibition, and state administrative reorganization—were superseded by national problems like social security, fiscal regulation, deficit spending, and employment. Yet in spite of these national concerns and persistent attempts by progressive governors to rally their colleagues behind New Deal programs, the governors remained largely hostile toward Washington. They advocated federal relief, but themselves practiced retrenchment.[21]

For nearly twenty-five years, 1938 to 1963, interrupted by a brief interlude of unity around their wartime activities, most governors were preoccupied with two principal issues. They demanded greater federal sharing of national tax sources with the states and also the return to the states of certain ongoing federal-state programs. These two issues were regularly formulated into various Conference resolutions and transmitted to federal officials for action. Unsuccessful though they proved to be until the passage of revenue sharing in 1972, they were aimed at separating governmental functions and taxable sources by government levels. From the time of the issuance of the Council of State Governments' *Federal-State Report on Taxes* in 1938 and in several major commission studies on intergovernmental relations, the governors persisted in viewing the federal system in terms of unwinding and separating functions and taxes. Whether liquor, excise, cabaret, gasoline, or telephone taxes were involved, the Governors' Conference characteristically supported any or all proposals advocating that the national government relinquish use of particular taxes to the states or provide for the greater sharing of tax sources among the states. In exchange for greater state authority over and usage of particular federal tax

[20] Glen Brooks, *When Governors Convene* John Hopkins, Baltimore, 1961. pp. 17–19.

[21] See James T. Patterson, "The New Deal and the States," *American Historical Review*, 54:71–84, October 1967; and Bernard Bellush, *Franklin D. Roosevelt as Governor of New York*, Columbia University Press, New York, 1955, pp. 148–149, 183–184.

sources, the states would assume greater responsibility for redelegated programs in highways, vocational education, and municipal waste treatment.

The outcome of these unsuccessful efforts, amply recorded in other sources, was essentially the same. The governors' proposals proved unfeasible in theory. Moreover, consensus among the governors rarely occurred, particularly where state inequities in returned federal revenues from tax sources would prevail. State governors demurred against full assumption of former federal-state programs such as those above when they were confronted with the full estimates of costs involved. The governors with traditional foresight, as one observer quipped, usually reversed their position on redelegation of federal programs when Washington added further financial incentives to the sharing of existing program costs.

The most celebrated case, of course, involved the governors' advocacy in 1953 of federal government withdrawal from highway financing, the abolition of the Federal Bureau of Public Roads, and the turning over of gasoline taxes to the states so that they could finance and construct their own national highway program. The outcome of this brief but important controversy between the governors and the federal government, like most previous cases, found states' chief executives reversing their previously held positions. Confronted by the economic dimensions of taking over the highway program as well as the fiscal disparities between wealthy and poor states, they opted instead for a much expanded, largely nationally financed interstate program. This illustrated the relative impotence of the Conference in affecting federal policy.[22]

If Conference-supported resolutions on key issues of federal-state relations are taken as benchmarks for evaluating the governors' national influence during the 1940s and 1950s, the ledger would record few if any victories and nearly all defeats. The Conference proved mildly obstructive on federal-state matters. It added rhetoric to the vestiges of states rights defenders, gained media attention for periodic recriminations against federal officialdom, and generally proved ineffectual as a national political interest group. No one seemed more aware of this situation by the early 1960s than the governors themselves.

The Kennedy-Johnson era in the White House produced a gradual modification in the governors' attitudes toward Washington. A grudging acceptance of the accumulating federal activity within state boundaries began creeping both into their statements and national resolutions. Pressures both indigenous and external to states—such as civil rights, reapportionment, constitutional reform, saliency of urban problems, and failure of state tax structures to keep pace with rising demands for ser-

---

[22] See W. Brooke Graves, *American Intergovernmental Relations*, Scribner, New York. 1964, chap. 13.

vices—eventually found an outlet in a Conference posture which became more receptive to national government activity. The governors' attitude of hostile dependency toward Washington, so prevalent in the 1950s, was largely replaced by one less critical of the substantive activity per se but directed more at the federal government's allocation of revenues and resources. Indications of these changes came from the governors individually and collectively. NGC resolutions, for example, were increasingly beamed toward Washington, in many cases requesting affirmative federal response rather than negative protestations against federal actions. Contacts between governors and Washington proliferated as grant-in-aid programs expanded and grant acquisition assumed larger importance. Individual governors established permanent state offices in Washington to carry on federal-state dealings on their behalf.

Futile attempts at unwinding the federal system or reassigning specific functions to state governments exclusively had become generally unpleasant memories of the past. Most governors acknowledged federal prerogatives in utilizing grants-in-aid as an instrument of federal influence and leverage upon the states. They turned their attention to the structure, form, and allocative procedures for distributing funds and programs. Instead of seeking to separate taxes and functions within the federal structure, the Conference in 1965 embraced a new policy calling for federal revenue sharing with the states.

Vast changes in organization, membership participation, and scope of activities characterized the NGC during the 1960s. The organization changed its name from simply the Governors' Conference to the National Governors' Conference and actively included the four territorial governors (Guam, Samoa, Virgin Islands, and Puerto Rico) in the association. Closer cooperation among state chief executives generally followed from greater homogeneity in state problems and common reaction to the new patterns in intergovernmental relations that had emerged. Cooperation also stemmed from individual awareness of the stakes involved in federal policy making. Transformation of the federal system during the sixties stimulated internal disturbances within the Conference as more active governors became increasingly concerned with the organization's lack of direction and influence in Washington. "We simply weren't going anywhere under the then existing structure," recalled one governor of this period, "while the mayors' and county officials' visibility in Washington became a source of constant embarrassment to us." One observer of the governors noted that the absence of their apparent interest in the federal school aid issue shocked the coalition of groups lobbying for federal aid in the early 1960s. "Here it was, education, the states' largest single functional expenditure, and the governors failed to testify or even lobby for the bill."

As to be expected in an interest group comprising such partisan members, the internal organization of the NGC greatly shapes policies and goals. It consists of an alliance of fifty prima donnas, the highest elected officials within the states, leaders and rarely followers. Governors are highly visible public officials, often loyal party members and frequently aspirants to higher federal office. These characteristics underlie much of the organization's internal dynamics and have significant consequences for the leadership and management of annual gatherings.

Not only personality and partisan differences but also the marked contrasts among states are important in viewing the NGC. These include political cultures, economic and industrial bases, population and geographic size, per capita income, taxing policies, and resource allocation. Population and income redistribution throughout the country as well as the nationalization of American politics have reduced individual differences among states. But their distinctiveness is often manifested in the recruitment, socialization, and personality of their chief executives. State chief executives' attitudes often reflect these differences. They may defend their states' diversity or deviation from the national norm and are not easily stampeded into supporting organizational policies which might be incompatible with the states' economic, social, and political traditions.

Centrifugal influences generally have outweighed integrating and socializing mechanisms. This is generally more characteristic of the governors than of the other government interest groups. Some annual meetings are more prone toward disruptions than others, especially during the period of midterm elections when a majority of the governors are up for reelection. Membership unity tends to be constantly undermined by the group's fairly evenly divided partisan composition. Personal ambitions, party rivalry, sectional and ideological cleavages, high membership turnover, and differences in constituencies and problems divide the governors internally. The media, White House, and national party pressures buffet the governors from the outside. These factors greatly limit prospects for effective action at their annual summer meetings. According to one governor's aide, a participant at several NGC annual meetings, "When you consider the innumerable forces pulling them apart, the fact that the governors continue to meet every year, regardless of what else they might accomplish, is a tribute to their perseverance."

The articles of organization, a terse, loosely drawn, and amendable Conference constitution, lodges much of the year-round responsibilities in a nine-man executive committee. Bipartisan leadership is assured by the provision that the NGC chairmanship alternate between the two major political parties and that a majority of the executive committee be of a political party other than the chairman's. Prospective presidential candidates, by tradition, are precluded from consideration as the Conference's chairman. Moreover, in that all governors vote for the chairman, contested elections within a single party find the out-party's members often voting for the person who might have less support among his own party members.

Regional governors' conferences, tangentially affiliated with the NGC and convened by each party, siphon off many regional concerns and issues from annual meetings. Similarly, the affiliated Republican and Democratic governors' associations meet annually as well. They gather for strictly partisan purposes and function as a platform for criticizing the opposition party. In-party caucuses or governors' meetings typically end with the governors calling upon the President to improve relations with his own party's governors. This is usually followed by an invitation from the President to meet at the White House, where harmony is temporarily restored. As presidential elections approach, the partisan governors may also seek unity behind one of their own as a presidential or vice presidential candidate and frequently screen other prospective party candidates.

Conference rules of procedure tend to be revealing of the internal dynamics and extraordinary tensions pervading the conduct of annual meetings. Prior to 1935, for example, the Conference did not permit the recording of resolutions, and for twenty years thereafter it operated under a unanimity rule, a sure deterrent to the adoption of any resolutions with opposition. A three-fourths majority was required on adoption of resolutions after 1955, and this was changed again to two-thirds after 1959. Later, greater flexibility was added when the suspension of any rule by a three-fourths majority vote was permitted. Conference rules function to minimize conflict, avoid controversial or partisan issues, and prevent the adoption of any resolutions found personally embarrassing or possibly injurious to any individual member. Such rules also debilitate the organization from gaining a sense of purpose or federal orientation, and this added to the mounting frustrations experienced by an expanding group of more nationally aggressive state chief executives.

Operating procedures played a key role in incipient insurrections at the 1962 Hershey and 1963 Miami meetings, where consideration of civil rights resolutions led to such extensive disruption that the Conference's future seemed in jeopardy. "No governor should be bound to any point of view," exclaimed Governor Grant Sawyer (D-Nev.), in an emotional plea for open discussion and Conference deliberation on controversial issues, "but it should be the purpose of the Conference to enunciate, dramatize, and to discuss matters with which the governors must deal."[23] Recurrent battles over rule changes occupied much of the discussions at annual meetings during the early 1960s. Indeed, the rules on adopting resolutions were changed at three successive meetings, with the governors eventually abolishing the resolutions committee which had screened and frequently emasculated policy statements prior to floor consideration.

As issues involving intergovernmental relations and support for federal revenue sharing assumed greater import at meetings, a movement emerged

[23] *State Government,* **36**:223, Summer, 1963.

among governors across party lines for overhauling the Conference and strengthening its then diminutive role as a government interest group. This movement eventually surfaced at the 1965 Minneapolis meeting, when controversy arose over the relevance of annual sessions. Detailing the historical inefficacy of the Conference as a government pressure group and enumerating the impressive array of domestic legislation affecting the states then pending before the 89th Congress, Governor Philip Hoff (D-Vt.) proposed a resolution directing the Conference's Executive Committee to study[24]

> *By what means would it be possible to assure state policy-making officials a greater measure of influence with respect to federal legislative proposals that have major implications for federal-state relations; to suggest the means whereby the influence of the states as a whole on matters of federal-state concerns may be strengthened; and to report its findings and recommendations, including personnel and financing to the next annual meeting.*

This resolution, passed by a unanimous vote, clearly indicated that the nation's governors wanted an organization different from the one they had belonged to in the past. They were uniformly dissatisfied over the services rendered by the Council of State Governments and particularly over its rather diminutive low-profile posture in the nation's capital. It proved a milestone in Conference history because restructuring of the entire organization and methods of seeking to influence national policy followed from its adoption.

The benefits and costs of several options for implementing the Hoff resolution were openly discussed at the following 1966 Los Angeles meeting. The period of 1965 to 1966 marked the low point of the governors' collective influence over federal policy. Great Society programs were enacted in a great flurry on Capitol Hill without Congress, White House officials, or federal departments paying much attention to the governors. Actual formulation of proposed changes, however, resided with the Conference's executive committee, which considered more sweeping changes than rank and file members actually debated. Meeting five times between the 1965 and 1966 meetings, the executive committee, led by Governors Hoff, Hughes (D-Iowa), Connally (D-Tex.), Volpe (R-Mass), and Scranton (R-Pa.), deferred final action until an unprecedented interim meeting of all governors convened at White Sulfur Springs, West Virginia, in December 1966.

At the historic Greenbrier Meeting, a critique committee comprising bipartisan regional conference representatives appointed by the NGC

---

[24] Ibid., **38**:235–245, Autumn 1965.

Chairman William Guy (R-N.D.)—after reviewing the Conference's purposes, structure, staffing, and financing—recommended to the thirty-eight governors and governors-elect in attendance the establishment of a National Governors' Conference Office for Federal-State Relations located directly in Washington. This office would be staffed, financed, and designed to serve the governors exclusively yet still remain nominally under the Council of State Governments. "Its purpose," states the critique committee's report, "shall be to improve the effectiveness of the states, and particularly the governors, in dealing with problems arising out of federal-state relations." Adopting the report through the formal authority specified in the articles of organization, the governors voted $240,000 annually from individual state appropropriations for supporting this new instrumentality under a revised membership dues schedule. According to the report[25]

> The Washington Office will be responsible to the executive committee . . . but it shall be available at all times to serve all member Governors and committees of the Conference. It shall also coordinate its work with the activities of offices representing the states in Washington.

By taking this major step the Conference embraced new organizational purposes aimed at directly influencing federal-state relations. Few governors seemed to grasp fully the significance of what they had done. In effect, they had put behind them the nonfederal functions and purposes of the organization so characteristic of the past. They had created a full-time governors' lobby in Washington. However, in specifying this office's missions, they avoided such nomenclature. Instead, the NGC noted that the Washington office's mission consisted of gathering and disseminating information on matters related to issues of federal-state relations. This information would be carefully reviewed, processed, and conveyed to governors and their staffs through a weekly "Governors' Bulletin" which informs them of congressional hearings of major interest and various executive decisions. Governors also receive "Box Score," a periodic report on federal budget items, appropriations, and impoundments. Special letters are sent to governors outlining congressional action calling for gubernatorial responses—including whom to write, call, or telegram. Besides acting as a listening post to gather and report intelligence—vitally important in providing governors with cues for action, secondary missions include occasional research on subjects of importance to all governors, the distribution of technical information, and the drafting of prepared testimony on behalf of governors appearing before congressional committees.

[25] National Governors' Conference, *Official Papers: Special Interim Meeting,* White Sulfur Springs, West Virginia, December 16–17, Chicago, 1967, p. 6.

The NGC office also represents the governors in such discussions or meetings as they cannot personally attend but that require Conference representation.

By late 1967 the NGC Washington office had commenced operation under a small but well-organized staff headed by Charles Byrley, former head of the New York COSGO office and a personal designee of Governor Guy. The Washington staff, jointly with the Conference's executive committee, developed a list of priority legislation to the states then pending before the 90th Congress which would be the specific targets of the governors' federal activities. The executive committee was granted discretionary powers to act for the Conference in the interim between annual meetings and they, in turn, empowered the staff to take necessary actions except where resolutions approved by the current NGC or Conference executive committee would be in effect. Moreover, through its weekly analysis and special research reports, the Washington office receives constant feedback from governors and their staffs on the anticipated effect of pending legislation upon state government. Based on this constant information flow between Washington and state capitals—direct communication between governors and NGC Washington staff, spokesmen for the governors now have sufficient information and support to provide a well-developed articulation of state chief executives' views before federal policy makers. By late 1967, the governors had become a fully operative Washington lobby joining the ranks of the mayors and county officials.

To sustain its new directions and offer greater policy direction, further internal Conference reorganization accompanied the move to Washington. Beginning in 1967 the NGC changed from its ad hoc committee structure, which had functioned primarily as a format for panel discussions at annual meetings, to year-round standing committees. Eleven standing committees were established initially, with all governors serving on at least one. Committee chairmen served as well on the Federal-State Relations Committee, which coordinated the work of the others. Each committee dealt with a specific functional policy area involving federal-state relations including such areas as transportation, education, manpower and labor, law enforcement, revenue and taxation, and human resources. Aided by foundation support, these committees became vital research sources for the NGC. Each probed fellow governors for their views and issued comprehensive reports detailing problems in federal-state relations, defining options for prospective federal-state policy in a particular field. The division of labor through committee structure, like that initiated by the NLC, had the effect of devolving power from the NGC executive committee to broad-based policy committees and of involving individual members. The committee structure was revamped further in the 1970s—consolidated and economized much along the lines of President Nixon's proposed reorganized plan for federal departments. Twelve committees were reduced to six:

(1) Executive Management and Fiscal Affairs; (2) Human Resources; (3) Law Enforcement, Justice, and Public Safety; (4) Natural Resources and Environmental Protection; (5) Urban and Rural Development; and (6) Transportation, Commerce, and Technology.

The committee system has resulted in wider membership participation, greater organizational cohesion, and less open cleavages than in the past. A certain reciprocity among overlapping committee membership and between committees emerged as their aggregate efforts became known as the "Policy Positions of the National Governors' Conference." These policy positions remain in effect from meeting to meeting unless amended or deleted by subsequent action. Thus, like the NLC's "Urban Policy" and NACO's "County Platform," the NGC had developed a comprehensive state policy of the governors.

Moreover, the committee system nurtured policy experts among chairmen and vice chairmen who were of opposite parties. This provided an organization resource used for congressional testimony, communication, and consultation with executive officialdom. Structurally, committee operations also moved interest and participation in the Conference away from an active minority, thus adding greater weight and substance internally and externally to Conference-passed policies.

To bring the Conference and its members in closer contact with federal policy makers, an annual midwinter meeting of the governors is now held under the aegis of the NGC Washington office. Forty-eight governors participated in the first Washington gathering in 1968, and subsequent sessions have been attended by nearly all state chief executives. These meetings serve to apprise governors of major legislative proposals expected to be taken up by Congress during that particular session and alert them to the probable consequences of this legislation for the states. Complementing formal sessions between governors and federal officials, individual NGC committees meet to discuss pending legislation in their policy areas, inviting congressional committee members, staff, and officials from the executive branch to participate in their deliberations.

The midyear sessions provide governors, as they do the other government interest groups which sponsor comparable meetings, with a firsthand understanding of the Congress and its particular climate at the time. By their fourth annual midwinter meeting in February 1970, the governors had virtually institutionalized these sessions on a permanent basis whereby the President, cabinet officers, and Capitol Hill leaders all participated in the three days of activities. The governors spend time on Capitol Hill discussing issues with congressional leaders, committee staffs, and their own delegations. They use these sessions to make their collective presence felt, demonstrating their continual concern with the course of domestic policy. The NGC Washington office also has sponsored since 1967 a national workshop for governors' coordinators of federal-state relations.

Governors' own staff members and high-ranking state officials assemble in Washington for briefing sessions on recently enacted legislation to gain information on how the states might participate in and take advantage of new laws or amended programs.

Thus outgoing NGC Chairman John Volpe, summarizing the governors' activities during 1967–1968, observed that the governors had at last established a firm foothold in the nation's capital. Reviewing the apparent success of the newly instituted NGC committee structure for making state chief executives' views known before Congress, Volpe stated, "The governors presented more oral testimony in Washington in the past twelve months than they had in the previous ten years."[26] During the preceding five months alone, Volpe noted in October 1968, fifteen governors testified on housing, crime control, pollution, health, education, transportation, welfare, and intergovernmental cooperation. Citing specific legislative enactments favorable to the states, he concluded, "It is through the National Governors' Conference . . . that we governors have been able to reassert the need for our own pivotal role in domestic policies and programs of this nation."[27] Volpe's efforts have been carried forth by successive NGC chairmen: Ellington (Tenn.), Love (Colo.), Hearns (Mo.), Moore (N.C.), and Evans (Wash.).

Finally, what has occurred for governors individually as well as the NGC is the institutionalization of their new roles as claimants before higher levels of government. In moving away from matters of interstate cooperation to concerns national in scope, the NGC has reordered resources and activities to reflect this focus. An accounting of NGC resolutions since 1946 underscores the declining interest shown by governors to interstate matters and to the substantial increase in attention directed toward national action.[28] State chief executives have accepted responsibility for concerns extending beyond their own state boundaries; they no longer passively accept federal activities affecting state budgets, policies, and priorities.

The new National Governors' Conference Washington Office for Federal-State Relations is the epitome of the governors' sustained interest in affecting federal policy. What began essentially as a center for information clearance, keeping the nation's governors abreast of federal developments in Washington, matured full force into a gubernatorial lobby. What began in March 1967 with a staff of five professionals and a budget

[26] National Governors' Conference, *The Modern State in the Federal System: Challenge and Responsibility*, Chicago, 1968; National Governors' Conference. "Summary of the Mid-Year Meeting on Federal-State Relations," mimeographed, Washington, D.C., 1968.

[27] *State Government*, **41**:220–221, Autumn 1968.

[28] Deil S. Wright, "Governors, Grants, and the Intergovernmental System," in Thad Beyle and J. Oliver Williams (eds.), *The American Governor in Behavioral Perspective*, Harper & Row, New York, 1972, pp. 192–193.

of $260,000 had grown to a staff of twelve professionals, and a $400,000 budget in 1972. The NGC operation became largely separate and independent from the Council of State Governments and its affiliates, relocating in a new downtown Washington office building at 1150 17th Street, N.W. From many reports around the country, especially from those governors and state officials whose memory predates the 1967 period when the governors were represented in Washington in name only, the NGC Washington office receives favorable comments, with considerable interest from some governors in expanding its operation further.[29]

COUNTY OFFICIALS

It is perhaps a paradox of the American political system that while the county serves as the principal organizing structure and base for political parties, it generally remains the weakest administrative link in the federal system. The once traditionally moribund condition of county administration is traceable to the constitutional position of American counties. They are invested with only such powers as state legislatures are willing to delegate or otherwise grant. Counties, in fact, stand as the oldest structural form of government in America and, according to some observers, they have "persisted the most in changing the least in responding to the needs and wishes of their citizens."[30]

While stereotypes of the Dark Continent and the courthouse gang persist, important administrative, fiscal, and political changes have overtaken county governments. These changes have touched most of the nation's 3,044 counties. Traditionally concerned primarily with law enforcement, tax collection, relief and election functions, counties today are involved in all the activities in which states and cities participate. Increased assumption of new services and expansion of old, functional consolidation and transfer of functions from lower to higher levels of government, and devolution of shared responsibilities from state and federal authorities are a few of the more perceptible trends producing a major place for counties in the American federal system.

By sharing in the governance of rural, suburban, and central-core cities, county government is inextricably involved in the financing and policy making of all three Americas. Some observers credit counties with the potential for solving national problems. Indeed, the Committee for Economic Development concluded in 1966 that "if the nation is seriously concerned about stronger and better local government, as it should be . . .

---

[29] *National Journal,* 5:935–943, June 30, 1973.

[30] Advisory Commission on Intergovernmental Relations, *Eleventh Annual Report,* Washington, D.C., 1970, p. 8.

weaknesses must be remedied to permit counties to play a major role."[31] At a time of rural depopulation and metropolitan repopulation, counties offer economies of scale, often a broader tax base, area jurisdictional purview, and a prospective structure offering political accountability for planning, management, and delivery of services.

"A major actor in changing the image of county government during the 1960's," states the Advisory Commission on Intergovernmental Relations' *Eleventh Annual Report,* "was the strengthening of the National Association of Counties—changing it from an organization staffed only with a part-time executive secretary in the late 1950's to an association with national prestige and considerable Washington influence."[32] A comparable judgment was made by W. Brooke Graves, a well-known author on American federalism, when he noted that "among the various forces producing change in county government, the National Association of Counties remains at the forefront, providing strong and effective leadership."[33]

Like the United States Conference of Mayors, the National Association of Counties (NACO) began as an organization during the Depression. Its original policies and programs were organized around public works and public welfare programs, its membership overlapping with the Chicago-based American Public Works Society and American Public Welfare Association. NACO was a Washington interest group, but in name only. Between 1936 and 1957 the Association remained a sleepy, rural-county, paper head organization run on a part-time basis by two Washington lawyers. It had an $18,000-a-year budget based on $6 annual dues paid by 3,000 individual county officials.

NACO's revitalization began in 1957 with the appointment of a full-time executive director, Bernard F. Hillenbrand, and the acquisition of staff and permanent office space. County officials from California, the strongest state member, threatened to pull out of NACO unless the organization found a full-time executive director. Hillenbrand fit the prescription for an energetic and experienced practitioner. After spending several years in state and local government, he joined the National League of Cities staff in 1954 to direct its congressional relations activities before moving on to NACO at the age of thirty-one.

Upon assuming the executive directorship, a position he still holds in 1973, Hillenbrand gained foundation support for research and service activities, broadened the organization's membership, and revamped its dues structure. In 1959 NACO was given an appreciable boost as bar-

[31] Committee for Economic Development, *Modernizing Local Government,* Committee for Economic Development, New York, 1966, p. 18.

[32] Advisory Commission on Intergovernmental Relations, *Eleventh Annual Report,* Washington, D.C., 1970, p. 8.

[33] W. Brooke Graves, "Changes in Suburban Counties," Washington, D.C., National Association of Counties, 1968, p. 40 (mimeographed).

gaining agent for county governments by its inclusion in the ACIR with status comparable to that of states and cities. NACO sponsored two urban county congresses, the first in 1959 which brought together elected and appointed policy-making county officials for the purpose of "finding practical solutions to urban problems." Building upon the success of this effort, a second congress held in 1963 moved the Association forward as a viable spokesman for metropolitan interests.[34] Using an initial $160,000 Ford Foundation grant as seed money, Hillenbrand gradually built up NACO's staff, publications, and service functions.

Membership base was transformed from individual county officials to county government membership in 1965, with dues prorated on the basis of population: one-fifth (raised to three-fifths by 1971) of a cent per capita up to a maximum level of $6,000 and a minimum of $100. Similarly, membership climbed from less than 400 in 1963 to 820 by 1973.

NACO's policy making is vested in ten committees in subject areas ranging from air pollution to zoning. Since 1958 these committees have held hearings, drafted organization policy, and built consensus around a NACO policy. The role of the Association's committees as specified in the *American County Platform* is "to carefully study federal, state, and local issues affecting counties and to recommend policy for consideration by the membership."[35] In practice the committee structure, largely controlled by Hillenbrand and NACO leaders, functions to develop consensus on policies and pass resolutions sufficiently ambiguous to generate membership agreement yet broad enough for mandating actions by the Association. The committee system, like that carried on by other government interest groups, promotes legislative expertise among county officials who frequently testify before congressional committees. Thirty-member steering committees direct the operations of each committee and are selected as a consequence of their members' expertise, political contacts, and on the basis of either national ambitions or future promise.

Annual NACO conferences attract as many as 3,000 elected and appointed county officials. To avoid inevitable cleavages among large and small counties, NACO officers and Hillenbrand structure these annual sessions around a specific theme previously agreed upon, such as planning or the development of county information services. Traditionally voting was conducted on the basis of one vote per county, but more recently voting is weighted according to dues—one vote per $500. Hillenbrand brought

[34] See Robert S. Duncombe, *County Government in America*, National Association of Counties, Washington, D.C., 1968; National Association of Counties, *The Urban County Congress of the National Association of Counties*, NACO, Washington, D.C., 1959; and *The Second Urban County Congress of the National Association of Counties*, NACO, Washington, D.C., 1963.

[35] National Association of Counties, *The American County Platform*, NACO, Washington, D.C., 1967, pp. 23–24.

NACO from a rural-dominated organization to a more urban and suburban foundation where counties above 50,000 population comprise roughly half the Association's membership. It was not until 1959, however, that an urban county official became a NACO vice president, moving on to president four years later. Since then, the presidency and four vice presidencies are divided between urban and rural counties, so that leadership alternates between them.[36] Like the executive directors of the other government groups, Hillenbrand aids those organization members aspiring to higher office or seeking publicity through NACO leadership positions. Organizational leadership is vested in a president, the four vice presidents, and a board of forty-eight directors without tenure limit. Promotion follows from vice president to president.

NACO's bylaws indicate that the primary goal of the Association is to stimulate and contribute to the continuing improvement of county government throughout the United States through increased efficiency and higher standards for public service. NACO's immediate goal, according to Hillenbrand, is twofold: (1) obtaining full home-rule authority from state government and (2) reorganizing county government to pattern it after municipal government, with a separate county executive position and separation of administrative and legislative functions as well an independent judiciary.[37] NACO's activities are directed as much at state and county objectives as at national goals. They are not mutually exclusive, however, NACO promotes federal intervention in state-local matters as a modernizing force upon states and counties: expanding county activities, gaining for counties a role in planning and administration of intergovernmental programs, and promoting joint county activities as well as city-county consolidation.

County reform depends largely upon state constitutional and legislative reform. Most state constitutional provisions relating to county government have changed little over the years, imposing inflexibility as to structural forms, prohibition of home rule charters, and limitations on types of services rendered and taxes levied.[38] Thus these impediments and obstructions have encouraged the balkanization of local governments by promoting special authorities, new regional bodies, and functional units other than county governments.

There are at least three basic forms of county government organization: the plural executive or commission form (80 percent of all counties); the county administrator form, where the governing body appoints the county administrative officer or county manager (18 percent); and the county executive plan (2 percent). NACO strongly promotes the county executive

[36] *National Journal,* **3:**130, May 29, 1971.

[37] "Urban Voice in Washington," *Public Management,* July 1968, p. 173.

[38] Advisory Commission on Intergovernmental Relations, *Profile of County Government,* Washington, D.C., 1972, chap. 2.

plan, the strong version whereby an independent county executive is elected by registered voters of the entire county, rather than the weak variation in which a board president is elected by fellow board members as the presiding officer. The number of elected county executives has increased from five to forty-five between 1950 and 1970. This structural form of governance still prevails in only a small number of counties, however. Table 2 indicates the states and population groups which have adopted the county executive form of government.

To promote membership and county reform, NACO publishes the *American County* (monthly) and a weekly newsletter entitled *NACO News and Views*. NACO also services 47 state leagues, 2,500 affiliated county members, and 14 functional affiliates through technical research, grants-in-aid information, and manpower training. Functional affiliates include county administrators, planners, public health officers, treasurers and finance officers, parks and recreation officers, engineers, recorders

T-2 Elected County Executives: Location and Population (Size of Counties)

State	Population Group				
	Under 100,000	100,000–199,000	250,000–599,000	Above 600,000	Total
Alaska	8	1	0	0	9
California	0	0	0	1	1
Colorado	0	0	1	0	1
Delaware	0	0	1	0	1
Florida	0	0	1	1	2
Georgia	0	1	0	0	1
Hawaii	3	0	0	1	4
Indiana	0	0	0	1	1
Louisiana	0	0	3	0	3
Maryland	1	0	2	2	5
Missouri	0	0	0	2	2
New York	0	3	1	5	9
Oregon	0	0	1	0	1
Tennessee	0	0	1	0	1
Washington	0	0	0	1	1
Wisconsin	0	2	0	1	3
	12	7	11	15	45

Source: National Association of Counties, 1972.

and clerks, attorneys, and others. The most active and influential of these is the National Association of County Engineers, which holds its annual meetings together with NACO. Besides seeking to upgrade county services and personnel, NACO runs joint activities with the National League of Cities in labor relations and regional councils. Roughly half of NACO's more than $1 million in operating funds is derived from research and training grants from federal agencies and foundations; the other half comes from membership dues, convention fees, and other services.

To further promote county modernization, NACO launched in 1969 its New County U.S.A. Center with foundation support. New County provides a major NACO thrust at county modernization directed at state governments and county clients around stronger political leaders (county executive movement), new county services and management reforms, and the promotion of intergovernmental reform. The center collects information about where county government is changing, what kinds of changes are taking place, and the results of these changes. The Advisory Commission on Intergovernmental Relations (ACIR) assisted New County in 1971 by publishing model statutes promoting recommendations both by the ACIR and NACO "for equipping counties to function effectively in the decades ahead."[39]

In 1971 NACO took another major step toward broadening its constituency by establishing its Council of Elected County Executives. Modeled after the USCM's Legislative Action Committee, this new lobbying arm included primarily large, populated, suburban counties and their executives. It augmented NACO's claims as representative of and spokesman for metropolitan and urban interests. Urban county executives from Westchester and Nassau counties (New York) served as officers, together with select members from suburban Baltimore counties (Prince Georges and Montgomery), Milwaukee, King County (Washington), St. Louis (Missouri) and the new city-county mayors from Indianapolis, Miami, and Jacksonville.

The greater portion of NACO's forty-five-man staff works on contract research in New County. In contrast to the mayor's dozen or so full-time lobbyists, NACO has a five-man lobbying staff. Where the mayors have a substantial backup research-policy analysis, NACO has little support except when New County or NACO's research foundation staff happen to be working in areas that might be useful to the lobbyists. Thus NACO lobbyists are spread rather thinly across congressional and executive agency work and are not now capable of covering the full range of activities that the mayors do.

Traditionally NACO policy has been supportive of a collaborative

39 Advisory Commission on Intergovernmental Relations, *County Reform*, Washington, D.C., 1971, p. 1.

partnership of federal, state, and local officials, with rigid adherence to the policy stance of greater involvement by the 75,000 elected county officials in local decision making. In stressing its vital role in the governance of urban, suburban, and rural America, NACO has been at the forefront of legislative coalitions supporting federal programs in highways, air and water pollution control, park and recreational services, Job Corps, area redevelopment, community development, and housing. According to the ACIR's *Eleventh Annual Report,* NACO's "influence on national policies had grown considerably by the end of 1969."[40]

NACO's emerging prominence among Washington lobbying organizations is in part a function of several factors. The federal government has accorded counties a greater role in intergovernmental programs through single and multiple county planning and operational grants. State and municipal governments are making greater use of counties to overcome problems of scale and organization for service delivery and consolidation of areawide functions. Also, as the *National Journal* maintains, "The best thing the nation's counties have going for them in Washington is Bernard F. Hillenbrand. [His] name and hustle have become synonymous with the county cause at the White House and on Capitol Hill."[41]

The National Association of Counties manifests many of the organizational characteristics of the National League of Cities. It has a somewhat unwieldy membership, open cleavages among large and small jurisdictions, and tensions between direct county members and state league affiliates. NACO, too, tends to avoid controversial issues, develop policy through a committee system, and delegate authority over day-to-day activities to a permanent staff. But significant differences nonetheless exist between the two.

The NLC built up its state leagues prior to recruiting individual member cities and engaging in national lobbying. NACO's Hillenbrand is trying to accomplish the same goals, but he begins with an anomalous situation where his organization tends to be stronger at the national level than at the state level. In contrast, NLC's statewide leagues are sufficiently well organized to concentrate on administrative modernization, recruitment of new members, and individual state activities, leaving the national association free to focus on federal affairs. NACO's state leagues generally are weak and disorganized. The strength of state leagues usually varies with the functions performed or services rendered by county governments. Where services are broad, paralleling those performed by the typical city, the state leagues are strong. California is the best organized by far because the state has made the county a stronger administrative and political unit

---

[40] Advisory Commission on Intergovernmental Relations, *Eleventh Annual Report,* Washington, D.C., 1971, p. 8.

[41] *National Journal,* 5:132, June 30, 1973.

than the city. California counties are responsible for health, welfare, criminal justice, pollution, housing, and transportation. Besides California, Western states like Washington, Oregon, and Utah have strong state county associations, as do several Midwestern states like Michigan, Wisconsin, and Minnesota. A handful of Southern states—Florida, Georgia, North Carolina, Tennessee, and Virginia—are well above the average. But only New Jersey in the East is considered a strong county state—and to an extent, New York as well. All told, only fifteen states, predominately Western ones, have more than half their counties represented in NACO.

NACO and counties have many things going in their favor at the national level, both actual and potential. Census figures for 1970 indicate that 85 percent of the population growth over the past decade occurred in suburban areas. Nearly all large cities, especially those east of the Mississippi River, experienced population losses over the past two decades, while their surrounding suburbs in most cases now contain greater populations than the central cities. Counties are the apparent political heirs of suburban growth and central-city decline, a force which has been significantly propelled by reapportionment. Once a distinct minority in population as compared to central cities and rural areas, suburbs are now dominant among the three. NACO increasingly seeks to capitalize on these population shifts and has achieved some significant successes thus far.

Supreme Court reapportionment applied to counties *(Avery v. Midland County)* and to Congress has had an interesting impact upon counties both at the state level and nationally. The Midland decision helped remove major impediments to making counties a more viable governmental unit. As a consequence of legislative reapportionment, counties lost some of their political control over state legislatures, especially the more rural-dominated ones. On the other hand, urban counties gained at the state level and suburban ones at the national level. The 92nd Congress, for the first time, was composed of more members from predominantly suburban constituencies (165 seats) than either the cities (136 seats) or rural areas (134 seats). The real weight of this suburban bloc has not yet materialized, but with gradual changes in seniority, its weight will increasingly be felt at the national level.[42]

Much of the counties' strength stems not from their significant strides in service delivery or problem solving but more from the basic fact of their being the fundamental organizing structure for political parties. The county is the building block in most cases for local, state, and national political structures. County politicians play a major role in nominating, financing, and electing members of Congress. They tend to be far more tied in to

[42] See Ralph G. Caso, "Counties: New Suburban Power and Influence," Report done for the National Association of Counties by the Nassau County Executive, New York, July 19, 1971 (mimeographed).

local congressmen and their activities than a mayor who may be outside this structure. Hillenbrand asserts this distinction more succinctly. "The political strength of NACO in terms of getting something done in Washington comes basically from the fact that NACO membership corresponds to the makeup of Congress."[43] Where governors have overlapping constituencies with senators and have the same coterminous political boundaries, many county officials share the identical constituency and boundaries with the congressmen. In the counties' situation, control of the local party structure is by far the most important factor, and here county officials can be much more effective in influencing a congressman than a governor his state's senators.

Modernization of county structure also may work to NACO's benefit. Urbanization trends are influencing, if not forcing, widespread reform of county governments. Numerous counties are in the process of improving and modernizing their structures, while states are proving more receptive to granting counties greater home rule powers and larger intergovernmental tasks than before. Increasing federal-state emphasis upon regional approaches to such problems as zoning, housing, transportation, environment, education, and planning has generated considerable enthusiasm concerning counties and the new functions that they may be capable of performing. Indeed counties provide an alternative to fractionated local governments, special districts, and councils of government (COGs) that fail to move beyond a voluntary, cooperative basis. However, counties have competition from other areawide instrumentalities. Who will win out is unclear. But one thing is certain, noted the ACIR in 1972, "the pressure for areawide mechanisms for areawide problems will not fade away."[44]

NACO is also riding the crest of strong support from the Nixon administration. Mr. Nixon's own experience in California politics makes him well aware of potential county strength based on this model. Former Vice President Agnew, his staff, and several White House Office staffers either served in county government or have ties to Republican county officials. The new executive director of the ACIR, William MacDougall — who came to Washington after nearly twenty years of directing the California State Association of Counties — has taken a strong interest in ACIR activities aimed at promoting county government. On Capitol Hill, NACO has moved away from its traditional brick and mortar interests by seeking greater county inclusion in programs aimed at community development, pollution, housing, criminal justice, and other matters. Strong supporters

[43] *National Journal,* **5:**132, June 30, 1973.

[44] Advisory Commission on Intergovernmental Relations, *Thirteenth Annual Report,* Washington, D.C., 1972, p. 14.

of counties within the GOP and executive agencies look upon counties as future administrative units for dealing with areawide problems and the cities as well as forming new political constituencies.

Nevertheless, NACO and counties still suffer from lack of identity, lack of a positive image, and outmoded structures. The multihead commission structure remains largely intact in most counties and in some states is mandated by state law. The lack of identifiable leadership except in those few counties with elected county executives severely handicaps counties in dealing with Washington and makes them look less effective than mayors from the vantage point of many federal agencies. Counties vary tremendously in structure, size, and functions—from do-nothings and near Neanderthals to highly progressive, well organized administrative units. Much of New England, for example, either has no formal county structures or extremely weak ones. This, to some federal officials, is indicative of all counties nationally. Thus counties and the county lobby are too amorphous for some to grasp fully, particularly the distinction between an Eastern and a Western county. Even more than the differences that exist among the fifty states, the diversity that prevails among county governments in terms of form of government, structure, and election of county officials suggests the enormous educational and reform problem confronting NACO both at the federal level and at the state-local level as well.

Finally, NACO's impact at the federal level is directly related to the organization's internal membership problems. Nearly 90 percent of the nation's population in 1970 lived within counties. NACO's 800-plus members comprise 60 percent of the U.S. population or some 65 percent of those who live in counties. NACO thus speaks for slightly more than half the residents within county governments. More than 400 nonmembers have populations above 50,000 and 26 nonmembers have populations exceeding 250,000. If NACO is to speak with greater authority in Washington, particularly for metropolitan interests, it must expand its membership to reach these counties and their officials.

NACO's problems are compounded by distribution among states in terms of numbers and populations served. Seven states have 100 or more counties, Texas having the most with 254; 18 states have fewer than 40, and 9 have fewer than 20. During each of the past three decades, half the nation's counties lost population, with the consequence that many rural counties are growing more rural and urban ones are becoming more urban. More than 40 percent of the nation's counties have populations of less than 25,000, and nearly 80 percent are below 50,000.[45] Translated into state-county composition, more than half the states have, in most of their counties, populations of less than 50,000. While many of these counties may be

[45] Advisory Commission on Intergovernmental Relations, *Profile of County Government*, Washington, D.C., 1972, p. 1.

inefficient and poorly organized, their capacity to resist state efforts toward consolidation or merger has been nearly uniformly successful.

NACO's constituency, divided as it is between largely rural and largely urban counties, often requires separate policy objectives for both. At times this extends to separate, individual services to meet their different needs. NACO's county modernization program typically stops short of threatening the existence of these smaller units. Thus Hillenbrand and NACO leaders pursue two strategies simultaneously: that of expanding membership, which is necessary both in terms of greater income for staff and for speaking with greater authority at the federal level, and that of reforming county structures nationally. These strategies are not always compatible and are often the source of considerable internal friction. In that greater income is necessary to expand the Association's staff and lobbying activities, Hillenbrand concentrates much effort on grant acquisition and the recruitment of new members. NACO could double its income from dues if all eligible counties became members. Focusing upon these activities exclusively, however, can detract from the Association's county modernization work. NACO officials recognize that their effectiveness at the federal level cannot be divorced from progress made at reforming counties at the local level. Thus Hillenbrand and NACO leaders try to strike a balance between county modernization and fund raising on the theory that both are necessary to promoting NACO's effectiveness as a national lobby.

THE COUNCIL OF STATE GOVERNMENTS

The Council of State Governments (COSGO) is a joint agency of all the state governments created, supported, and directed by them. The objectives of the Council are as follows:[46]

> *To assist the states in improving their legislative, administrative, and judicial practices, to promote interstate cooperation, and to facilitate and improve state-local and state-federal relations.*

Since its inception in 1933, the Council has functioned primarily as a service organization. It conducts research; maintains an inquiry and information service for state agencies, officials, and legislators; and serves as a clearinghouse for information exchange among state public officials and agencies. It also holds national and regional meetings in which state officials and legislators survey common problems, provides staff for affiliated organizations, and issues publications and proceedings for use by states in

[46] Council of State Governments, *The Council of State Governments and Affiliated Organizations,* COSGO, Chicago, 1965, p. 1.

respect to all aspects of governmental affairs. Governed by a board of managers comprising representatives from all three governmental branches, the Council is organized to represent directly each of the states, affiliated organizations, and others that cooperate closely with it.

. The Council, like many other national associations of government officials and organizations interested in public administration, established its headquarters on the University of Chicago campus to become an integral member of the famous but now defunct Public Administration Clearing House (PACH). Attracted to Chicago by Spelman Foundation support and the enterprising activities of such men as Charles Merriam and Louis Brownlow, the Council emerged out of the American Legislators' Association, an earlier organization, which was founded in 1925 by Colorado State Senator Henry W. Toll. Under Brownlow's organizational talents and guiding philosophy more than twenty separate, distinct, and autonomous associations were assembled eventually under one roof. They were united by common interests and purposes rather than hierarchical relations and reflected concern with the improvement of administration, organization, technique, and methods as opposed to promotion of reform or political improvement at the polls.[47] The Council was clearly the largest and most important of the organizations that had their offices at the famous 1313 East 60th Street location on the University of Chicago campus.

Modeled on previous efforts coordinating functional associations, like education officials assembled in Washington and health officials in New York, PACH served as a central secretariat for organizations and officials. It provided for the interchange of information and experience, with the expectation that greater interdependency might improve government practices and procedures. Two of Brownlow's basic tenets, which are fundamental to PACH's operations and the assemblage of public officials' groups, suggest its orientation. Brownlow believed in the then dominant political science tradition "that there is and always will be a difference between politics on the one hand and administration on the other, no matter how closely they may be related in a democratic society." This philosophy was reflected conspicuously in member groups' information exchange and service functions, precluding national lobbying activities and other forms of political activity. Brownlow felt that government administration and management could be upgraded through instilling greater professionalism in its employees. His other conviction was that if the public officials' groups were located in Washington instead of Chicago the "overshadowing presence of the federal government would compel the staff to

---

[47] Louis Brownlow, *A Passion For Anonymity*, University of Chicago Press, Chicago, 1958, p. 237. For a brief but incomplete history of the "1313" complex, see Barry D. Karl, *Executive Reorganization and Reform in the New Deal*, Harvard University Press, Cambridge, Mass. 1963.

think federally," rather than in terms of state and local government administration, as they did for the greater part of their history.[48] Brownlow and Merriam alike envisaged improvements in social science and public administration due to the interaction of academia and government practitioners.

These tenets served the purposes of PACH and affiliated members well through the early 1950s, but they came, in time, to lay the seeds for dissolution. "The sisters never married," concluded one government official long familiar with PACH. The federal system had become larger, more complex, and centrist, while federal-state relations had assumed greater importance to constituent members than the improvement of state administration or the promotion of interstate compacts. National associations of public officials found federal orientation, contact, and information services too important to be directed any longer from Chicago, necessitating relocation in the nation's capital. Moreover, rivalry among the groups proved a more powerful centrifugal force than the centripetal activities involving professionalism, information exchanges, and research.

The National Governors' Conference remained unattached to the "1313" complex until 1938, when the need to acquire staff, research services, headquarters, and a permanent secretariat compelled it to join. Affiliation with COSGO was placed on a more permanent basis with the naming of Frank Bane, Brownlow's protégé and a man known to be friendly to several governors, as director of the Council. Serving in a dual role as director of COSGO and secretary to the governors, Bane's skillful leadership produced a harmonious relationship between the two government groups from 1938 to 1958.

Moreover, during the two decades of Bane's leadership, the activities and reports of the organizations were barely distinguishable. Joint operation followed from overlapping membership and staff as well as interlocking leadership. COSGO greatly expanded its operations in the 1940s, adding new affiliates of state executive, legislative, and judicial associations like chief justices, attorneys general, state budget and purchasing officers, lieutenant governors, state legislators, juvenile, parole, and other court officials. It also expanded its service functions by opening regional offices in New York, Washington, San Francisco, and Atlanta.

The Council and affiliates tended to view their stakes in federal legislation during the 1940s and 1950s as largely inconsequential. It, like the National Governors' Conference, believed in keeping Washington at a distance. COSGO opened a Washington office in 1938, which, outside of prominent wartime regulatory activity, operated on a shoestring basis with little visibility. It followed federal legislation in such areas as water resources planning and highway safety, where membership consensus was

[48] Louis Brownlow, *A Passion for Anonymity*, pp. 254–259, 237.

attainable and the Council could record a moderate impact upon federal policy.[49]

Frank Bane ran both the Council and the Conference on a highly personal basis, promoting personal relations with state and federal executives rather than with Congress. He had served for several governors early in his career and received appointments to government commissions under four Presidents. "The governors didn't view the cities' lobbying buildup in Washington with any great alarm," recalled Bane.[50]

> Cities were still referred to as political subdivisions of the states. Besides, with something like twenty former governors in the Senate, we were confident that direct federal-urban programs wouldn't move much beyond housing and urban renewal—at least not until the passage of the 1946 Federal Airport Act—a landmark in intergovernmental relations.

The 1960s found COSGO adjusting to new pressures, problems, and conditions. With Bane's retirement in 1958 and appointment as the first director of the newly established Advisory Commission on Intergovernmental Relations, his successor, Brevard Crihfield, assumed leadership of a soon embattled NGC and a Council with several disgruntled affiliates. Much of the problem was the groups' location. PACH had ceased operations, while several urban groups like the American Municipal Association and the National Association of Housing and Redevelopment Officials had vacated "1313" for a Washington address.

The example set by the NGC in opening its Office for Federal-State Relations in Washington was soon followed by other COSGO affiliates, which did likewise. COSGO, too, changed its headquarters in 1969, making "1313" into its Midwestern office and moving its major operations into a spacious new center on the University of Kentucky campus at Lexington. For a brief period the NGC and COSGO had difficulty in sorting out their respective political and administrative services. The former eventually turned into a full-time lobbying operation servicing the governors exclusively, while the latter broadened its traditional strengths in research, training, and general service functions.[51] Once this transition was completed, the NGC and COSGO arrived at a division of labor whereby this new balance and diversity complemented one another.

---

[49] Rochelle Stanfield, "Intergovernmental Relations: The Role and Program of the Council of State Governments in Perspective," internal working document for the National Governors' Conference, Washington, D.C., 1968.

[50] Frank Bane, private interview conducted at the Office of Emergency Planning, Washington, D.C., January 3, 1969.

[51] See Brevard Crihfield, "Future Operations of the Council of State Governments," *State Government*, **40**:16–20, Winter 1967; Council of State Governments, "Budget for Future Operations," COSGO, Chicago, 1967 (mimeographed).

Like the other government interest groups, COSGO has benefited from a much expanded federal system. Federal departments and agencies utilize COSGO for grant research, manpower training, technical service dissemination, and for general clearinghouse activities. To its Consulting Clearinghouse Service, COSGO added in 1971 a large technical service program to aid state agencies in problem solving, promoting state planning, and sharing experiences from one state to the next. COSGO remains heavily service-oriented, providing extensive study of state legislative, administrative, and judicial practices. More recently, it has become involved in the actual delivery of services through training, loaned staff, and as a repository of information for and about the states. The Council of State Governments' publications include *The Book of the States* (biennial), *State Government* (quarterly), *State Government News* (monthly), and *Suggested State Legislation* (annual). It also publishes proceedings of conferences, issues pamphlets, and publishes major works in such state service fields as education, mental health, planning, and judicial reform.

2

CHIEF EXECUTIVES IN
THE FEDERAL ARENA

★ ★ ★

Intergovernmental lobbying is not a new phenomenon. Constitutionally, it was institutionalized in the federal structure with equal state representation in the Senate and national representation based on population in the House of Representatives. In a larger sense, intergovernmental lobbying has persisted over time through interbureaucratic communication, the earliest of federal-state programs, among professional associations of government employees, and recently through the collective activities of governors, mayors, and county officials.

The term *intergovernmental* signifies various types of interjurisdictional relationships, like interrelationships found throughout government, each with its own constitutional and legal basis and each with its own practical and political considerations. Federal-state, federal-local, and federal-state-local relations, which are among the primary concerns of this study, by no means began fifty years ago with the first large federal grant program or even with the institution of the Governors' Conference at the turn of the century. Contrary to nineteenth-century court interpretation and to the perpetuation of myths about the glorious past, considerable evidence supports the contention that federal and state governments worked together in many important spheres and activities during the previous century. A great deal of cooperation between state and nation existed in this period. Not only that, but also more substantial continuity between the past and present has persisted than supposed.[1]

Contact between public officials at all levels was generated in a variety of institutional, programmatic, and professional forms. Paralleling, if not

---

[1] See Daniel J. Elazar, *The American Partnership,* University of Chicago Press, Chicago, 1962, and "The Shaping of Intergovernmental Relations in the Twentieth Century," in Robert E. Crew, Jr. (ed.), *State Politics,* Wadsworth, Belmont, Calif., 1968, pp. 53–68.

preceding, the federal government's involvement in national improvements—such as commerce, communication, education, and the general economy of subnational governments—is the widespread activity of professional associations. These groups, comprising public officials in research, education, engineering, science, and health, formed early clienteles around embryonic federal programs and agencies. According to Elazar, the new form of federal relations began developing in the 1840s, over time growing "to be a significant means of improving government services at both levels and of forging strong, if not informal cooperative lines between Washington and localities."[2]

The Departments of Agriculture and the Interior were the first of the major clientele-oriented departments to be established in response to demands from the states and from rural America. Yet the cities of the nineteenth century were not without their claims upon federal departments for commerce routes, freight and passenger services, government buildings, or appeals to the Army Corps of Engineers for waterway and harbor dredging and other internal improvements. Tariff concessions on specific items were said to be able to make or break individual cities whose survival depended on particular industries. In several cities party machines built durable alliances with banking and commercial interests for tariff preferences, government contracts, and various subsidies which were amply represented through Washington lobbying.[3] Indeed, tracing federal-local relations through the nineteenth century, Elazar concluded that "direct federal-city relations created by the river and harbor improvement programs . . . were possibly as extensive in proportion to the total amount of intergovernmental activity of the time as are direct federal-city relations in contemporary redevelopment programs."[4]

Likewise, intergovernmental lobbying as carried on by elected federal representatives has long been a characteristic of legislative life and executive-congressional relations. Boardinghouse or mess groups of senators and congressmen who lived and dined together in Washington—often by regional, state, or smaller groupings—constituted reference blocs in voting, negotiation, and bargaining in the earliest Congresses.[5] When election to the Senate resided with state legislatures and not the popular vote, great party battles ensued in many states for control over the instructed senators sent to Washington—frequently for the protection of

[2] Daniel J. Elazar, "Urban Problems and the Federal Government: A Historical Inquiry," *Political Science Quarterly,* **82**:516, December 1967.

[3] See Harvey C. Mansfield, "Political Parties, Patronage, and the Federal Government Service," in Wallace S. Sayre (ed.), *The Federal Government Service* Prentice-Hall, Englewood Cliffs, N.J., 1965, pp. 131–133.

[4] Daniel J. Elazar, "Urban Problems," p. 513.

[5] See James S. Young, *The Washington Community,* Columbia University Press, New York, 1966, chap. 5.

vested state interests in patronage, land disposition, traction franchises, commerce routes, and business.[6] Sectionalism, long characteristic of the past century's politics, is another lively manifestation of subnational government groupings which still raises its head on contemporary issues of civil rights, water rights, defense spending, and in other areas. It, too, has emanated from state-local politics, often with governors and mayors promoting regional cleavages at the national level.

Partisan mutual adjustment in the form of logrolling—wherein legislators exchange support for each other's demands—for decades has been a distinctive operation of the legislative process. "Pork barrel," the designation given the allocation of miscellaneous projects lumped together in the rivers-and-harbors bill, is perhaps the classic example of congressional logrolling in the allocation of dams, levees, and other construction projects among congressional districts and states. Congressional interest in pork barrel is undiminished by time yet often overshadowed in the post-1950 period by the more visible and conflictual pursuit of national government procurement, defense-aerospace contracts, and project grants like water and sewer programs. Governors and mayors, largely on an individual basis, have been participants in these congressional activities. Intergovernmental lobbying as conducted by public officials—be they federal representatives, professional associations, or chief executives of state-local governments—cannot therefore be considered something entirely new. It is rich in antecedents, functional equivalents, and gradual institutional developments. In practice this system of intergovernmental lobbying is not a widely recognized aspect of American federalism. Nevertheless, it is no less a real one, fundamentally important to maintaining the positions of subnational governments.

PHASES IN GROUP RELATIONS

What has changed in scope, intensity, and organization, however, are the activities by state and local government chief executives aimed at influencing their federal constituency. What some assert to be the basic patterns in the development of American federalism have not always been reflected in corresponding behavior by state-local executives in their Washington relations. By and large governors and mayors were not very interested in what transpired in the nation's capital prior to the 1930s. Before that time, after all, states and localities outspent the federal government in domestic activity and indeed, as the record of the progressive era suggests, preceded the national government in efforts to regulate corpora-

6 See William H. Riker, "The Senate and American Federalism," *American Political Science Review* **49**:452–469, June 1955.

tions and deal with social reforms. What activities existed betweeen these subnational officials and Washington tended to be narrow and unsustained. The Governors' Conference, for example, had extremely limited agendas, largely devoted to the technical business of state government such as administrative reform and interstate cooperation. State governments still had rather simple housekeeping responsibilities, budgets were small and often surpluses existed, taxes were low, and legislatures typically met briefly on a biennial basis.

The principal competition and tension in intergovernmental relations were restricted mainly to issues of state versus federal powers. The governors persisted in their belief that they had sufficient collective power to block or otherwise frustrate unwanted federal intrusion in state matters. To the extent that governors were concerned with national policy, their principal interest traditionally was confined to keeping Washington out of state business.[7]

Phase One

The Depression introduced the first phase of sustained group relations with Washington, but more from the perspective of large-city mayors than governors or county officials. From the New Deal era through the early sixties, the first phase of government interest group dealings with their federal constituency, their attention to federal matters remained fragmented, specialized, and discontinuous on the one hand, rarely competive or cooperative on the other. This phase is not only a reflection of most subnational officials and their attitudes toward Washington but also a commentary on the rather meager federal expenditure on intergovernmental programs operating on the state-local government level. From the vantage point of most governors, nothing of much intergovernmental significance occurred in Congress during this period except by way of the federal highway program, housing, and welfare.

For the mayors, the year 1932 constituted what Roscoe Martin termed a "sort of geological fault line" in the development of the American federal system. Where formal relations between the federal government and subnational governments had been limited substantially to dealings with the states, the cities became partners with the states.[8] What had previously been a covert and indirect recognition of the cities as members of the federal system now rapidly emerged as overt and direct. Direct federal-local ties multiplied under the New Deal recovery programs and were fur-

[7] Glenn Brooks, *When Governors Convene*, John Hopkins University Press, Baltimore, 1961, chap. 1.

[8] Roscoe C. Martin, *The Cities and The Federal System*, Atherton, New York, 1965, p. 111.

ther promoted by the Conference of Mayors, which organized to sustain, protect, and nurture these newly established bonds.

The greater significance of direct federal-city relations lay in the patterns it established. In addition to sharing with the states partnership in the federal system, the cities became direct competitors with the states for sharing in the allocation and redistribution of national resources. State governments and governors may have regarded with cold, unfriendly eyes all direct contact between their local subdivisions and the federal government; but as these relations expanded, they could no longer ignore them. To the extent states tightened their controls over cities and blocked direct aid, cities only redoubled their end runs to Washington, often hastening the development of legislative and administrative bypass. While direct federal aid bypassing the states had not developed on a very large scale prior to the early sixties, it nonetheless provided the basis for a future urban strategy, the counterinfluence exercised by city leaders in bargaining with their states and federal constituency in gaining aid. City leaders sought to loosen state ties, enlarge on their separateness and the uniqueness of their problems, and promote direct federal aid as a defensive weapon against state intransigence. Also, where large cities began engaging in the practice of playing state governments off against their federal constituency, so nearly all local governments eventually joined the game in the expectation that they, too, might gain federal assistance at less risk than dealing with their states would involve.

Other distinguishing characteristics of the first phase need to be set in context so that the distinctiveness of later developments may be more fully appreciated. The Depression obviously shattered many a governor's confidence in the individuality of each state and its capacity to cope independently with its problems. While the Depression did force upon the states changes in taxation and relief administration, it did not radically transform them. The nationalistic interpretations of Roosevelt's New Deal programs to the contrary, the period of 1933 to 1940 "witnessed neither federal dictation, a completely cooperative federalism, nor a dramatically new state progressivism."[9] Federal aid to state and local governments in 1937, the height of the New Deal, did not increase over the next fifteen-year period, and, in fact, declined precipitously during the war years. As a percentage of total federal outlays for domestic purposes, federal aid to subnational governments declined from 1941 through 1952.

During the postwar period, federal aid to states and localities climbed slowly but distinctly up through 1964. In aggregate, federal aid as a percentage of total state-local revenues increased by less than 5 percent in the ten-year span between 1954 and 1964. Even through 1964, nearly 80

[9] James T. Patterson, "The New Deal and the States," *The American Historical Review*, **54**:77, October 1967.

percent of federal aid to the states could still be accounted for in terms of public assistance contributions and the federal-aid highway programs. Martin observed of this period that three federal programs—housing, slum clearance, and aid-to-airport programs—constituted the "essence of federal-city relations."[10] If one adds to the above brick-and-mortar programs various others for school construction and educational aid to impacted areas, these federal programs comprised roughly three-quarters of all direct federal aid to local governments.

The lobbying activities of the Conference of Mayors during the 1950s centered nearly exclusively on housing and urban renewal. The renewal program was the first large-scale federal effort in assistance designed to deal with problems largely confined to the nation's urban centers. Title I of the Federal Housing Act of 1949—the sections dealing with urban development and slum clearance and later broadened by Title IX of the 1954 Housing Act—became the key urban elements in the national housing programs directed toward the goal of a "sound home and a suitable living environment for every American family." These urban programs were to be achieved through federal aid, state enabling legislation, local government planning, and largely private real estate and building initiative. The mayors were extremely aggressive in expanding urban renewal, gaining congressional appropriations for its support, and broadening its scope and administrative guidelines. They were partially successful in fighting the Eisenhower administration's long but futile search for an entrepreneurial substitute for public housing and periodic Presidential vetoes over federal housing legislation.

To sustain support for the program, the mayors acquiesced to certain basic changes while supporting other aspects of the program. Its direction and scope were altered away from its housing orientation to commercial, industrial, and institutional developments. Also, through a series of legislative and administrative changes, the program was expanded to include smaller cities and towns. The expectations governing urban renewal and low-income housing often far exceeded results. Many mayors recognized that these programs were inadequate to meet actual urban needs. They were slow, unwieldy, and ineffectual in proportion to the magnitude of the cities' growing problems. Nonetheless, these programs were all that the federal government had to offer at the time. For large-city mayors concerned with protecting the city's tax base and promoting central-city viability, urban renewal remained the principal if not only tool provided by higher-level governments to attain these results. Thus many a mayor's problem-solving staff was totally consumed by dealing with its federal constituency in these narrow programmatic areas, even though the actual

[10] Roscoe C. Martin, "Washington and the Cities," in *The Federal Government and The Cities*, George Washington University, Washington, D.C., 1961, p. 11.

results in some cases ceased having much relevance to what the city needed.

In sum, for the period of the 1930s through the early 1960s, with the exception of the brief interlude of big-city mayors' activities and the governors' wartime prominence, state-local chief executives were simply not much concerned about Washington and their federal constituency. These attitudes are amply reflected in the resolutions passed by the various national government interest groups and from their various federal-related activities. Whatever relations existed between subnational chief executives and their federal constituency tended to be parochial. Each group jealously guarded the prerogatives and advantages it had accrued in early periods and sought to expand upon them. Each tended to specialize in the specific federal programs and policies that most preoccupied its level of government: governors and state bureaucracies in health and hospitals, education, highways, and employment; the counties in agriculture, highways, conservation, and economic development; the mayors in housing, urban renewal, and welfare assistance.

Even the much-touted mayors' relations with Washington during the thirties can only be considered in light of later developments to represent a rather robust childhood that is only slowly developing into maturity. La Guardia's leadership of the big-city mayors constituted a highly personal lobby, largely reflecting the unbounded energies and enthusiasm of this city leader. It was born out of the cities' fiscal destitution and was grounded in the mayors' allegiance to President Roosevelt and his New Deal programs. The mayors, however, failed to sustain the crisis-generated unity, tenacity, and dedication characteristic of this earlier period. With the exception of housing and urban renewal, the mayors had a rather insignificant impact on federal legislation from the postwar period through the early sixties.

Phase Two

By the middle 1960s a second phase of relationships between subnational executives and Washington had clearly emerged. This second phase did not correspond to any single event like the Depression or a clear demarcation line like 1932. This second phase grew out of a pattern of events and federal policies both internal and external to the groups which since 1964 stimulated vast changes in their organization and activities. It affected their relations with federal officialdom and also radically transformed their relations to each other.

"It is not too much to say," observed Davis and Sundquist of this period, "that federalism, as it has been known in the preceding seventeen decades of the American republic, had been revolutionized."[11] What occurred at the federal level was a massive breakthrough in domestic legislation directed at states, local governments, and other public-private instrumentalities for the purpose of achieving national programs and goals. These new programs not only promoted significant departures from preexisting intergovernmental relations—as measured by scope, magnitude, and attendant responses required of other jurisdictions—but also brought governors and mayors into direct competition with one another over the control of federal programs and funds. New constituencies, claimants, and instrumentalities for conducting government business were stimulated, and these had a sweeping impact upon state-local governments and their chief executives.

Between 1964 and 1966 an entire generation's backlog of ideas and programs swept through Congress and became law. These new domestic programs asserted national purposes in such areas as racial discrimination, educational opportunity, eradication of poverty, the rebuilding of cities, jobs for the unemployed, health care for the aged and indigent, and the abatement of air and water pollution. The sheer number of programs distinguishes this period from others. Though the tabulation of federal grants and separate programs is often confused by exactly what one is counting or attempting to demonstrate (individual programs, categories of programs, subcategories, separate authorizations), the number of grant programs and/or separate authorizations for subcategories doubled between 1964 and 1968. According to separate authorizations, the number climbed from 225 to 438 by early 1969 count, and this is the most frequently cited figure for federal grant-in-aid expansion. More significant perhaps than sheer numbers are the demonstrable changes that occurred in the philosophy of federal aid, types of grant programs, directional bias, and functional concentration.

Briefly, federal grant programs date back to the nineteenth century, when federal aid in the form of land grants, technical services, and assistance promoted shared functions between government levels. These were continued into the next century. Federal grants-in-aid are a judicially approved device for achieving national purposes by spending federal tax moneys for general welfare purposes. Generally most federal grants involve the payment of federal funds to a lower level of government for a specified purpose, usually on some matching basis and in accordance with prescribed standards or governing requirements. Federal grants are allocated to all eligible jurisdictions for selected functions on the basis of some formula which prior to the 1930s was typically a flat matching con-

---

[11] David W. Davis and James L. Sundquist, *Making Federalism Work*, Brookings Institution, Washington, D.C., 1969, p. 1.

tribution, but since then this formula has increasingly included such criteria as fiscal capacity of the recipient government, population, number of poor people, or a combination of these.

Federal grants also have a wide variety of purposes: to stimulate activity where little or none existed before (mental health), to guarantee certain minimum service levels (vocational education), to ease special hardships (federal impacted areas), to equalize resources (hospital construction), and to support economic stabilization or development (Appalachian programs, public works acceleration grants).[12] Grants are also given on a project-type basis for demonstration, research, or experimentation (mass transit, juvenile delinquency), and planning or coordination (glue money for discretionary use by chief executives as in the Safe Streets Program). Since 1966, two other types of grants have come into prominence, namely bloc grants and revenue sharing. The former involves large categorical grants for use in broad functional areas (Partnership for Health; Safe Streets), and the latter entails sums of federal funds returned to states and localities—sums largely unrestricted as to use and devoid of any matching requirements.

From the 1920s through the 1950s federal assistance progressed from flat grants for minimum service levels to variable matching ratios to promote equalization among the states through categorical programs. Federal grants generally concentrated upon rural American and many of the poorer states, in terms of per capita income, for purposes of promoting certain basic service levels and redistributing federal revenues from above-average-income states to below-average-income states. However, a significant break with the past occurred in the sixties: a shift in program focus away from the historical bias favoring rural America to a more metropolitan base, the bypassing of states and even local jurisdictions to deal with specific groups or problems, and the emphasis upon project types of grants as compared to the more traditional formula based grants of the past. Project grants provided federal officials considerable flexibility, selectivity, and discretion—subject, of course, to budgetary cycles and congressional manipulation—in determining recipients and conditions. In that Congress delegated more discretion to executive departments and agencies over broad rule-making authority under project grants than in older formula grants, federal authorities had greater opportunities to bypass state governments and even general-purpose units of government to focus on specific localities, groups, or conditions. Project grants introduced a demonstrable change in federal development, the era of so-called private federalism, when federal funds were channeled to nongovernmental bodies, nonprofit organizations, and individuals.

---

[12] See Deil S. Wright, *Federal Grants-in-Aid: Perspectives and Alternatives,* American Enterprise Institute, Washington, D.C., 1968, chap. 4.

The change of philosophy, still basically pragmatic but nonetheless altered, is evidenced by the federal government's new relations to states and localities. Rather than emphasizing its role in assisting these governments in developing programs of demonstrated nationwide interest, the federal government largely shifted to the initiation and development of "hundreds of detailed new programs at the instigation of relatively narrow sectors of the population and then demanded that the states and localities implement them in all their specifics under threat of direct federal action if they did not."[13] In the earlier model of federal grants, national goals were rarely stated. Instead, policy making for the established functions remained where it had resided before the functions were assisted. In most cases federal assistance aided the states and localities in achieving their objectives—building hospitals, schools, or highways. The older model, however, was largely superseded by the newer model, whereby federal grant monies were being extended for purposes of aiding the federal government to achieve its objectives. Programs were being tailored largely to national policies, to the attainment of federal purposes often by proxy through a variety of instrumentalities, many of which were not to be general-purpose governments. Thus states and local recipients tended to be viewed as one among several instrumentalities assisting the federal government to achieve national objectives and goals, rather than the reverse.

The newer model invested greater reliance on instrumentalities more or less autonomous from subnational government control. In 1965 Congress enacted, for example, sixteen separate grant programs. Seven of these were channeled exclusively through the states, six went through the state or directly to local or private agencies, and three were designed to bypass all general-purpose governments. The Advisory Commission on Intergovernmental Relations (ACIR) estimated that by 1967, some sixty-eight federal grants for operational purposes allowed direct payments to local governments, though local governments were the sole recipients for only thirteen. However, it is notable that of the half dozen or so landmark programs enacted from 1964 to 1968, only one, Medicare, was to be administered exclusively at the national level. The remaining programs were delegated to a wide variety of public and private institutions.

Between 1964 and 1969, the number of project grants nearly tripled— from 120 to 380, as measured by separate authorizations, or from two-thirds of all federal grants to five-sixths. In terms of federal fiscal aid to states, localities, and others, the total aid accounted for by project grants increased from 25 percent of all aid to nearly 50 percent.[14] The directional focus of federal grants, though somewhat difficult to tabulate with any

[13] Daniel J. Elazar, American Federalism, 2d ed. Crowell, New York, 1972, p. 71.

[14] ACIR, Fiscal Balance in the American Federal System, vol. 1, Washington, D.C., 1967, p. 151; Special Analyses, Budget of the United States Fiscal Year 1973, Government Printing Office, 1972, p. 249.

definitive accuracy, shifted increasingly toward metropolitan areas. Between 1964 and 1970, total aid for urban areas had tripled from $5.6 billion in 1964 to an estimated $16.7 billion.[15] The composition of the total federal grant program shifted significantly during the sixties, with a tremendous upswing in human resource program expenditures—education and manpower, health, income security—accompanied by a rapid decline in expenditures in the commerce and transportation categories. Table 3 traces this transition from FY 1950 through FY 1974.

During the 1964–1966 period, Congress asserted federal interest and authority in a wide range of government functions that until then had been the province, exclusively or predominantly, of state and local governments. A notable example of this intervention was extraordinary federal involvement, measured in fiscal terms and accompanying conditions for functional sharing, in some of the most sacrosanct confines of state-local authority like education, health, and law enforcement. Major national programs were undertaken as well in such new fields as area redevelopment and manpower training and in established domains of local government like transportation, solid waste treatment, and water-sewerage systems. In addition, in the Economic Opportunity Program and Demonstration Cities Act, Congress for the first time provided massive federal funds to localities

[15] *Special Analyses, Budget of the United States Fiscal Year 1970,* Government Printing Office, 1969, p. 202.

T–3 Percentage Distribution of Federal Aid to State and Local Governments by Function

Function	1950	1960	1970	(est.) 1974
Agriculture and rural development	5	4	3	2
Natural resources and environment	2	2	3	5
Commerce and transportation	21	43	21	13
Community development and housing	0.4	3	11	8
Education and manpower	11	10	18	14
Health	5	4	15	15
Income security	55	33	26	26
General revenue sharing	—	—	—	14
General government and other	1	1	3	3
Total	100	100	100	100

Source: *Special Analyses, The Budget for Fiscal Year 1974,* Washington, D.C., 1973, p. 212.

on a virtually unrestricted basis subject only to a general definition of purpose in the former and limit by geographic basis in the latter.

The newer model had created, in sum, differing systems of actors and claimants. These systems involved some programs and funds that went directly to the states; some that bypassed states to go directly to local governments; and others that circumvented all general-purpose governments to go directly to special-purpose agencies, quasi-governmental units, private institutions, and individuals. Indeed, the vast number of local governments in this country, already considered by some to be the Achilles' heel of governmental reform, experienced further balkanization as a consequence of the appearance of new or expanded special districts and functional empires aided by federal intervention. These new actors, institutions, and organized interests whose loyalty and fiscal existence were often tied to Washington support added to the jurisdictional confusion on the state-local level. Comprehensive planning and coordination were the immediate casualties. Elected chief executives frequently became referees in their political systems as a further consequence, devoid of sufficient authority to rectify the situation. At times, in fact, they were even more degraded, written out of the contest for prizes—as occurred initially in the poverty program.

The war against poverty most clearly manifested federal intentions to bypass directly state governments in dealing with local agencies. The animus toward state government by federal policy makers was plainly evident as the program developed and the governors reacted. Democratic governors in the early part of the second phase found themselves in an awkward position. Wishing to avoid collision with their party's President, many grudgingly acquiesced to federal programs which bypassed state governments and governors essentially on the grounds, as the ACIR suggests, that "the poor and the Blacks would never get a fair shake from state governments, especially in the South."[16] Governor George Wallace's obstructionist tactics to block federal authority in Alabama not only greatly influenced Northern liberal governors who might otherwise have opposed increased federal-local programs but also fundamentally reinforced many federal officials' determination to penalize state governments.

However, following a succession of new federal-local grant programs in poverty, education, and Model Cities, the governors' resistance hardened, further bolstered by Republican statehouse victories in the 1966 elections. The churlish mood of the governors, alarmed by their impotence to influence federal policy and programs, was typified by one Midwestern governor who protested that "if the present trends continue, our major cities will just become islands with bridges to Washington, and State legislatures will be left only to deal with smaller places that don't qualify

[16] ACIR, *Eleventh Annual Report*, Washington, D.C., January 1970, p. 3.

for Federal Aid to big urban areas."[17] In light of these sweeping developments, the nation's governors resolved to terminate further extension of
direct federalism where they could agree that the states had a role to
play in the administration and implementation of national programs.

With the proliferation of new grant programs, many bypassing states
and dealing with their subdivisions or the specific problems within these
jurisdictions, the consequences to governors and legislators seemed
abundantly clear. They were losing control over their governments at the
expense of grant recipients and the administrators of functional programs
through the narrow and direct channeling of federal assistance. State and
local governments, moreover, were now being confronted by a situation
whereby they welcomed, if not encouraged, new federal funds, but sensed
that accompanying federal guidelines and grant conditions were hampering
the capacity of these governments to govern.

New programs introduced myriad problems: choosing among virtually
hundreds of programs, often duplicative or overlapping; responding to
virtually dozens of narrow functional planning requirements; and coping
with the indeterminacy of what grants are available to whom, at what
time, and when the actual funds will be transferred to the recipient government. With fifty or so federal grant programs in operation prior to this
period, "Most governors, mayors, or city managers could, if asked,"
asserted the ACIR, "enumerate all or most of the types of Federal aid for
which their jurisdictions were eligible." Up to the early 1960s the intergovernmental grant-in-aid programs seemed "sensible, comprehensive,
and manageable." By 1966 the situation had changed significantly,
prompting the same ACIR to observe: "From the point of view of grant
recipients, the sheer number, variety, and complexity of grants makes it
all but impossible for eligible recipients to be fully aware of what aids are
available, which federal agencies administer them, and how they suit
particular needs."[18] To underscore the acute frustration of client members,
the ACIR compiled in 1966 a "catalog of catalogs," a bibliography of information sources regarding various federal grant programs which alone
ran to eighteen pages.

During this period, the National Governors' Conference (NGC) became
a heated platform for gubernatorial criticism of the seemingly runaway
grant system. Congress had ignored the governors in passing these programs; the President and federal policy makers had dismissed the states
and their chief executives as not being significant to their implementation.
With growing recognition of the nation's urban problems, the states were
being held accountable for the kinds and magnitude of these problems,

---

[17] Arlen J. Large, "States, Long Weary of Being Bypassed, Open a Lobbying Office," *Wall Street Journal,* September 1, 1967, p. 6.

[18] ACIR, *Eleventh Report,* p. 2, and ACIR, *Fiscal Balance,* p. 151.

leading some federal officials to argue that they had to pay the price for the neglect, ineptitude, and unresponsiveness of the past. The governors' annual meetings of 1965–1966 reflected this tremendous turmoil and upheaval at the state level, leading eventually to the governors' decision to establish an independent gubernatorial voice in Washington, one separate from the Council of State Governments (COSGO).

For the mayors, the Democratic landslide of 1964 and the activists' control of Congress provided the opportunity to gain national recognition for urban problems on a scale and magnitude unsurpassed in previous Congresses. The United States Conference of Mayors (USCM) took the lead in promoting programs that bypassed state government and encouraged the diversification of eligible grant recipients and the multiplication of project grants, especially to the extent they assumed an urban orientation. Beginning with the Los Angeles riots of 1965, media attention increasingly turned to the cities in what became known as the "urban crisis." Urban-oriented programs like the war on poverty, rent supplements, Model Cities, residential rehabilitation, and massive housing bills passed through the 89th Congress, often carried "piggyback" by more popular programs like medical care for the aged and federal support for education. The mayors' visibility in Washington was further bolstered by the establishment of the Department of Housing and Urban Development in 1965, to be followed by continuous task forces and commissions dealing with cities and their problems.

The mayors rode the crest of the Democratic party's hegemony over the institutions of government, the windfall of Great Society programs, and heightened public consciousness of and concern over urban problems. For many large-city mayors, their attitude was generally one of enjoying the feast before the famine once again set in. They encouraged these new federal efforts on all fronts, seeking to take maximum advantage of federal largesse as long as the congressional floodgates remained opened. However, the mayors, too, discovered that they had major problems in coping with these new departures in federalism, especially the bypassing of general local units of government. The war on poverty and its direct federal-local emphasis that circumvented city hall at first generated a strong unfavorable reaction from many mayors. They welcomed the experimental grants and demonstration programs but expressed considerable apprehension concerning new organizations and programmatic structures whose survival was tied to Washington rather than city hall. Also, city leaders indicated their growing concern over the endless new federal programs that provided support for other than basic, rudimentary municipal services which the cities desperately needed.

County officials reacted even more strenuously than the governors to direct federalism and the bypassing of general-purpose units. They rallied around the cause of local elected official control over federal-local programs. NACO generally encouraged the metropolitan focus of federal programs as long as counties were the preferred units of planning, funding, and administration. On the other hand, NACO objected to federal stimulation of new planning districts and the special-function instrumentalities which many federal programs and agencies encouraged in service delivery. These often became competitors with county governments in all aspects of local governance.

The 1964 to 1968 period also produced a significant reaction by the government groups against Washington's apparent inattentiveness to the disjointed and competitive activities of federal agencies and programs operating at the state-local level. During this second phase, there arose a loose alliance comprising, in addition to the groups and their members, the Bureau of the Budget, cabinet members, the ACIR, and congressional leaders. All these were concerned in one way or another with effecting major changes in intergovernmental relations, particularly at the federal level. Senator Muskie launched his extensive congressional hearings on *Creative Federalism* in 1966, observing that what Washington had helped create was almost "a fourth branch of government, but one which had no direct electorate, operates from no set perspective, is under no specific control, and moves in no particular direction."[19] HEW Secretary John Gardner echoed the complaints of federal department heads, stating that the reshaping of intergovernmental relations had led to a "crisis of organization."[20] The ACIR, a major interpreter of American federalism, summarized the views of these political actors in the late 1960s, railing against what it termed creative feudalism. It observed that practically all the new federal grant programs were functionally oriented, with power, money, and decisions being vertically dispersed from program administrators in Washington to program specialists in regional offices to functional department heads in state and local governments. From the Commission's perspective, this left "cabinet officers, governors, county commissioners and mayors less and less informed as to what was actually taking place and making effective horizontal policy control and coordination increasingly difficult."[21]

Consequently, governors, mayors, and county officials were being united by their common problem: that political executives were being undermined by functionalist ties between Washington and their governments. They also expressed frustration over the new fiscal, administrative, and man-

---

[19] *"The Federal System as Seen by State and Local Officials,* A Study Prepared by the Staff of the Subcommittee on Intergovernmental Relations, Senate Committee on Government Operations, 89th Congress, 1st session, 1965, p. 2; see also *Congressional Record,* vol. 112, 89th Cong., 2d Sess., 1966, p. 6834.

[20] *Creative Federalism Hearings,* Senate Government Operations Committee, Subcommittee on Intergovernmental Relations, 89th Cong., 2d Sess., 1966, part 1, pp. 270.

[21] ACIR,*Eleventh Report,* p. 2.

power demands upon their government that had made the objectives and goals of these new programs impossible to meet. One White House task force leader on intergovernmental relations arrived at the same conclusion in 1966. He observed that the Great Society programs had at least three things in common: their implementation cut across existing departmental and agency lines with little prospect of resolving interagency disputes; they demanded almost heroic responses from state and local governments in order to succeed, which would necessarily be a slow process; and they required a combination of technical and administrative skills that are critically scarce in the society at large.[22]

Thus the second phase in group relations with their federal constituency prompted intense and widespread competition among government levels and their chief executives. Beyond competition, however, this phase also stimulated growing bonds, stemming from their common needs and problems, among subnational executives. Political executives gravitated toward one another, cooperating on problems whose remedy lay in part with federal officialdom. These problems included some of the following:[23]

1. Proliferation of federal grants, agencies, and new programs which were deemed excessive in number and too narrow in functional orientation

2. Multiplicity of planning requirements and rigid funding arrangements under federal grant programs which had created rampant confusion over variable matching requirements and involved too much duplication and overlap in structure and purposes

3. Bypassing of general-purpose units of government which, at times, entailed open discrimination against their participation

4. The systematic undermining of elected executives and their authority due to unnecessary limitations placed on their involvement in intergovernmental programs as well as the inadequate consultation with them on program structure, funding, administration, and implementation

5. Inordinate program delays and uncertainties as to eligibility, funding, and actual transference of federal funds, as well as enormous red tape in the total grant acquisition process

[22] Stephen K. Bailey, "Co-ordinating the Great Society," *Reporter,* **34**:24–40, March 24, 1966.

[23] See Harold Seidman, *Politics, Position, and Power,* Oxford, New York, 1970, chap. 4; *Creative Federalism Hearings,* part 1, 2A, and 2B; *Intergovernmental Cooperation Act Hearings of 1971,* Senate Government Operations Committee, Subcommittee on Intergovernmental Relations, 90th Cong., 2d session, 1968; and *Grant Consolidation Hearings of 1969,* House Government Operations Committee, A Subcommittee, 91st Cong., 1st Sess., 1969, part 1.

The transformation of group relations from the first to second phase amounted to a passing from infancy to maturity. Their narrow, episodic contacts with federal officialdom had expanded in scope and substance to encompass a wide range of issues. Indeed, a new reformist enthusiasm propelled the groups and their members in this second phase, one predicated on their overriding need for fiscal assistance and the strengthening of general purpose-governments and their chief executives.

Phase Three

The third phase in group relations with Washington begins with the changeover from the Johnson administration to the Nixon presidency. This phase is punctuated by the internal strengthening of the groups: their structure, staff, resources, and lobbying activities. Externally, it is characterized by their attention to funding of existing programs and competition among them for control over program benefits rather than substantial lobbying for new programs. The passage of federal revenue sharing with states and localities marks the culmination of group efforts during the four year period from 1969 through 1972 and the likely beginning of a new phase in federal relations as well.

By 1969 the governors had come to Washington to stay. The NGC Washington Office for Federal-State Relations had become a recognized force in Washington lobbying, a new entrant into federal policy making, an institutionalized resource actively tied in to the operations of individual governors' offices. The mayors' organizations bolstered their national role and visibility by joining forces in 1969, creating not only a more unified urban voice but also increased political resources through consolidated activities and services. The National Association of Counties (NACO) passed through a major period of reorganization, becoming a stronger, more balanced organization as a consequence. All four groups had expanded their lobbying activities, more fully developed their research and analytical capabilities in reviewing public programs and policies, and greatly increased their service functions to member governments and their officials.

Multiple benefits flowed from these changes. Federal agencies increasingly utilized the groups for research, training, and service functions. Congressional committees paid greater attention to group policies, their analysis of legislation and past experiences under various federal programs. The efforts by President Johnson to open communication lines with state-local executives and enhance their roles in matters affecting state-local jurisdictions were continued and expanded during the early Nixon administration. Indeed, the new administration looked to the groups and their members for assistance and support in developing the President's

New Federalism programs, which, among other things, involved the ambitious effort to change the balance of power in American federalism by shifting money and authority from Washington to state and local governments. At the forefront of these changes were efforts aimed at strengthening state and local governments, especially their elected chief executives.

During this third phase the groups found their areas of interest overlapping and often competitive with one another. Their frequent confrontations at the national level contributed to the stalemate that developed in the 91st and 92nd Congresses over the President's programs. The governors, with their heavy Republican domination, experienced a brief interlude of high access to the White House, but the mayors had sufficiently strong congressional allies to frustrate any preferential treatment by the Nixon administration. The governors, mayors, and county officials divided on nearly every major Presidential program in special revenue sharing that would have consolidated existing categorical grants into broad functional areas, with federal funds returned to states and localities.

The mayors' suspicion that special revenue sharing and New Federalism might lodge administrative control over them by the states and their governors immediately received confirmation in the administration's manpower program. Congress overhauled the President's proposed legislation which would have placed control with governors and state bureaucracies, instead turning it into a public-service employment bill directed at large urban areas. President Nixon vetoed Congress's version (which gave the mayors control of manpower programs in cities of 100,000 or more and the states over those in nonmetropolitan areas) in 1970. A compromise in 1971 between Congress and the executive led to passage of a version much along the lines Congress had initially passed, once the governors dropped much of their opposition and the forces of the recession compelled the government groups to collaborate on an employment strategy. Much of the same division between governors and mayors also occurred in other programs like the transportation revenue sharing, where congressional committees, the administration, and the government interest groups were all far apart on a single approach on how to channel additional federal funds into alternative modes of transit. The mayors failed to embrace fully the urban community-development revenue sharing, particularly after the prospects of less funds rather than more became fully known. NACO, too, objected to consolidation of major urban fund programs in the Housing and Urban Development Act of 1972, because the bloc grants provided preferential status to central cities at the expense of counties. Thus, in case after case, the government groups fought one another over benefits and control of the administration's proposals to regroup categorical programs into bloc grants or special revenue-sharing programs.

Group leaders and members were constantly divided as to strategies: whether to go along with the Democratic-controlled Congress by seeking increased authorizations and appropriations for special categorical and project grant programs, of which they were the major clients and direct beneficiaries, or to side with the Nixon White House in seeking grant consolidation and strengthening of general-purpose governments and their chief executives. Typically the groups did both, but they often shifted back and forth according to funding and ambiguities of outcomes. Against this background of few victories, many standoffs, and growing fiscal need, the groups rallied around the cause of federal revenue sharing. Its enactment became their single most important accomplishment during this third phase.

Where fiscal issues divided the groups, fiscal exigency provided the basis for reconciliation. Growing fiscal imbalance in the federal system and revenue shortfalls in many state-local budgets required the groups to direct their activities at Congress and the White House for general fiscal relief rather than against each other. Politics of scarcity gave rise to politics of collaboration where previous efforts had produced rather meager results. What follows is a brief but not definitive synopsis of the more salient factors leading to revenue sharing's passage. This is not a definitive case study, an exploration into the merits of the plan, or even a record of what fully transpired at the White House or in Congress. Rather, it is a view of revenue sharing essentially from the perspective of the government interest groups and their members. It not only provides insight into this third phase of group dealings with their Washington constituency but also serves as a background for later analysis of intergovernmental lobbying by state-local chief executives.

REVENUE SHARING

Three essential events led to the passage of revenue sharing; the absence of any of these would likely have meant defeat. Individually, the government interest groups had to reach agreement that this program constituted their highest legislative priority. After that, they had to build consensus around a plan that their members would accept. The President also had to decide whether or not to make revenue sharing his administration's top domestic legislative priority and, once having made this decision, how to develop legislation that would be found acceptable both to the government groups—its principal supporters—and Congress. Finally there was Congress, highly partisan in composition, with the Democratic leadership rather unfavorably disposed toward any major domestic victory for the Republican President and the GOP. It, too, had to support revenue sharing. Thus the key actors and decision centers involved the government interest groups, the President and his advisers, and the Congress and those committees that would oversee revenue sharing's disposition.

Revenue sharing's history dates from late 1963, when Walter Heller, chairman of President Johnson's Council of Economic Advisers, raised with the President the general proposition of sharing with the states some of the annual "fiscal dividend" from federal income taxes rather than using such funds for federal tax reduction. President Johnson approved further exploration of the idea through a White House task force chaired by Dr. Joseph Pechman of the Brookings Institution which, in July 1964, strongly recommended the adoption of a federal revenue-sharing plan.

However, further discussion of revenue sharing was terminated within White House circles for a variety of reasons. Organized labor reacted strongly against the idea, as did federal agency heads and program administrators, all fearful that such a plan might undermine the future growth and vitality of federal categorical grants. The mayors expressed apprehension about whether the cities would get a "fair share" from federal funds channeled through the states. The Vietnam war heated up, defense spending and inflation rose, and the "peace dividend" envisaged by the authors slowly eroded.

The Governors' Conference became the first of the government interest groups to discuss and then endorse revenue sharing in 1965, to be followed by NACO. The USCM-NLC also endorsed a form of revenue sharing calling for unrestricted bloc grants to cities. The NLC Committee on Revenue and Finance undertook serious consideration of revenue-sharing proposals in March 1967, especially following the report of the General Electric Center that stated "over the next decade solutions to problems that beset U.S. cities will require a total incremental expenditure of $262 billion in excess of present revenues and those funds generated from normal growth."[24] The League hammered out the general principles for a plan which later established the basic guidelines for all the groups in their negotiations: it should be simple, understandable, and fair, focusing on the commonly accepted public service responsibilities of muncipalities; it should be direct, equitable, and continue sharing of federal revenue according to a fixed percentage of the federal income tax base; it should supplement local funds rather than substitute for local tax effort; and it should augment federal grants, and not merely substitute for such aids.[25]

The Governors' Conference moved on revenue sharing at the same time, creating a special committee under Governor George Romney to come up with recommendations and a plan. By spring 1967, the NGC promoted staff negotiations on revenue sharing among the various government in-

[24] Robert E. Weintraub, *Options for Meeting the Revenue Needs of City Governments,* Report by TEMPO-General Electric for the National League of Cities, Santa Barbara, Calif., January 1967, p. vi.

[25] National League of Cities, "Background Paper and Chronology of Progress on Revenue Sharing," NLC, January 1969 (mimeographed).

terest groups. The Romney committee together with similar committees from NACO, the USCM, and NLC met periodically often joined by outside economists from Brookings, the Urban Institute, and elsewhere. By 1968, both national party platforms and presidential candidates had endorsed revenue sharing, and in 1969, it had become a component of President Nixon's legislative program before Congress.

President Nixon called for a revenue-sharing plan that would have made $500 million in federal revenue available to state and local governments in FY 1971, with the total rising to $5 billion by FY 1976 and with distribution based on population and revenue raised. Funds were to be unrestricted as to use. Congress did not act on the proposal as initial enthusiasm surrounding the idea dissolved on nearly all fronts. The White House, according to reports, was not fully committed to revenue sharing. Romney, Treasury officials, and the White House staff exhorted the government interest groups to work out their version, but they generally failed to take the lead. Also, welfare reform outranked revenue sharing on the President's domestic agenda, making some observers feel that the Nixon budget really could not accommodate both if enacted, so emphasis was placed on the former at the expense of the latter.

Congress was unconvinced of the general need for the plan. Wilbur Mills, chairman of the powerful House Ways and Means Committee, under whose auspices revenue sharing and all tax plans pass, openly opposed it, even going so far as to denounce the idea from the steps of the White House. The congressional Appropriations Committees viewed any plan tied to federal tax receipts as a circumvention of their authority and opposed any back-door raids on the federal Treasury. To a large extent, it was a matter of political power and partisanship within the Congress. Generally, congressmen were concerned about relinquishing control over federal funds to states and localities, leaving no restrictions as to their use. Moreover, a Democratic Congress was not enamored of the idea of allowing a Republican President to take "their program," reaping the political benefits from its passage. Congressmen and senators were not about to go rushing to the aid of governors and local executives—many of whom were their rivals and adversaries, let alone agree to any apportionment of large sums of federal revenues without a critical sense of whose constituencies would be the principal beneficiaries.

Substantial cleavages existed within the government interest groups themselves. Many governors initially assumed the stance that they were entitled to the lion's share of federal funds, and they were somewhat cool toward any guaranteed pass-through of substantial funds to local governments. Riding the crest of their statehouse domination, Republican governors seemed confident that strong presidential and public support would be sufficient to achieve their goals. The mayors and their large block of congressional sympathizers viewed the Nixon plan as a direct aid to the states and GOP governors, shortchanging the cities in the pass-through of federal funds from states to localities. Their initial fears seemed warranted when the NGC endorsed a resolution in 1969 calling for 80 percent of the federal funds to be distributed to local governments through the states. NACO remained more flexible, first endorsing sharing through the states to localities and later siding with the mayors in demanding that at least 50 percent of the funds be passed through directly to local governments. All the groups were further dissatisfied by the low base figure of $500 million set by the President and by the administration's apparent unwillingness to raise this amount.

During the 1970 period it became evident to state and local officials — governors, mayors, county officials, state legislators, and city managers — that they wanted revenue sharing or some form of fiscal relief far more than Congress did. Between late fall and January 1971, a durable alliance was consummated between the White House and the government interest groups over revenue sharing which, in spite of obvious partisan tensions and periodic cleavages within and between the groups, persisted through revenue sharing's passage in late 1972. Led by Murray Weidenbaum, the Assistant Secretary of the Treasury for Economic Policy, and White House envoys, the White House agreed to increase revenue sharing substantially and apportion federal funds evenly between states and localities if and when the government interest groups worked out a general plan that they would all agree to.

The White House and the government groups launched their joint efforts before the 1970 elections by sending letters, outlining their proposal and requesting a commitment to revenue sharing, to every congressional candidate. During fall 1970, representatives of the NGC, USCM, NLC, and NACO together with the International City Managers Association (ICMA) and three groups representing state legislators met on several occasions, eventually reaching agreement on a bill in early December 1970 — an agreement acceptable both to the groups and the White House. This coalition had its difficulties in remaining intact, split briefly by the President's plan which gave local governments something less than half; by a short-lived insurrection among Democratic governors in spring 1971; by the mayors' brief enchantment with Congressman Mills's alternative to provide federal funds to local government exclusively; and by indecision and bickering among them over formulas. Nonetheless, the coalition maintained adherence to the agreements worked out among them, though congressional architects attempted on several occasions to play one group off against the other or to promote partisan differences. As the NLC President Richard Lugar stated before the Ways and Means Committee in June 1971, "We have arrived at agreement through a series of conferences, and the formula adopted in the administration's bill is the formula that was found acceptable as a compromise by all of the areas of government involved."[26]

In securing the cooperation and support of the government interest groups in late 1970, the White House promised not only an all out effort on revenue sharing's behalf but also the assurance that more federal funds would be offered in the President's new proposal. Following the 1970 midterm elections, the President ordered a thorough review of revenue sharing. Between then and early January, he decided that revenue sharing would be the administration's top domestic priority and that the initial base figure would be lifted to $5 billion. Instrumental to these decisions was the role played by Nelson Rockefeller. He launched a campaign for a $10 billion revenue-sharing base in November, got the Republican Governors' Association to endorse this proposal in December, and then fought for revenue sharing before the White House staff.[27] The New York Governor argued that an expanded revenue-sharing plan, supported by the GOP administration, the governors, mayors, and local officials and opposed by the Democratic Congress, could spell the difference in the forthcoming 1972 elections. The President and his party needed an issue, and revenue sharing, successful or not, could be the issue. With Vice President Agnew's assistance, the $5 billion figure prevailed—the difference between Rockefeller's $10 billion advocacy and the President's budget advisers' figure of $2.5 billion.

On January 22, 1971, President Nixon outlined the administration's domestic program in his State of the Union Message, in which he proposed to make "a $16 billion investment in renewing state and local government." General revenue sharing divided among states and localities on the basis of their population and tax effort would begin at $5 billion during the first year of operation. The remaining $11 billion would be passed on to these same governments in special revenue-sharing funds for six broad purposes by consolidating about 100 existing federal-aid programs. Under the general revenue-sharing proposal, 90 percent of the $5 billion would be allocated according to each state's percentage of total U.S. population, adjusted for state tax effort, and the remaining 10 percent would be available to states that had negotiated a formula for sharing their funds with local governments. Roughly 50 percent of each state's share would be passed on to general purpose local governments, excluding school districts and special purpose units, according to the ratio of local revenues to state revenues or a negotiated state-local sharing formula within the state. The President's bold package took Congress by surprise and began the long up-

[26] General Revenue Sharing Hearings, House Committee on Ways and Means, 92d Cong., 1st Sess., part 2, 1971, p. 237.

[27] Interviews with staff of Governor Nelson Rockefeller conducted at the Governor's New York City Office with Mary McAniff Kresky and Jim Cannon, February 8, May 24, and June 15, 1973.

hill struggle by the government interest groups to get Congress to enact revenue sharing.

With the government interest groups and the White House working together, their combined attention turned to Congress. For the government groups the tactic became one of mobilizing sufficient outside pressure upon the House to break down Democratic party resistance to revenue sharing. The President's revenue-sharing bill introduced in February confronted strong partisan reaction, with 37 cosponsors in the Senate—only 4 of whom were Democrats, and 133 House cosponsors including only 8 Democrats. Chairman Mills denounced the President's bill as being inflationary, defective as to approach, and he further indicated that he would hold hearings to put an end to the President's revenue-sharing bill.[28] In light of these obstacles, the government groups pursued several related tactics: (1) personal negotiations conducted by leaders with Mills; (2) mobilizing pressure from Democratic governors, mayors, and state-local officials upon fellow congressional Democrats; (3) direct appeals by Democrats and Republicans alike upon other members of the House Ways and Means Committee; (4) full-scale lobbying of all House members by virtually hundreds of state-local officials in spring 1971, just prior to the Mills hearings; and (5) stimulation of grass-roots support for revenue sharing from statewide and locally based citizen groups to raise its visibility and manifest public support for its enactment.

Group mobilization began shortly after the President's January 22 message. NACO rallied rank and file members through a series of regional "jet ins," where administration officials explained the President's bill to an estimated 1,500 county officials. NACO and the NLC conducted a joint session on revenue sharing in Indianapolis in February. This was followed by the NGC midwinter meeting in Washington, where the governors formed a special revenue-sharing committee and organized a National Citizens Committee for Revenue Sharing comprising governors, mayors, county officials, state legislators, and others. Later that spring, the USCM, NLC, and NACO came to Washington in full force, sending virtually hundreds of local officials to pressure local congressmen on behalf of the bill. Democratic presidential contenders Muskie and Humphrey, each with his own revenue-sharing bill, encountered hostility from many Democratic state and local officials when they suggested alternatives to revenue sharing, such as providing welfare relief to state and local governments.[29] In late April, a Democratic party summit meeting attended by congressional leaders, governors, and mayors resulted in open criticism of House Democratic leaders by their own party mayors due to their un-

---

[28] *The New York Times*, January 27, 1971, p. 1. See also *National Journal*, 3:704–708, April 3, 1971.

[29] See *Nation's Cities*, May 1971, pp. 8–15, and *National Journal*, 3:761–769, April 10, 1971.

willingness to support revenue sharing.[30] In the meantime, President Nixon actively joined the revenue-sharing campaign, addressing several state legislatures to request their assistance in moving Congress.

Not only were Democratic leaders subjected to the wrath of state-local party officials but Chairman Mills found himself under intense pressure from urban members of his own Ways and Means committee. They let Mills know that if some general relief for large cities was not soon forthcoming, several might be in trouble with their constituents in the 1972 election. Still Mills insisted that the hearings would be used to kill the administration's proposal, exposing the dangers and weaknesses of the revenue sharing concept. Ways and Means began revenue sharing hearings on June 2, 1971, one day after Senator Muskie commenced his own hearings on his ACIR revenue sharing plan and that of Senator Humphrey, which proposed to use revenue sharing essentially as an incentive to modernize state and local governments.

Beyond partisan objections to revenue sharing, Wilbur Mills and others felt that such a program would be fiscally irresponsible, divorcing taxing and spending authority. It would promote wasteful state-local spending and would undermine much of the federal control system. He recognized that an obvious revenue problem existed for the ten or so highest-tax-effort states and for most large cities, but he viewed indiscriminate rewarding of all general-purpose units of government, including low-tax-effort and highly regressive tax systems, as being unwarranted. Midway through the hearings, Mills indicated that Ways and Means would consider a multiyear direct federal aid plan for cities and needy rural communities. However, Mills soon abandoned this idea, even though the partisan appeal of tying direct federal aid to a community's needs—uniting the urban rural constituencies of Hubert Humphrey and George Wallace from the 1968 election—seemed most attractive. Governor Nelson Rockefeller and urban members of Mills's committee reportedly convinced the chairman that this plan would prove counterproductive. Not only would cities end up being "federal reservations" and further dependents of the federal government as a consequence but state legislatures would probably react by reducing their urban aid in proportion to the increased federal grants. Once this one-shot federal infusion of direct aid had expired, the states would send the cities back to Washington for further assistance.[31]

For nearly a year Mills and his staff pored over revenue-sharing formulas and mechanisms for apportioning funds among states and localities. The government interest groups provided backup support, using their own economists to cost out alternatives, while the Treasury Department ran one computer printout after another using various formulas to detail how

[30] See *National Journal*, **3**:19–733, April 3, 1971.

[31] *The New York Times*, December 1, 1971, p. 28; Ibid., July 16, 1971, p. 31.

much each level of government would receive. Nelson Rockefeller as well, engaged his state's Budget Division in feeding the Mills staff alternatives and options. On November 30, 1971, Mills and nine other members of Ways and Means introduced his long-awaited substitute to the President's version, the Intergovernmental Fiscal Coordination Act of 1971, a title which avoided specifying revenue sharing. It deviated in detail but not substance from the administration's bill. According to the Mills bill, funds would be divided one-third to the states and two-thirds to local government rather than on a fifty-fifty division. Funds would be drawn from a permanent five-year appropriation placed in a trust fund over which the Appropriations Committees would have no control, rather than being tied to a set percent of federal income tax receipts or an annual appropriations process.

During the first six months of 1972, Mills and the Ways and Means Committee brought the government interest groups, their allies, and the Treasury into agreement on final formulas and specific details of the bill. In April 1972, the House Ways and Means Committee reported a clean bill, the State and Local Fiscal Assistance Act, based on Chairman Mills's earlier bill. It provided a first year amount of $5.3 billion in federal funds to states and local governments. At the insistence of Rockefeller and other state-local officials, payments were made retroactive to the beginning of the calendar year. The states would receive one-third of this amount, or $1.8 billion, unrestricted as to use, based on two formulas: one-half according to state income tax collections and the remainder according to combined general tax effort of state and local governments. Local governments' share, $3.8 billion, would be divided among the states with distribution to local governments based on three equally weighted factors: general population, urbanized population (cities of 50,000 or over and the metropolitan areas surrounding them), and population inversely weighted for per capita income (the so-called poverty index). The Committee justified the allocation of the larger proportion of funds to local governments on several criteria: severity of fiscal need, increased need for services at the local level especially in urban areas, inflation and lower than average increase in local revenues due to the recent stagnant economy.

The House formula—with its five-factor combination based on state-local tax efforts, state income tax effort, population, urbanized population, and per capita income—reflected a number of trade-offs among factions and was geared to the House's population-based composition. The Mills formulas favored heavily urbanized states, poor states, and those states helping themselves through high tax efforts. The key to passage of the Ways and Means' bill involved obtaining a closed rule from the House Rules Committee governing its disposition on the House floor and then sustaining the closed rule on a House vote. Ways and Means' revenue bills customarily received closed rules because of their complexity and be-

cause of the problems that would develop from an open amendatory process. The government groups rallied their pressures around key members
of the Rules Committee, gaining a closed rule for the bill in late May by a
narrow 8 to 7 vote margin. The closed rule limited alternatives to passing
the bill as written, killing it, or returning it to Ways and Means. Among the
issues at stake were the prerogatives of the House Appropriations Committee whose chairman George Mahon opposed revenue sharing on the
grounds that it increased further the federal budget deficit and it violated
House rules by appropriating funds in a legislative bill rather than following the usual dual-authorizations appropriations route. The Mills bill
in a single stroke established the revenue-sharing program and appropriated necessary funds for its implementation, bypassing the appropriations process and Mahon's committee.

Twice, Mills and his allies postponed floor action fearing insufficient
votes to sustain the closed rule. With last-minute lobbying muscle provided
by state and municipal public employee unions, Mills eventually prevailed
on the key procedural vote when the House voted 223 to 185 to terminate
debate on the controversial closed rule which virtually assured passage.
On the next day, June 22, 1971, the House voted to pass revenue sharing
by a vote of 274 to 122. The bill was then sent to the Senate, where revision
seemed all but certain.

The Senate Finance Committee, the upper body's counterpart to the
House Ways and Means Committee, began revenue-sharing hearings in
July 1972, even though most committee members considered welfare
reform of higher priority. When committee members shifted their attention to revenue sharing, they tended to be far more preoccupied with
the issue of distributing federal funds among the states than with other
aspects of the plan. In the Senate, where poorer and less populous states
had an equal vote with the large states, the House version seemed blatantly
inequitable. Governors and senators from the nine or so non-income tax
states objected vehemently to the House action, which penalized them and
amounted to a serious federal intrusion into their states' politics. Moreover, the administration did not pass up the opportunity to lobby for
Senate revisions more closely approximating the President's original bill.
It felt that the House's version seemed overly generous to highly populated
states and large cities, which constituted much of the Democratic party's
core constituency. In that Congress was to adjourn early for the forthcoming election campaign, the groups redoubled their efforts to maintain
cohesiveness in spite of difficulties some had with the House bill. The
governors caucused prior to their Senate testimony, where high-tax-effort
state governors conceded to the objections by low-tax-effort state governors
that the House income tax factor should be replaced in the Senate version
by total state tax effort. Senate Finance Committee members probably
would have insisted on this change anyway, but the governors agreed to it

so as to reduce whatever cleavages might develop within the Senate over this issue.

The same jurisdictional dispute among House committees also erupted on the Senate side between Finance and Appropriations Committee as the Senate Finance Committee adopted a revenue sharing measure financed through a permanent appropriation geared to income tax receipts for the five years of the legislation. The Finance Committee like the House Ways and Means prevailed. What then emerged from the Senate Finance Commitee and Chairman Russell Long, its principal revenue sharing architect, was not surprising in light of the commitee's composition. Only one of its members represented any of the ten most populous states, with the preponderance from the least populous states, the South, Southwest, and Rocky Mountain region.[32] The Senate formula, based on total population, total tax effort, and the "poverty index," favored poorer rural states, especially those in the South. By emphasizing income and tax effort, the Senate version channeled funds tc large cities and poorer rural areas.

Senator Long and Finance Committee members used the revenue-sharing legislation as a vehicle to accomplish another goal—that of imposing an annual $1 billion federal ceiling on the open-ended social services program by way of amendment to the bill. The explosive growth of this program—dating from its enactment in 1967—had been a boon to the more progressive states and high-service cities but a matter of deep concern both to Congress and the administration. The governors had long expected Congress to terminate this open-ended funding as the program expanded from $345 million federal reimbursement in FY 1969 to $1.7 billion in FY 1972; but together with social service directors, the welfare guilds and other lobbying groups had successfully blocked committee action in prior sessions. Thus the Senate Finance Committee voted out a revenue-sharing bill that included a $600-million limit on child care and family planning services, repealed authorizations for other social service programs, and— as a trade-off to urban states and localities for this prospective revenue loss—added to the bill one billion dollars extra funds that could be spent for social services and other purposes. Through the supplemental grant program for social services geared to population, Long argued that these funds would offset losses to most populated, urban states from the Senate bill compared to the House version. After rejecting several amendments to the Long bill to provide greater apportionment of revenue-sharing funds to larger states, the Senate passed the bill by a wide margin and sent it to conference committee, where House and Senate members reconciled the two separate versions.

What the conference committee approved was a highly unusual compromise which allowed each state the larger of the revenue-sharing al-

32 *National Journal*, **3:**779–784, April 10, 1971.

locations its state and local governments would receive under the conflicting House and Senate approved distribution formulas. Each state
amount is determined by the formula—the House five-factor version or
the Senate three-factor plan—that maximizes its share. If the total of the
shares is greater than the available authorizations, all shares are reduced
proportionately. The governors successfully appealed to Wilbur Mills to
protect the states from a loss of nearly all social service funds and to reject
the Senate-approved repeal of specified program funding. House-Senate
conferees, largely at Mills' insistence, deleted much of the Senate bill's
language regarding social services and instead placed a $2.5 billion ceiling
on annual federal 75 percent matching grants to state and local governments for social services, with each state's percentage geared to population.[33] With the dual-formula alternative, revenue sharing readily passed
the House by a vote of 281 to 86 and the Senate by a margin of 59 to 19.
On October 20, 1972, President Nixon signed the State and Local Fiscal
Assistance Act of 1972 into law, stating that this bill would begin the
process of renewing the federal system and restoring the balance among
government levels.

Beginning in early December 1972, all fifty states and more than 38,000
local communities began receiving their first installments on revenue-
sharing allocations. Total payments amounting to $30.1 billion are
scheduled to be made between 1972 and 1976 unless Congress revises,
terminates, or increases the amounts. Beginning with $5.3 billion and
increasing gradually to $6.425 billion in 1976, states will have substantial
new funds to spend on anything they went as long as they maintain the
level of aid they are now giving to local governments from non-revenue-
sharing monies and with the proviso that these funds cannot be used to
substitute for state income or to match other federal grants. Local governments are allowed to use these federal funds to substitute for existing
expenditures and to pay for maintenance, operation costs, and capital
expenditures. They may also use these funds for basic services including
public safety, environmental protection, public transportation, health,
recreation, social services, and other functions.

Passage of revenue sharing reflects the product of many labors. The
NLC laid down the broad principles for the bills, while the USCM helped
fill in major details. Treasury officials spent endless hours with the
groups in developing apportionment formulas, using its computers to keep
all actors informed as to what amounts could be expected under each
variation. Nelson Rockefeller played a major role in the bill's passage,
keeping the governors and the government interest group alliance together,
feeding all parties alternative formulas, and eventually gaining Mills's
commitment to push for revenue sharing's enactment. Finally, Wilbur

---

[33] Ibid., **4**:1564–1566, October 7, 1972.

Mills constructed the eventual House version, shepherded the bill through floor passage, and negotiated the compromise over the differing House-Senate versions in conference.

The enactment of revenue sharing, in effect, marked the high point thus far in joint work of the government interest groups to influence their federal constituency. The combination revenue-sharing program and social-service provisions holds the prospect of channeling more than $40 billion to state and local governments over a five-year period, making it the largest domestic aid bill ever enacted. Congress, for the first time, experienced the collective weight of the group's united effort on major legislation. What implications this may have—as well as what the consequences of revenue sharing itself may be—will be discussed in the final chapter. In the meantime, it is important to turn to the fiscal and programmatic dimensions of intergovernmental policy as they relate to the activities of the government groups during this third phase.

TAX POLITICS

The 1960s were years of defining new objectives for the nation and for allocating resources to achieve them. The transformation of the federal system, according to most published reports and testimony, did not correspond to or follow any single plan or strategy. The intergovernmental sharing of functions grew precipitously as political institutions responded to particular programs in a largely ad hoc manner. "The very significant change in governmental arrangements and practices took place without any systematic doctrinal justification, as have most such changes in American history," observed Derthick.[34] Nevertheless, vast changes did occur, especially following enactment of Great Society programs, leading many observers, especially state and local chief executives, to feel that the balance among government levels had become severely and perhaps irreparably strained.

By its expansionist national policies, the federal government became an even more important actor in state and local political systems than it had been in the past. By shaping the political environment and altering the distribution of influence and resources among political actors, it affected a great range of management concerns, fiscal and programmatic, facing chief executives. From their perspective, federalism transformed saddled them with insuperable responsibilities for implementing national programs without commensurate resources, both political and fiscal, for their attainment.

---

[34] Martha Derthick, *The Influence of Federal Grants: Public Assistance in Massachusetts,* Harvard University Press, Cambridge, Mass., 1970, p. 219.

It has been asserted, with good justification, that the essential differences between politics on the federal level and that on state and local levels is largely a function of fiscal resources. The federal income tax, progressive and dependably incremental, provides federal policy makers with sufficient sources of annual revenue to enable them to be largely preoccupied with "program application politics."[35] State and local governments, laboring under a mixture of less progressive and less incremental taxes than the federal government, find themselves engrossed with "tax politics," namely the continual search for new or expanded sources of revenue.

Such distinctions between types of taxes occasion much of the activity by elected chief executives within and without their own political systems. For mayors, governors, and county officials the question "who shall pay?" tends to be more senstive than "for what?" For them, tax politics consume a disproportionate amount of time as compared to other concerns. It cuts across every major program and problem of state-local government.[36] The political consequences of tax politics are precarious and unpredictable for incumbent executives. Tax policy changes constitute bread-and-butter or gut issues for voters, with varying outcomes and hazards for executives pursuing sizable tax increments. "Recent political history," notes the ACIR, "is replete with such an eclipse of state political careers following tax actions."[37] In choosing between pursuit of new revenues and reduction of government expenditures or activities, many a chief executive has found the latter to be a time-consuming and often unproductive enterprise.[38] Caught between the legal restraints and curbs upon budgetary powers through agency exemption, earmarked revenues and accounts, fragmented taxing authorities, and debt service limitations on the one hand and preoccupation with the quest for new revenues on the other, governors and mayors find that they have little flexibility in initiating changes in expenditures and priorities. They also find that they have to abandon much of their informal power that might be used to act as a brake on public spending.

Mayors confront a somewhat different situation than that faced by governors. Most large cities have little potential for equitable and efficient taxation. This stems from their already high reliance on often

---

[35] *Creative Federalism Hearings,* statement by Dean Alan K. Campbell, Dean of Maxwell School, Syracuse University, Syracuse, N.Y., pp. 858–859.

[36] Thomas Anton, "Roles and Symbols in the Determination of State Expenditures," *Midwest Journal of Political Science,* 11:27–43, February 1967.

[37] ACIR, *Fiscal Balance,* p. 115. See also Austin Ranney, "The Governor," in Herbert Jacob and Kenneth Vines (eds.), *Politics in the American States* Little, Brown, Boston, 1965, p. 91.

[38] See Anton, *The Politics of State Expenditure in Illinois,* University of Illinois Press, Urbana, Ill., 1966; Ira Sharkansky, *The Politics of Taxing and Spending,* Bobbs-Merrill, New York, 1969, chap. 4.

regressive property taxes and the economic fact that differential tax increases may cause both investors and the income-earning population to vacate the city. In light of often critical urban problems and rising financial deficits, mayors have had little recourse but to encourage and to promote federal-city ties. "We depend on Washington far more than on our own state government," Mayor Thomas Currigan of Denver proclaimed in 1966. "Matter of fact, we even have better rapport with the federal people than the state people and the state house is right across the street."[39] While cities may have found a more sympathetic ear in Washington than in the state capital, their pursuit of large federal grant programs like urban renewal, housing, and Model Cities often brings with it certain disrupting consequences. "A Mayor soon discovers," notes James Q. Wilson, "that he has to hurt the poorest and weakest citizens in order to provide for the general welfare."[40] With financial relief largely out of the large-city mayor's hands, resting instead with state and federal governments, mayors no less than governors are frequently trapped politically by the fiscal consequences of the job.

Tax politics, in sum, tends to be the most pervasive and inescapable political pressure operating upon state-local chief executives. Little political mileage is generally gained for executive leadership in taxation even in the name of reform. Chief executives must contend with fragmented taxing structures and fiscal disparities among governmental units. Where taxation and the pursuit of new or expanded revenue sources are difficult within one's constituency, funds may be more easily acquired from without. Governors and mayors look eagerly to the national government as the constituency from which they hope to win the most at the least cost.

The single most important factor to shape intergovernmental fiscal relations involves the Sixteenth or Income Tax Amendment which broadly affected the balance of power between the federal government and the states by assuring the former of a continuing source of revenue in substantial amounts. The personal income tax is the nation's prime revenue source and by far the most responsive to economic growth. For every 10 percent of growth in the national economy, it has been estimated, federal income tax receipts increase about 15 percent. In that 80 percent of state-local tax revenues as of 1969 were derived from property, sales, and excise taxes as opposed to income taxes, their collections responded sluggishly to economic growth. Economic growth gave the federal government the revenues—it collects nearly 90 percent of the income taxes nationally—producing a fiscal mismatch of needs and resources between

[39] Jules Loh, "Beleaguered Cities Turn to Washington for Aid," *Nashville Tennessean*, January 16, 1966, cited in Daniel R. Grant and H. C. Nixon, *State and Local Government in America* 2d ed., Allyn and Bacon, Boston, 1968, pp. 70–71.

[40] James Q. Wilson, "The War on Cities," *The Public Interest*, 3:31, Spring 1966.

national and subnational governments. States and localities are left with the problems. Federal domination over the nation's taxing and fiscal resources without greater redistribution to subnational governments than deemed necessary by these units made restoration of the fiscal balance their key demand by the end of the sixties.

Fiscal disparities between government levels and jurisdictions expanded geometrically as service demands and expenditures mounted. Meanwhile, Congress consistently cut taxes since World War II—in 1948, 1954, 1962, 1964, 1965, 1969, and 1971—taxes which would have produced billions more in government revenues, while states and local governments continuously increased their own taxes faster than the growth in the GNP.[41] The federal government further enjoyed the luxury, which states and localities did not, of being able to respond to shortfalls in tax collections, particularly during the high inflation and economic recession period of 1969 to 1971. It did this in part by absorbing increases in the national debt and smoothing out the rate of expenditures by changes in the levels of capital outlays.

Where state and local governments may be criticized for their somewhat laggard rate of expenditure increases prior to 1950, the overall rate of expenditures climbed at nearly twice the rate of the federal government's domestic outlays between 1950 and 1970. State and local government spending increased fourfold from 1950, while their aggregate indebtedness increased at nearly the same rate. Figure 2 indicates the tremendous growth in state and local government spending from their own funds during this two-decade period.

These subnational governments may also be faulted for their lack of greater reliance on income taxes. For many states, however, such taxes

[41] *General Revenue Sharing Hearings of 1971*, part 6, pp. 1026–1027.

F–2   Total State and Local Government Expenditures, 1950–1971

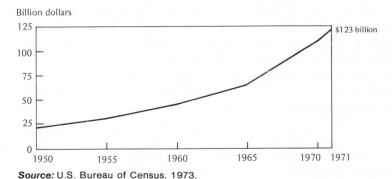

Source: U.S. Bureau of Census, 1973.

involved economic competition, taxpayer revolts, and politicians' survival. Making the point that the ten highest-tax-effort states had virtually reached their practical taxing maximum in relation to the other states, Governor Nelson Rockefeller informed the Senate that in his state "Any further substantial increases in taxes . . . is going to drive out its job producing industries, and individuals who have to pay high income taxes."[42] The growing disparities in state and local tax structures not only heightened competitive economic positions among governments but also further balkanized governmental units nationally.

Another intergovernmental fiscal problem experienced by subnational chief executives during the late sixties is what may be termed "rising expectations." This refers to situations where federal intervention spurred state-local hopes that congressional declarations of national purposes in housing, poverty, medical care, environmental action, and elsewhere meant a federal commitment to provide sufficient funds to support these efforts. The plethora of new national programs and the overwhelming pressure upon states and localities to participate affected their own budgetary allocations. This constituted a drain on existing programs and new areas of activity. When federal programs experienced reductions, state and local governments often had to compensate for this by funding the particular activity from their own budgets. Where programs stopped and started, particularly capital construction financing under executive impoundments and stretch-outs, lower governments incurred the consequences. Where federal stipulations required "maintenance of effort" as a condition for receipt of additional federal funding, states and localities had to lift their standards even higher to be eligible for additional federal funds. In some cases, these were states whose program standards and spending already far exceeded the national average.[43]

Under feast and famine conditions, contradictory or competitive federal policies, many governors and mayors reluctantly joined in the competition for new federal monies, only to be left disenchanted and at times embittered by the results.

Supporting the governors' and mayors' contention of "rising expectations and dashed hopes," the ACIR documented the "dollar gap" between federal authorizations and appropriations between 1966 and 1969. "We are concerned," observed the ACIR, "primarily with the impact upon those state and local administrators of federal aid programs, who—rightly or wrongly

---

[42] *Intergovernmental Revenue Act Hearings of 1971,* Senate Committee on Government Operations, Subcommittee on Intergovernmental Relations, 92d Cong., 1st Sess., 1971, p. 216.

[43] See statements by New York Governor Nelson A. Rockefeller before Congress, *Water Pollution Control Legislation Hearings of 1971,* House Committee on Public Works, 92d Congress, 1st session, 1971, pp. 482–484; *Grant Consolidation and Intergovernmental Cooperation Hearings of 1969,* Senate Government Operations Committee, Subcommittee on Intergovernmental Relations, 91st Cong., 1st Sess., 1969, pp. 87–91.

—plan their programs on the basis of congressional 'promises' as reflected in program dollar authorizations."[44] The gap between authorizations and appropriations increased steadily from $2.7 billion to an estimated $8.5 billion on some forty or so programs in this period. Similarly, federal aid appropriations fell from approximately 80 percent of full authorizations in 1966 to an estimated 65 percent of the full amount by 1970.

This disparity between federal authorizations and appropriations created enormous problems for subnational executives, their budget advisers, and program managers by way of planning their own budgets. Executive impoundment and budget freezes added another. Presidential declination to spend appropriations previously signed into law has a long historical precedent, especially in the military area, but not in terms of the scope and magnitude reflected by President Nixon's actions in the domestic area. For Congress, such Presidential action generated a constitutional crisis. For state and local executives, it amounted to a breach of confidence between national and subnational units of government. Beginning in FY 1964 and on through FY 1971, executive impoundments rose from $4 billion to more than $13 billion. This amount still constituted only 6 to 7 percent of total federal outlays but nonetheless had a significant impact upon the areas affected—such as highways, urban renewal, water and sewer programs, mass transit, public housing, and others. These were among the most favored federal programs for hard-pressed governors and mayors.[45] The government interest groups responded by filing protests, passing ringing denunciations of the practice, and resorting to legal tests of these actions in the federal courts. Probably no Presidential course of action made the government interest groups and their members more suspicious of Mr. Nixon's new federalism than did Presidential impoundments and freezes imposed on major domestic programs. It produced often chilly relations between the groups and the White House, a chill that was only briefly interrupted by their common efforts on behalf of federal revenue sharing.

Inflation is the most conspicuous cause of rising governmental expenditures. The powers of governors and mayors to cope with this problem are negligible in comparison with those of federal officials. Costs for federal government purchasing inflated by about 40 percent between 1960 and 1970, and costs for state and local government purchasing inflated by 54 percent. For all general expenditures combined between 1955 and 1969, inflation accounted for well over 40 percent of the increased outlays by local governments, the remainder accounted for in terms of workloads and scope or quality of services. Expanding government services had an

[44] ACIR, *The Gap between Federal Aid Authorizations and Appropriations, Fiscal Years 1966–1970*, Government Printing Office, June 1970, p. 1.

[45] *National Journal*, 3:1027–1039, May 15, 1971.

enormous impact on state-local government employment as well, which increased from 4.3 million persons in 1950 to nearly 11 million in 1970 (several times the rate of employment growth in the economy as a whole), while federal civilian employment during this same period increased rather gradually. Basic salaries and retirement benefits for state-local employees constitute roughly one-half of the aggregate state-local expenditures, which totaled $130 billion in 1970. Wages and salaries for public employees rose substantially over the past decade, especially since 1966, when the rate of increase, averaging 5 percent, jumped to slightly less than 8 percent.[46] These increases have been due in large part to the trend toward equalization with the private sector's compensation levels of state-local wage scales, to the persistent inflationary trend in the economy, and to greater unionization and militancy among public employees.

Thus the fiscal side of federalism prompted state-local government reactions on the programmatic side. By the late sixties and early seventies, state-local chief executives were in various stages of revolt against further categorical grants. The newer grants of the sixties had required subnational governments to match federal funds to gain these additional monies. Requirements to use scarce resources for new efforts constantly inflated their budgets, while many states and local governments were not even meeting the costs of basic services. On the average, grant recipients had to raise directly $1 for every $2.50 coming from the national government, which amounted to roughly 10 percent of their general expenditures. Thus as federal aid to states and localities climbed from $13 billion in 1966 to $24 billion in 1970, the costs to the subnational governments for acquiring these funds went from $5.5 billion to an estimated $12.5 billion.[47] If one includes increased public employment, administrative costs, and indirect expenditures, many states and localities paid, on the average, more to obtain federal monies than they in turn received.

These same grants were restricted largely to new enrichment or innovative programs, making rather minor contributions for the most part to fundamental services performed either at the state or local government levels. More than categorical grants and programs, which many chief executives nonetheless supported because of the partial relief they provided, nearly every governor, mayor, and county official who testified before Congress on revenue sharing argued that he needed basic operating funds. That is, these officials made the case for general, unrestricted federal support to hire police, firemen, sanitation workers; to operate parks and recreation centers; to aid primary and secondary education; and for other basic services.

Against this background of the late sixties and early seventies, chief

[46] See *General Revenue Sharing Hearings of 1971*, part 2, p. 257.
[47] See *Special Analyses, Budget of the U.S. Fiscal 1970*, p. 209.

executives nationally pleaded fiscal destitution. "If this desperate situation is not resolved," Nelson Rockefeller informed the Senate in 1971, "this country is going to experience a domino wave of bankruptcies spreading from cities to states all over the nation during the next five years.[48] "American cities are being squeezed in a financial vise as never before since the Great Depression," warned the USCM, NLC, and ICMA that same year.[49] The mayors cited studies indicating that the prospective revenue gap between future needs and existing state-local expenditures and revenue trends could well exceed $200 billion over the next decade. Later calculations, based on 1970–1971 state-local expenditures of $130 billion, indicated that these governments, at a growth rate of 12 percent per year, would need $100 billion in additional funds alone by 1975–1976.[50]

Thus governors, mayors, and other state-local officials came to organize around the cause of federal revenue sharing, and, to a lesser degree, bloc grants and grant consolidation and the elimination of federal grant matching requirements. Economic recession and inflation compounded revenue problems. State and local governments were victims of national cyclical fluctuations: unemployment rose, tax receipts fell off from anticipated yields (particularly where income taxes existed), and expenditure requirements continued to mount. They had neither control over national business conditions nor real countercyclical remedies, which remained the federal government's responsibility. More states increased taxes in 1971 than in any other previously recorded year, while many states and localities cut back existing personnel, closed facilities, delayed capital expenditures, or reduced services.

Mayors and governors—their positions and performance in office—are more conspicuous than ever before in an era of tax politics. It well may be that their vulnerability is not greater but that their visibility has measurably increased.[51] Governors are caught in a crossfire between growing demands for services and protests against rising taxes, between the problem of fiscal imbalance in the federal system and inadequate or politically unpalatable revenue options. It is local executives, however, mayors and county officials, who are on the immediate firing line. They are the officials who must contend with often static or shrinking tax bases, the front line for service demands and problems involving the inequitable

[48] Intergovernmental Revenue Act Hearings, p. 215.

[49] General Revenue Sharing Hearings, part 2, p. 250.

[50] Ibid., p. 268, and Intergovernmental Revenue Act Hearings, p. 224.

[51] See J. Stephen Turett, "The Vulnerability of American Governors, 1900–1969," in Thad Beyle and J. Oliver Williams (eds.), The American Governor in Behavioral Perspective, Harper & Row, New York, 1972, pp. 17–30.

taxing systems. Summarizing the dilemmas of local executives, the mayors and city managers issued a joint statement in 1971 which read:[52]

> *In maintaining a balance between revenues and expenditures in the face of unionization, inflation, and citizen demands for services on the one hand, and state constitutional and statutory limits on municipal taxation and debt, and citizen tax rebellion on the other, cities have had to reduce their attempts to finance adequate programs to meet both the old and new problems confronting them.*

Thus as the 1970–1971 period concluded, prior to revenue sharing's enactment and a significant upturn in the general economy, the revenue picture as seen by state and local executive appeared to be bleak. This situation added a new intensity to their collective appeals to their federal constituency for fiscal relief.

PROGRAMMATIC POLITICS

Many factors are related to the opening up of the federal system during the sixties: favorable economic conditions, growth of federal tax receipts, rising public service demands, reapportionment, Democratic party domination of Congress and the executive led by an activist President, and the recognition of national problems that required federal intervention. However, in explaining the scope and types of federal response during this era, one must look to the organization both of Congress and the federal executive.

Two of the major legislative reforms undertaken by Congress thus far in the century have been significant in determining the distribution of power within the legislative branch. The curbing of the powers of the House Speaker in 1910 ended elected leaders' domination of the House Rules Committee and the Speaker's appointive powers of majority party members to committees. The other reform, the Legislative Reorganization Act of 1946, intended, among other things, to revivify the disintegrating committee system by reducing drastically the number of standing committees from 48 to 19 in the House and from 39 to 15 in the Senate. Both reforms had the effect of reinforcing the powers of committee chairmen, measurably increasing the capacity of senior leaders to frustrate the elected leadership.[53]

In choosing between centralization of legislative power around elected leaders and further decentralization of power through committees and sub-

[52] *General Revenue Sharing Hearings*, part 2, p. 273.

[53] See Douglass Cater, *Power in Washington*, Knopf, New York, 1965, p. 156.

committees, Congress since at least 1946 has consistently opted for the latter. By most any score—growth of subcommittees, committee assignments, segmented flow of legislative business, elected and senior leaders' relations, and the hardening of committee jurisdictions—the trend continues, seemingly unabated, toward dispersing power to individual members and subcommittee structures. In the Senate this trend is manifested in the maximum freedom allowed to individual senators in carving out areas of expertise and gaining subcommittee chairmanships to forward these interests.[54] In spite of the House's obvious differences in size and stature, much the same thing has occurred, further propelled by the opening of subcommittee chairmanships to more members. Since 1946, in fact, the number of subcommittees in both bodies nearly doubled from 150 to 250, and the number of separate subcommittee chairmen more than doubled.

"To understand the organization of the executive branch," observed a former Bureau of the Budget (BOB) official, "one must first understand the organization and culture of the Congress and the high degree of congressional involvement in administrative decisions."[55] Congressional organization and executive branch organization are interrelated and constitute two fundamental components of a single system. Congress provides the legislative authority to create new departments, agencies, and programs. It establishes these agencies's missions, defines their goals, investigates their behavior, and allocates funds for their operations. Balkanization of Congress into subcommittees and narrow jurisdictions has meant that each separate unit typically develops its manner of operations and set of relationships to executive agencies, subject to oversight and mandated responsibilities. Each executive agency—whether engaged in regulatory activity, technical services, or distributive programs—has its beneficiaries, and established supporters among the congressional committees that oversee the agency's activities and fund its programs. The tie between Congress, agencies, and agency clientele is known as the "triple alliance." This term refers to the shared and interlocking aims of the constituent groups, congressional committees and subcommittees, and the administrative agency responsible for the conduct of the program.

The growth of congressional bureaucracy and the institutionalization of committees have functioned to deepen the divisions among legislative fiefdoms, resulting in the development of rather narrow, functionally confined subsystems. To the extent that broader policy, administrative, and fiscal concerns are raised within these insulated subsystems, typically such pressure comes from outside: from cabinet heads; Office of Manage-

---

[54] See Randall B. Ripley, *Power in the Senate,* St. Martin's, New York, 1969.

[55] Seidman, *Politics, Position, and Power,* p. 37.

ment and Budget (OMB), the President and his staff, and state-local chief executives. Analogizing the growth of these policy subsystems to the political structure of the middle ages, the ACIR in its 1968 annual report concluded that "Feudalism in the federal system is on the rise with middle management administrators at all levels, congressional subcommittees and pressure groups which coalesce around individual grant programs carrying the day more times than top policy-makers."[56] Not only state and local political executives but also the President are generally unwelcome intruders in these policy subsystems—except in cases where they are the beneficiaries, protectors, or direct constituencies of the programs. Indeed, President Nixon's efforts in the early 1970s to overhaul the federal grant-in-aid system and control federal expenditures led to innumerable setbacks and constant frustration. In his FY 1974 budget message, the President stated:[57]

> *A momentum of extravagance is speeded by requirements created initially by legislative committees sympathetic to particular and narrow causes. These committees are encouraged by special interest groups and by some executive branch officials who are more concerned with expansion of their own programs than with total Federal spending and the taxes required to support that spending.*

Congress is well aware of its organizational problems but generally resists taking actions that might disrupt congressional fiefdoms and their barons. Indeed, it would rather blame the executive for structural and managerial deficiencies. In a recent action—the Federal Advisory Committee Act of 1972, for example—Congress sought to curb the proliferation of an estimated eighteen hundred councils, commissions, boards, and similar groups which had arisen in the executive to adjudicate agency disagreements, provide advice, and coordination across program and agency lines. It is not that these advisory committees have been successful generally, but that Congress dropped the responsibility for meshing inter-governmental programs—coordinating and managing them—clearly on the White House steps, while resisting delegation of power to the executive to take action commensurate with the magnitude of the problems.

One consequence of federal organizational structure has been the continuous proliferation of new federal programs—narrow categorical or project-type activities. For nearly every one of the 550 or so categorical programs operating in 1972, organized beneficiaries existed, particularly among professional associations whose members often administer the

---

[56] Advisory Commission on Intergovernmental Relations, *Tenth Annual Report*, Washington, D.C., January 1969, p. 8.

[57] *The United State Budget in Brief, Fiscal Year 1974*, Office of the President, Office of Management and Budget, Washington, D.C., 1973, p. 8.

grant programs. These beneficiaries and supporters—often middle-management functionalists and professional guilds—obviously have much greater interests in protecting, maintaining, and expanding these special benefits than unorganized taxpayers or even political executives who are generalists rather than program specialists. As they see it, observes Seidman, "successful intergovernmental relations are chiefly successful bureaucratic relations."[58] As Edward Banfield noted, "From the standpoint of organized interests, dealing with Congress and the Washington bureaucracies (a few key congressmen and administrators are usually all that matter to any particular interest) is vastly easier and more likely to succeed than in dealing with the legislatures and governors of 50 states, not to mention the officials of countless cities, counties, and special districts."[59] The opposition by organized labor and numerous national interest groups to revenue sharing, bloc grants, or presidential grant consolidation authority provides considerable insight into the organized group pressure directed at keeping the existing structure intact and power concentrated in one place. The federal grant system therefore has played a significant role in nationalizing and institutionalizing lobbying activity in Washington. It is further reflected in the shift of much power from Congress to the executive, where interest groups, especially professional associations, expend a large amount of their resources and energies— often with congressional encouragement.

Interest groups, federal agencies, and intergovernmental program administrators are key defenders of the federal grant system. Congressmen are even more so. Many reasons account for the federal government's utilization of grants-in-aid as a key mechanism for redistributing funds from higher levels to lower-level governments, but one essential justification is the influence of the benefactor upon the decisions and behavior of the beneficiary. Supporters of the existing apportionment system may defend federal grants in terms of state-local government incompetence, venality, or as a pressure for administrative and personnel reform. However, many congressmen tend to view the grant allocation process in terms of augmenting their personal influence. For them, especially for senior leaders and committee and subcommittee chairmen, the benefits are often conspicuous, including (1) general and specialized media recognition as well as national interest group support when a congressman's name is attached to a program or where he is identified as the promoter, defender, and benefactor of a particular program; (2) local media attention and visibility where the congressman announces the tending of a federal grant to his district; (3) the channeling of aid, directly or indirectly, to a special-

[58] Seidman, *Politics, Position, and Power*, p. 138.

[59] Edward C. Banfield, "Revenue Sharing in Theory and Practice," *The Public Interest*, **23**:38, Spring 1971.

ized, organized segment of their constituents where they may take the credit; and (4) the exercise of control over the program through interference in administrative rule making often favorable to local conditions and constituencies.

Several consequences flow from programmatic politics in terms of state-local political executives. Efforts to change the grant system tend uniformly to meet opposition to the extent that they involve elimination or consolidation of grants, presidential reorganization authority, congressional provision of long-term authorizations, budgeting strategies that cut across agencies and congressional committees, and decentralization of federal grant decisions out of Washington. Attempts by the President, state-local chief executives, and their budget officers to break open these established fiefdoms confront near overwhelming opposition from the alliance of congressional committee leaders, grant constituencies, and federal agencies. Outsiders are actual or potential enemies and the hostility to them, explicitly or implicitly, is shared and encouraged by these same actors and what the ACIR terms "functional autocracies."

The consequences of the vast changes in the federal grant system during the sixties are significant, therefore, in understanding the government interest groups' activities during phase three. Federal programs confined in scope, administration, and channeling generally aided the state or local grant recipient, increasingly insulated chief executives from budgetary and organizational influence, and frequently thwarted efforts at reorganization. "The Governor," concluded one study of state chief executives and the federal grant system, "to a considerable extent, is bypassed in this line of communication and finds that his control over both policy and management of agencies which administer these programs at the state level is weakened considerably."[60]

During the Senate hearings on *The Federal Role in Urban Affairs,* every large-city mayor who testified expressed comparable concerns regarding federal grants, reflecting problems which were further compounded by the vicissitudes in state-city relations. Mayors indicated that they could render neither an accounting of the magnitude and scope of federal activities in their cities nor any specification of how much federal money was spent annually in their jurisdictions.[61] A Housing and Urban Development (HUD) survey of Oakland, California, further underscored the mayors' arguments, finding that Oakland's mayor had no control whatsoever over 85 percent of the federal money coming into the city and that this situation was typical of most large cities. The Oakland study was expanded and replicated by OMB in several other cities. OMB concluded,

[60] Coleman B. Ransone, Jr., *The Office of Governor in the United States* University of Alabama Press, University, Ala., 1956, p. 249.

[61] See *Federal Role in Urban Affairs Hearings,* Senate Government Operations Committee, Subcommittee on Executive Reorganization, 89th Cong., 2d Sess., 1966.

as a result, that federal programs were operating in a chaotic fashion with practically no effort on the federal level to mesh program dollars to provide a comprehensive attack on community problems, and that local officials had no idea of the range of federal programs in their jurisdictions and little ability to influence the operation of these programs.[62] These findings only reaffirmed the contentions by mayors and governors that programs and policies outside their purview were weakening executive authority or, at least, were a sufficient deterrent to their strengthening.

CHIEF EXECUTIVES AS LOBBYISTS

A changing partnership characteristic of twentieth-century federalism thus far has vastly expanded previously existing sharing patterns through a wider scope of intergovernmental activities and a more complex system of administration. While intergovernmental lobbying of the past might be considered rather negligible by contemporary standards, it was considerable nevertheless. But today, greater dependency by state-local governments of federal resources exists. Arenas of conflict are much expanded, and prizes have assumed more demonstrable proportion. The competition between governmental levels and between these units and other actors is measurably enhanced.

One consequence of increased federal activity has been the delegation of discretionary rule-making authority to federal administrative agencies whose impact upon intergovernmental relations is nearly as great as formal legislative and judicial interpretation. Another consequence, directly related to the first, is the growth of government interest groups: elected, appointed, civil service, union, and professional associations. The latter groups—professional associations—have grown at a tremendous rate, extending into health, education, highways, public works, welfare, urban renewal, housing, and other areas. Close links have emerged between the professional associations, from whose ranks bureaucratic agencies are often staffed and dominant work force is drawn, throughout government levels. These associations often exhibit strong unity formed by training, skills, and professional concepts of status and autonomy. They constitute almost a private form of government the consequences of which are not readily appreciated, with the added importance of setting detailed standards for day-to-day operations of intergovernmental programs.

One may distinguish between the basic types of government interest groups of state and local origin. The five general groups, comprising governors, mayors, and county officials, are for the most part political and administrative generalists. In the Washington community they are

[62] See *National Journal*, **4**:1914, December 16, 1972.

frequently referred to as the public-interest groups or the "PIGS." This designation carries no intrinsic prescriptive value except that they are representing the interests of the highest elected officials of subnational governments. However, their claim as being the public-interest groups, self-alloted in part, serves multiple purposes related to the groups' overall activities. It functions to play down their lobbying, essential to the maintenance of a tax-exempt status, and distinguishes them from other organizations both public and private in membership. Such designation also enhances their own collective identity if not legitimacy as political actors.

However, several other types of government groups comprising public officials operate in Washington, also under the rubric of public interest groups. They can be distinguished from the former by their dissimilar attitudes, interests, and degree of public accountability—factors arising from their different positions, constituencies, and often training of members as well as historical relations with governments on all levels. One category of public officials includes representatives of professional organizations or associations concerned with specific government programs in health, education, welfare, and the like. When broadly defined in terms of public service professions rather than general professions, most of these are organized like guilds and hence are referred to as guilds. These assist government agencies and bureaus in developing and nourishing clientele support, often negotiating regulations and jurisdictional arrangements among other guilds unimpeded, for the most part, by elected or top-level appointed policy makers. The professional associations and guilds groups, frequently referred to in the Washington community as the "PORGS" (an abbreviation for public official organizations), are perhaps best distinguished by their involvement in social welfare, education, and science policy areas.

Another category of government officials—made up essentially of "specialists" and "functionalists"—is analogous to overhead agencies on state and local government levels such as finance, auditing, planning, and budgeting. It includes hardware and line agencies such as police, fire, traffic, and housing as well as special authorities such as airport operators; bridge, tunnel, and turnpike specialists; public power, highway, and port authorities. More than thirty organizations, predominantly Washington-based, comprise these latter "special-purpose" government interest groups. They, too, have national organizations with state and local affiliates. They elect officers, hold conventions, and employ full-time Washington staffs.

The national professional associations, guild groups, and functional government interest groups tend to comprise nonelected government officials, frequently middle-management administrators or professionals on all government levels pursuing the advancement, expansion, and/or autonomy of a particular program or professional specialty. The chief elected officials' organizations, on the other hand, whose members constitute the general-purpose government interest groups, are political executives pursuing the general interests of chief representatives of duly constituted governments. Typically the generalists pursue annual substantial increases in federal funding in bloc-grant form, with federal funds available for distribution at state or local discretion under chief executive control. In the political contest over stakes, the generalists and functionalists (including guilds and professional associations) often clash and compete with one another. They also collaborate on select areas of public policy where their mutual interests are involved. The presence of functionalists and the guild system are fundamental to understanding intergovernmental lobbying. Indeed, many argue that their influence is more durable and encompassing in the policy areas within which they operate than that of the government interest groups.

Nonetheless, the five general groups (who are referred to as the government interest groups rather than the "PIGS") enjoy thus far certain lobbying advantages over other government-interest groups as well as private interest groups. They are immune from the 1946 Lobbying Act in that they qualify as tax-exempt organizations under the Internal Revenue Code, Title 26, Section 501 (c) (1 and 4).[63] They are, in effect, considered employees of state, county, and municipal governments; hence to tax these instrumentalities would also be to tax state governments and municipal corporations. Other government interest groups such as the National Association of Housing and Redevelopment Officials (NAHRO) and the American Association of State Highway Officials (AASHO) are tax-exempt under Section 501 (c) (3) of the Internal Revenue Code but are forbidden by the same section from lobbying Congress directly. In practice, however, these advantages tend to be marginal because they do not restrict lobbying of the executive or deter AASHO, NAHRO, and other government official organizations from making their views known before Congress. On the other hand, the latter hesitate to become too highly visible in lobbying, often deferring to other groups, both public and private in composition, in taking the initiative as the lead group.

Intergovernmental lobbying as conducted by public officials, be they federal representatives, professional associations, or chief executives of state-local governments, suggests a further development of the American political system and its basically decentralized structure. Each of the government interest groups strives to enhance its role and autonomy, and each is constrained at the federal level by congressional fiefdoms and programmatic bureaucracies. These state-local interests pursue their activities in Congress through routinized legislative interference as well as through the executive in administrative collaboration on rule making.

---

[63] See *The Washington Lobby*, Congressional Quarterly, Inc., Washington, D.C., 1971, pp. 95–96.

Each of these outlets is vitally important in maintaining the positions of states and localities and each is fraught with tensions between elected officials, professional administrators, and the competition between them.

The historical development and institutionalization of agency liaison to Congress invites analogies to intergovernmental lobbying by subnational chief executives. While House-legislative liaison first reached its institutionalized form during the Eisenhower Presidency, it has been vastly expanded by Presidents since. Skilled bureau leaders long acted to bridge the gaps between Capitol Hill and downtown, courting congressional good will, cultivating key congressional committee leaders and staff, and building program support. Presidents learned from the example of executive officialdom that they too needed liaison to serve as spokesmen on behalf of their total programs rather than submit to agencies who often are claimants for their own programs.

In the intergovernmental arena a situation comparable to that of the President's late entry into congressional liaison has persisted. Dependent upon congressmen, senators, agency administrators, and federal field personnel for dealing with Washington as they have been, state-local chief executives have recognized that federal relations are too important to be left to others. Like the President, subnational chief executives found, individually and collectively, that they were belated entrants into federal lobbying. They often were competitors with other federal, state, and local officials, largely guilds, in the most important arenas of public policy. They, like recent Presidents, were threatened with subordination in their roles as chief legislators and chief administrators by the permanent government—the bureaucracy with its more institutionalized ties with Congress.

Thus the entrance of the White House into formal legislative negotiation and day-to-day working relations with Congress corresponds in function to the emergence of state-local chief executives as individual and collective claimants in the Washington community. Congress, in fact, formally sanctioned this liaison by establishing the Advisory Commission on Intergovernmental Relations in 1959. In charging the Commission with duties both to the executive and to Congress, the Congress nurtured an agency independent of itself and the President. But by composition, structure, and operation, the ACIR instead has functioned as a research arm, in ad hoc advisory capacity, and as a lobby of Congress on behalf of state and local governments, especially their chief executives.[64] While the President may appoint three private citizens and three officers of the executive branch to the ACIR, he also must select fourteen state-local

[64] See Deil S. Wright, "The Advisory Commission on Intergovernmental Relations: Unique Features and Policy Orientation," *Public Administration Review*, **25**:196–198, September 1965. Also see *10-Year Record of the Advisory Commission on Intergovernmental Relations Hearings,* Joing Hearings by the Intergovernmental Relations Subcommittees of the House and Senate Government Operations Committee, 92nd Cong., 1st Sess., 1971.

representatives on the Commission from a list of names submitted by the government interest groups (four governors, four mayors, three county officials, and three state legislators). This designation process has elevated the government interest groups and enhanced their recognition as official bargaining agents on behalf of subnational chief executives. Moreover, a built-in legislative liaison to Congress is maintained for the ACIR through the appointment to the Commission's board of six members, three from each chamber.

The most significant aspect of the changing relations between state-local governments and the national government and between subnational chief executives and federal policy makers is the growing dependence of these governments upon federal funds. As Table 4 indicates, federal aid as a percent of state-local expenditures in FY 1973 amounted to an estimated 23.8 percent, an aggregate increase of nearly 10 percent alone in the past decade. Federal grants more than doubled as a percent of state-

T-4 Federal Aid Outlays in Relation to Total Federal Outlays to State-Local Expenditures, 1930–1974

| | | Federal Aid | | |
| | | | As a Percent of | |
Fiscal year	Amount (millions)	Total federal outlays	Domestic federal outlays*	State-Local expenditures
1930	$200	4.9	5.8	2.7
1945	901	1.0	6.0	8.9
1952	2,393	4.3	11.2	10.0
1960	7,040	7.6	16.4	13.5
1965	10,904	9.2	18.4	14.6
1967	15,240	9.6	19.5	16.3
1969	20,255	11.0	21.3	17.4
1971	29,844	14.1	23.5	19.8
1972	35,940	15.5	24.5	21.3
1973 (est.)	45,008	18.0	27.0	23.8
1974 (est.)	44,825†	16.7	24.8	21.3

Source: Special Analyses, Budget of the United States, Fiscal Year 1974, Table N–5, p. 217, and Special Analyses, Budget of the United States, Fiscal Year 1970, Table O–3, p. 209.

* Excludes outlays for defense, space, and international programs.

†Excludes $1.7 billion representing direct federal payments to adult public assistance recipients starting January 1, 1974, under Public Law 92-603.

local expenditures between 1930 and 1952, indicated by Figure 3; rose gradually between 1952 and 1963; and since then climbed sharply in the late sixties and early seventies. Indeed, the entire process of federal redistribution of revenues transformed intergovernmental relations, making states and local governments into client groups of federal programs and their chief executives into federal lobbyists.

The scope and magnitude of this client-lobby relationship is significant. Not only the 50 states and larger cities were turned into dependents and clients but also virtually thousands of local governments, special districts, and authorities, many of which became eligible for federal funding for the first time. One-half the states received, in 1971, more than 20 percent of their revenues directly from federal grants, and one-quarter of them received more than 25 percent. If one includes the $100 billion in federal purchase of goods and services (defense and nondefense) as well as $85 billion in federal transfer payments (retirement and disability, food stamps, unemployment benefits, veterans' services and benefits, medical insurance), federal expenditures are a major force in state-local economies. A major shift in federal expenditures has occurred with the rise of domestic programs. Total domestic transfer payments and grants-in-aid were larger in 1971 for the first time in four decades than the total federal purchase of goods and services.[65] The client-lobbyist relationship between subnational executives and their federal constituency far exceeds, therefore, the federal grant system alone.

The dramatic upswing in federal aid to large cities as a percentage of their expenditures represents a major departure from the past in most cases. New York City, for example, whose budget and municipal employees exceeds that of the other 75,000 or so units of government in this country below the federal level, experienced an elevenfold increase in federal aid between 1963 and 1973. The nation's largest city carries on a range of government functions unsurpassed in magnitude and kind by any state or local government. As Table 5 indicates, the city financed these functions largely on its own, plus state contribution, until the early sixties, when federal aid as a percent of its overall expense budget rose precipitously from less than 5 percent to nearly 20 percent. Acknowledgedly, the New York City example is not typical of most large cities. Nonetheless, its increased reliance on federal funds does make the point that this federal dependency overtook many states and localities during the past decade at an extraordinary pace.

Governors, mayors, and county officials have multiple options and strategies to choose from in dealing with Washington. They can take a visible, lead role in negotiations. They can convey problems personally to the highest executive levels—the President, White House staff, Office

[65] *Special Analyses, Fiscal Year 1973*, p. 9.

T-5   Federal Aid to New York City as a Percent of the City's Expense Budget for Selected Years, 1952–1974 (est.)

Fiscal year	1952– 1953	1963– 1964	1966– 1967	1969– 1970	1971– 1972	1973– 1974
NYC expense budget (millions of dollars)	$1,469	2,785	4,554	6,701	8,472	10,595
Federal aid to New York City	$ 56	142	508	1,068	1,496	2,055
Federal aid as percent of the New York City budget	3.8	5.5	11.2	15.9	17.7	19.4

Source: City expenditure figures are taken from Citizens Budget Commission Fiscal Summaries, 1952–1973; the 1973–1974 budget estimates are taken from the Mayor's Annual Report and Expense Budget Message, May 1973.

of Management and Budget, and department heads—or they may work with congressional leaders, staff, committee chairmen, and the state's or unit's delegation in the Congress. To avoid being a persistent mendicant and to legitimize their demands, they may mobilize citywide or statewide elected officials, nongovernmental interest groups, business associations, or even the media in supporting their case before national policy makers. Also, they may employ professional envoys who do their government's bidding for them.

The concentration of Congress upon overseeing legislation and providing constituency services has provided legislators with ample devices for monitoring state and local grant requests, administrative decisions, and federal guidelines which apply to subnational units. Institutional interference has come to play a major role in mayor-governor contact with Congress involving "casework" on behalf of their governments. Through congressional powers to review, investigate, and fund federal agencies, committee members can extract concessions for their constituent governments as a price for supporting an agency and its program. Whether in the form of state or city delegation or individual legislators performing casework for their states and localities, an institutionalized system of intergovernmental lobbying has been built into the legislative process. Some delegations, in fact, have a well-developed sense of "real estate" on how federal funding, policies and decisions affect their turf and frequently join forces without regard to party for bargaining collectively on behalf of their states' interests.[66]

However, for the governor or mayor dealing with Congress, his sense of

[66] See David B. Truman, The Congressional Party, Wiley, New York, 1959, chap. 7, and Barbara Deckard, "State Party Delegations in the U.S. House of Representatives," Journal of Politics, 34:199–222, February 1972.

F–3 Federal Aid as a Percent of Aggregate State and Local Government Expenditures, 1930–1974 (est.)

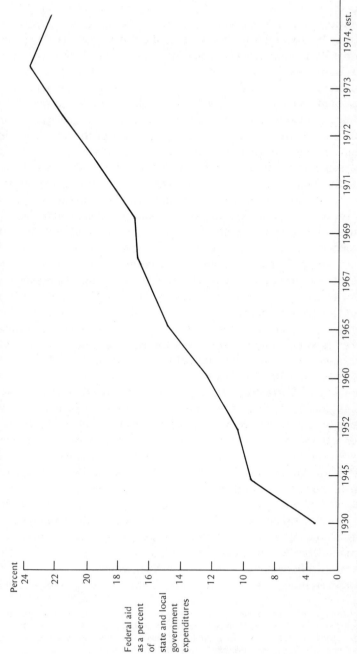

Source: *Special Analyses,* Budget of the United States, Fiscal Year 1974, Table N–5, p. 217, and *Special Analyses,* Budget of the United States, Fiscal Year 1970, Table O–3, p. 209.

priorities and an agenda may be radically different from that of his delega-tion. House members and the two senators may be of opposite parties, rivals of the state-local chief executive either for his job or for control over the party's machinery. They are frequently not members of the relevant committees with which the chief executive is concerned; or, if they are, they may be too junior to do anything about his concerns. They also may lack the skills, information, or—for reasons of their own—leave the governor or mayor to carry the effort without their help.

During phase two of the governments groups' relations with Washing-ton, subnational chief executives individually strengthened their "Potomac pipelines." Between 1964 and 1969, nearly half the governors instituted a state liaison office in the nation's capital. Nine of the ten most populous states, for example, each maintain a full-time Washington office staffed by personal representatives of the state's governors, while perhaps twenty or so others have a comparable full-time or contractual outlet. Most large-city mayors and a few large counties have similar emissaries either opera-ting through NACO, USCM-NLC's Man in Washington Service, or through management consultant operations. Federal aid coordinators attached to a chief executive's office also have emerged in governors' and mayors' staffs, forming national organizations with their parent govern-ment interest group. Nearly all the governors and most large-city mayors have a single agency or person tied to their staffs charged with federal aid and program responsibilities dealing as the chief executives' surrogates in the intergovernmental area. These "intelligence outlets," "coordinators," and "emissaries" function ideally as the chief executives' counterpart for Washington negotiation, looking out for their interests, stakes, and future as affected by federal policies.[67]

Individual efforts by chief executives to expand and promote their Washington contacts notwithstanding, governors and mayors have in-creasingly acknowledged the need for a collective strategy in dealing with Washington. A governor or mayor is typically not an effective contact with the national political system that dispenses grants unless he learns how to get at the grant decision process of agencies and how to persuade pro-gram administrators and bureau chiefs. Even then, leaders of federal bureaus that administer federal programs also must respond to other pressures: the executive chain of command through departments up to the White House, and—more important—the congressional committees and subcommittees in Congress that, to a considerable degree, control and influence the behavior of agencies and their leaders.

Moreover, many governors and mayors attest to a changing era in White

[67] See Jerry Udell, "The Governor's Ambassador: A New Concept of Representation," unpublished master's thesis, American University, Washington, D.C., 1966; Billy L. Charl-ton, "A Study of State-Local Governmental Liaison Activities in Washington, D.C.," un-published master's thesis, American University, Washington, D.C., 1967.

House intervention—an era in which preferential treatment for them is declining. No longer does a single call to the White House or one channeled through the Vice President's liaison office for dealing with state-local chief executives produce immediate aid and results. That is not to say that someone like Chicago's Richard Daley does not still have sufficient clout in White House circles to get a President to overrule his Commissioner of Education, as in the case of the confrontation between the Chicago Mayor and Commissioner Francis Keppell in 1967 over a cutoff of education funds due to the city's slow progress in desegregating its public schools. But such power to intervene is increasingly the exception rather than the rule. State-local executives recognize that successful interference requires more formal and durable pressure.[68]

The grant-based intergovernmental economy of the late 1960s and early 1970s has profoundly affected state-local chief executives. The fiscal and political consequences of federal grant programs carry over to the rising administrative, managerial, and control problems they confront. The positions of chief executives in relation to the proliferating grant system is both anomalous and ambiguous. Since grants constitute a major portion of these government budgets, chief executives must compete for and actively pursue them at the apparent risk of political suicide if they refuse. As Governor Nelson Rockefeller observed of this situation, "If you don't apply for this money, somebody will get up and say, 'Why don't you ask for this money? Here is this free money in Washington you are not using.' Then it becomes a political issue."[69] Nevertheless there are positive political payoffs from a chief executive's perspective in obtaining as much federal aid as possible. Federal grants do help meet demands for services, expand programs, and perhaps more importantly, are generally regarded by voters as "free" money, a substitute perhaps for paying higher state and local taxes.

The two-edged sword of federal grants, however, is readily apparent to these executives in the recognizable trade-offs required to obtain them. On the one hand the grants are popular and may temporarily alleviate the fiscal drain on state-local revenues that is involved. On the other hand, grants contribute to the headaches chief executives suffer in performing their political and administrative leadership roles. Most observers agree that grants contribute to the fragmentation of participating governments, undermine what executive controls may exist, and dilute chief executives' policy, coordination, and budgetary roles. The financial and administrative problems that accompany most grants, for some, may far outweigh whatever fiscal, political, and programmatic advantages they intrinsically have.

---

[68] *National Journal*, **4:**1144, July 15, 1972.

[69] *General Revenue Sharing Hearings*, part 5, p. 833.

Grant entrepreneurship by governors and mayors also gets mixed reviews as to its individual importance. San Francisco's Mayor Joseph Alioto has been quoted saying that "No mayor can really do his job unless he spends at least one day per month in Washington."[70] Alioto, like some other prominent large-city mayors and several governors, has perhaps enhanced his political attractiveness by nature of his reputation as a successful grantsman. Others have lost, however, Being too preoccupied with federal grant acquisition can also go hard on a chief executive. Commenting on the demise of its city's four-term Mayor Arthur Naftalin, the *Minneapolis Star* editoralized in 1968, "The mayor lost press support because he spent too much time away from the city on his missions seeking federal aid."

Thus for state-local executives, the increased dependency upon federal funds and a vastly expanded allocative and acquisitive process has intensified their problems in competing over the disposition of contemporary $300-billion-dollar federal budgets. Collectively they pursue annual substantial increases in the amounts of federal money made available to their governmental level; individually they seek to secure for their own government the maximum allowable share under the most favorable terms possible.

Faced with partisan differences and competition from other governments, subnational chief executives have come to rely increasingly on the least risk-laden and most economical strategy in dealing with the national government—that of working with fellow chief executives. The governors, mayors, and county officials depend on the size of this coalition, its obvious visibility, and its national scope to gain concessions in funding and administration. This often works to their collective benefit.

The recognized need for this collective strategy and its gradual but distinctive development has played a fundamental role in making the government interest groups into stronger lobbying instrumentalities. By the third phase in their Washington relations, the groups' activities had become organized, sustained, and seemingly institutionalized by way of dealing with their national government constituency.

POLITICAL PARTIES AND THE GOVERNMENT GROUPS

While chief executives may be central political figures in their respective political systems, this does not assure that they will be recognized as central spokesmen for their government in dealing with higher government levels. Because of institutional, constitutional, and historical factors, chief executives confront many rivals—elected, bureaucratic, party, and interest

[70] *National Journal,* 4:1924, December 16, 1972.

groups—who may have more established pipelines and more receptive audiences at these levels.

Similarly, rivalry between political executives within state boundaries often extends nationally. Participants in this rivalry may include the states' federal representatives—congressmen and senators—as well as officials elected to statewide executive offices, often with separate constituencies, elections, and followings independent from those of a chief executive. Intra-party and interparty competition among elected officials varies according to personal ambitions, loyalties, alliances, and party position as well as other factors. The multitude of elected positions in our political system combined with the absence of clearly defined and recognized paths from one position to another finds mayors, governors, federal representatives, and senators pursuing the prizes one another may hold or have claims upon. This pursuit further adds to the problems of our decentralized, fragmented political parties and the vagaries in relations among office-holders.

Nevertheless, governors and mayors are integral components of, leaders in, and primary products of national political parties, local in origin. Gov-ernors are even more important, then, because their office is established by the state constitution, not the party, and is one of the essential reasons for the existence of the party itself. State political parties nonetheless remain, for the most part, alliances of autonomous and sometimes feuding factions with several barons and fiefdoms. Thus one can perhaps appreci-ate better the consequences of this rivalry and competition, insofar as what subnational chief executives desire may also be what other elected officials want as well. In politics one does not readily give advantages to actual or potential rivals, regardless of how compelling the need may seem.

In Congress, the government interest groups' assertion of "representa-tive" status confronts an already established, formal system of state and local participation. Federally elected officials are sensitive to their own representative status. Many if not most congressmen have "trustee-oriented" role conceptions, viewing themselves as free autonomous agents, to use their own judgment in determining the public interest.[71] Even those representatives who consider themselves "politicos" or "delegates" view roles primarily in terms of reflecting as well as defining territorial stakes in the legislative process. These territories, of course, are not necessarily contiguous with city, county, or even state lines. Presumably, friction between government interest groups and Congress, in a collective

---

[71] See John C. Wahlke, et al., The Legislative System, Wiley, New York, 1962, chap. 12–13; Lewis A. Dexter, "The Representative and His District," in Robert Peabody and Nelson Polsby (eds.), New Perspectives on the House of Representatives, Rand McNally, Chicago, 1963, pp. 3–39; and Aage A. Clausen, How Congressmen Decide, St. Martin's, New York, 1973.

sense, is built into their relationships: it is an outgrowth of interparty and intraparty rivalries; separate constituencies and followings, responsibilities and roles; and conflicting views of the public interest. "Hostility to political executives," notes Seidman "is shared and encouraged by committees and subcommittees of the Congress and state legislatures which are preoccupied as the administrators with protecting and promoting the purposes of the individual programs under their respective jurisdictions."[72]

Certainly the fact that mayors and governors are not national officials enjoying an institutional foothold in the federal bureaucracy reduces any formal competition that may arise between Congress and the government interest groups over legitimate roles and policy leadership. More subtle and enduring frictions tend to be built into these relations as a result of the decentralized structure and nonprogrammatic nature of political parties. The implications of this locally based party system surface in the ongoing rivalries and often conflicting ambitions among the nation's more visible officeholders: governors, large-city mayors, United States senators, congressmen, and even the President. In more populated states, both a governor and senator may entertain presidential ambitions or the governor hold a claim on a senator's seat; a senator or congressman, though occupying a national office, may hope to move to the governorship; and a large-city mayor may aspire to be a senator or a governor.

The consequences of this rivalry for governors and mayors on the national scene are not readily apparent but nonetheless real. "Egger's Law"— that governors hold senators with the same level of contempt as senators hold their states' governors—persists more than ever today, as evidenced by how assiduously some senators operate to keep various intergovernmental programs from flowing directly through the states and their governors as opposed to supporting programs which bypass the states.[73] As more than one senator has remarked in private interview concerning federal-state-local relations under federal grant programs, "I don't want my governor to get his hands on it." On the other hand, certain Southern legislators, congressmen and senators alike, often favor federal-state programs over federal-local ones in the expectation that Southern governors and state bureaucracies can better resist federal pressures, especially where integration is concerned, than can local governments or instrumentalities.

A comparable attitude is often evoked from suburban and rural congressmen in opposition to "flow-through" programs to the cities when

[72] Seidman, *Politics, Position, and Power*, pp. 136–137.

[73] My thanks to the late Wallace S. Sayre, Chairman of the Department of Political Science, Columbia University, for this quote, which probably dates back to the war years when the Office of Price Administration created enormous conflict between senators and governors.

urban-rural cleavages come into play. Relations among individual members of government interest groups can be no less intense. "Governor Richard Ogilvie (R-Ill.) made it quite clear to President Nixon and Cabinet officials alike," noted one White House observer in 1969, "that he must be privy to any federal agency dealings with Chicago's Mayor Richard Daley." Tensions between governors and senators are equally high in competition for federal contracts, programs, or state patronage. In addition, cleavages, rivalries, and interests are exacerbated often by party organizations whose structure may differ from city lines or congressional districts and frequently require separate sets of machinery for handling nominations, campaigns, and allocation of rewards.

For the government interest groups whose members are products of these confederated, truncated political structures, relations with Congress exist on several levels. As interest groups comprising elected officials with a broad scope of political interest, they have distinctive liabilities vis-à-vis other public and private groups, which have a more narrow scope of interests and greater power to intervene in a particular policy area. Thus the government interest groups seek to capitalize on their potential political influence as leaders of state-local party structures with attendant importance to Congress, the President, executive agencies, and other political actors.

Thus one set of relationships exists between elected chief executives and federal legislators which is tied to what V. O. Key called "party and the electorate," namely their competition for voter allegiance and constituency following. These relations may be harmonious or competitive depending on personal ambitions and the structure of party ties. In an aggregate sense, governors and mayors also deal both with "party-in-the-government" at the federal level and the national party organization seeking to influence both to their collective advantage.[74]

From the postwar period until the early 1960s, Congress had debated as a matter of national policy the question of whether or not the federal government should become involved in areas and functions considered the province and responsibility of state and local governments. By the late sixties, such questions had largely been resolved. Broad national support for and congressional enactment of major intergovernmental social programs in employment, education, civil rights, housing, air and water pollution control, consumer protection, health care, crime control, and the like decided these issues.[75] Since federal involvement per se no longer constitutes a major issue, Congress has increasingly turned to such matters as how, for what purposes and aims, in what forms, on what basis,

[74] See V. O. Key, *Politics, Parties, and Pressure Groups*, 5th ed., Crowell, New York, 1964.

[75] See congressional voting scores on the issue of larger federal role in the national government's relations with states and local communities. *Congressional Quarterly*, 26: 3123–3127, November 15, 1968.

through which channels, and with what consequences the federal government assists state and local units in achieving certain goals and attaining national policies.

The ongoing debate over how the national government can best combine its resources with those of state and local governments, in fact, underpins much of the competition and conflict among the government interest groups. The issue of which instrumentalities the federal government should stimulate and support in implementing national programs presents no small problem for public officials at all governmental levels. The issue of federal relations with a panoply of public and private actors is further complicated by the fact that decisions and programs, once established, have a certain momentum of their own. Once federal policy makers agree to deal with the states exclusively or bypass all general-purpose units whatsoever, constituencies develop, professional associations organize, and programs tend to be staunchly defended against change. At times, these programs are modified, updated, or adjusted for the entry of new claimants, but rarely are they comprehensively overhauled. Which government level and agencies become the recipient, executor, and reallocator of federal monies is often crucial to political executives. It can influence revenues and budgets, planning and priorities.

By tradition and preference, most domestic public services are actually performed at the level of government closest to the intended beneficiary regardless of which level finances them and in spite of the fact that all levels might participate in shared administration. One calculation of service delivery in 1970 estimated that states administered 25 percent of civilian domestic services—mainly highways, higher education, and welfare; local governments provided 43 percent—predominantly elementary and secondary education; and the federal government provided 30 percent —primarily postal services, agriculture, and natural resource programs.[76]

States find themselves in a somewhat ambiguous position. As the federal government has moved into national politics affecting traditional local functions and service forms, the states, in a sense, are steadily becoming retail distributors of funds that the federal Treasury distributes in a more wholesale fashion. States also are becoming more the bankers for local governments because of their superior revenue-raising and bonding powers, passing along to local governments anywhere from 50 to 80 percent of their funds. As retail distributors of federal funds and banker of state monies, they too, want their pound of flesh for performing the brokerage role between national and corporate entities under their control. Municipalities and counties, often justifiably so, feel outraged at the overhead costs taken from their consumers by the states. Mayors term this allocative process, by which each government level skims funds off

---

[76] Special Analyses, Budget of the United States, Fiscal Year 1970, p. 201.

the top of distributive or redistributive programs as they pass down through the federal system, the "sticky-fingers routine." Alternative types of federal aid where the states are involved—such as bloc grants and revenue sharing—may compound, in one way or another, the local government's dilemma of shedding services and freeing themselves from state bondage. Thus mayors grasp at panaceas like municipal bloc grants, "flow-through" programs, and even extremes like city-statehood or federal incorporation of large cities as seemingly preferable to their existing situation.[77]

One of the very first postwar debates over the issue of federal aid to the states as opposed to localities erupted in the National Airport Act of 1946. Strong congressional support existed for federal promotion of civil aviation through federal aid for airport construction. Much debate centered around the issues of who would be the beneficiaries and what public agencies would be eligible for federal grants—state agencies exclusively or state and local government agencies alike. The senate-passed version championed by Senator Owen Brewster, a former NGC leader, required mandatory channeling of federal funds through state agencies. The House-passed bill left the mandatory channeling decision up to any state's initiative but otherwise permitted municipal and county governments' direct participation in the program. Following strong lobbying by the mayors, aviation trade groups, contractors, and commercial airlines in support of the House bill, the Senate-House conferees from the Public Works Committees adopted the House version, which was subsequently approved by both chambers.[78] The 1946 Federal Aid to Airports program created, in effect, a federal-local program in which states could participate and exert control if they established a state airport agency and contributed matching funds. Few states did, however. This act constituted the first of major channeling debates to be revived in many forms over the next several decades.

The Airport Act is not a particularly significant program, but various patterns emerging from its resolution are. Presidents and their advisers are frequently drawn into disputes involving the channeling issue. Democratic presidents and administrations since 1933 have proved more receptive to promoting federal-local relations in government programs. They are cognizant, to be sure, that much of their electoral and congressional support resides in large cities and metropolitan areas. On the other hand,

[77] See Suzanne Farkas, "Federal Role in Urban Decentralization," *American Behavioral Scientists,* **15**:15–35, September 1971; and Murray Weidenbaum, *The Modern Public Sector,* Basic Books, New York, 1969, chap. 4.

[78] See Randall B. Ripley, "Congress Champions Aid to Airports, 1959," in Frederic N. Cleaveland (ed.), *Congress and Urban Problems,* Brookings Institution, Washington, D.C., 1969, pp. 20–71; Morton Grodzins, "American Political Parties and the American System," *Western Political Science Quarterly,* **13**:976–980, December 1960.

Presidents Eisenhower and Nixon invested considerable prestige in promoting federal-state relations. Once again, this may be accounted for in terms of constituency and congressional support, but basic philosophies are involved as well. Indeed, President Eisenhower expressed concern over increases in federal programs and activities at the expense of states which, he felt, transgressed upon "our most cherished principles of government, and tend to undermine the structure so painstakingly built by those who preceded us."[79] President Nixon's rhetoric has far surpassed his Republican predecessors, stressing, since 1969, that too much power, too much money, and too many bureaucrats have become concentrated in Washington and that it is time to reverse the flow.

Other significant patterns can be traced from 1946 or earlier in terms of party cleavages and voting alignments, dividing Democrats and Republicans on the federal-state-local issue. Such patterns varied with party strength, leadership support, administration involvement, and policy. But the Democrats generally supported programs containing direct federal-local involvement, while congressional Republicans have advocated stronger federal-state ties and using the states in dealing with local governments. Defections predictably occurred in both parties over the issue. Urban Republicans often sided with the federal-local position, and Southern Democrats supported the federal-state stance.

Intercameral relations between the House and Senate on this issue underwent changes during the postwar period as well. The Senate characteristically was more supportive of the federal-state position from 1933 to 1953 than the House. The Senate gradually became the stronger advocate of the two for direct federal-local relations, particularly since the 1958 elections. The Senate not only became the more liberal of the two bodies in the sixties but also the institution more disposed toward using federal aid as a defensive weapon in bypassing states unsympathetic to urban needs.[80]

For the mayors and their urban allies, the greater part of their activities during the 1950s was directed at Congress. They gained congressional assistance for the consolidation and preservation of existing programs and worked with liberal activists in building a favorable legislative climate for many national programs eventually enacted during the following decade. The governors, in contrast, champions in rhetoric of the administration's commitment to devolution of powers and programs to the states, failed in practice to attain any working consensus around specific programs. Much of the attention they gave to what transpired in Congress was aimed at frustrating the mayors' efforts to expand federal-local programs. From the governors' perspective, their interests were well protected by an administration adamantly opposed to bypassing state governments. The governors

[79] Quoted in Glenn Brooks, *When Governors Convene*, p. 94.
[80] See Davis and Sundquist, *Making Federalism Work*, chap. 9.

had the added protection that anywhere from one-sixth to one-fourth of the Senate's composition since 1946 included former governors. They were once referred to as the "governors' bloc" because of their high degree of unanimity regardless of party affiliation.[81] As this bloc declined in number and unity, the states' veto power within Congress was taken up by various state guilds such as the state health officers in their extensive lobbying against congressional passage of a proposed federal-local water-pollution-control bill.

While the government groups perform valuable political functions directed at shaping federal policy, they also seek to influence national parties internally. Yet this influence tends to be tactfully applied, often partisan-based, with coalitions of mayors and governors operating upon both national parties. The government groups attempt to maintain a bipartisan stance in spite of natural leanings toward one party or the other. They appear before the platform hearings at both parties' national conventions and develop position papers for use in campaigns, but they refrain as organizations from endorsing candidates or actively campaigning for either party or its candidates.

Nonetheless, organization behavior dating from at least the New Deal period suggests that a favorable predisposition occurs toward one of the parties. However, this situation has become somewhat more fluid than in the past. The USCM has operated within the Democratic party's inner circles on matters of urban policies and programs, while the governors have found the Republican party to be generally more favorably inclined towards its policies and goals. These group differences are rooted historically. Urban political machines have been the foundation of much of the Democratic party's national support since the late 1920s. Between 1932 and 1964, for example, Democratic presidential candidates received pluralities in each of the nation's fifteen largest cities, with the Eisenhower elections of 1952 and 1956 being the principal exceptions. Democratic presidents have not been unmindful of the contributions made by large-city voters and their political leaders in national elections, electoral college tabulations, and urban congressional delegation support in Congress. They have, accordingly, rewarded these leaders and cities with various perquisites. Moreover, between 1946 and 1971, Democrats have held the mayoralty position in thirteen of these cities with few exceptions (Los Angeles, San Francisco, and Detroit are the major ones), clearly demonstrating the almost unbroken line of postwar Democratic hegemony in big-city leadership.[82]

[81] W. Brooke Graves, *American Intergovernmental Relations*, Scribner, New York, 1964, pp. 185–186.

[82] Charles E. Gilbert, "National Political Alignments and the Politics of Large Cities," *Political Science Quarterly*, **79**:25–51, March 1964. Samuel Lubell, *The Future of American Politics*, Harper, New York, 1952; Richard Scammon (ed.), *America Votes: A Handbook of Contemporary American Election Statistics*, vol. iv, University of Pittsburgh, 1962.

Large-city mayors anticipated harsh treatment from the Nixon administration, a harshness heightened by the President's commitment to New Federalism and the governors' domination of cabinet posts. One White House source indicated to the mayors the significance of the new GOP administration less subtly, noting the political adage "reward your friends and punish your enemies," which, translated, meant the mayors are Democrats, the governors are Republicans. Mr. Nixon declined invitations to attend the mayors' annual meetings which his Democratic predecessors frequented, preferring to meet with delegations of mayors privately at the White House. Their early relations were combative in spite of the efforts of NLC President Richard Lugar to quell the growing anti-Nixon feeling among mayors. Nonetheless Mr. Nixon's initial policies—impoundment of urban funds, hostility toward Model Cities, and curtailment of categorical programs—seemed to confirm the mayors' worst suspicions.

However, fears of a highly partisan and anticity Republican President failed to materialize as far as most mayors were concerned. The anti-Nixon sentiment so prevalent at USCM gatherings in 1969–1970 had subsided, and by 1972 the mayors were openly expressing their favorable reaction toward many of the administration's policies. "We've been treated as well by the Nixon administration as we would have been by a Democratic administration," observed Pittsburgh's Democratic Mayor Peter Flaherty. "It hasn't hurt us at all."[83] For large-city mayors, the existing alignment of a GOP President setting policies and strengthening mayoral powers and a Democratic-controlled Congress funding urban programs at levels higher than the administration's requests had obvious advantages.

Thus what began in the first two years of the Nixon administration as a concerted strategy for dealing with the states and their governors resulted in greater attention being given to cities and a mayoral constituency. Not that the governors were excluded from New Federalism experiments, especially in executive waiver of federal grant regulations and attention to substate regional planning, but that HUD and other federal departments found accomplishments more readily attainable at the local level. The administration's experiments with planned variations and chief executive review instruments aimed at vastly augmenting mayoral powers at the expense of functional bureaucracies in control over federal programs sparked a most enthusiastic reaction from these cities and their mayors. The USCM lauded the President's plans to get federal funds to cities on a regular, sustained basis and, in fact, openly applauded Mr. Nixon's commitment to a $30-billion revenue-sharing plan in early 1971 which proposed to divide federal funds evenly between the states and local governments.

The mayors' gradual conversion to a more even disposition toward the Republican President became fully evident at the time of the 1972 election.

[83] National Journal 4:1143, July 15, 1972.

One mayor summed up the difference between Mr. Nixon and his Democratic opponent Senator George McGovern by saying that the former was anticity but pro-city hall while the latter was procity but anticity hall. President Nixon received the endorsement of prominent USCM-NLC officers in his 1972 campaign, something that few would have predicted back in 1969. USCM 1972–73 President Louie Welch of Houston, past USCM President Jack Maltester of San Leandro, Norfolk's Ray Martin, Nashville's Beverly Briley, Philadelphia's Frank Rizzo, Miami's David Kennedy, and virtually hundreds of mayors nationally lined up behind Mr. Nixon's reelection.[84]

The National Governors' Conference, for the most part, has found a greater philosophical compatibility, a more receptive ear, and increased policy direction for the states from within the Republican party. Even though they were a minority within the NGC for most of the past two decades, Republican governors generally have taken a more active role in the association than Democratic governors. Also, GOP governors have been more visible and important as an interest group within their party than Democratic governors within theirs. GOP state chief executives have been instrumental in forwarding party alternatives, shaping party platforms, and, in fact, have long operated as a separately constituted unit within the Republican National Committee.

During the early 1960s, Republican governors were strongly identified with the party's liberal wing as opposed to the more conservative congressional faction. It was they who survived the 1964 Democratic landslide election victory better than any other public official grouping within the GOP and subsequently led the fight to break the Goldwater faction's grip on the party machinery. Republican Governors Romney, Volpe, Guy, Hatfield, and others were a primary force in rejuvenating the National Governors' Conference in the sixties and led efforts to bolster the governors' Washington influence.[85] Also Republican governors, as Figure 4 indicates, scored a major breakthrough in party strength during the 1966–1969 elections. This marked a highly unusual period where GOP governors far exceeded, in percentage terms, the percentage of Republicans in either the House or the Senate. Table 6 indicates this, and it also shows how party control of governorships tends to increase or decrease in a more volatile manner than party in Congress. In spite of differences in state and federal elections and the attempt by many states to keep them separate, gubernatorial composition still is subject to national trends, often preceding shifts in congressional alignments.

The Republican governors were among the key supporters of President

---

[84] Pete Wilson, "Nixon's Urban Record," *City*, Fall 1972, pp. 7–8.

[85] Stephen Hess and David Broder, *The Republican Establishment: The Present and Future of the G.O.P.*, Harper & Row, New York, 1967, chaps. 1–2.

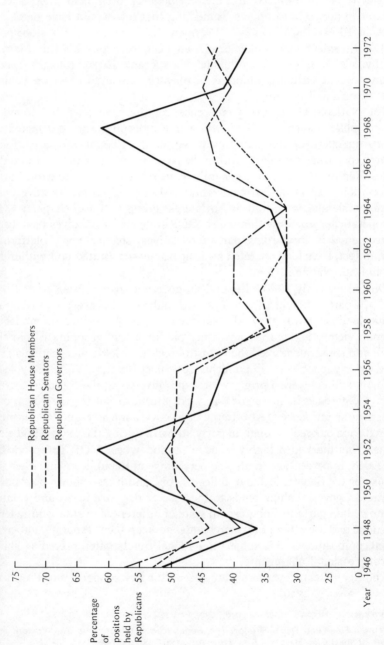

F–4   Republican Federal Officeholders and Republican Governors Compared, 1946–1972

Percentage of positions held by Republicans

Republican House Members
Republican Senators
Republican Governors

Year   1946 1948 1950 1952 1954 1956 1958 1960 1962 1964 1966 1968 1970 1972

Source: Congress and the Nation, 1945–1972, vols. I–III, Congressional Quarterly Service, Washington, D.C.

Nixon's New Federalism and presumably, at least in 1969, were viewed as its main beneficiaries. GOP governors were riding an all-time high at that point, controlling nine of the ten largest states' governorships — states which contained more than 40 percent of the country's population. Nelson Rockefeller had taken over as policy director for the Republican Governors' Association, and he and other governors used the Association as an internal lobby for position and policy within the national party. Moreover, Republican governors dominated President Nixon's earliest cabinet appointments, a situation unprecedented among recent administrations, reflecting in part Mr. Nixon's efforts to unite his party by mollifying the more liberal factions.

Changeover in gubernatorial composition between 1969 and 1972 had a definite impact upon the President's domestic programs and his cultivation of a gubernatorial constituency. The 1970 midterm elections transformed the NGC from a GOP-dominated forum to a Democratic-controlled one. The Republicans lost control of thirteen statehouses, reducing their number from thirty-two governorships — a postwar high — to nineteen by 1973. The consequences of this partisan realignment within the NGC were immediate. Democratic governors took the lead in attacking the Republican President and his domestic policies. Repeating the script of the Republican

T-6 Republican Officeholders as a Percentage of Incumbent Officeholders, 1946–1972

Position	1946	1948	1950	1952	1954	1956	1958	1960
Senate	53	44	49	50	49	49	34	36
House	57	39	46	51	47	46	35	40
Governors	52	36	52	62	44	42	28	32
Variance among the three by percent	5	8	6	12	5	7	7	8

1962	1964	1966	1968	1970	1972
32	32	36	42	45	43
40	32	43	44	41	44
32	34	50	62	42	38
8	2	14	20	4	5

Source: Congress and the Nation, 1945–1972, vols. I–III, Congressional Quarterly Service, Washington, D.C.

governors from the sixties, they criticized the White House's inattentiveness to state matters and the breakdown in communication between the President and the governors. In spring 1971, a special caucus of Democratic governors convened to openly oppose the President's revenue-sharing plan, joining congressional Democrats in developing alternative programs. In spite of the long-standing NGC policy supportive of bloc grants and greater gubernatorial discretion over federal-state programs, the Democratic governors denounced the Nixon administration's special revenue-sharing plans and further efforts to provide governors with greater powers over intergovernmental programs. The 1973 annual NGC meeting found a faction of several Democratic governors dominating the session's proceedings by calling for Mr. Nixon's immediate resignation in light of his involvement in the 1972 Presidential campaign irregularities. What began in 1968 as a key support group for President Nixon's domestic policies had turned into a heated platform for criticism of the GOP administration, forcing the President to look more to the mayors and county officials for assistance.

Indeed, the cases of attempted or actual influence of partisan groupings of mayors and governors within the national party suggest that the line between party and interest group can become blurred, even producing a reversal of roles. Such incidents have arisen in the slating of local candidates where the Democratic party has lobbied organized labor to shift its position on candidate selection.[86] To a degree, a comparable situation has occurred where blocs of governors or mayors operating within the national party structure have exerted sufficient pressure or threats of veto upon candidate selection or party platform, compelling the party organization to actually lobby these blocs to change or otherwise modify their stance. Such developments, of course, remain the exception rather than the rule. Republican governors have not recently attained the eminence in party circles that emerged in 1968, and they are unlikely to do so again. Southern Democratic governors led by Georgia's Jimmy Carter tried in vain to reverse the all but inevitable nomination of Senator George McGovern in 1972 as the party's Presidential nominee. McGovern supporters and party officials moved quickly to heal party cleavages, courting the governors by suggesting that one of them might be selected as the party's Vice Presidential candidate. With the decline of big-city machines and the population shift away from most large cities, mayors are also unlikely to regain the organized power they possessed within the Democratic party from 1932 through at least 1960.

For governors and mayors, individually and collectively, their national party influence is generally declining. Their positions have been weakened

[86] See J. David Greenstone, "Party Pressure on Organized Labor in Three Cities," in M. Kent Jennings and Harmon Zeigler (eds.), *The Electoral Process*, Prentice Hall, Englewood Cliffs, N.J., 1966, pp. 55–79.

by presidential primaries, new delegate selection methods, and more open national conventions. The governors' once advantageous position in presidential nominations through control of large-state delegations at national conventions and the lack of involvement in controversial national issues have been greatly diminished by the growing pains of state governments. Some governors may still hold presidential ambitions and control party machinery necessary to indulge in such aspirations. However, the line of presidential succession appears to have reverted once again to the senate. This may be a temporary phenomenon, but it has persisted in recent times.[87] Large-city mayors, too, no longer command the respect within Democratic party circles that they once did. Their control over party resources and organization structure is nowhere near commensurate with their predecessors. Moreover, few mayors seem to have much political future beyond their present local party office. Not more than a handful of large-city mayors since World War II have gone on either to the state governorship or the U.S. Senate: Senator Joseph Clark, formerly mayor of Philadelphia, and Senator Hubert Humphrey, a past mayor of Minneapolis, are the two principal exceptions from the fifties. "The lack of political future in being mayor has made the office most unattractive," observed one political scientist, "so that the more astute politician will guide his career around, not into, the office."[88]

These trends suggest all the more why governors and mayors have acted upon the political necessity of banding together to deal with their federal constituency. The importance of individual governors and mayors within their respective parties may have declined, but their collective identity has increased. This is particularly the case at the groups' annual meetings, where scores of congressional and administration officials are visible, lobbying group members for support of particular programs and policies. White House envoys keep close tabs on each of the groups' resolutions. Department heads and their assistants spend considerable time courting the good will of governors, mayors, and county officials in light of the groups' enhanced visibility and lobbying influence.[89]

Case Studies

Earlier sections of this book have concentrated upon the history and organization of the government interest groups as well as the evolutionary development in their relations with Washington. Another related focus has

[87] Louis Harris, "Why the Odds Are against a Governor's Becoming President," *Public Opinion Quarterly,* **22**:361–370, fall 1959.

[88] Marilyn Gittell, "Metropolitan Mayors: Dead End," *Public Administration Review,* **23**:20, January/February 1963.

[89] See Martin and Susan Tolchin, *To the Victor: Political Patronage From the Clubhouse to the White House,* Random House, 1971, pp. 253–254.

emphasized the consequences of federal programmatic and fiscal policies upon state-local governments. The latter have increasingly become clients of the national government and their chief executives have turned into lobbyists of federal officialdom. Increased dependency of lower governmental levels upon higher ones has resulted in systematic changes throughout the federal system which have not only overtaken state-local governments but also profoundly affected the behavior of highest elected officials. It is next important, however, to demonstrate the linkages between the government interest groups and their members to actual federal policies.

The following cases will explore the roles and functions the government interest groups perform at the national level. They will shed some light upon the strategies, tactics, and resources employed by the groups, cooperatively and competitively, in pursuit of their goals. Each of the cases examined ranked high on the government groups' agenda both as to investment of resources and consequences for their members. The first three — Budget Bureau directive A #85, the Intergovernmental Cooperation Act of 1968, and Section #204 of the 1966 Model Cities Act — constitute essentially nonmaterial, regulative policies in which the groups generally anticipated that the outcome would increase benefits for each group and its members. These policies generated the least intergroup conflict and the broadest consensus among the cases studied where joint policy making and extensive collaboration characterized much of the groups' negotiations with one another.

A second series of cases differ from the first in intergroup relations and substance. These entail a middle-range variety, situated somewhere between the relatively harmonious relations of the first type and the conflictual ones of a third type. They comprise essentially a nonzero type of group relationships where the actors involved anticipated that policy decisions would lead to mutually acceptable compromises, wins, and losses held to tolerable levels. In these three cases — the regulation of Industrial Development Bonds, the Federal Aid Highway Act of 1968, and the antipoverty program — stakes were significant but the groups did not anticipate dramatic changes in established federal policies, with massive benefits suddenly shifted from one government level to another. The groups generally pursued a strategy of changes in programmatic emphasis and power relations, but with the exception of the poverty program, they did not seek a total overhaul of existing federal policies.

Predictably new social programs, both distributive and redistributive in thrust, produced the fullest range of group differences where prospective fiscal benefits and control were expected to flow to one governmental level predominantly at the expense of others. Considerable intergroup conflict prevailed in the two cases selected to probe this third type of intergroup relations: the Omnibus Safe Streets and Crime Control Act of 1968 and the Juvenile Delinquency Prevention Act of 1968. Governors and mayors fear-

instructions for implementing the President's directive to all federal agencies and bureaus.

One week preceding the President's historic directive mandating federal agency consultation with representatives of the chief executive officials, Mr. Johnson signed into law the Demonstration Cities Act of 1966, later to be called Model Cities. The major thrust of this multibillion-dollar program was to establish "showcase" neighborhoods demonstrating how public and private resources might eliminate urban blight on a limited but comprehensive basis. The legislation also contained far-reaching planning requirements. Senator Edmund Muskie, principal sponsor and Senate floor manager for the Model Cities legislation, had incorporated into the administration's proposed bill a provision which required local government officials to submit to an areawide planning agency for review all applications for federal loans and grants to assist in carrying out activities under ten major aid categories.

The areawide planning requirement contained in the legislation did not allow a planning agency to veto applications by local governments. Instead, the legislation directed the reviewing agency to submit its recommendations and comments upon the grant application for consideration to the appropriate grant-reviewing agency at the federal level. This sweeping and controversial provision, found in Section #204 of Public Law 89-754, touched off major disputes among the House and Senate, federal agencies and their clientele groups, and within the government interest groups over its intent, scope, and implementation.

A third major achievement, perhaps one in the outcome of which the government interest groups were even more substantially involved, was the congressional passage of the Intergovernmental Cooperation Act of 1968 (PL 90-577). This legislation represented the first congressional program aimed exclusively at improving the administration of federal grant-in-aid programs by all government levels. It contained provisions simplifying federal grant practices, improving communications between federal officials and state-local chief executives on federal grants, and permitting these nonfederal officials greater discretion and authority in managing intergovernmental programs.

The three have much in common. All dealt with the problems of federal grants, specifying their administration and coordination. Each involved state-local chief executives and their relations with federal agencies and the Bureau of the Budget. Little or no money was at stake, hence minimal blood was spilled among governors, mayors, congressional committees, and others in resolution of differences. And each involved a wide range of participant actors: select congressional committees and subcommittees of Congress, individual congressmen and senators, the White House and the Bureau of the Budget (BOB), the Advisory Commission on Intergovernmental Relations (ACIR), and outside interests.

A-85: THE PRESIDENT ORDERS CONSULTATION

Congressional passage of grant-in-aid programs takes place without much consultation, either in drafting or in legislative review, between federal officials and the chief executives of state-local governments. Governors, mayors, and county officials often appear before congressional committees to deliver prepared testimony or to communicate with their jurisdictions' congressmen and senators on pending bills. But most such occurrences characteristically have been haphazard and discontinuous until the middle 1960s. As Grodzins observed, "It is characteristic of the grant programs that they have offered no full-dress discussion between state and national officers representing their respective levels of government with respect to matters of administration and budget before the final enactment of the bills."[2] However, considerable discussion and consultation usually occur, as previously noted in Chapter 2, between federal agencies and their state-local counterparts and between program administrators and their clientele or professional associations. The ties between intergovernmental program administrators and professional associations foster informal alliances whose growth and importance is often sanctioned and even controlled by congressional committees and subcommittees. The often interlocking aims of federal agencies, congressional committees, and their clientele or support groups place mayors, governors, and county officials at a distinctive disadvantage in gaining access to somewhat inaccessible information and insulated policy systems.

Several government commissions and congressional studies have directed their attention to the impact and growing influence of federal grants upon state and local governments. The Kestnbaum Commission in 1955, for example, took note of the apparent lack of consultation between federal officials and nonfederal chief executives in the design and implementation of these programs, citing the Budget Bureau for its limited contact with state budget officials.[3] It was not until the early 1960s, however, that congressional and executive leaders, under mounting pressure from state and local chief executives and their surrogates, took action to deal with the problem. The proliferation of new grant programs and rapid increase in federal aid to state and local governments added further momentum to efforts aimed at broadening intergovernmental consultation.

Of greater significance to many state-local chief executives than the rampant confusion surrounding proliferating grant systems and lack of

---

[2] Morton Grodzins, *The American System,* Rand McNally, Chicago, 1966, p. 65.

[3] See *Report to the President by the Commission on Intergovernmental Relations,* Meyer Kestnbaum, chairman, Government Printing Office, 1955, chap. 4. Between 1953 and 1955 this Commission undertook a comprehensive review of the federal system and intergovernmental relations. It reaffirmed the utility of federalism but specified that better cooperation was needed between federal and state governments.

coordination was their impact upon them. Chief executives were finding that these programs were undercutting their authority and executive powers. Surveys of state administrators of grant programs had long acknowledged that agencies and programs were less responsive to the governor and legislature because of federal grants.[4] Yet few chief executives enjoyed the luxury of enough time in office to gain a clear sense of what was occurring. Furthermore, ample evidence supported their contention that federal grants were distorting expenditure patterns, increasing federal influence over their budgets, and often skewing programs and allocations in directions which did not correspond to these governments' priorities and needs.

The Groups Force Action

Pressures aimed at upgrading the administration of grant programs and strengthening the resources of elected chief executives converged upon the White House from several sources. These included officials within the White House Office, Congress, and notably the government interest groups. President Johnson assured independent access to the White House to the government groups and their members through his staff organization and assignment of duties. In March 1965, he named Vice President Humphrey as the administration's designated liaison to local government officials, especially the mayors, to serve as their communications link with federal officials and agencies. Correspondingly, former Governor Buford Ellington, a former National Governors' Conference (NGC) president, was appointed Director of the Office of Emergency Planning (OEP) to serve as the White House's liaison to statehouses, a communications channel between governors and the federal government on matters of federal-state relations. Not that previous Presidents did not also have such high-level counterparts for dealing with the governors, but President Johnson gave more attention to the matter than his predecessors. The contact point, once spread among several White House staffers, eventually gravitated toward the Vice President's office, where it became one of this official's major responsibilities.

Both Humphrey and Ellington, and the latter's successor Governor Farris Bryant, went to extraordinary lengths to nurture good relations with their assigned constituencies. Humphrey's aides, in fact, claim that the Vice President spent more time on his liaison responsibilities to local governments than on any other assigned duty during the Johnson adminis-

---

[4] See *Replies from State and Local Governments to Questionnaire on Intergovernmental Relations,* Sixth Report by the Committee on Government Operations, U.S. House of Representatives, 85th Cong., 1st Sess., 1957; Deil S. Wright, "Executive Leadership in State Administration," *Midwest Journal of Political Science,* 11:1–26, February 1967.

tration.[5] Ellington and Bryant attended all the governor's national meetings and regional conferences, visited statehouses, and arranged periodic sessions at the White House between the NGC's executive committee and the President. Similarly the Vice President, a former mayor himself, convened or attended virtually hundreds of sessions—in Washington, regionally, and on a city-by-city basis—for local officials. There he explained the administration's programs, expedited individual requests from local chief executives, and generally aided these officials in gaining attention to their problems.

Both OEP directors and the Vice President elevated the concerns of chief executives and their national organizations to White House officials, the Bureau of the Budget, and heads of executive agencies and departments. Humphrey and Schultze were among the strongest advocates of reforming the grant structure within the inner White House circles. Humphrey labored diligently to gain greater BOB attention to the complaints made by local government officials. Budget Director Schultze, a personal friend and worker in Humphrey's early mayoral campaigns, collaborated extensively with the Vice President in 1966–1967 by way of redirecting BOB's efforts.

The Bureau of the Budget also received considerable pressure from the National Association of State Budget Officials (NASBO), its state counterpart and working ally, for turning its attention to the problems of state-local executives and the consequences of federal grant programs. NASBO, representing budget directors and officials in all fifty states, informed BOB officials that federal grant programs were undercutting what little oversight they and chief executives might exercise over budgets and programs. In spite of admonitions by NASBO that the functionalists and program administrators were running all over the governors, BOB made rather piecemeal responses by way of simplifying budget forms, aiding timely transference of funds, and modifying some regulations, but it demurred on moving farther. The attitude of the agency was perhaps best typified by one BOB official who indicated that the Bureau would "no more think of consulting state officials on clearance or construction of federal guidelines than a Supreme Court Justice would tell reporters in advance of how he was going to vote on an important case."[6]

Budget Director Schultze got a more comprehensive perspective on the rising complaints from state-local officials concerning federal grants programs. In August 1965, an intergovernmental task force headed by Stephen Bailey, dean of the Maxwell School of Public Affairs, made several

[5] See Hubert H. Humphrey, *The Vice President and Local Government: A Report to the President,* Washington, D.C., August 1968.

[6] Tom Graves, private interview conducted at the Bureau of the Budget, Washington, D.C., January 13, 1969.

recommendations to the director for BOB action: strengthening the co-ordinating capability of the Executive Office and the Bureau, improving interagency coordination in the field, and making resources available to state and local chief executives for improving grant administration. The Bureau gained greater firsthand experience and insight into the problems being encountered by governors and local officials in doing business with the federal government when it participated, in the summer of 1966, in a five-state field study of the situation. From BOB's perspective, this study revealed that state-local chief executives were most disturbed about the impact of fragmented government programs; their overlapping and complex planning requirements; the uncertainty regarding availability of funds and information on programs; and the failure of federal officials to consult with political executives about program decisions, administrative requirements, or about grants made to agencies under their jurisdiction.[7] This study also pointed out what NASBO had long told BOB: that the average governor, mayor, or county official had only limited authority to deal with state and local problems and that their positions need strengthening through statutory or constitutional revisions. The Bureau, executive agencies, and even the President could do little about the latter.

By late 1965 and early 1966 the Bureau began forwarding proposals to President Johnson and to Congress for action in the intergovernmental grant and administration area. The Bureau shifted additional personnel into the intergovernmental area, and legislation emerged. As Harold Seidman, Assistant BOB Director for Management and Organization commented on the earlier period of the Bureau's obvious indifference towards these problems, "Prior to 1965 the Bureau of the Budget's concern [in intergovernmental relations] was limited almost exclusively to the fiscal impact of Federal assistance programs."[8] Further impetus for action lay not in the Bureau, however, but in pressure from Congress and the government groups.

In Congress, Senator Edmund Muskie, who had ascended to the chairmanship of the Government Operations Subcommittee on Intergovernmental Relations, became one of the most outspoken proponents for legislative action in the intergovernmental area. Surveys, hearings, and investigations conducted by his subcommittee underscored those by the ACIR, NASBO, and the Bureau of the Budget. Muskie added further pressures upon BOB in March 1966, when he announced the findings from a three-year study conducted by his subcommittee which detailed the

---

[7] *Creative Federalism Hearings*, part 1, pp. 390–399.

[8] Harold Seidman, *Politics, Position, and Power* Oxford, New York, 1970, p. 161. For additional information on the Bureau's role, see "The Bureau's role in the Improvement of Government Organization and Management," part IV, draft of chapters prepared by the Bureau of the Budget for the Lyndon B. Johnson Library, Washington, D.C., 1968.

rampant confusion, lack of coordination, and general program mess that had developed in grant administration.[9] Muskie's findings prefaced the beginning of a more extensive study by his subcommittee on *Creative Federalism,* which served, among other things, as a sounding board for state-local chief executives in attacking federal programs.

Muskie's hearings with respect to the organization, management, and coordination of federal aid programs and their implementation at state and local levels were accompanied by other less friendly ones investigating individual programs and often aimed at dismantling or otherwise altering newly enacted Great Society legislation. In fall 1966, for example, Senator Abraham Ribicoff (D-Conn.) concluded his preliminary investigation of the *Federal Role in Urban Affairs* with a resounding blast at the Bureau of the Budget. "The task of coordination and a unified view," reported Ribicoff, "had been sadly ignored in our headlong rush to adopt bigger and newer programs. And this failure must be laid squarely on the doorsteps of the Bureau of the Budget."[10] Ribicoff's pyrotechnics were no less successful than Muskie's careful probing in gaining executive attention.

Operating with congressional pressure for BOB action and under the weight of endless recriminations pouring in from the governors, Budget Director Schultze broached the subject to the President in early fall. The President, apparently eager for new announcements on forthcoming legislation, jumped upon Schultze's suggestion that he issue a directive dealing with program consultation and coordination by federal agencies and departments on federal grant programs and their guidelines. Well briefed on the need for such action by Humphrey, OEP officials, and the NGC executive committee, he instructed Schultze to prepare a Presidential message on his recommendations.

The President issued this far-reaching order mandating consultation with state and local officials in November 1966, with guidelines and procedures for implementation to follow. But Schultze's work had just begun. It was one thing to issue the directive, quite another to develop procedures for its implementation, and still a third to gain compliance. Circulation of the President's directive to federal agencies and departments stunned agency and bureau heads, undersecretaries, and program administrators, who responded that "prior consultation" had already occurred. BOB, however, made it quite clear to involved parties that these new regulations would include clearance of regulations, guidelines, and procedures with elected officials—not just agency counterparts, professional societies, or agency guilds on the state-local level.

Agency and bureau heads sensed immediately the implications of the

[9] *Congressional Record,* 112, 89th Cong., 2d. Sess., 1966, p. 6834.

[10] *Federal Role in Urban Affairs,* Hearings before the Subcommittee on Executive Reorganization, Senate Government Operations Committee, 90th Cong., 1st Sess., 1967, part 20, pp. 4317–4318.

directive which might jeopardize the careful negotiations worked out between them and their state-local counterparts. They balked at recommendations for compliance, raising such objections as costs, delays, and problems of paper shuffling. They even threatened to overload the procedure with inordinate amounts of regulations and procedures. The Department of Agriculture allegedly complained, for example, that it could not possibly implement the directive since several important members of the Agriculture Committees were of opposite parties from the state governors they would have to deal with. Advanced clearance, therefore, would threaten their working relations with overseer committees in Congress. HEW was even more severely shaken. Its health and education guilds, typically, had little regard for state governors, while it felt that rules and guidelines ought to be constructed by professionals themselves. Comparable debates were touched off throughout the executive establishment as agencies and guild groups alike sensed the danger of greater chief executive involvement in grant administration and control.

The government interest groups, instead of welcoming the President's directive as the administration had anticipated, expressed dissatisfaction that it had not gone far enough. The mayors' organizations, represented by USCM's Gunther, asked that the regulation be extended to include prior consultation with BOB in drafting legislation, program clearance, and even budgetary considerations. The governors went one step farther in their demands, requesting that they, not individual congressmen and senators, be allowed to announce forthcoming federal grants for their states.

Thus the government groups and their leaders kept the pressure on the White House to ensure that A-85's implementation would meet with their full satisfaction. In a much reported "governors' revolt" led by Harold Hughes (D-Iowa) in late 1966, Democratic governors blamed the President's lack of communication in domestic programs as one of the causes for the party's losses in the fall midterm elections nationwide.[11] The governors' public attack upon the President, in fact, helped BOB to secure White House blessing for the sweeping scope which emerged in A-85. Assuring the governors in January 1967 that much progress was being made in federal-state relations, the President indicated that "every governor soon will have a chance to review and consult with federal departments on every federal regulation involving programs in their state."[12]

Nevertheless, Schultze and BOB officials were in a quandary about how best to implement the directive. BOB did not want to handle it for fear of being saddled with line functions and riding herd on all agencies and departments for advanced clearance and full compliance. Budget sug-

[11] *The New York Times*, December 16, 1966, p. 1.

[12] *Ibid.*, July 2, 1967, p. 1.

gested that the ACIR or some intermediary be found. The ACIR did not want the full responsibility either, lest it lose its own protected autonomy and freedom in dealing with Congress. Furthermore, this atypical, quasi-legislative agency viewed its role as a mediary one between Congress, the executive, and state-local chief executives on substantive policy. A direct role in implementation would inundate its budget and small staff with full-time activities to the neglect of other congressionally mandated responsibilities. For a brief period, it appeared that A-85 might lead nowhere.

However, following months of negotiation between the BOB, ACIR, and the government groups—under pressure from the White House—an agreement was reached. Henceforth, the ACIR would serve as the clerical and administrative intermediary on draft regulations from agencies to the government interest groups and the latter's comments back to the issuing agencies. Functioning as middleman between federal agencies and the associations of state and local executives, the ACIR would receive draft copies or summaries of guidelines and regulations from an issuing agency (forty-five days in advance of promulgation) and distribute them to the United States Conference of Mayors-National League of Cities (USCM-NLC), NGC, the Council of State Governments (COSGO), and the International City Managers Association (ICMA). They, in turn, would be responsible for securing and presenting the views of their clients on the drafts. Unless an earlier response were required, the groups desiring to comment would, upon consulting their members, transmit their views within three weeks to the federal agency concerned through the ACIR. Where comments and differences occurred, negotiations would commence between the groups and agencies involved. This latter procedure, in practice, encouraged direct negotiation between the government interest groups and the issuing agency.[13]

On June 28, 1967, more than six months after the President's directive, the Bureau of the Budget formally released Circular A-85, specifying its scope and purpose as well as the procedures executive agencies and departments would have to follow in obtaining "advice and consultation with state and local elected officials." The new regulation went into effect thirty days later, not only covering new regulations and revisions of old ones but also directing that agencies would "give constructive consideration to requests from heads of state and local governments to review and revise regulations already in effect, and to consult with such officials on request."[14]

---

[13] See *Advisory Commission on Intergovernmental Relations*, "Annual Report on Operations Under the Bureau of the Budget Circular A-85" Washington, D.C., 1969.

[14] U.S. Bureau of the Budget, "Bureau of the Budget Circulars of Interest to State and Local Governments," Washington, D.C., 1968, Memo from the Director of the Bureau of the Budget Charles L. Schultze to the Heads of Executive Departments and Establishments, dated June 28, 1967.

Testifying before Senator Muskie's *Creative Federalism hearings* in late November 1966, Budget Director Schultze noted that A-85 "started a whole new force for change in the workings of intergovernmental relations . . . by requiring that federal agencies find out what the other partners have to say before proceeding with programs and procedures."[15] By way of following up on A-85 and calming the dissident governors, the President dispatched squads of top-level federal officials led by Farris Bryant, Ellington's successor as OEP director, to forty state capitals to discuss problems associated with federal grant programs. Beginning in Delaware in January 1967, these sessions involving BOB, OEP, and individual department heads who lectured governors and more than 2,000 state officials on the importance of being attuned to federal grants and their stakes in these programs. They also emphasized the need for governors to strengthen their own positions and control over state budgets.

What began for some as a gravy train, with governors concerned about how they could obtain more federal revenues, developed in many cases into an "educational device." As BOB's Seidman observed:[16]

> *In many instances, governors and mayors discovered to their embarrassment that what they had assumed to be Federal problems were problems within their own households. Guilds were misinterpreting Federal regulations as a means of negating directives promulgated by the central executives.*

At each statehouse conference, the problems of individual governors, general or specific, were recorded and later acted upon by federal officials through a follow-up report to the governors by OEP. Furthermore, the governors were fully briefed by BOB officials on the meaning of A-85 and how it could be utilized by a governor and his immediate staff to resolve specific problems in coordinating grant programs for their state.

THE INTERGOVERNMENTAL COOPERATION ACT OF 1968

On March 17, 1967, President Johnson sent to Congress a message—the draft of which had sat around the Bureau of the Budget for nearly a year—entitled "Quality of American Government." This historical and unprecedented message, following in the wake of A-85, marked an attempt by the President to gain congressional support for legislation aimed at improving the quality of government itself including its machinery, manpower, and

---

[15] *Creative Federalism Hearings,* part 1, p. 397.

[16] Harold Seidman, *Politics, Position, and Power,* p. 155. See generally Farris Bryant, *A Report to the President: Nine Months of Progress in Federal-State Relations,* Washington, D.C., August 1967.

methods. Listing general factors which had expanded red tape, delays, and diffusion of channels through which federal assistance comes to state-local governments, the President requested that Congress approve recommendations for improving relations among governors and mayors. This general list involved the consolidation of categorical grant programs; simplification of grant procedures; consolidation of grant authorizations, appropriations, and statutory requirements; and additional proposals in the area of management-cost reduction.[17] For the government interest groups and the Bureau of the Budget, the President's message signaled, at last, White House support for the Intergovernmental Cooperation Act, portions of which had been before Congress since the early 1960s.

Interest in intergovernmental cooperation dates back at least to the studies of the nature and impact of grant-in-aid programs upon subnational governments conducted by the First and Second Hoover Commissions, the Kestnbaum Commission, and President Eisenhower's Joint Federal-State Action Committee.[18] In Congress, however, it was the House Government Operations Committee which, under the Legislative Reorganization Act of 1946, was given the responsibility for studying intergovernmental relationships between the federal government and the states and municipalities. Beginning with the Kestnbaum Commission's Report in 1955, the Intergovernmental Relations Subcommittee of the Government Operations Committee under Chairman L. H. Fountain (D-N.C.) reviewed the Kestnbaum report, addressing its attention specifically to two general problems: (1) Was the existing division of responsibility between the national and other levels of government proper and satisfactory? (2) By what means could intergovernmental cooperation be improved in the grant-in-aid programs and their operation made more efficient and economical?[19]

The first set of considerations was quickly subordinated to the second when the Fountain subcommittee laid to rest the proposition that federal-state functions could readily be redelegated to the states exclusively. Thus Fountain focused upon improving federal grant programs, reporting out of his subcommittee legislation which called for the periodic review by Congress of all grants-in-aid. This proposal ended there, however. The full Government Operations Committee failed to take action largely because of vehement opposition from organized labor, which feared that a five-year expiration limit placed upon grant programs might lead to a rollback of

[17] U.S. President, "Quality of American Government," Message by President Lyndon B. Johnson to Congress, H. Doc. 90, March 20, 1967.

[18] See *A Report to Congress by the Commission on the Organization of the Executive Branch of Government*, Government Printing Office, 1949; and *A Report to the President of the U.S. and to the Chairman of the Governors' Conference by the Joint Federal-State Action Committee*, Government Printing Office, 1958.

[19] See *Federal-State-Local Relations*, Hearings before a Subcommittee, House Committee on Government Operations, 85th Cong., 2d. Sess., 1958; and W. Brooke Graves, *American Intergovernmental Relations*, Scribner's, New York, 1964, chap. 25.

New Deal programs (a position that the AFL-CIO repeated years later in its opposition to revenue sharing).

Fountain's interest in intergovernmental relations following his initial efforts declined as leadership passed to Senator Edmund Muskie's Subcommittee on Intergovernmental Relations. Out of his subcommittee's studies of metropolitan planning activities and surveys of state and local officials with respect to grant programs, Muskie developed the initial recommendations for the Intergovernmental Cooperation Act. Since his subcommittee was given the responsibility to examine, investigate, and make a complete study of intergovernmental relationships, Muskie used his own studies and those by the ACIR to build a strong case for this legislation. It contained five basic provisions:[20]

1. *It authorized full information for governors on grants made to their states and provided for more uniform administration of grant programs.*

2. *It provided for federal technical assistance and training services to states and local governments.*

3. *It established a coordinated intergovernmental policy and administration of grants and loans for urban development.*

4. *It provided for congressional review of future grant programs in a systematic fashion.*

5. *It prescribed a uniform policy for urban land transactions undertaken by the General Services Administration.*

This original bill, introduced with the cosponsorship of forty-two senators and supported by the government interest groups that assisted in its drafting, passed the Senate by a unanimous vote in August 1965.

On the House side the Muskie proposal was introduced by Fountain and Congresswoman Dwyer (R-N.J.) and was followed by similar bills. Jurisdiction over the legislation, however, passed from Fountain's investigatory subcommittee to the Government Operations Subcommittee on Executive and Legislative Reorganization, which, according to full-committee Chairman William Dawson, had review over substantive legislation. The Executive and Legislative Reorganization Subcommittee, chaired by Chet Holifield (D-Cal.), conducted hearings on the proposed legislation, deleting provisions for periodic congressional review of grant programs and a Muskie-backed proposal for payment of uniform relocation assistance to persons and businesses affected by federally assisted real property acquisition, such as for highways. The latter proved too controversial in both

[20] *The Effectiveness of Metropolitan Planning,* Study prepared for the Subcommittee on Intergovernmental Relations, Senate Committee on Government Operations, 87th Cong., 2d. Sess., 1962.

House and Senate, cutting into the carefully guarded jurisdiction of the Public Works Committees. Once again, the full Government Operations Committee failed to act upon the bill. Chairmen Dawson and Holifield apparently awaited more positive approval of the legislation from BOB and the White House.

The President's 1967 "Quality of American Government" speech provided a substantial impetus behind the legislation. Negotiations over a new, more comprehensive intergovernmental cooperation bill began immediately between Budget Director Schultze, Senator Muskie, Congressman Blatnik (who replaced Holifield as subcommittee chairman), their staffs, the ACIR, and representatives of the government interest groups. The USCM-NLC and NGC worked closely with the principal White House and congressional actors, as did the ACIR, in developing a balanced bill with benefits for governors and the mayors alike. All participants agreed that it was absolutely necessary that the new omnibus bill be kept within the jurisdictional boundaries of the Government Operations Committee, lest it be splintered into several bills and placed among several legislative committees for review.

Muskie reintroduced, in early 1967, the Intergovernmental Cooperation Act. In addition to the five basic titles previously passed by the Senate, it contained several new titles. One provision gave the President authority to submit to the Congress plans for the consolidation of individual categorical grants into a single program. Another involved uniform relocation assistance, strongly supported by the mayors, and a measure providing for conformity in the federal acquisition, use, and development of urban land with local governments, also advocated by the mayors.

The Senate began final hearings on the Cooperation Act in May, a matter of weeks before its House counterpart did the same. Muskie labored to develop as strong and comprehensive a bill as possible for enhancing the Senate's bargaining leverage with the House. The latter was expected to enact a much weaker measure, as it eventually did. He included in the scope of his hearings two related measures: one, a bill (S. 458) sponsored by Senator Karl Mundt (R-S.D.), the Senate committee's ranking minority member, which broadened periodic congressional review of grant programs through use of the ACIR, the Comptroller General, and other committees. The other bill (S. 2981) sought to expedite procedures for certain federal assistance programs. This latter measure, developed by the Bureau of the Budget at the President's request, would make it possible, in the President's own words, "for Federal agencies to combine related grants into a single financial package, thus simplifying the financial and administrative procedures—without disturbing, however, the separate authorizations, appropriations, and substantive requirements for each grant-in-aid program."[21] The purpose of this legislation was to remove or simplify ad-

<hr>

[21] *Creative Federalism Hearings*, part 2B, p. 956.

ministrative impediments which hamper or prevent the administration and approval of projects drawing upon resources available from more than one federal agency, program, or appropriation.

Both Joint Simplification Funding and Muskie's Title VI (Sec. 601–602), grant consolidation were new departures in the intergovernmental area designed to deal with proliferating federal grants programs: one by way of executive consolidation, the other by simplifying federal grant programs in making them more amenable to joint utilization in single projects. Nevertheless, while grant consolidation was considered a top-priority item by all the government interest groups, it, like Joint Simplification Funding, was an early casualty when congressional committees engaged in markup sessions. Grant consolidation, whereby the President would be empowered to merge duplicating or related programs in a manner similar to that by which the President reorganized executive agencies, was vehemently opposed by House and Senate committee members. Confusion existed over how to resolve disputes involving committee and agency jurisdiction as well as grant equalization formulas. Several legislators, in fact, opposed the measure simply on the grounds that it might remove a program that was widely identified with an individual congressman's name. Furthermore, congressional critics of the grant consolidation provision argued that the President already had sufficient authority under the Reorganization Act of 1949 to achieve the purposes of this measure—a position backed by the Bureau of the Budget.[22] Similarly, both congressional committees refused to incorporate Joint Simplification Funding (S. 2981 and H.R. 12631)—legislation strongly supported by the President, Bureau of the Budget, and the government groups—into the Cooperation Act for reasons similar to their opposition to grant consolidation.

Besides grant consolidation and grant simplification, the governors were most enthusiastic about three provisions in the legislation: (1) full information to chief executives on the nature and amount of federal grant funds flowing into a state; (2) authorization to federal departments to provide technical training and other services to states on a reimbursable basis; and (3) modification of the "single-state-agency" requirement.[23] The latter provision, a particularly sensitive one to several governors, would modify a much-used federal requirement that a particular program had to be administered by a single state agency with sole responsibility for the activity. This requirement, found in about one-quarter of all federal grant programs, had been used by federal departments, especially HEW, for establishing direct relationships between a designated state agency and its federal

[22] *Intergovernmental Cooperation Act of 1967 and Related Legislation,* Hearings before the Subcommittee on Intergovernmental Relations, Senate Committee on Government Operations, 90th Cong., 2d. Sess., 1968, p. 98.

[23] *Intergovernmental Cooperation,* Hearings before a Subcommittee, House Committee on Government Operations, 90th Cong., 2d. Sess, 1968, pp. 96–103.

counterpart. While the requirement had made state administration of grant programs orderly and had upgraded personnel systems, it functioned as a deterrent against gubernatorial reorganization of state agencies. It also prevented governors from exercising greater fiscal control over state programs and grant administrators.

Governors had chronically complained about the single-state-agency provision. Governor Mark Hatfield had unsuccessfully fought HEW over the issue in a much-publicized case in 1961.[24] Attempts by governors at creating multiagency or multidisciplinary reorganization of existing programs and agencies for purposes of effecting budgetary, management, and fiscal control over intergovernmental programs were stifled time and again through an alliance of federal-state program administrators invoking the single-state-agency requirement. Seidman observed of the effects of this requirement, "For the professional guilds, these statutory provisions are the equivalent of corporate charters, the indispensable source of both power and legitimacy."[25] Thus for many governors, the waiver of the single-state-agency, board, or commission provision contained in Title II of the Intergovernmental Cooperation Act was the single most essential provision in the bill. Their support for the overall legislation was largely contingent upon retention of this item.

Mayors and county officials, on the other hand, had their own list of priorities in the bill. Staunchly supportive of measures aimed at simplifying grants or consolidating them, they saw the crux of the legislation as residing in three titles: (1) Title IV, which contained the intent of Congress to achieve coordinated intergovernmental policy and administration of grants for urban development, and a provision authorizing preference in assigning grants to general purpose units of local government rather than special districts; (2 and 3) Titles VIII–IX, which related to uniform relocation assistance and uniform land acquisition policies. USCM-NLC were especially concerned about uniform relocation assistance for those forced to move as a result of the property acquisition for federally aided programs. This measure, passed unanimously by the Senate in the 88th Congress and referred subsequently to the House Committee on Public Works, was intended to correct what many mayors considered to be serious deficiencies and inequities in the Federal Aid Highway Act involving payments for the relocation of displaced residents.

The uniform relocation assistance provision was deleted in the House, however, and sustained in conference when BOB objected to the costs involved and failed in efforts to develop agreement on a policy with affected agencies. Title IX, which provided for a uniform policy for the acquisition of real property by the federal government and was supported by both

[24] See Council of State Governments, "State Organization and Federal Grant-in-Aid Requirements," Chicago, 1951.

[25] Harold Seidman, Politics, Position, and Power, p. 144.

mayors' groups, underwent a similar fate in the House, foregoing further consideration in conference committee.

Blatnik's Subcommittee on Executive and Legislative Reorganization not only deleted Titles VIII and IX but also diluted or eliminated other provisions found in the Senate bill. As one staff man on the Government Operations Committee later observed, "The Chairman was apprehensive about letting the bill out of committee altogether since he felt considerable differences existed between federal agencies and the Bureau of the Budget on the legislation and we would have liked more time to smoke these out."[26] But a vastly emasculated Cooperation Act nonetheless was reported by Government Operations and passed by the House, according to several sources, as a result of administration pressure. One version has it that the Vice President intervened on behalf of the government interest groups, getting Mayor Daley to specifically request of Chairman Dawson that the bill be let out, while Humphrey appealed to fellow Minnesotan John Blatnik to do the same.

In the final showdown over the bill, House conferees led by Blatnik, Holifield, and Erlenborn (R-Ill.) won out on nearly all differences between them and their Senate counterparts. Muskie, without much support from Senate conferees, battled the often hostile House members in order to achieve the mere skeleton of the Senate's original bill.[27]

As enacted, the Intergovernmental Cooperation Act of 1968 favored neither the governors nor the mayors. The governors attained most of what they wanted except for joint funding and grant consolidation, which they really had not held much hope for. The mayors, acknowledgedly, achieved far less than they had desired. The key to the passed legislation from their perspective was Title IV, the intergovernmental policy coordination section. This title containing related sections required the federal government to establish policy to promote "the sound and orderly development of urban communities" through the establishment of regulations governing the formulation, evaluation, and review of federal programs and projects having significant impact on these areas. As Peter Harkins, the NLC staff man who developed the mayors' policy on the legislation commented, "Title IV offered real potential for developing coordinated federal policy in urban areas if the Bureau of the Budget would give it teeth."[28] Nonetheless, many mayors were pleased with the provision. They felt it might aid the President in giving the Bureau of the Budget the mandate to develop an overall urban strategy and policy, a goal of both mayors' organizations.

[26] Elmer Henderson, personal interview in the House Office Building, Washington, D.C., February 4, 1969.

[27] See Intergovernmental Cooperation Act of 1968, 90th Cong., 2d. Sess., H. Rept., 1845, 1968, and Intergovernmental Cooperation Act of 1968, 90th Cong., 2d. Sess., H. Rept. 1934, 1968.

[28] Congressional Quarterly, 27:202, January 31, 1969.

COUNCILS OF GOVERNMENT

Congress in 1966 passed the Demonstration Cities and Metropolitan Development Act (PL 89-754), the most comprehensive federal program yet undertaken for community renewal of American cities and for the orderly development of metropolitan areas. While the final legislation, as characteristic of federal housing programs, distributed benefits to a multitude of interested parties, two principal features of the legislation, as its title suggests, involved demonstration cities and planned metropolitan development.

The basic concept of the demonstration plan emanated from recommendations made by a special White House Task Force on Urban Problems headed by political scientist Robert C. Wood, who was appointed Undersecretary of the Department of Housing and Urban Development in early 1966. Departing from the "bricks and mortar" approach of existing urban renewal programs, the demonstration plan envisioned a restructuring of the "total environment," physically and socially, of a select number of particularly deteriorated neighborhoods through a concentration of public and private resources, locally administered, with "demonstration neighborhoods" sharing in the program's decisions. The President originally requested $2.3 billion for this program, with one year of preparatory planning and five years of implementation.[29]

A second major component of the bill provided for "sound and orderly" development and organization of metropolitan areas. Portions of this provision are attributable to the Wood Task Force and HUD officials, namely metropolitan expediters who were to be a liaison between localities and federal agencies in areas served. The greater portion embodied the efforts of Senator Edmund Muskie and his staff in collaboration with congressional and executive actors. The Muskie provisions found in Title II, Sections 204–205, required that all applicants (including special-purpose units) for federal assistance in certain specified programs within any metropolitan area be submitted for review and comments to a metropolitan-wide planning agency and—in their absence—a state agency named by the governor. These planning agencies were to have review, not veto functions and were to be to the greatest extent practicable responsible to the elected officials of general local governments. As a companion measure, Section 205 provided a fiscal incentive to local governments which created such agencies and complied with the review procedures. Participating local governments would be eligible for supplementary grants for up to 20 percent of the local share of the costs for the specific program or project.

While controversy over the demonstration cities portion of the legis-

---

[29] U.S. President, "City Demonstration Programs", Message from the President to Congress, 89th Cong., 2d. Sess., H. Doc. 368, 1966.

lation initially obscured the planned metropolitan development provisions, the latter were to be termed a "red herring" and even worse things by House and Senate critics. A brief chronicle of the passage of these Title II provisions, albeit a small but important component of the entire legislation, suggests an interesting case of congressional initiative and the activities of the government interest groups in the intergovernmental area.

Background

In 1962 Senator Muskie's Subcommittee on Intergovernmental Relations undertook an extensive investigation into metropolitan planning activities. The Senator, his staff, and outside researchers were concerned with two major questions: To what extent does federal financial assistance for urban areas promote the creation of special districts or otherwise affect the structures of local governments? And to what extent do federal programs require coordination of federally aided projects with local decisions and comprehensive development plans?[30]

In response to the former, the subcommittee discovered that almost all of the federal aid programs were available to special districts and almost half were available to nongovernmental persons or groups. A further study by the subcommittee, *The Federal System as Seen by State and Local Officials,* underscored the problems inherent in the proliferation of grants and eligibility. More than half of the responding county officials, city managers, and mayors indicated that statutory and administrative requirements attached to grant programs hampered flexibility in the organization of local government.[31]

Studying the latter, Muskie's subcommittee found that studies by the ACIR on the *Impact of Federal Urban Development Programs on Local Government Organization and Planning* revealed little evidence supporting the existence of a "unified Federal policy or organizational machinery for coordinating aid programs in the field of urban development." The ACIR, in fact, produced evidence to the contrary. Federal programs were found to be encouraging special-purpose units of government rather than promoting general-purpose units. Federal programs encouraged or required functional planning, but not comprehensive areawide planning, and planning requirements varied according to type of financial aid given,

[30] *Impact of Federal Urban Development Programs on Local Government Organization and Planning.* Report prepared by the Advisory Commission on Intergovernmental Relations in cooperation with the Subcommittee on Intergovernmental Relations, Senate Committee on Government Operations, 88th Cong., 2d. Sess., 1964, pp. 1–5.

[31] See *Federal System as Seen by State and Local Officials,* A Study prepared by the staff of the Subcommittee on Intergovernmental Relations, Senate Committee on Government Operations, 89th Cong., 1st Sess., 1965, pp. 203–214.

participant receiving aid, and the nature of the function being assisted. To encourage more effective planning processes among state and local recipients of federal assistance, the ACIR recommended that:[32]

> *Congress favor general purpose units of government as grant recipients over special purpose ones and require that special purpose recipients coordinate their aided activities with general purpose governments;*
>
> *Congress, the executive, and the states encourage joint participation by local governmental units where common objectives or overlapping boundaries exist;*
>
> *Congress and executive agencies promote effective planning at the local levels in all programs affecting urban development through the #701 Section of the 1954 Housing Act;*
>
> *Congress promote federal interagency coordination on urban programs as well as a unified urban development policy.*

These recommendations and others which came before the Muskie subcommittee in the early 1960s were to find their way into legislation proposed by the Maine Senator both in the urban field and in intergovernmental relations during the 89th and 90th Congresses. As early as 1962 Muskie, building upon earlier ACIR recommendations, introduced legislation calling for review of federal aid programs by metropolitan planning agencies. In 1963 the Senate approved, without commensurate House action, a Muskie bill, S. 855, which provided for more effective utilization of federal assistance programs by encouraging coordinated local review of state and local grant-in-aid applications. Again in 1965, Muskie unsuccessfully sought congressional passage of the Intergovernmental Cooperation Act, which included provisions for preferential treatment for general-purpose units of government as grant recipients and favored areawide review by planning agencies. In each of these proposals Muskie incorporated the concept that federal grants to local governments in metropolitan areas be conditioned upon an advanced review and comment by an areawide agency whose functions involved planning. In the absence of such an agency, review and comment functions would be carried out by a state agency designated by the governor.

Pursuing his objectives through the Banking and Currency Committee, the Maine Senator—as a junior member of the Housing Subcommittee—gained committee and later congressional approval for financing these metropolitanwide planning councils. Section #701 (g) of the 1954 Housing Act was amended under the Housing and Urban Development Act of 1965 to make these planning councils eligible for urban planning assistance

---

[32] *Impact of Urban Development Programs*, chap. 4.

grants up to two-thirds of their operating costs. This amendment provided an important boost to these embryonic, voluntary, and fiscally needy councils. But Muskie still awaited the opportunity to further strengthen the role and functions of these organizations.[33]

It is notable, by way of further background on this case, that planning has been an integral part of housing and development programs since the Housing Act of 1949. Under the 1954 Housing Act a citywide workable program and comprehensive planning were required for urban renewal, public housing and renewal-related FHA housing programs. Metropolitan-wide planning as a condition to federal assistance was applied in later years to open-space land programs, highways, mass transportation, water and sewer facilities. Such planning, however, operated more in theory than actual practice. It was used as a necessary device to meet federal specifications, but not as an instrument for overall planned development. Indeed, similar plans emerged in almost all cities and metropolitan areas as planners went from city to city to market those of their blueprints that had previously received federal approval. Against this background, Senator Muskie attempted to make planning and orderly urban development meaningful.

The mayors and county officials tried to influence the Senator's ideas and legislation on metropolitan planning. The National Association of Counties (NACO) and the NLC, for example, established in 1961 a voluntary information exchange center on councils of government and similar planning bodies operating under various names which eventually blossomed into a National Service to Regional Councils operated jointly by the two groups. NACO and county officials were the staunchest supporters of Muskie's efforts for gaining congressional legislation which supported metropolitan planning councils. NACO's executive director, Bernard Hillenbrand, acknowledging the limited possibilities of further city-county consolidation, argued persuasively before Muskie's sub-committee that counties would and could plan a more important role in metropolitan planning if given encouragement to do so by federal and state legislation. "To our way of thinking, this is the only approach that does make sense since it is predicated on the use of existing cities and counties and other general purpose governments," Hillenbrand informed his organization's members.[34]

Counties expected to be beneficiaries of Muskie's legislation in that more than half of the country's metropolitan areas fell within the boundaries of county government. The mayors' organizations, especially the USCM,

[33] Don Nicoll, personal interview conducted in the office of Senator Edmund S. Muskie, Washington, D.C., February 12, 1969, and personal interview with Hugh Mields in his Washington office, October 24, 1968.

[34] See "The County as a Regional Government," *American County Government,* September, 1966, p. 49.

were extremely apprehensive about planning councils, however. Considering the mayors' real fears that these agencies would be dominated by
planners, as was the case in most instances, Muskie amended his proposal,
stipulating that metropolitanwide planning agencies be responsible to the
elected officials of the general local governments where located. Still,
large-city mayors and the USCM were not altogether appeased. In spite of
elected official control, regional councils yet might be controlled by elected
suburban and county officials, as eventually occurred in several cases.
Furthermore, these mayors instinctively opposed any planning legislation
that might allow suburban officials to pass judgment upon housing and
urban renewal programs. These are still the most prized of federal-city
programs and ones already impeded by reviewing boards and other
seemingly interminable delays.

Muskie Reshapes Model Cities

The Demonstration Cities Program, or Model Cities as it was later called,
seemed in trouble from the very beginning, with the administration nearly
abandoning the program altogether at several points during 1966. While
the program had considerable support from its drafters and sympathizers,
which included a mixture of intellectuals, academics, journalists, consultants, and what Wood has termed "intervening elites," Model Cities,
much like its antecedent legislation, the poverty program, had little corresponding support in the Congress. Wearied by Great Society legislation
and concerned about further inflationary spending on new programs,
potential supporters and even traditional allies of housing legislation
shied away from sponsoring it. John Sparkman (D-Ala.), the stalwart defender of liberal housing legislation, declined the administration's request
that he manage the bill. The Senator not only viewed the legislation as
potentially harmful to his reelection campaign but chided the administration for its lack of prudence in proposing a bold new housing law so soon
after the passage of the comprehensive 1965 program, which had included
the controversial rent supplements provision. Sparkman's reaction was
widely shared among fellow senators.

Complicating matters further, conditions inside the House were equally
unsettled. Albert Rains, Chairman of the Housing Subcommittee and long-
time friend of the mayors as well as liberal housing programs, had retired
to be replaced by William Barrett, aptly described as a "devoted, amiable,
but inexperienced Philadelphia ward politician."[35] Moreover, Democratic
House leaders were still smarting from a rebuff by a Senate filibuster when
in late 1965 they had gone all out to repeal the right-to-work provisions in

[35] The New York Times, November 4, 1966, p. 1.

the Taft-Hartley Act. They were not about to throw themselves so prodigiously behind another controversial legislative measure, especially in an election year, without firm assurances, even preceding their action, that the Senate would act favorably.

As a matter of recourse, administration officials inveigled Senator Muskie in June to be the bill's manager both in the Senate Banking and Currency Committee and on the Senate floor. But Muskie had a price for management, which included (1) broadening the legislation's eligibility to be more acceptable to his Maine constituency and that of other legislators and (2) the incorporation of his own metropolitan planning provisions. Executive officials exhibited guarded enthusiasm over Muskie's metropolitanwide planning councils and provisions of financial inducements for their growth. Housing and Urban Development (HUD) was supportive but preferred its own "expediter" approach. BOB worried about who would implement these provisions. It would be the likely contender for prescribing rules and regulations for administration—a responsibility that it wished to avoid. And White House staff opposed all-out support for fear that their inclusion might sabotage the entire legislation.

Muskie was not to be deterred. The White House desperately needed his backing. Thus the planned metropolitan development provisions, Title II, were worked out through a series of meetings between his administrative assistant Don Nicoll, HUD's legal staff, and Carl Coan, the staff director of the Senate Housing Subcommittee. To make the legislation more acceptable to the mayors, Muskie exempted housing and urban renewal programs from the list of federally assisted grants which would pass under the areawide reviewing councils, but he stiffened his resistance to further exemptions.

Following hearings on the legislation, the Senate Housing Subcommittee reported out a slightly revised version of the administration's bill—cutting the $2.3 billion program spread over five years to a $900 million over two and eliminating the provisions on new towns. The full Banking and Currency Committee approved its subcommittee's action in late July, and the Senate, after considerable debate over the bill's authorizations, passed the legislation in mid-August by a 53 to 22 vote.

More formidable opposition to the bill resided in the House, however, where Housing Subcommittee members were inclined toward scrapping the controversial legislation altogether. They considered eliminating the new towns provisions and Muskie's planning agencies and reducing the $2.3-billion demonstration cities section to a one-year, $12-million grant program for planning. What produced a change of heart in the Banking and Currency Committee, according to several observers, was a combination of administration pressures and inducements. Vice President Humphrey reportedly assured Barrett and Democrats on the committee that the administration would spare nothing in fighting for House passage. Moreover, Barrett was informed that the mayors' organizations would head up an alliance of outside interest groups during the summer to lobby on behalf of the committee-reported bill. The committee voted out the bill on a strictly party basis, with the Republicans labeling the metropolitan planning provisions a "Trojan horse" and disguised "federal control."[36]

The mayors were the key to successful floor action. Eleven large-city mayors testified favorably on behalf of the legislation before Barrett's subcommittee, including Mayor James Tate, a personal friend of the chairman's. Yet it was no secret to Congress that they objected to several provisions in the bill, especially the new towns provision, which many thought might divert from urban renewal monies. But HUD's promise in June to the mayors of an additional $600 million in urban renewal funds mitigated much of their substantive opposition. The prospect that the Housing Subcommittee might report out of committee a substitute bill containing no new funds proved the ultimate stimulant for mobilizing their support behind the legislation. Once the administration's bill cleared the Banking and Currency Committee, the mayor-led lobbying organization headed by USCM's John Gunther, and comprising faithful allies of federal housing programs with labor, religious, business, civil rights, and welfare groups, united to fight for floor passage. This coalition of sixty organizations, named the Urban Alliance, proved, according to some published records on the bill's passage, tremendously successful.[37]

Considering the differences between the Senate-passed bill and the House Banking and Currency Committee's version, the House's Subcommittee on Housing reconvened at the administration's request to accept the Senate bill with its scaled-down authorizations. Besides including in their bill the new towns program, the subcommittee added several amendments from a separately passed Senate bill (S. 3711) in the housing area, including provisions on FHA insurance, mortgages, more generous urban renewal regulations, and related measures. Thus the legislation indeed had become an omnibus housing act containing sufficient benefits for legislators and lobbying groups alike to bolster its chances for successful passage.

House approval came in October, only after what many considered to be one of the most acrimonious floor fights in recent memory. Extending into late evening, much debate centered upon the metropolitan planning provisions which critics charged were a disguised means of furthering civil rights objectives and gaining further federal control over local governments. HUD's "metropolitan expediters" provision was deleted, largely

[36] See Housing and Urban Development Act of 1966, 89th Cong., 2d Sess., H. Rept. 1699, part 1, 1966. pp. 59–68, and Demonstration Cities and Metropolitan Development Act of 1966, 89th Cong., 2d. Sess., H. Rept. 1931, 1966, pp. 135–156.

[37] Congress and the Nation, 1965–1968, vol. 2, Congressional Quarterly, Inc., Washington, D.C., 1969, pp. 195–209.

at the insistence of the mayors, while conservatives attached an antibusing amendment to the legislation. Otherwise the legislation passed intact, including Muskie's provisions for metropolitanwide planning agencies, by the narrow margin of 178 to 141.

Conferees from the House and Senate Banking Currency Committees met the following day, October 15, to reconcile the differences between the two versions of the legislation. Muskie's provisions still remained in doubt, however, as ranking House conferees advocated deletion based on the argument that their committee had really never considered the subject in hearings. But Muskie and Senate conferees held their ground, backed by Chairman Wright Patman, who wished to go along with the administration on the entire bill. Lining up essentially along party lines, conferees voted to retain the planning provisions and restore the new towns provisions deleted on the Senate side. The House and Senate both approved the conference bill. The President signed it into law, calling the Model Cities program one of the "most important pieces of legislation for all mankind."

But the battle over Muskie's amendment was not over. Representative William Cramer (R-Fla.), having lost the floor fight over deleting metropolitanwide planning provisions, invoked the argument that they usurped the jurisdictional authority of the Public Works Committee and prevailed successfully upon the House Appropriations Committee to prevent their funding under Section 205 of the legislation. Supplemental funds for planning were thus cut out altogether. An amendment to HUD's appropriations in 1967 and 1968 stipulated that the department could not use any of its funds or time to administer the provisions in the Model Cities Act that required review of certain kinds of federal grant applications by a metropolitan planning agency. As a result of this action, the responsibility for general administration and implementation of the planning agency review functions is, at the time of this writing, being handled by the Bureau of the Budget.[38]

It is ironic, however, that this is what Muskie had advocated in the first place—a redirection of BOB's activities into management, planning, and coordination of federal programs directed at metropolitan areas. For BOB, the outcome was what it had originally feared. As the managerial and staff arm of the President, the agency had carefully avoided being the recipient of delegated congressional authority. It was now saddled with congressionally mandated responsibilities—a new task that would not likely ingratiate the Bureau with Congress and executive agencies. However, from the mayors' vantage, this is exactly what they also wanted and gained in Title IV of the Intergovernmental Cooperation Act. The #204 provisions thus were reinforced by the mandate given BOB under the Cooperation Act.

[38] See U.S. Bureau of the Budget Circular A-82.

COORDINATING EFFORTS

The passage of the Intergovernmental Cooperation Act and the issuance of Budget Circular A-85 were seen as positive gains by the government interest groups. They marked a turning point in intergovernmental negotiations. Governors, mayors, and county officials had been elevated to positions of more equal footing with a host of well-established actors who influence federal program guidelines and establish grant-in-aid patterns. The rules of the game governing grant acquisition, administration, and substate planning underwent significant change. Chief executives gained certain resources to use in dealing with federal officialdom. To borrow Clinton Rossiter's phase regarding growth of presidential resources, state-local executives were now given more of a "sporting chance" in making their individual and collective weight felt in the federal grant system.

Immediate benefits flowed from these precedent-setting cases. A-85 rendered the groups greater formal recognition throughout the executive, further legitimizing their role as bargaining agents for elected chief executives of state-local governments. The President's executive order stimulated communication among the groups and also encouraged them to work together as watchdogs upon federal agencies that circumvented the order's intent by using the *Federal Register* for issuing guidelines and regulations. The groups carried a certain sanction to rely on, a basis for claiming "bad faith" on the part of federal agencies that failed to comply with clearance procedures. Greater consultation between agencies and the groups followed immediately, since the agencies found it easier to deal directly with the groups than to resort to the cumbersome arrangement of using the ACIR as an intermediary. Even the professional associations and guild groups found clearance procedures changed. They began contacting the government interest groups regarding new regulations and procedures, where previously the reverse had generally been the case.

The Intergovernmental Cooperation Act of 1968 represented a milestone in ACIR, BOB, and government interest group negotiations. Congress had finally given its approval to the simplification of federal grant programs and the strengthening of chief executive control over program management and planning. It signaled to all interested parties that further changes were possible, with Congress being an active rather than a passive participant in the process. Though Congress had nonetheless emasculated the original intergovernmental legislation, those items which failed to pass became the pending agenda for future consideration. The passage of legislation establishing the councils of government (COGs) and prior efforts to make them eligible for federal funding stands as a testimony to the persistence of Senator Muskie and the government groups. COGs manifested the growing recognition by all government levels of urgent and emerging metropolitan problems and the need for new governmental machinery safeguarding general-purpose local governments and their elected officials. "The potential of COGs for metropolitan cooperation and planning," notes one subsequent evaluation of their import, "has won them an official place and function in the expanding federal system."[39]

Together the three—A-85, ICA, and COGs #204—became the building blocks for other developments in intergovernmental cooperation between elected chief executives and federal officialdom. They opened the way for a backlog of federal legislation dealing with intergovernmental problems: grant-in-aid reform, grant consolidation, reorganization, and the development of state and local government planning and managerial capabilities. They were precursors of major shifts within the President's own family — the White House office and the Bureau of the Budget. What the Johnson administration set in motion by way of attentiveness to governmental machinery and the plight of state-local executives, the Nixon administration furthered.

As one of his first official acts, President Nixon established an Urban Affairs Council to advise and assist in the development of a national urban policy. In March 1969, he created by executive directive coterminous federal boundaries and identical headquarter locations for the field operations of several federal agencies, and later he extended this to others. Chronic complaints by chief executives over the then twelve regional office structures of federal departments—spread over several states and many cities in the same region—had set in motion this reorganization during the last days of the Johnson administration, only to be implemented during the first year of the Nixon Presidency. President Nixon established ten separate regions together with Federal Regional Councils (FRCs), which were given monitoring, coordination, evaluation, and general problems-expediting responsibilities. The visibility and responsibilities of FRCs were upgraded both in the field, through a designated chairman, and in Washington by an Undersecretaries' Group for Regional Operations. In February 1972, the President furthered the cause of FRCs by giving them formal standing and assigning to them major functions for developing program delivery strategies, integrating federal programs under state-local chief executives, and resolving interagency disputes.[40]

Regional councils of government also prospered under the Nixon administration as federal programs began assuming a greater regional dimension. A Joint Service to Regional Councils formed by NACO and the NLC became a national service agency and administrative clearinghouse

[39] Jeanne R. Lowe, *The Near Side of Federalism,* The Ford Foundation, New York, 1972, p. 28. Also see Committee for Economic Development, *Reshaping Government in Metropolitan Areas,* New York, 1970.

[40] Executive Order 11647, February 11, 1972; See Melvin B. Mogulof, *Federal Regional Councils: Their Current Experience and Recommendations for Further Development,* Urban Institute, Washington, D.C., 1970.

for COGs. The number of COGs increased from 100 to nearly 200 between 1968 and 1969, and by 1971 there were more than 300.[41] With nearly 600 COGs operating by late 1973, most of the nation's 200-plus Standard Metropolitan Statistical Areas (SMSAs) had an identifiable COG known as an A-95 agency. Typically, their responsibilities had grown where new federal responsibilities had been piggybacked to the agency's initial functions.

Using his reorganization authority, President Nixon also sought to strengthen his own managerial and fiscal authority by centralizing departmental clearance and broadening the responsibilities of the Bureau of the Budget. In 1970 he created the Domestic Council, superseding the functions of the Urban Council, to provide him with a "streamlined, consolidated domestic policy arm, adequately staffed, and highly flexible in operation." The President also changed the name of the Bureau of the Budget to the Office of Management and Budget (OMB), reflecting its broader emphasis upon fiscal analysis and management needs of the President. The new office, Mr. Nixon observed, "will place much greater emphasis on the evaluation of program performance; on assessing the extent to which programs are actually achieving their intended results, and delivering the intended services to the intended recipients."[42] Making the A-85 procedures a high-priority of the new Domestic Council, its director, John Ehrlichman stated:[43]

> *The President views the participation of State and local officials in the formulation of Federal policy as essential. It is his desire that as you develop your recommendations for our Fiscal Year 1973 domestic programs you take appropriate steps to ensure consultation with State and local government officials. . . . They should be included at an early stage of development.*

In July 1969, OMB issued administrative regulations implementing #204 (areawide review regulations) and Title IV of the Intergovernmental Cooperation Act (ICA), which authorized the President to establish rules and regulations governing formulation, evaluation, and review of federal grants having a significant impact on area and community development. Both were incorporated into OMB Circular A-95, which led to many #204 agencies being known as A-95 agencies. This directive detailed the range of state and areawide review functions, which included assessing the likely

[41] Melvin B. Mogulof, *Governing Metropolitan Areas.* Urban Institute, Washington, D.C., 1971, p. 1.

[42] Text of President Nixon's Reorganization Message of the Executive Office of the President, March 12, 1970, in *The Congressional Quarterly,* **28**:825–826, March 20, 1970.

[43] Memorandum for the Domestic Council, Executive Office of the President, from John Ehrlichman, dated May 21, 1971.

impact of some fifty separate grant programs. The intended purpose of these regulations was to fit federally sponsored programs into state, regional, and metropolitan plans under elected chief executives through a process of intergovernmental evaluation. With the passage of the National Environmental Policy Act of 1969, the environmental impact of federally assisted projects also was brought under the A-95 review process. In early 1971, OMB issued A-95 revisions tying the "review and comment" functions together to include impact of federally assisted programs upon state and local affairs in management, organization, and planning.[44]

The 1968 Intergovernmental Act provided the statutory basis for numerous OMB directives dealing with information to governors and legislatures on federal grant allocations, reduction of grant processing time, and simplification of grant applications. Federal agencies were required to develop consistency and uniformity in administering federal grants. These new procedures also gave impetus to efforts by HUD and other departments to develop their own forms of joint simplification funding, as in HUD's "planned variations" and "annual arrangement" experiments. The latter were directed at packaging federal programs, waiving federal requirements, and giving mayors greater control over and more flexible use of federal funds within their cities.

Further fallouts from the ICA involved intergovernmental legislation either deleted from the act or blocked in Congress during the sixties. Senator Muskie's Intergovernment Personnel Act, first introduced back in 1966 and long tied up in the House, passed Congress late in 1970. The Uniform Relocation Assistance and Land Acquisition Act (PL 91-646), originally included in the Senate's version of ICA and twice previously passed by the Senate, also was enacted. Congress carried the principle of federal interagency coordination in programs affecting urban development, found in Title IV of ICA, one step further when it included Title VII provision in the 1970 Housing and Urban Development Act. This provision, largely the work of Congressman Thomas Ashley and the House Banking and Currency Committee, placed clearly in the President's office the responsibility for developing a national urban growth policy which is to be transmitted to Congress biennially beginning with 1972.[45]

Further Presidential efforts to gain grant consolidation authority and joint simplification procedures remained stymied in the 91st and 92nd Congresses.[46] Once Democratic legislators fully appreciated the signifi-

---

[44] U.S. Government, Bureau of the Budget, Circular A-95, July 24, 1969; Executive Office of the President, Office of Managment and Budget, Circular A-95 revised, February 9, 1971.

[45] National Growth Policy, Hearings before the Subcommittee on Housing, House Banking and Currency Committee, 92nd Cong., 2d. Sess., 1972, part 1, pp. 1–74.

[46] See Intergovernmental Cooperation Act of 1972, Committee on Government Operations, U.S. Senate, 92nd Cong., 2d. Sess., 1972, S. Rept. 92-1109, pp. 2–5.

cance of President Nixon's domestic strategy of dismantling Great Society programs and recasting them in Republican mold, their receptiveness toward intergovernmental cooperation programs cooled. If Congress delegated to the President authority to consolidate or merge grants (including statutory formulas, interest rates, eligibility requirements, and other conditions he requested), it would have sanctioned the already apparent Nixon efforts to restructure the entire federal grant-in-aid system. By the 92nd Congress at least, the President's resolve to overhaul federal grant programs without prior congressional approval had become evident. As Congress shunned the President's reorganization of federal departments and turned back special revenue-sharing plans, the President resorted on a broad scale to executive fiat to implement his domestic design. Several departments instituted their own versions of joint simplification funding and bloc grants. Also, some FRCs began experimentation with the Integrated Grant Administration (IGA) program to package various categorical grant programs on a regional basis, simplifying the grant process and reducing state-local contact with federal agencies in Washington. The President relied on the "implied powers" of his office to impound congressionally appropriated funds, and he moved to decentralize federal programs under state-local chief executives without prior congressional approval. Even Senator Muskie, the key sponsor of the Intergovernmental Acts of 1970 and 1972, seemed to lose much enthusiasm for these programs in light of the President's actions and their partisan implications.

Finally, the three cases have a broader significance. Their importance lies in the new processes emerging in intergovernmental relations which began following their adoption. Nonetheless these processes have not yet become institutionalized. A conspicuous gap still exists in 1973 between executive orders mandating consultation with state-local executives and adoption of their recommendations; between "review and comment" or planning-evaluation functions and the enforcement of these clearance procedures upon federal policy makers; and between rhetorical dedication to uplifting political executives and the practices of federal agencies and bureaus.

The federal government's attitude toward COGs is still evolving. No apparent federalwide consensus exists concerning the role and functions of regional authorities, the extent to which they should be encouraged, and activities supported by federal policy makers.[47] COGs are praised by their advocates as a boon to state-local executives and the wave of the future in federalism's evolving structures. Critics condemn them for being another layer of government, a new impediment between states and localities in resolving their outstanding differences. COGs tend to be only as effective thus far as the authority granted them by member governments — states,

[47] See Melvin B. Mogulof, *Governing Metropolitan Areas*, chap. 8.

municipalities, and their chief executives—as well as the degree of support they generate from federal officialdom. Some are paper tigers devoid of power and organized defensively to fight metropolitan governments; others are more substantial, growing in visibility and importance. Nevertheless, with the exception of only a few cases, the mirage of regional governance still is greater than its actuality.

Government interest groups and their clients have found A-85 on the federal level and A-95 and its revisions on the state, regional, and local levels to be much more of a tedious, paper-shuffling endeavor than anticipated.[48] Sufficient staff and resources to monitor and to evaluate federal agencies do not exist in most cases. Governors have new authority over designating substate regional planning boundaries, which federal agencies are supposed to heed prior to designating their own planning and development districts. Where states are moving into substate regional planning in a big way, several are replicating the problems generated by competing federal agencies. They, too, have created multiple planning districts, overlapping metropolitan and statewide agencies which compete with one another over territorial prerogatives and planning responsibilities. These problems are compounded by the fact that federal grant programs continue to proliferate and the march of federally supported mechanisms into new functional areas continues unabated. The two federal agencies which most highly influence COGs in their development at the federal level—HUD with fiscal assistance and programmatic support and OMB which administers the A-95 process and develops rules governing its application—have not fully integrated their operations either.

The three cases stand as pioneering initiatives in the intergovernmental arena between the government interest groups, their members, and federal officialdom. The immediate benefits from their adoption have not been commensurate with initial expectations. Governors, mayors, and county officials, no less than the Nixon administration, seem ambivalent about future courses of action. Meanwhile, Congress, executive agencies, and their clients cautiously guard their own territorial, functional, and programmatic stakes in the disposition of these intergovernmental experiments.

---

[48] See Editorial, *Nation's Cities*, November 1971, p. 6.

4

COMPETITION, BARGAINING, AND COLLABORATION

The constitutional immunity of state and local government from federal taxation has long been one of the more inviolable privileges preserved in the name of dual sovereignty in the federal system. The importance of this immunity for subnational governments is attested to by the fact that, between 1960 and 1970, close to half of all state and local government capital outlays were financed by long-term borrowing, essentially through general obligation and revenue bonds.[1] Cities, in particular, have become increasingly dependent upon revenue borrowing through municipal bonds to finance the major portion of their capital construction and general operating expenses as well. Tax exemption on interest on state and local bonds enables these governments to borrow at interest rates well below those of the private sector or even the federal government. Thus costs to these governments in providing services would be considerably greater without the benefit of this subsidy.

Tax immunity also has become the source of considerable friction between national and state-local governments. Since the late 1930s Treasury Department officials have looked eagerly upon means for curbing the benefits accrued from these interest-free bonds and stemming the loss of otherwise taxable revenues. It has been estimated, for example, that the federal government loses $2 for every $1 of interest subsidy received by state-local governments.[2] This has led many a tax-reform-minded official to contemplate less costly mechanisms and institutions for subsidizing state-local government borrowing.

---

[1] Advisory Commission on Intergovernmental Relations, *Fiscal Balance in the American Federal System,* Washington, D.C., 1967, p. 55. See also *Financing Municipal Facilities Hearings* before the Subcommittee on Economic Progress, Joint Economic Committee, 90th Cong., 1st Sess., 1967, 1.

[2] Joseph Pechman, "The Rich, the Poor, and the Taxes They Pay," *The Public Interest,* **17**:37, Fall 1969.

INDUSTRIAL DEVELOPMENT BONDS

From the Treasury's perspective, one of the greatest modern abuses involving state-local immunity stemmed from Industrial Development Bonds (IDBs). These are bonds issued in the name of state or local governments to finance the construction of industrial plants for occupancy by private corporations. In contrast to utility revenue bonds or those where the full faith and credit of unlimited tax obligations are pledged for public purposes, industrial aid bonds use public credit for essentially private purposes. These bonds typically are debt obligations of private corporations which, because of local or state sponsorship, gain the full interest exemptions and lower interest rates than regular corporate securities. What usually occurs is that the municipality issuing these bonds for building a corporation's factory agrees to "lease" the municipally owned plant to the private company, with rental payments to the local government used to offset interest and amortization requirements.

Quite clearly, then, IDBs constituted an improper use of tax immunities by state and local governments, a fact of which they were fully aware. Such abuses, in fact, reached absurd proportions when sleepy little Southern towns of a few thousand people began selling bond issues of $50 million or so to construct enormous factories when they could not possibly compensate bondholders upon actual default of payments. In effect, the exemption of interest on IDBs from federal income tax involved a federal subsidy to private corporations—a boon to commercial banks, underwriters, and investment banking houses as well as a tax break for bondholders and a loss of federal income. What made the situation all the more alarming to Treasury was the fact that a constituency supportive of IDBs began emerging nationwide as their use spread from state to state.

Many comparable cases of the improper use of bond tax immunity occurred in the previous century, so the rather limited use of industrial aid bonds prior to the 1960s really was not considered too disturbing by most observers of the situation before that time. Between 1936 and 1950, in fact, only Mississippi and Kentucky permitted the practice for attracting industry to low-income and high-labor-surplus communities within their states. But following Treasury's 1954 ruling, which reaffirmed the legality of the tax-exempt status of these bonds, more Southern states joined in the practice to entice Northern industries to relocate. By 1960 some thirteen states had approved the use of industrial aid bonds at an annual rate of $70 million. But by 1967 the practice had spread from coast to coast. Forty-two states authorized IDBs, with their combined value of new issues exceeding $1 billion. The Depression-spawned incentive for luring small industry into rural states had clearly mushroomed into a common practice for cutting factory costs and engaging in industrial competition.[3]

[3] See Richard W. Epps, "Strategy for Industrial Development," *Business Review*, The Federal Reserve Bank of Philadelphia, November 1966, pp. 3–18.

Yet the criticism of industrial aid bonds also increased in proportion to their growth. By the early 1950s the Investment Bankers Association of America (IBA) cautioned members about the hazards involved in the extensive underwriting and marketing of these bonds.[4] A decade later, the organization was calling for national action to deny interest deductions accrued from their use. Fearing the loss of jobs and companies to nonunion areas in the South, the AFL-CIO demanded action. In 1961 they urged Congress to "end the improper use of the revenue raised from the tax free state and local bonds to entice runaway employers." The Advisory Commission on Intergovernmental Relations (ACIR) in 1963 also warned against the expanding practice of using public credit for private purposes, the federal tax loss, and the counterproductive tendencies of states pirating one another's industries.[5]

But with most states involved in the practice, Congress, especially the Senate, was not receptive to taking the leadership on the issue. Thus the Johnson administration took up the cause, beginning with encouragement from the "economic triumvirate" which involved the Secretary of the Treasury, the Chairman of the Council of Economic Advisers, and the Director of the Bureau of the Budget. They uniformly condemned the practice of using tax-exempt bonds for industrial purposes.

Nevertheless, responsibility for executive action resided in the Treasury. As the amount of new public issues of IDBs rose from $200 million in 1965 to more than $500 million in 1966, Treasury—under the leadership of tax reform advocate Stanley S. Surrey, the Assistant Secretary for Tax Policy—began moving on bond abuses. In 1966 the department indicated that it would cease providing rulings as to the exempt status of interest on certain arbitrage bonds, which all but ended the practice of "oversells" by certain municipalities. Arbitrage transactions involved the floating of bonds by municipalities in excess of the estimated costs of the specific capital construction to be financed. This enabled additional funds raised through the bonds to be reinvested by the municipality for paying off the costs of the facility constructed.

Treasury's action placed IDBs in jeopardy as well. If the arbitrage theory applied to cities for capital construction, it could, so tax reform advocates claimed, be extended to industrial aid bonds. But Treasury officials decided against extending this ruling for fear of probable counter-action by Congress, which might foreclose future options for tax reform.

---

[4] See Investment Bankers Association of America, "Report of the Subcommittee on Municipal Industrial Financing," Hollywood, Fla., 1963, mimeographed. See also American Federation of Labor and the Council on Industrial Organization, *Labor Looks at the 90th Congress*, Legislative Report by the Department of Legislation, Washington, D.C., December 1968, p. 11.

[5] *Wall Street Journal*, October 10, 1967, p. 1. See Also Advisory Commission on Intergovernmental Relations, *Ninth Annual Report* Washington, D.C., 1968, p. 11.

The Groups Get Involved

For chief executives of state-local governments and their national organizations, the issue of IDBs and their tax-exempt status became a highly emotional and divisive problem. Bond rates were rising at an unprecedented rate, reaching a thirty-three-year high in 1967. The number of IDBs had increased 50 percent between 1965 and 1967 alone. Their total amount as calculated in dollars tripled, which constituted an increase from 2 percent of all new state and local tax-exempt financing to more than 10 percent by 1967. Interest rates were up from 1/4 to 1 percent in some cases. Most observers of the situation agreed that the bond market had become increasingly unstable.[6] Something had to be done, and quickly.

Treasury attempted to draw these major vested interests into concert on a position for curbing IDBs before going to Congress to request specific action. It invited the government interest groups to a series of meetings beginning in early 1967, for the purpose of building a coalition. The invitation carried with it the credible threat that if these groups did not cooperate, Treasury might proceed independently, through administrative action which might extend far beyond industrial aid bonds.

Governors and mayors were thus united out of mutual apprehension that the constitutional immunity on federal taxation extended to all state and local government bonds was endangered. Both parties felt that the matter of IDBs could be regulated on the state level. The mayors urged "the states to enact legislation regulating local government's use of industrial development bonds."[7] The governors called for resolution of the problem by interstate agreements. Moreover, state and municipal chief executives wanted to keep both the courts and Treasury out of the picture for fear that abridgement of tax immunity might be the first step toward more extensive action. The government interest groups were not in complete agreement on this issue, however. The National Association of Counties dissented, requesting immediate action on revenue bonds regardless of whether it was national or state legislation. The differences among the groups thus proved to be irreconcilable.

The governors acted in a Janus-faced manner. Publicly, they condemned the uses of IDBs but continued to request their use from state legislatures. Privately, they admitted to Treasury officials that action was required. But many had assumed a new and growing role for state chief executives — that of industrial supporter.[8] The governors of Alabama, Kentucky,

[6] See Investment Bankers Association of America, *Tax Exempt Corporate Bonds: A Tax Abuse,* New York, 1967.

[7] National League of Cities, National Municipal Policy of 1965, Washington, D.C., 1966, p. 83.

[8] See Alan J. Wyner, "Governor-Salesman," *National Civic Review,* **56**:81–83. February 1967.

Mississippi, and Arkansas, the principal users of IDBs, had achieved considerable success as business promoters. Northern states like Ohio, Michigan and Iowa had countered with their own generous offerings of IDBs. Latecomers to the competition like Virginia, Louisiana, and Massachusetts were just beginning underwriting procedures and were not about to relent to fellow governors' pressure until some form of parity had been achieved.

Typical of state ambivalence on the issue was the case of North Carolina. Its legislature in May 1967, acting, as it said, "reluctantly as a defensive measure with reservations," adopted a bill to permit the use of such bonds by communities. In doing that, the legislature also adopted a resolution denouncing the practice it was authorizing and calling on the President, Congress, and fellow states to stop it. [9]

The mayors were ambivalent as well. Gunther and Healy, the executive directors of the United States Conference of Mayors (USCM) and the National League of Cities (NLC), though privately opposed to the use of IDBs, feared that collaboration with Treasury in curbing the tax-exempt status on these bonds might produce a rank and file revolt. "We might find ourselves working against our members' best interests, especially if Treasury used our compliance as a precedent to move against all tax-exempt bonds," was how one NLC staff man viewed the situation. The USCM had organized originally to safeguard "the interests, rights, and privileges of municipalities," and the tax immunity from federal taxation on municipal bonds was deemed by most mayors one of the most sacrosanct privileges needful of safeguarding.

The mayors' groups also were affiliates of another organization devoted entirely to the protection of this immunity—the Conference on State Defense. This organization, essentially a coalition of governors, attorneys general, mayors, state and local finance officers, state development corporations, and independent government authorities was led by Daniel B. Goldberg, a counsel to the New York Port Authority. Goldberg successfully disrupted meetings between Treasury and the government interest groups by raising for members' consideration a constant parade of horribles as to the possible scope and coverage of any Treasury action. Appearing at the USCM and NLC annual conventions, he reminded the mayors that revocation of tax-exempt status on municipal bonds would mean spending perhaps 2 percent more on bond interest rates and a 25 to 30 percent increase in debt service. [10] Thus, the mayors, too, were incapable of sustaining unity, instead deferring to a veto posture against any Treasury action whatsoever.

[9] U.S. News and World Report, June 12, 1967, p. 94.

[10] United States Conference of Mayors, Proceedings of the Thirty-Third Annual Meeting Washington, D.C., 1966, 135–137.

However the National Association of Counties (NACO), led by its executive director Bernie Hillenbrand, remained adamant in its stand in spite of pressure from some county officials and fellow government interest groups to change position. Hillenbrand staked out a position of leadership on the issue, perhaps in advance of rank and file members, asserting that the use of IDBs threatened "the very continuation of counties' tax-exempt status on its bonds and was impairing the ability of local governments to finance its capital expenditures."[11] In effect, NACO assumed a posture in direct opposition to that of the mayors. The later argued that any abridgement of tax immunity constituted a first step toward complete revocation, while NACO argued that if the tax immunity on IDBs was not terminated immediately, all state and local bonds were in trouble.

Congress Acts

Treasury discussions with the government interest groups proved fruitless. Both Treasury and the groups were too split on positions and strategies to attain agreement sufficient either for administrative or legislative action. Treasury avoided independent legislative action through congressional "tax reformers" for fear of offending Ways and Means Chairman Wilbur Mills, whose own state was steeply entrenched in the IDB business to the amount of $130 million between 1963 and 1966. Thus an outside coalition of interests emerged, formed by such unlikely bedfellows as NACO, the AFL-CIO, the National Association of Real Estate Boards, and the Investment Bankers Association. Organized under IBA leadership, the coalition sought legislative action through the taxation committees of Congress. Through Representative John Byrnes (R-Wisc.), ranking minority member of Ways and Means, and Abraham Ribicoff (D-Conn.) of the Senate Finance Committee, legislation was introduced by these members in November 1967, seeking revision of the Internal Revenue Code to remove tax exemptions on the interest of IDBs. Two months later Treasury Secretary Joseph Barr decided to throw in with the coalition and formally endorse the Byrnes and Ribicoff bills, even without Mills's prior approval.

By late February Treasury realized that neither Chairman Mills nor Russell Long, Senate Finance Committee Chairman, would hold hearings or report out legislation dealing with IDBs. Long's home state of Louisiana was in the process of issuing some of the largest IDBs yet underwritten, while Arkansas' commercial banks, principal benificiaries of their state's IDBs, would not view kindly any assistance Mills might lend to the Treasury's campaign against these bonds.

[11] Bernard Hillenbrand, "The Snake Pit of Revenue Bonds," *American County Government*, July 1967, pp. 8–9.

In a bold move, Treasury decided to act on its own. On March 6, it announced that it would soon propose a rule to remove the tax exemption on the interest of IDBs and, in conjunction with this announcement, the IRS declared that it would no longer issue ruling letters on such bonds.[12] These ruling letters were Treasury certifications that a specific bond issue complied with the requirement for tax exemption, and inability to obtain one had the effect of precluding the selling of the bonds. Treasury and the IRS had another ally. The Securities and Exchange Commission tightened its control over IDBs by announcing that these bonds were no longer exempt from registration with the SEC, which was required of the other municipal bonds. Thus, by reversing its 1954 decision covering IDBs, Treasury was clearly legislating taxation and was extremely vulnerable, as it realized, to strong congressional reaction.

Treasury correctly anticipated that Senate reaction would be swift and the outcome of any showdown seriously in doubt. Its announcement produced a torrent of letters and telegrams from mayors, governors, state development commissioners, and affiliates of the State Defense League, especially from those states and communities in the process of negotiating plant acquisition based on IDBs. These communications denounced Treasury's administrative action and called upon Congress to assume its legislative prerogative in the matter. What emerged was vast Senate confusion over the issue and what its impact might be on each Senator's state. The first challenge came only five days after Treasury's announcement. Between March 11 and 28, the Senate took three different roll-call votes on the tax exemption question and on each occasion assumed a position different from that on the previous vote.

Senator Mike Monroney (D-Okla.) was the first senator to seek reversal of Treasury's action by legislative means. He proposed an amendment to the Supplemental Appropriations that would provide additional funds for Treasury to be used exclusively for "continuing examination" by the IRS of requests for rulings on IDB's tax-exempt status. This amendment was defeated by a close vote of 42 to 38, more a reflection of the Senate's disapproval of forcing Treasury's retreat by this circuitous method than objection to the intent. Two weeks later Senator Carl Curtis (R-Neb.), a Finance Committee member, forced the issue of Treasury's preemption of a legislative prerogative by proposing an amendment to the Tax Adjustment Act of 1968 that would block further Treasury action pending congressional review. This amendment, passed by a 51 to 32 vote, preserved the tax exemption for IDBs and required Treasury to issue the ruling letters needed to sell the bonds.

Yet all was not lost. Only two days later, on March 28, the Senate com-

---

[12] U.S. Internal Revenue Service, "Announcement of Rulings on Issuing Letters for Industrial Development Bonds," *Federal Register*, 33(56):4950–4952, March 23, 1968.

pletely reversed its earlier action by a 50 to 32 vote. It accepted an amendment by Senator Ribicoff, a modified version of his original bill, which ended existing tax exemption on interest from IDBs in excess of $1 million.[13] This reversal, which caused seventeen senators to switch their positions between the Curtis and Ribicoff votes, stands as a superb testimony to the round-the-clock lobbying operations conducted by Treasury, the investment bankers, NACO, and organized labor. NACO helped neutralize the mayors' and governors' opposition. Its staff contacted each opposing senator, indicating that "the irresponsible continuation of the unchecked issuance of industrial development bonds poses a disastrous threat to the entire state and local government bond market."[14] The IBA, joined by numerous Wall Street allies, further underscored NACO's assertion, as did the AFL-CIO, which rallied their affiliates to pressure Northern and Western senators for reversing, in several cases, their pro-IDB stands.

By accepting modifications to his amendment which extended the proposed cutoff date for five months to January 1, 1969 (allowing partially completed bond arrangements in several states to be concluded), Senator Ribicoff turned around a handful of senators who otherwise would have voted against the amendment. The Connecticut Senator made another concession found acceptable to Treasury and its allies, and that was to allow interest exemptions to stand on industrial revenue bonds of less than $1 million. Treasury, the bankers' groups, and labor next focused on the Senators from Hawaii, Maryland, and Virginia, who apparently were confused about what implications the amendment might have for their own states. Five sets of state senators eventually shifted their position from one vote to the next when assured that the IDB cutoff would constitute minimal damage to their own states. Thus, the Ribicoff amendment, attached to the Tax Adjustment Act (later termed the Revenue and Expenditure Control Act of 1968), after passing the Senate successfully, cleared a much harried conference committee and was signed by President Johnson into law (PL 90-364).

The case of IDBs, the congressional limitation placed upon federal tax immunity on interest from these securities, illustrates the defensive posture often assumed by the governmental interest groups when protecting benefits previously distributed to them. The case also points to an interesting characteristic of the groups' leadership-membership relations. NACO, the less prestigious and visible member of the government interest groups, asserted its independence from the others rather than bargaining with each over specific concessions. Its executive director moved out ahead of rank and file, while the governors' and mayors' leaders were constrained by

[13] For original bill and remarks by Senator Ribicoff on proposed legislation relating to amendment of Internal Revenue Code, see U.S. Congress, Senate, S. 2326, 90th Cong., 1st. Sess., November 8, 1967, *Congressional Record*, 113, S. 16023–16027.

[14] *Congressional Quarterly*, **26**:1200, May 24, 1968.

previous policy and fear of membership revolt. USCM-NLC leaders eventually discovered, however, that membership opposition to Congress's action was considerably less than had been anticipated. While House-Senate conferees were still reviewing the final legislation containing the IDB amendment, the USCM passed a resolution at its June convention supportive of the legislative action. The mayors noted that industrial development bonds jeopardized the immunity of the interest "on all true state and local debt obligations."[15] The governors also swung in line behind the congressional action, but in an ambivalent fashion. They both praised and condemned what Congress had done. In a resolution at their July meeting, they demanded public hearings in advance of any Treasury ruling on the definition and scope of IDB exclusions.

Final decision on the application of Congress' action limiting the use of IDBs rested with Treasury. Defeated in the legislative arena, the government interest groups centered their efforts upon Treasury to influence the forthcoming guidelines and regulations. Treasury, once again, extended an invitation to the groups to participate in determining these regulations, only this time they were all too eager to participate. Treasury had the upper hand.

THE 1968 HIGHWAY ACT AND MASS TRANSIT

The nation's mayors served notice upon Congress in 1968 that their routine support for the Federal Highway Program could no longer be counted on. Prior to the late 1960s, the mayors' threat of withdrawing support for the biennial authorizations covering the highway construction program would probably have had little impact upon the "subgovernment of highways." Moreover, such action would have been unlikely, given the mayor's traditional support for the program. But the years 1967 and 1968 were different. Urban highways were jammed, traffic was poorly regulated, alternative forms of transportation were often nonexistent, planning among government jurisdictions was fragmented, and opposition to highway expansion was on the rise everywhere.[16] Indeed, the consequences of the highway program were becoming all too apparent to some large-city mayors, accentuating the wrong-way migrational patterns of people and business and forging a white middle-class ring around the growing black and poor inner city.

The Highway Trust Fund, the self-liquidating trough established in 1956 through gasoline and highway-related user taxes to finance highway

[15] United States Conference of Mayors, *Proceedings of the Thirty-Sixth Annual Meeting,* Washington, D.C., 1969, p. 154; and *Nation's Cities,* December 12, 1968, pp. 11–14.

[16] See John Meyer, John Kain, and Martin Wohl, *The Urban Transportation Problem,* Harvard University Press, Cambridge, Mass., 1968.

construction, became the focus of attack by those who wished to divert its funds into other forms of transportation. The prestigious national organization of road-building specialists, the American Association of State Highway Officials (AASHO), emerged as the target of those interests concerned with highway safety, the environment, and the relationship between urban problems and inner-city highway construction. AASHO, often referred to as the "Army Corps of the Highways," is a national association of highway officials, many of whom are engineers, organized on the federal, state and local levels. They have been an integral component of the highway policy-making system which included the Bureau of Public Roads, the Public Works Committees in Congress, and myriad support groups with some vested interest in the expansion of the nation's highways.

Acute awareness of urban transportation problems and the consequences of past policies had disturbed the once noncontroversial system of highway interests. The mayors and others demanded admission, if not dramatic changes in highway programs. A coalition of critics was emerging, and by 1968 these interests were being heard in Congress.[17]

For years the focus in national highway policy was on rural, interstate, and intercity routes, with primary attention given to interstate commerce and the establishment of post roads. Federal aid for highways grew from $5 million in 1917 to nearly $5 billion in authorizations by 1967. Billions had been earmarked from the Highway Trust Fund to finance a nationwide network of highways linking cities horizontally from coast to coast, with diminishing benefits for inner cities. Mayors were keenly aware of the disparities involved in the allocation of benefits in federal highway funds, both the two-to-one differential favoring nonurban areas over urban and the imbalance existing among alternative modes of transportation. Cities were continuously short-changed in the redistribution of the nearly $14 billion in user taxes collected by federal and state authorities. Most states, through their highway departments, exercised strict controls over intra-city use of these monies, often requiring project-by-project approval. Mayors felt particularly aggrieved by these historical biases, since 70 percent of the nation's population lived in urban places and more than half the mileage covered by motor vehicles was covered there. Yet, allocation formulas written into federal and state laws continued to favor rural areas, even disqualifying most urban streets and expressways from eligibility for participation.

Nonetheless, the history of the Federal Highway Program does reflect the shift from rural to urban attention, but in a limited interstate or inter-city context rather than intracity movement of traffic. The first major highway legislation, the Federal Aid Road Act of 1916, established durable

[17] See Helen Leavitt, Superhighway-Superhoax, Doubleday, New York, 1970; and A. Q. Mowbray, Road to Ruin, Lippincott, New York, 1968.

patterns in federal-state cooperation when the Secretary of Agriculture was authorized to aid state highway departments in the construction of rural post roads. In 1944 Congress shifted emphasis to interstate travel by earmarking highway funds for three basic kinds of projects under the so-called ABC program. These included primary road support such as major highways, which were given 45 percent of the funds; the secondary road system of rural, farm-to-market, and feeder routes, given 30 percent; and urban roads such as inner-city and metropolitan types, alloted 25 percent. Prior to 1944 only a small amount of federal-state funds went for urban projects and in fact, before 1934, states were prohibited from spending any federal highway monies in municipalities of more than 2,500.[18]

The Federal Highway Act of 1956 authorized the biggest road-building program in the nation's history. It included a 41,000-mile Interstate System to be financed by a $60 billion federal-state fund and operated under the "pay-as-you-go" Highway Trust Fund. The massive new system was to be paid for out of the Trust Fund on a 90 to 10 federal to state-local government basis for the interstate component and on a fifty-fifty basis for the expanded ABC system. It was further provided that the Highway Trust Fund should not show a deficit, that the ABC system be given priority in funding, and that no trust funds be used for other than highway construction.

Mayors Challenge the Highway Interests

Local officials were among the first and strongest supporters of the program to direct highway user taxes to highway trust funds reserved exclusively for highway construction. Intercity freeways and the Interstate System were then viewed by many mayors as instrumental to the city's economic well-being. Highways often aided urban renewal efforts, connected city markets with buyers and suppliers, and functioned as a boon for commerce and industry. Yet by the 1960s early returns on the highway program demonstrated its negative externalities and often counterproductive tendencies — economically, socially, and politically. Almost all city chief executives confronted one or more of the program's effects, including traffic congestion; drain on city finances for construction and maintenance; a net displacement of businesses and jobs; reduction in land use, housing, and taxable property; inadequate relocation provisions; rising awareness of pollution; and citizen groups' opposition to further highway expansion. Thus the Interstate System reflected a shift from rural to urban areas, but, to municipal officials it had provided little

---

[18] For a brief history of the federal highway program, see W. Brooke Graves, *American Intergovernmental Relations*, Scribner, New York, 1964, pp. 675–676.

assistance in coping with intracity travel, mounting traffic problems, and alternative forms of transportation.

By 1967 the mayors, county officials, and their national organizations resolved that the urban transportation problem had to be met head-on. City officials recognized that transportation had become an integral part of urban and metropolitan development affecting the total urban environment. Efforts directed at gaining federal approval for a separate mass transit fund or sufficient appropriations to support subways and other forms of transportation construction had thus far proved unsuccessful. So had attempts to support coordinated transportation programs through state financing or even limited commutation taxes in large cities.

But the nation's mayors had to develop a consensus around a strategy and targets for their lobbying efforts if they were to be successful in changing priorities in the nation's transportation policies. Their organizations were rife with factions. Some wished to attack the Highway Trust Fund and others wanted to bargain for greater urban inclusion. Some even opposed further federal spending for highways altogether, and many demanded a greater share for the cities.

Strategies and tactics were further delimited by the congressional committee system and its separate fiefdoms. Appropriations Committees, heretofore opposed to the creation of another transportation trust fund, could be expected to block circumvention of their authority. Ways and Means viewed bond financing as a raid on the public treasury and was not kindly disposed toward earmarking further highway user taxes for a mass transit system. The House Public Works Committee and its Subcommittee on Roads were seen as captives of Washington lobbies and were often called "the road gang." The eventual decision to focus their attention upon the Federal Highway Program, though made in several stages, resulted more from events within the highway subsystem than internal pressures and emerging consensus inside the mayors' ranks.

First, Congress directed in 1965 that the Department of Commerce, later the Department of Transportation, issue a biennial report, beginning in January 1968, of estimates of future highway needs for the nation. Next, in anticipation of this report, AASHO jumped the gun by delivering to Congress in early 1967 its own *Preliminary Report on Federal-Aid Highway Needs After 1972.* With the Interstate Highway Program nearing two-thirds completion and the Highway Trust Fund scheduled to expire in 1972, widespread debate had erupted within and without the highway subgovernment over the future development of the nation's federal-aid highway system. Most observers of the regular biennial authorization for highway construction anticipated a rather perfunctory review of the program in 1968. The AASHO and forthcoming DOT reports, coupled with rising congressional concern that the future program be mapped out in advance of the 1968 elections, dramatically changed the situation. If the mayors and their urban allies were to influence the direction of the highway program, they concluded that it would have to be done during the 1968 congressional review.

The Mayors' Plan

In June 1967, the National League of Cities formed a special Transportation Committee under the leadership of J. D. Braman, Mayor of Seattle. The steering committee met several times prior to the NLC's Congress of Cities convention to formulate a comprehensive transportation policy, later adopted by the NLC, which called for a new federal highway program to help urban areas improve their major streets. The mayors had long advocated a more equitable distribution of highway user revenues on the basis of road use, but beginning in late 1967 they specified the need for a new federal-aid urban highway fund to be financed on the same 90 to 10 basis as the Interstate System. Moreover the mayors' updated policy called for a totally new State, Urban, and Rural (SUR) highway program and classification system to replace the existing ABC highway program with greater planning requirements, federal takeover of relocation payments, and a general redirection of the entire highway program following the completion of the Interstate System.[19]

To gain acceptance of their proposed program and to broaden their constituency, NLC officials focused their lobbying efforts upon key interests in the highway program — which included officials in the Federal Highway Administration, the staff and members of House and Senate Subcommittees on Roads, AASHO, and fellow public official organizations. AASHO presented the most immediate challenge. It had already issued its preliminary report on highway needs for the 1975 to 1985 decade, a report which suggested, among other things, that the existing rural-urban system of allocating highway funds be maintained essentially intact even after the completion of the Interstate System.[20] The NLC joined forces with the National Association of County Officials to use their combined forces to get AASHO to change major sections in its preliminary draft before issuing a final version in early 1968. In September 1967, Braman and Mayor C. Beverly Briley, NLC's vice president, continuing a long NLC-AASHO policy relationship dating from 1956, met with AASHO representatives to see if the two organizations might come closer together in their positions. Basic differences between the two existed, however. AASHO felt completion of the Interstate System should take precedence

---

[19] "AASHO Fires Opening Salvo and the Post-1975 Highway Battle Begins," *Nation's Cities*, September 1967, pp. 45–48.

[20] *Preliminary Report of ASSHO on Federal-Aid Highway Needs after 1972*, Hearings before the House Committee on Public Works, 90th Cong., 1st Sess., 1967.

over all other highway construction, that uses of the Highway Trust Fund should be narrowly applied, and that rural priorities should be maintained over urban ones. The mayors took fundamental issue with all three of these positions.

Yet AASHO mayors' differences proved negotiable. AASHO's once powerful influence upon Congress had decreased. In the opinion of many mayors, several members of the Public Works Committees, and others, it had long acted as proprietor, not steward of the highway program. Where the Public Works Committees and their then executive counterpart, the Federal Highway Administration, had long deferred to AASHO's judgments concerning routes, construction, building specifications, and technical matters, the professional organization no longer carried the day on substantive policy.[21] AASHO needed allies and sought to placate the mayors.

AASHO thus agreed to collaborate with the mayors and NACO as long as the latter did not seek to dismantle or divert uses of the Highway Trust Fund to rapid transit programs. Moreover, a strong minority faction within AASHO—namely, county and municipal public works and highway officials—advocated closer cooperation for purposes of maximizing their collective strength before Congress. In revising its initial report, AASHO sent to the Public Works Committees in June 1968 an *After 1975 Highway Program.* In this report, AASHO now supported the mayors' quest for a separate transportation trust fund without specifying how it was to be established. It also supported the use of the Highway Trust Fund after completion of the Interstate System to finance improvements of a new urban arterial street system on a 90/10 basis, and it even proposed greater urban emphasis in future allocations of highway funds.[22]

AASHO's turnabout was greatly facilitated by numerous meetings conducted between it and representatives from NLC-NACO, congressional staff, officials of the Department of Transportation, and the Federal Highway Administration (abbreviated FHW to distinguish it from the Federal Housing Administration, or FHA). The Bureau of Public Roads, a relatively autonomous agency in the Department of Commerce, became the Federal Highway Administration when it was transferred to the Department of Transportation (DOT). FHW was beginning to feel pressures from the secretary level to incorporate urban transportation needs into its overall planning, and in 1967 FHW Administrator Francis Turner had introduced a pilot TOPICS program (an acronym for Traffic Operations Program to Increase Capacity and Safety) for urban projects to improve the capacity of existing urban arterials without major construction. This new

---

[21] Staff of House and Senate Public Works Committees, interviews with selected members, Washington, D.C., August 16, 1969.

[22] *After 1975 Highway Program of AASHO,* Hearings before the Subcommittee on Roads, House Public Works Committee, 90th Cong., 2d Sess., 1968.

traffic-control program spawned in the bureau and sold to the NLC, NACO, and AASHO, coincided with the mayors' insistence on a separate and identifiable urban highway program. The mayors' case for a more balanced and equitable sharing in the Federal Highway Program was given a further boost when the secretary of DOT sent to Congress the long-awaited report entitled the *1968 National Highway Needs Report.* Besides endorsing the TOPICS program, a more balanced redistribution of federal highway funds to urban needs, the report emphasized that "the federal interest in highways . . . now appropriately must focus strongly where the problems are most critical—in the urban areas."[23]

Thus, by the time extensive congressional hearings on the Federal-Aid Highway Act began before the House Public Works Subcommittee on Roads in February 1968, the principal actors had been able to achieve closer harmony on overlapping interests and general agreement to support the mayors' position on greater attention to urban needs. Where subcommittee members had expected hearings to involve merely standard authorizations and extension of the completion date for the Interstate System, they now had to contend with major revisions and planning for a new highway program to follow completion of the Interstate System.

In advocating an overhaul of the existing highway system, NLC's executive director Pat Healy informed House members that "our cities badly need funds to improve streets and highways that are not part of the Interstate System."[24] Healy called for a more balanced highway development strategy in which urban highway development would be given comparable emphasis to that of completing the Interstate System. So as not to offend committee members unnecessarily or retreat from the NLC's agreement with AASHO, Healy assured committee members that the Highway Trust Fund should be reserved for highways and "highway related activities." Two months later, Healy would return to the same subcomittee with the support of the Conference of Mayors to have Mayor Braman argue the case for the new TOPICS program, expansion of the ABC system, and greater federal control over highway relocation activities.

The mayors and county officials directed the greater part of their efforts at the House Subcommittee on Roads. The Senate counterpart was viewed as being more sympathetic to urban needs, and, in fact, broadened the scope of its highway hearings to include environmental ramifications, especially the relationship between urban problems and urban highway construction. Senator William Jennings Randolph (D-W. Va.), its chairman, had assured the mayors and their allies of greater committee atten-

---

23 U.S. Congress, House Committee on Public Works, *1968 National Highway Needs Report,* Committee Print, 90th Cong., 2d Sess., 1968, p. 3.

24 *Federal-Aid Highway Act-1968,* Hearings before the Subcommittee on Public Roads, House Committee on Public Works, 90th Cong., 2d Sess., 1968, pp. 26–27.

tion to urban problems. He proved supportive of their demands as long as they did not conflict with highway building programs in the Applachian Program, partly ABC-financed, for which the chairman was the principal protector.

Decision making in the House Public Works Committee, as one observer noted, is "profoundly influenced by its internal partisan structure and by the patterns of support in the House for its legislative proposals."[25] The Committee's Subcommittee on Roads generally reflected this partisan structure with rural and urban members in both the majority and minority composition. Neither the full committee nor the subcommittee were likely to be supportive of overhauling the complete highway program and fundamentally shifting its allocation from rural and interstate priorities to inner-city and metropolitan ones. Yet, they were accommodating to demands for small shifts in programs and resource allocations insofar as the overall program remained untouched.

NACO, NLC, USCM, AASHO, DOT, and the FHW supported the TOPICS program. The mayors, in their next appearance before the House Subcommittee on Roads, used both Mayor Braman and fellow NLC-AASHO member Milton Pikarsky, the Commissioner of Public Works for the City of Chicago, to argue their case for TOPICS. Pikarsky, a long-time political compatriot of Subcommittee Chairman Thomas Kluczynski of Chicago and a person well known to committee members, had proved extremely helpful to the mayors' organizations. He had linked highway officials, AASHO, and congressional staff together in working out legislative strategy. Once again, Braman assured committee members that the NLC's advocacy of a coordinated and balanced transportation was not directed "toward a raid on the highway trust fund for anything other than roadways upon which rubber-tired vehicles can roll."[26] The mayors merely wanted what they, AASHO, and DOT had all called for—greater highway financing responsiveness to urban needs. Mass transportation, Braman assured members, would be pursued through different legislative means other than diversions from the Highway Trust Fund.

One of the mayors' key allies on the House Subcommittee was Representative Don Clausen (R-Cal.), a former county supervisor and NACO official. Clausen proposed, successfully, two key amendments to the administration's legislation during the closed committee markup session—the authorization of $224 million for 1970–1971 for the urban TOPICS program, and the same amount for additional use on the primary and secondary road systems exlusive of their urban extensions. Both amend-

[25] James T. Murphy, "Partisanship and the House Public Works Committee," paper presented at the Sixty-Fourth Annual Meeting of the American Political Science Association, Washington, D.C., September 4, 1968, p. 23.

[26] Federal-Aid Highway Act—1968 Hearings, p. 502.

ments were adopted by the committee and, in effect, neutralized the clash of urban and rural forces by apportioning separate and equal authorizations from the Highway Trust Fund.[27]

The Outcome

As it developed, the House and Senate passed substantially different versions of the Federal-Aid Highway Act. The Senate legislation contained environmental deprivation provisions allowing Highway Trust Fund expenditures for damages produced as a result of highway construction and operation. It also authorized funds for highway beautification, more generous allocation for TOPICS, and relocation payments and procedures as well as more stringent requirements governing proposed hearings on highway route location. The House bill gave little attention to the social aspects of highway construction such as public hearing requirements, deprivation funds, or beautification payments. Instead, it gave completion of the Interstate System top priority, including a 3,000-mile addition to the 41,000-mile system, and it directed much of its attention to a local dispute involving the District of Columbia. The House bill required the Secretary of Transportation and the D.C. Government to complete part of the Interstate System in the District, including the construction of an additional, highly controversial bridge over the Potomac River. The D.C.-Interstate controversy, in fact, so consumed committee members and later House-Senate conferences that one or more of the provisions previously objected to by the House committee members, such as federal control over relocation assistance and mandatory equal employment provisions on bids for federally aided highway projects, passed along with the punitive D.C. measure.[28]

The Federal-Aid Highway Act of 1968 (PL 90-495) included several demonstrable achievements for the mayors and their allies. The legislation contained a separate authorization within the Highway Trust Fund for the TOPICS program, with a combined two-year funding of $400 million and funds for a "fringe parking facilities" program advocated by the mayors. The mayors had succeeded in gaining a slightly greater urban orientation to the non-Interstate System component of the highway program than previously was the case. It was likely that federal funds for the TOPICS program would be applied not only to the "systematic and comprehensive application of traffic operations," as called for, but also to capital improvements and other minor construction that would alleviate

---

[27] U.S. Congress, House, *Conference Report on the Federal-Aid Highway Act of 1968,* H. Rept. 1970, 90th Cong., 2d Sess., 1968.

[28] See *Congressional Quarterly,* **26:**1796–1800, July 19, 1968.

congestion and improve traffic flow. The mayors further gained approval for a federally directed and financed relocation assistance program, a measure long advocated by local officials. This provision would probably aid local approval of proposed interstate highways, many blocked by the courts and citizen groups until provisions guaranteeing just compensation and actual relocation prior to construction were achieved. Most important, however, the legislation broadened the uses for which the Highway Trust Fund might be spent, with the prospect that more highway-related activities might be funded in the future. It was a precedent which the mayors viewed as an opening to wider uses of trust funds.

The provisions gained in the 1968 Highway Act made its enactment one of the NLC's most important successes during the 90th Congress.[29] It was expected from the onset of its lobbying activities that the likelihood of even moderate gains was minimal. The success of this venture could not be attributed exclusively to the League. NACO had contributed immensely by working with the NLC in building a consensus among agency, interest group, and congressional committee members. It also helped reduce the anxieties of House Republicans who feared a mayors' grab for easy trust fund monies. The large-city mayors' organization, the USCM, had operated most successfully on the Senate side, where its traditional allies proved useful. But the key to the entire lobbying operation, according to many observers, was the NLC-led effort to bring the major highway interests together, namely AASHO, DOT, the Federal Highway Administration, and congressional staff. Even more important, perhaps, was timing. AASHO and the Highway Trust Fund were under attack. The House and Senate reviewing committees decided to take a hard look at the total highway program, and the mayors were there, organized with their own program and list of priorities.

THE POVERTY PROGRAM

The Economic Opportunity Act of 1964 consisted of ten separate programs designed to combat national poverty. It was the first major legislation originated under President Johnson—indeed, the core of his 1964 election-year program. The legislation's most controversial features were found in Title II, which authorized, first, the creation of the community action program and, second, community action agencies (CAAs), which were comprehensive organizations, either public or private, formed to mobilize available resources for a coordinated attack on poverty. These multi-purpose CAAs were essentially undefined as to geographic and political

[29] Allen E. Pritchard, "The National Municipal Policy," *Nation's Cities*, November 1968, pp. 14–21.

boundaries and even composition and responsibility. Their sole original directive—for operating community action programs—was found in the clause specifying that they were to be "developed, conducted, and administered with the maximum feasible participation of residents of the areas and members of the groups served."[30]

In designating CAAs as the institutional vehicle for planning and implementing poverty-related programs, Congress allocated funds to local communities directly, subject only to general definition of purpose. It also delegated to the Office of Economic Opportunity (OEO) and its director extraordinary discretion in setting up and administering the entire program. It was thus an uncommon grant of power and funds. Congress enabled private community groups and organizations to be eligible recipients for up to 90 percent of the costs of a local poverty program, which become 100 percent to most, and left to OEO the choice of which organizations were to be funded.

As little understood or untested as the community action concept was, however, a highly partisan Congress approved the entire program without really probing the meaning, intent, or commitment of the community action section.[31] The "maximum feasible participation" provisions contained the seeds of trouble that were to plague public officials on all governmental levels, touching off bitter disputes over who should run, be represented upon, and have the say in controlling antipoverty programs. Given time, other OEO programs like Head Start, Upward Bound, and health and legal services were to achieve their separate identity as well as to gain support groups, congressional defenders, and even popularity. The poverty program, for many, was left synonymous with the controversial community action.

Nonparticipation and Cooptation

The poverty legislation was the product of the executive branch and the Democratic administration. Unlike many sweeping national programs with substantial pressures for enactment and many congressional advocates, the program had neither a broad congressional base nor widespread public approval.[32] Indeed, it was born amid formidable opposition, both ideological and partisan. Adversaries included a large number of Republi-

---

[30] Public Law 88–452, Title 2, sec. 202 (a) (3).

[31] See James L. Sundquist, Politics and Policy, Brookings Institution, Washington, D.C., 1968, chap. 4.

[32] See Richard Blumenthal, "The Bureaucracy: Antipoverty and the Community Action Program," in Allan P. Sindler (ed.), American Political Institutions and Public Policy, Little, Brown, Boston, 1969, pp. 129–179.

can congressmen, some Southern Democrats, old-line agencies like the Department of Health, Education, and Welfare, as well as social workers, educators, health officials, and other state and local guilds which had been precluded from a primary role in the program.

Congressional leaders participated cursorily in developing this legislation. But political executives of state-local governments, with few exceptions, were peremptorily bypassed. OEO Director Sargent Shriver had noted, with some pride, that more than 135 persons were consulted by the poverty task forces in formulating the program, including 8 elected state-local officials.[33] All were loyal Democrats: one ex-governor, one lame-duck governor, and several mayors like Lee of New Haven and Oakland's Houlihan, who had participated in antecedent foundation-sponsored poverty efforts.

The administration rounded up six mayors and five governors, all but one a Democrat, to testify favorably on behalf of the legislation before Congress. None found the bill's language inconsistent with their having a significant role in the program. Seemingly unaware of the profound impact that the program would have upon intergovernmental relations, the mayors, so as not to disturb existing political relations, placed almost abiding faith in the federal government's administration of the program. Syracuse's Mayor Walsh assured the House Education and Labor Committee that "if we could not have direct control of the program, we did not want it."[34] Chicago's Richard Daley put down Republican warnings about the absence of guarantees for public official participation by stating that as far as he was concerned, the legislation allowed for this. The nation's mayors, in fact, fully supported the program from the beginning. The United States Conference of Mayors pledged "front-line service," as did the National League of Cities. Both, however, urged that "appropriate local governmental units be designated as the channel through which projects in the antipoverty program be proposed, submitted, and co-ordinated."[35]

Similarly, the five Democratic governors who rendered favorable testimony displayed, according to one observer, "almost unmitigated optimism concerning the poverty proposals; and, whatever the vagueness of the guarantees, all seemed confident of their ability to deal with the federal

[33] *Economic Opportunity Act of 1964,* Hearings before the House Committee on Education and Labor, 88th Cong., 2d Sess., 1964, 1, pp. 22–25. See also Roger Davidson and John Bibby, *On Capitol Hill,* Holt, New York, 1967, chap. 7.

[34] *Economic Opportunity Act of 1964 Hearings,* vol. 2, pp. 766–767, 825. Mayors included Daley (Chicago), Walsh (Syracuse), Cavanaugh (Detroit), Tucker (St. Louis), Wagner (New York), and Briley (Nashville).

[35] Ibid., pp. 780, 790. See National League of Cities, *National Municipal Policy of 1964,* Washington, D.C., 1965, p. 22.

government."[36] Kentucky's Breathitt expressed no apprehension whatsoever that the legislation was drafted to circumvent state government. Governor Edmund Brown of California admitted, on the other hand, that "it might be well to spell out certain safeguards to preserve . . . the appropriate role for state government."[37] As important as the poverty program was to become to federal-state relations, the governors gave the legislation only fleeting consideration at the 1964 National Governors' Conference meeting, passing a rather weak resolution which called for a measure of state control over the new program.

The poverty program thus received the endorsement of state-local political figures and their respective national organizations. The momentum behind the legislation permitted little time for extensive hearings and debate. Public officials' support, or even their reservations concerning guarantees for participation by state-local-county political executives, had scant impact upon the final shape of the legislation or its enactment.

General expectations of these subnational political leaders, of course, varied considerably depending upon their position, party, region, size of constituency, and ideological disposition. Thus many city-county officials envisioned community action to be something analogous to the New Deal's public works programs, only directed at human development stressing jobs and education. Like the New Deal programs, the emphasis would be upon dispersement of perquisites as expeditiously as possible, requiring such new political machinery as found in CAAs, with sufficient flexibility to bypass recalcitrant state officials and bureaucracies where necessary to do so. Large-city mayors, mostly liberal Democrats, expected to gain most from the federal-local program. The party would be able to maintain or expand its urban constituency while its political leaders would be rewarded by the program's beneficiaries. The governors, predictably, were split along party lines. Most were unaware of the degree to which the states had been cut out of the program by design and intent. Some were satisfied with the State Technical Assistance provisions in the legislation (federal funds, in part for the governors' personal use) and the protection of a gubernatorial veto over programs and contracts. In any event, state-local chief executives tended to read in the legislation what they chose to, many confident that OEO under congressional surveillance would work eventually to their benefit.

OEO began operations under considerable congressional pressure to show immediate results. It quickly dispensed the greater part of its one-year, $800-million appropriation to often hastily constructed and planned

---

[36] Roger Davidson, "Creative Federalism and the War on Poverty," paper delivered at the Sixty-Third Annual Meeting of the American Political Science Association, Chicago, Ill., September 6, 1967, p. 4.

[37] Economic Opportunity Act of 1964 Hearings, vol. 2, p. 993; 3, pp. 389–390. Governors included Breathitt, Brown, Sanford (N. Carolina), Hoff (Vt.), and Welch (Ind.).

local agencies. It became readily apparent, however, in OEO's initial grants and contracts, that general-purpose units of government, public agencies, and elected officials were being barred from the planning, development, and administration of antipoverty activities. Then occurred a series of events in 1965 which produced a national outcry from state-local chief executives. Militants captured antipoverty agencies. OEO refused to designate Midwest public agencies as local poverty units. Confrontations flared in Newark, Syracuse, San Francisco, Oakland, and dozens of other cities between antipoverty organizations and city hall. Widespread rioting rocked Los Angeles and other places.

The mayors were irate and turned their wrath upon OEO. A resolution at the USCM's 1965 meeting accusing OEO's Shriver of "fostering class struggle" was barely tabled in favor of a high-level meeting between the mayors' special antipoverty committee, headed by Mayor Daley, with Vice President Humphrey and OEO officials to seek resolution of these matters.[38] Both mayors' organizations endorsed resolutions exhorting OEO to recognize city hall-endorsed local agencies as the proper channel for community action projects.

The worst fears of many local officials had been confirmed. They had sensed at the outset that if the poor, minority groups, civil rights organizations, and militants were given outside impetus to organize and direct their own interests, the mayors' control if not their political support base would be jeopardized. If the mayors possessed the power at that time to abolish community action altogether, they likely would have chosen to do so.

The attitudes of governors and county officials differed in degree rather than kind. They had awakened to the antistate and anticounty bias built into the structure and implementation of CAAs. Moreover, with state-local welfare, health, planning, and employment agencies subjected to attack in several areas by community action groups, these public officials and their professional organizations appealed to political executives, to Congress, and to their federal counterparts to put an end to OEO's circumvention of traditional governmental structures and bypassing of general-purpose units of government.

Following Congress's amendment of the governors' veto power—which was replaced by a discretionary "override" provision for possible use by the OEO director—the governors were equally rebellious. They fought determinedly for retention of the existing veto provisions, threatening open warfare on the program if further diminution of the governors' power to veto proposed antipoverty projects continued. Both Shriver and the President were compelled to intervene. They assured the governors, especially the Democratic ones, that their opinions on future programs would be solicited.

[38] See John Donovan, *The Politics of Poverty*, Pegasus, New York, 1967, chap. 3.

Large- and small-city mayors also joined forces against the poverty program from a diversity of motives. In addition to ideological or partisan reasons, many saw it as a diversion of jobs, patronage, and federal monies from municipal treasuries. But for most, it was a question of political power, couched in terms of public accountability, responsibility, and governmental authority. While even strong city mayors had difficulty in asserting control over local agencies and municipal employees, they could hardly be expected to support quasi-public, independent instrumentalities and a new federal bureaucracy which were threatening to undermine their control and the legitimacy of public institutions. Indeed, the program spelled a further breakdown in traditional federal structures and the downgrading of state governments to governors and state officials. It represented to them a siphoning off of federal funds. Republican governors were even more hostile, convinced that the program was a partisan effort designed by Democrats to reward their urban constituency through a special pipeline to the cities.

Mayors Get the Upper Hand

By late 1965 more than 600 CAAs were in operation, less than 15 percent run directly by city or county governments. The low point in relations between OEO and political executives had been reached. But the politics of federalism began taking hold. Protests, sit-ins, street confrontations, and civil disturbances, justifiably or not, were linked to community action programs. Cases of corruption and waste, impressions that distributive benefits were for minorities exclusively, and urban riots—all fanned by the media—contributed to the mounting opposition to the program. Public outcry against the program was translated into demands upon Congress for action, undermining the fragile consensus upon which the legislation had been constructed. Angry denunciations by state-local public officials added further to the growing disenchantment. Governors, mayors, and county officials organized to use party, bureaucratic, and congressional allies in bringing the program more under their control. During the next twelve months, OEO's personnel, guidelines, operating procedures, and administration underwent significant changes both at the local and national levels.

Beginning with the naming of Vice President Humphrey as the Administration's liaison to local officials, the mayors were to have, as Humphrey himself put it, "a built-in special agent" on the poverty program.[39] Meeting with mayors, county executives, and their national organizations, he em-

---

[39] See Jules Witcover and Erwain Kroll, "Politics and the Poor: Shriver's Second Thoughts," *The Reporter,* December 30, 1965, pp. 22–25.

phasized that no group, not even the poor, was to control local poverty efforts. The mayors, if attentive in performing their executive functions, could set the boundaries and control the direction of Community Action Programs (CAPs) through appointments to their governing boards. OEO formalized its own liaison with the Washington-based government interest groups by creating a Public Officials Advisory Council (POAC) comprising mayors, governors, county officials, and city managers. In setting the agenda for the POAC, the interest groups met frequently with OEO officials to review the agency's guidelines, publications, regulations, and pending congressional amendments to the poverty legislation. OEO also tightened administrative controls over CAPs. It instituted checkpoints procedures to ensure that project applicants cleared proposals with local chief executives, firmly prohibited any further partisan political activity by OEO employees, and transferred certain OEO regional personnel found objectionable by local officials.[40]

Thus by 1966, most mayors, directly or indirectly, were in full command of local antipoverty programs. It had become clear that an independent CAP controlled by the poor was not a viable organization. A CAP could not serve two masters: the poor on the one hand and established agencies and local public officials on the other. Experiences differed, but generally, where OEO had first attempted to mediate between militant takeovers and city hall, it was now siding with the latter by forcing the merger of competing applications and programs. The balance of power had clearly swung in the direction of the mayors. By 1966, in fact, the USCM openly encouraged its members to carry out effectively the spirit of the participation requirement.[41] To many observers this indicated that the mayors had ascended to position of control over local CAAs.

Moreover, bureaucratic and congressional forces had successfully split the various OEO programs into separate entities, obviating any possible coordination function CAPs may have provided. Community action agencies were stripped of an identifiable constituency and hence were vulnerable to congressional and local official pressures. OEO was embarked on a survival strategy. Its protector, ironically, became the nation's mayors. Community action in most cases had constituted much less of an actual political challenge than originally believed. Local political systems proved more resilient to challenges than expected, more accommodating, cooptive, and absorptive of OEO activities than the mayors had figured. In the

---

[40] U.S. Office of Economic Opportunity, *Community Action Guide*, vol. I, Government Printing Office, 1965, pp. 40–41. See also U.S. Office of Economic Opportunity, "Memo 23–23 Governing OEO Personnel," Washington, D.C., March, 1966.

[41] See United States Conference of Mayors, *Economic Opportunity in Cities*, U.S. Conference of Mayors, Washington, D.C., 1966; and Advisory Commission on Intergovernmental Relations, *Intergovernmental Relations in the Poverty Program*, Government Printing Office, 1966, pp. 54–55.

wake of the 1966–1967 riots, many mayors had concluded that if CAAs did not exist, they would have to be invented.[42] Some functional equivalent was needed to sustain liaison between public officials and the ghettos, and CAAs often filled the need.

It was the 1966 congressional debates over the poverty program which galvanized this turnabout and the fear of the loss of federal funds and riots which sustained it. The President proposed a mere $250-million in-increase in OEO's budget for fiscal 1967, which signaled the administration's retreat from its domestic war and the impact of its foreign one. While both houses approved the full $1.75 billion requested by the President, the House Appropriations Committee sliced up the program, scaling appropriations down to $1.56 billion. The impact of this cutback was made patently clear by OEO's Shriver, when he detailed publicly how much each major city would stand to lose if the cuts were sustained. Subsequent House-Senate battles over OEO funding and earmarking of programs unified the riot-weary mayors into a full-scale lobbying operation in support of the program. Mayors Lindsay and Cavanagh declared the USCM-NLC's enthusiastic support for the continuation of the community action program before congressional committees. Thus was completed the mayors' nearly total reversal from positions held the previous year.[43] As OEO's legal counsel Don Baker observed of the OEO-mayors alliance, "They became our strongest and most effective support before Congress and, in effect, saved the program on several occasions from complete emasculation."[44]

Governors and NACO against the Mayors

The anti-city hall attitude having been subdued, OEO confronted a new alliance of state and county officials who sought further restructuring of the program to meet their needs. From their perspective it seemed as if OEO had established its own system of local government, one bent on disrupting and competing with traditional state-county services and agencies. The National Association of Counties, with members and functional affiliates in nearly all the nation's counties, launched a formidable grass-roots attack upon OEO, calling for total involvement of existing county

[42] Daniel P. Moynihan, *Maximum Feasible Misunderstanding*, Free Press, New York, 1969, pp. 156–157.

[43] *Hearings on Amendments to the Economic Opportunity Act of 1964*, before the Subcommittee on Employment, Manpower and Poverty, Senate Labor and Public Welfare Committee, 89th Cong., 2d Sess., 1966, p. 742; and *Federal Role in Urban Affairs*, Hearings before the Subcommittee on Executive Reorganization, Senate Government Operations Committee, 89th Cong., 2d Sess., 1966, pt. III, p. 636.

[44] Don Baker, personal interview at the U.S. Office of Economic Opportunity, Washington, D.C., January 31, 1969.

structures and agencies in the poverty program. Reflecting the views of its affiliated organizations in the health and welfare guilds, NACO reasserted its policy that the alleviation of poverty should begin at the county level.[45] Even in 1967, three-quarters of the counties had not organized CAP programs, while existing programs usually lacked elected county representatives. In effect, few of the measures that had appeased the mayors had reached the counties. They had lost employees to higher-paying OEO positions, been called upon to fund discontinued poverty activities, and been generally bypassed in planning and administering portions of the program.

The governors also felt new political muscle in a setting more conducive to making their claims felt upon OEO. Midterm elections had given Republicans control of several statehouses and governorships and had left a Congress more sympathetic to the states' position. Seeking to reverse Great Society programs that had bypassed the states, the governors' NGC lobbying operation focused upon the poverty program as one of its principal targets. Governors and county officials thus were united by a common goal, that of reorganizing the poverty program. Their collaborative efforts centered upon two issues: how to enable elected public officials to participate meaningfully in the poverty program. and how to cut in the states, and thereby the counties, on a greater portion of control and responsibility for the total poverty effort. Both these issues were to come up before succeeding Congresses.

Elected Official Control

The controversy over who should run community action agencies intensified in 1967 in spite of congressional efforts to clarify the situation the previous year. Predictably, the crucial test was decided in the House, where opposition to OEO had always been the strongest. An amendment proposed by Representative Edith Green (D-Ore.), the second-ranking Democrat on the Education and Labor Committee and perennial OEO critic, provided that CAAs be a state or political subdivision of a state. It further specified that community action boards be limited to fifty-one members, one-third of whom would be public officials, including chief elected officials. The so-called Green amendment weathered acrimonious House debates and a House-Senate Conference on the poverty legislation, tempered only by minor modifications.[46]

---

[45] See James L. Martin, "Let's Reorganize the War on Poverty," *American County Government,* February 1967, pp. 14–18; and National Association of Counties, American County Platform, National Association of Counties, Washington, D.C., 1967, pp. 11–12.

[46] *Public Law 90-222,* sec. 210-211. Modifications included that OEO could fund private groups where public officials failed to carry out a program and the effective date was moved ahead to February 1, 1969.

The mayor's organizations initially supported the amendment provided that control be optional, not mandatory as originally proposed. But the mayors, who had called for a provision like the Green amendment since 1964, eventually shied away from lobbying for its passage. Most mayors were able to control CAAs by this time through the appointive process and by other means. The Green amendment might upset the delicate balance many had worked out by requiring public hearings, enabling legislation, and official mayoralty involvement in the controlling agency. Heat also would be taken off OEO, the favorite whipping boy of local officials, and instead placed upon local government officials who would be held accountable for scandals and all CAA activities. Another reason for backing off from this amendment was the mayors' fear that local government control over OEO programs would lead to congressional requirement of local fiscal support.[47]

Thus, once the implications of this amendment were fully understood, the mayors sought modifications of its restrictive intent and greater flexibility in its application. It is notable that in spite of successful enactment of the Green amendment, few mayors opted for transfer of OEO programs from the private, nonprofit corporation to local public agency control.

In addition to congressional and bureaucratic supporters of the amendment, governors and county officials were its principal backers. The governors operated most effectively upon Senate Republicans and the House Republican leadership, especially Congressman Quie, ranking Republican on Education and Labor, and Charles Goodell, Director of the Republican Planning and Research Committee. NACO, the most persistent OEO critic among the government interest groups, organized county officials nationally behind the amendment. In short, far from being a "city hall provision" as some observers maintained, the passage of the Green amendment was largely attributable to the work of county and state officials operating in a congressional setting ripe for reprisals against the program.[48]

The passage of the Green amendment in 1967 may have saved the program temporarily from more drastic revisions. A state-run and state-administered poverty program, whether administered directly by OEO or—as in the Republican's "Opportunity Crusade"—by old-line departments, had been advocated by House Republicans and a handful of Democrats from the very beginning. In 1969 Congress again debated extension of the poverty program. But the legislative climate had changed consider-

---

[47] See U.S. Comptroller General, *Review of the Economic Opportunity Programs,* Comptroller General's Office, Washington, D.C., 1969, p. 54. It is notable that only 34 of 1,012 community action agencies were governmental instrumentalities by June 30, 1968.

[48] See *Congressional Quarterly,* **25:**254, December 15, 1967; and Bernard Hillenbrand, "Why We Support the Green Amendment," *American County Government,* February 1968, p. 10.

ably in the wake of a new Republican administration, one dedicated to a New Federalism in which the states were to be given a more prominent position in intergovermental programs.

Fulfilling his campaign pledge to restructure the poverty agency, President Nixon called for the transfer of four OEO programs to regular line departments; Head Start, Health Services, and Foster Grandparents were given to HEW and Job Corps to Labor. He otherwise proposed a two-year continuation of existing OEO programs, including community action, pending further study and review. But following an apparent agreement among the White House, liberal Democrats, and congressional leaders over this compromise with retention of community action under city control, a bipartisan group of OEO critics led by Representatives Green, Quie, Ayres, and Giaimo unveiled a substitute bill that would give the states control over the entire program. Indeed, the issue of state versus local control had emerged at the forefront of congressional debate. For nearly two weeks in December the resolution of this issue remained unclear.

Once again, the government interest groups and their members lobbied vigorously, this time with the mayors opposed by the governors and county officials. The governors and their allies argued the advantages of greater state involvement, the benefits of maintaining the federal system, the importance of public official accountability. Mrs. Green charged OEO with a "serious breach of congressional intent" by not fully implementing the 1967 amendments.[49] For NGC, whose ranks included the postwar high of thirty-one Republican governors, it was a final showdown in its efforts to achieve state control by congressional fiat. The USCM-NGC, led by Mayors Daley, Lindsay, Stokes, and Lugar, protested bitterly over a possible takeover by the states, arguing that the states had demonstrated their unresponsiveness to the needs of the poor, particularly those in urban slums.

Caught between the pressures of the Republican governors, a new OEO director who called the substitute crippling, and the various congressional factions, the President emphasized that OEO Director Don Rumsfeld deserved the opportunity to develop his own program. Apparently placating some Republican opponents, Rumsfeld promised Republican House leaders he would see to it that the Green amendment would be revived and the states provided with a much stronger voice in OEO programs.[50] Thus the two-year extension of OEO passed Congress, its defenders in retreat.

---

[49] Public letter from Congresswoman Edith Green to Carl Perkins, Chairman of the House Committee on Education and Labor, dated February 17, 1968. See also Edith Green, "Who Should Administer the War on Poverty," *American County Government,* January 1968, pp. 9–10.

[50] Public letter from OEO Director Donald Rumsfeld to Representative John Anderson, Chairman of the House of Republican Conference, dated December 12, 1969.

Remaining programs clearly were to be shared in some way with state and county governments.

The poverty program, from the perspective of the government interest groups, passed through at least three stages of development between 1964 and 1969. In its early phase, state-local chief executives were essentially nonparticipants. This was followed by a period where public official control was on the ascendancy, led first by the mayors and then soon after by governors and county officials. Next, a new phase began where state and urban forces battled over the distribution of federal resources, both political and economic. Each of these periods coincided with legislative fighting within Congress over OEO, in the House especially, where the issues of public official control and state-run as opposed to local-run programs were brought into sharp perspective. These stages also had counterparts to infighting within the executive over changing policies at OEO, its increased dependence on the mayors for support, the spinoff of OEO programs to old-line departments, and transition to a Republican administration.

FURTHER DEVELOPMENTS

With regulatory discretion over IDBs delegated to the Treasury Department, the government interest groups' fears that advocacy bureaucrats might work against their interests materialized. Industrial aid bond financing virtually dried up in 1969, shrinking from $1.6 billion in the previous year to roughly $50 million the next. In its enthusiasm to close off IDBs, Treasury included several traditional areas of bond financing which governors, mayors, and county officials felt had transgressed congressional intent. They appealed to Congress to redefine IDBs lest Treasury move unimpeded into all areas of tax-exemption in state-local bonds.

The tax-exempt issue arose in Congress once again in 1969, when the House Ways and Means Committee reviewed the Nixon administration's tax reform legislation. Ways and Means devised a federal subsidy plan to encourage state and local governments to issue taxable bonds in competition with corporate bonds, with the differences in higher bond interests being subsidized by the federal government. The ABA, Municipal Finance Officers' Association, and the government interest groups joined forces to get the Senate Finance Committee to drop consideration of this Treasury-backed subsidy plan. Led by Governor Dan Evans (R-Wash.), Chairman of the NGC Executive Management and Fiscal Affairs Committee, the governors descended on Capitol Hill to help beat back this proposed tax reform. The coalition played down Treasury's estimate of federal savings and prospective tax yield, emphasizing instead the long-term consequences for state and local taxpayers in higher borrowing costs. Prevailing in this round, the government groups awaited the next, which would surely come.

Treasury, the government groups, and the financial community seem to agree that the existing municipal bond market, as presently constituted, would not likely to able to satisfy the growing capital financing needs of states, localities, and other public-related institutions in the near future.[51] Congress had earlier considered a proposed federal Urban Development Bank, a new federal agency which would be authorized to purchase, service, and sell taxable obligations of state and local governments to finance capital expenditures for public works and facilities serving community needs. This proposal and others are being considered by Congress as all interested parties seek to develop a workable program that would provide a subsidy to state and local bonds that are sold on a taxable basis and would compete in the bond market with corporate bonds. The government groups probably will not offer too much opposition to such a plan as long as participation is strictly voluntary, free of delay and federal interference in local matters, and the financial advantage of tax exempts are not diminished.[52]

Meanwhile, the IDB issue was not finished. When Congress cut off all large municipal financing for privately owned companies, it left open a gray area: that of financing state and local air and water pollution control improvements through tax-exempt pollution-control bonds. The imposition of stricter federal, state, and local government pollution-control standards created enormous problems for government and industry in financing improvements necessary to meet these standards. A marriage of convenience was struck, therefore, between local industry, state-local governments, and Treasury whereby IDBs could be used by local governments to finance pollution-control programs. Municipalities are permitted thus far to sell corporate bonds as long as they use the money to build pollution-control equipment like scrubbing towers, sludge handlers, dust-bag houses, and the like. Money raised from bond sales goes to the local government that is putting up the equipment. The government then leases the facilities to a corporation under contract designed to pay off interest as it comes due and finally the principal. The company's lease money goes to the municipality which, in turn, sends the investor the tax-free interest.

Bond ratings are based on the corporation instead of the community, which means that large corporations like Ford Motor, U.S. Steel, Union Carbide, and others gain high ratings while the companies gain a considerable cost saving. Mayors and county officials as well as major unions

[51] See Advisory Commission on Intergovernmental Relations, *Federal Approaches to Aid State and Local Capital Financing,* Government Printing Office, 1970.

[52] *Housing and Urban Development Legislation 1971, Hearings before the Subcommittee on Housing,* House Banking and Currency Committee, 92nd Cong., 1st Sess., 1971, pp. 512, 524.

supported this form of bond exemption, in contrast to the 1968 IDB controversy, in that funds are used to retain existing companies instead of
pirating new industry from state to state. Corporations are allowed to de-
duct depreciation on the pollution-control facilities as if they owned them
and to take advantage of federal investment tax credit. Neither Congress
nor state-local governments were prepared to fully and directly finance
pollution abatement programs to meet prescribed standards, so they too
seemed to accept, if not encourage, this financing arrangement.

Thus by early 1973 pollution control financing through tax-exempt
bonds exceeded $1 billion, with the likelihood that it would surpass the
high of $1.6 billion in IDBs reached in 1968. Wall Street observers, in fact,
ventured that the amount of pollution-control bonds through privately held
offerings far exceeded public offerings, which means that the total amount
of bonds outstanding is more like several billion dollars' worth. With the
backing of these bonds by the credit standing of the corporate recipient
rather than the municipality, many prestigious bond houses that had
previously spurned IDBs could be found in the pollution-control underwriting business. Indeed, what Treasury had helped take away with one
hand was returned with another. This time, however, industry, Wall
Street, labor, and the government interest groups could be found in
support.

Returning to group involvement in OEO, their interest in its programs
peaked in 1969. This marked the high point in the governors' efforts to
gain state control over the agency's programs. The House barely defeated
a state control substitute amendment in 1969, while the Senate approved
a gubernatorial veto over OEO's legal services programs. Conferees deleted this amendment and earmarked all the agency's FY 1970 funds to
hamper the Nixon administration's reorganization efforts.

OEO Director Don Rumsfeld tried to move the agency in a new direction
in 1969–1970 by bringing governors, mayors, and county officials into
the agency's programs on a more supportive basis. This met with strong
congressional opposition. OEO discontinued many community action programs while merging others with Model Cities programs under mayoral
control. To legitimize this move, OEO contracted with the USCM-NLC
to survey members, requesting their opinions on whether the merger
should take place. The mayors overwhelmingly supported this action as
long as the transfer did not involve a net reduction in community action
funds. To assure this, USCM quietly reversed its earlier opposition to
congressional earmarking of OEO funds by siding with congressional
efforts to maintain strict earmarking.[53]

Nevertheless OEO was embarked on a survival course from the very
onset of the Nixon Presidency. The President reluctantly agreed to a two-

[53] National Journal, 3:1869–1875, September 11, 1971.

year extension for OEO in 1969 to give the director time to remodel the agency into "an incubator" for the administration's new policies.[54] Congress remained steadfast in efforts to block reorganization, which only further added to the administration's resolve to terminate the agency. The Nixon administration wished to approach the nation's social-welfare problems from an income maintenance strategy, as in the President's proposed family assistance plan, rather than through a federal service strategy such as community action.

OEO continued to flounder in this clash between the White House and Capitol Hill Democrats over the agency's mission and programs. The President informed Congress that he wanted to make OEO's social research and demonstration operations part of his staff. Congressional Democrats had other ideas.[55] They preserved OEO as an operating service agency by specifying in the 1971 OEO extension that the administration could make no further transfer of programs. Funds for all fifteen OEO categorical programs were earmarked to impede budgetary shifts or cutbacks by the White House.

Failing to gain approval for his proposals, the President called for further retrenchment and dissolution of the agency in 1971. Some of OEO's programs were to be folded into new Departments—Community Development and Human Resources—while others would be discontinued. OEO would cease to exist, in effect, through reorganization and special revenue-sharing programs unless states and localities wished to fund these programs themselves. More than a hundred national organizations came to OEO's defense during the 1971 congressional hearings on OEO's extension. Congress challenged the administration by doubling the agency's budgetary requests, earmarking all funds in a strict manner, and adding to its authorizations a new multibillion-dollar comprehensive child development program. The President vetoed the bill in December 1971, only to have Congress approve OEO funding in a supplemental appropriation through June 30, 1973.

After nearly a decade of controversy, OEO, once hailed as a major instrumentality for alleviating the nation's poverty, passed from center stage in Congress to a sideshow of executive-legislative wills. The government interest groups had, for the most part, lost interest in the outcome. Several major OEO programs that they supported had previously been spun off to old-line departments, and in the cases of Head Start and manpower programs, were likely to survive in one form or another. CAPs had become a hollow shell, with the great majority of federal support siphoned off into salaries and overhead. Some mayors, of course, were concerned

---

[54] See President Nixon's "Welfare Speech," August 8, 1969, as reported in *Congressional Quarterly*, **28**:1018, April 17, 1970.

[55] See *National Journal*, **2**:2550–2553, November 21, 1970.

precisely about this aspect of OEO. Loss of funds would probably mean considerable pressure upon city hall from unemployed poverty workers and community organizations to get local funding for these programs. A handful of governors still complained about the intransigency of OEO legal workers and OEO-led class-action suits pending against states. But the government interest groups had moved on to concerns over cutbacks in other federal programs where the prospects of winning seemed better.

President Nixon's announcement that no further funds would be made available to OEO after June 30, 1973, caught few observers by surprise. After five OEO directors, the President appointed one who was committed to physically dismantling the agency and thoroughly discrediting its programs. Once again, however, Congress seemed determined to keep OEO alive, even if it meant continuing the agency as a shadow of its former self. Aided by court rulings and congressional opposition to executive impoundment of OEO funds, OEO seemed destined to struggle along, but it was still on a survival course.

Finally the 1968 Highway Act, as it developed, constituted a mere battle skirmish for what followed. As public opposition to the highway program mounted, exacerbated by the emerging strength of the environmental lobby, the mayors gathered new allies in their quest for mass transit funding. The battle cry became "balanced transportation," which meant for mass transit advocates that the $5-billion-a-year highway trust fund expenditures be counterbalanced by a comparable expenditure for other modes of rapid transit. Indeed, mass transit began replacing urban renewal by the early 1970s as some mayors' highest federal priority. Former Secretary of Transportation Alan S. Boyd would go so far as to proclaim that "cities have no future without mass transit facilities."[56] Many large and even smaller cities and their mayors came to believe in this prophecy.

Congress deferred action in 1969 on the highway program, in part to await congressional action on the Urban Mass Transit Act (UMTA). The 1964 Mass Transit Act authorized federal grants and loans to states and localities for improvements to rail, bus, or other transit systems which operated through a public transportation authority. The program remained vastly underfunded, with only $200 million being expended annually as of 1970. This was spread among dozens of cities on a two-thirds federal and one-third local matching basis. In light of the mayors' earlier involvement in seeking UMTA appropriations and the 1968 Highway Act battle, they at first were convinced that nothing short of a separate mass transit or shared transportation trust fund would meet their growing needs. Stymied by the Appropriations Committees' opposition to another trust fund and providing long-term contract authority to localities in advance

[56] *Congressional Quarterly*, **28**:1018, April 17, 1970.

of specific congressional appropriations, they confronted the rather bleak prospect of seeking incremental gains through UMTA authorizations. Thus the mayors, joined by NACO, pressured Congress on two fronts: increasing mass transit funding through the regular authorization-appropriations process and breaking open the Highway Trust Fund for mass transit use.

The mass transit trust fund idea had a host of supporters. Mayor James D. Braman, USCM-NLC leader on the 1968 Highway Act battle, was named Assistant Secretary of Transportation in 1969 and emerged as the leading in-house advocate for mass transit within the new Nixon administration. Braman and DOT Secretary John Volpe argued the case within the White House for a new trust fund—later a unified trust fund covering all modes of transportation—and a much expanded UMTA program. To the mayors' surprise, President Nixon responded to their appeals by asking Congress for a $10-billion, twelve-year mass transit program to be financed from general revenues instead of a separate trust fund.

The mayors and their allies agreed to work within the confines of the Nixon proposal as long as they could gain a favorable disposition of the key contract authority issue. Only Congress generally, and the Appropriations Committees specifically, could grant such authority to executive agencies or departments, which allows them to incur obligations prior to actual appropriations. Without such authority, states and muncipalities would have to rely on a year-by-year federal commitment to fund the program. This, among other things, would be a deterrent to local business community support and likely voter support for approving mass transit bond issues. The Nixon administration, cognizant of the budgetary implications of long-term authority, reluctantly agreed to congressional approval of the $3.1 billion proposed for the first five years of the program being obligated in the first year lest the mayors and their allies withdraw support. A realignment of congressional subsystems enabled the mayors to achieve what they had been denied in the past. The transfer of the Urban Mass Transit Administration from HUD to DOT in 1968 meant that appropriations oversight shifted from Joe Evins's Independent Offices Subcommittee —a largely rural-dominated subcommittee—to a new Transportation Subcommittee with greater urban representation and the pro-transit leadership of Representative Edward Boland (D-Mass.). Negotiations between Boland, the mayors, and other members of the full committee gained approval for the five-year contract authority, provided that DOT and UMTA supply the subcommittee with a detailed work plan for obligating funds in subsequent years. Thus the subcommittee retained its influence to oversee the transit agency's operations, which the White House feared might turn into a multibillion-dollar pork barrel arrangement with DOT subjected to congressional logrolling. Nevertheless, Congress passed and the President signed the 1970 Urban Mass Transit Act. The mayors responded by providing both the administration and the Appropriations Committees with a waiting list of local public authorities in seventeen states which fully expected first crack at the funds.[57]

This act amounted to a significant victory for the mayors and their mass transit allies. However, it was only an opening wedge in meeting their transit problems. Rising costs, increased fares, reduced services, and fewer riders were killing off local transit. Only massive federal subsidization of operating transit deficits would reverse this cycle in many mayors' eyes. "Federal subsidies are the only way," noted NLC's Pritchard. "If we don't get some blood transfusions this year for mass transit, we'll need embalming fluid next year."[58] Efforts to gain federal subsidies failed in 1970, when a House-Senate conference struck $150 million from a three-year authorization for this program. The mayors renewed their efforts to gain inclusion of subsidies in the Housing and Urban Development Act of 1972, only to have the effort once again fall short as the bill failed to pass at the session's end.

The alternative strategy pursued by the mayors in gaining congressional commitment to long-term mass transit financing was through the Federal Highway Act. With the multibillion-dollar Highway Trust Fund (HTF) Act up for renewal in 1972, heated debate erupted in Congress over its future course. The stakes were sizable, since decisions might well shape the nation's transportation system for decades. Among the principal issues before the Congress were these: Should the HTF be continued past 1972, and if so, in what form and for how long? If the fund continued, how would the funds be allocated between competing highway programs — interstate, urban, state, and rural? Should the HTF be merged in favor of a total transportation fund including highways, air, and mass transit, or should trust funds merely be diverted to other transportation programs? If the latter, should they be restructured to highway-related transit systems and uses like bus transportation, or should they be used for rail systems as well? Congress and the Nixon administration were divided internally on these issues, and there were shifting alliances with outside groups ranging from defenders of the status quo to those who advocated abolition of the HTF or significant transformation of its use to more pressing transit priorities.

The well-organized highway lobby — oil, auto, and construction industries; state highway engineers and others — insisted that the HTF be maintained and used only for highway-related purposes. They would cite studies indicating that billions were presently needed for completion and updating of the nation's highways as well as to provide for national economic consequences from diverting the HTF for other purposes. The opposition consisted of the mass transit coalition which originally included the mayors, the American Transit Association, the Institute for Rapid Transit, and the Railway Progress Institute; these had been joined by conservationists, environmentalists, urban planners, and the Highway Action Coalition. As evidenced from the successful mass transit legislation, the mayors tactfully broadened their coalition, directing their mass transit appeal at suburban interests and suburban congressmen.[59]

Not only the highway lobby but also the government groups were divided as to strategies. The USCM-NLC supported the use of HTF funds for highway-related purposes as long as it contained a greater urban emphasis. However, several large-city mayors wanted to go all out for breaking open the HTF for mass transit use. NACO wanted the interstate share limited and emphasis instead placed on secondary or county roads, with a new metropolitan aid system for highways which the mayors also supported. The governors, on the other hand, began their gradual march toward support for a unified transportation trust fund with distribution allocated through states and governors in accordance with each state's own transportation needs. DOT Secretary Volpe promoted the idea of a unified transportation trust fund inclusive of all modes of transit, even though the Federal Highway Administration within his own department bitterly denounced the idea. The White House seemed more concerned with controlling HTF spending and the economic implications of rising federal expenditures on transit than on developing a comprehensive policy governing the nation's transportation systems.

The White House and Volpe thus pursued a moderate, flexible course, that of curtailing any long-term highway commitments and that of expanding the use of the highway fund for highway-related purposes. The passage of the 1970 Urban Mass Transit Act removed temporarily some of the pressure inside and outside of Congress for breaking open the HTF. Thus bargaining within Congress and between the Public Works Committees over the 1970 Federal Aid Highway Act led to rather minor changes in the overall highway program. The Senate, White House, and mayors combined to beat back the more profligate and longer-term House version. The compromise reflected emphasis upon the ABC system and a new urban system rather than priority to completing the interstate system. This pleased NACO and the mayors. The federal share of the noninterstate component was raised from 50 to 70 percent, something the governors supported. The HTF was extended from FY 1974 to FY 1977, with its uses liberalized to include highway safety and bus-lane construction and an expanded TOPICS program. This compromise essentially bought time for all interested parties to regroup—to develop positions and alternatives.

The 92nd Congress convened amid a rash of new proposals to convert

[59] Ibid., 2:1193–1206, June 6, 1970.

the HTF into a transportation trust fund and to give states and metropolitan areas more flexibility in using their share of trust funds. In March 1971, President Nixon proposed a special transportation revenue-sharing program which combined 23 categorical grant programs dealing with transportation into one $2.6-billion package. As a fallback to this controversial overture, the administration proposed a single urban fund for mass transit and highway projects in metropolitan areas beginning with $1 billion in FY 1974 trust funds and progressing to $2.25 billion for FY 1976 through FY 1979. As far as the mayors were concerned, this plan amounted to a sleight-of-hand.[60] The Urban Mass Transit program, passed in the 91st Congress, would be collapsed into one limited pot together with HTF monies apportioned to metropolitan areas. Not only would these funds be spread among 267 SMSAs on a population basis, thereby reducing the concentration of mass transit funds in major metropolitan areas as anticipated from the 1970 Act, but the overall use of these funds would be left to state and metropolitan discretion. The mayors might be disadvantaged on both scores. With the prospect of no new funds and possibly less for mass transit, and funds being scattered broadly instead of concentrated, the city transit interests opposed the Nixon program.

The USCM-NLC were determined to keep the highway and mass transit programs separate at the time both to maximize funding opportunities and to play down the mayoral differences over rail rapid transit versus highway mass transit issues. The mayors then turned to the Banking and Currency Committees, first to increase authorizations for mass transit and then to gain support for funding a mass transit subsidies program. To promote logrolling with the highway interests or at least not unnecessarily antagonize them, the mayors informed Congress that the nation's highway and highway-related mass transit needs were sufficiently great that it would be inappropriate at the time for rail transit to be funded from the HTF. The mayors, nonetheless, applauded Volpe's plan insofar as the HTF was to be used for highway-related programs, assume a greater urban and intracity focus, and place greater control over transit planning and priorities on a metropolitan basis.[61]

Once again the government interest groups were divided. NACO called for a separate mass transit trust fund, which represented a break with the mayors' policies. The NGC supported a single unified transit fund with state allocations placed under the governors. They too opposed the administration's urban fund concept because it downgraded the states' role in urban transportation. Congress also found itself in a muddle as to a course of action. The Senate voted to allow states to use part of the HTF

[60] Ibid., **4**:264–275, February 12, 1972; **4**:484–492, March 18, 1972.

[61] For the government interest groups' positions, see *Proposed 1972 Highway Legislation, Hearings before the Subcommittee on Roads,* Senate Committee on Public Works, 92nd Cong., 2d Sess., 1972, pp. 525–532, 725–737, 792–798.

designated for urban areas to construct subways and rapid rail systems as well as to buy buses. The House barred use of trust funds for these purposes and passed a two-year $16.8-billion highway bill through a parliamentary maneuver which prevented a trust fund diversion amendment from even being voted on. A heated conference produced a one-year extension, but the House failed to obtain a quorum to vote on the compromise, so the legislation did not pass. Also, with the failure of the 1972 Housing Act containing increased federal funds for mass transit and operating subsidies program, all key transit issues were held over to the 93rd Congress.

Repeating the script of the previous session, the House and Senate passed completely different versions of the highway bill. The Senate voted to permit urban areas to use their portion of the trust fund, some $800 million a year, for buying buses, improving rail transit systems, and for other forms of mass transit at local discretion. By a close vote the House voted an extension of the existing legislation devoid of nonhighway diversions from the HTF. After more than two months of negotiations and some twenty-nine meetings among the conferees, House-Senate members agreed upon a three-year extension of the trust fund which allowed $200 million of a reduced urban share from the trust fund to be spent beginning in FY 1975 for express buses; beginning in FY 1976, urban areas could use all or part of the $800 million for any form of mass transit whatsoever. Operating subsidies for mass transit were deleted from the bill, which passed both chambers, so that the mayors, county officials, and urban governors had to pursue operating subsidies through another route. The outcome of this effort remained in doubt by mid-summer 1973.

Thus since 1968 the mayors and their allies have been successful in broadening the use of the Highway Trust Fund beyond highways and roads specifically. In spite of obvious cleavages among the mayors and between them and the other government groups, they have all pulled closer together in pressuring Congress for major changes in the nation's transportation policies. The gradual transformation of public policy involving highways, more than a decade in the making, seems destined to take that long in its gradual but nonetheless significant revision. At the forefront of these changes have been the government interest groups in their federal lobbying activities.

5

GROUP COMPETITION AND WARFARE
IN THE CONGRESS

Probably no single national issue in the period of 1965 to 1968 generated more conflict between governors and mayors in Washington than the 1968 Crime Control and Safe Streets Act. The National Governors' Conference (NGC) proclaimed the outcome of this battle to be its single most important legislative victory during the 90th Congress. The mayors, on the other hand, viewed the final legislation as by far and away their most decisive setback. For President Johnson and the Justice Department, it may well have been the most serious rebuff by Congress on a major administration program during the entire Johnson Presidency.

The very heart of the President's anticrime program involved a series of proposals to provide project grants to local communities for upgrading their law enforcement capabilities. The governors advocated changing this program from its categorical grant form to bloc grants to be distributed by the states to their local communities, with statewide planning placed under the governors' control. The mayors enthusiastically supported the administration's original proposal, however, which would have provided direct federal assistance to localities for such interrelated activities as police recruitment, training, modernization of equipment and facilities, and the reorganization of local law-enforcement agencies.

Mayors and governors and their national organizations disagreed bitterly over such fundamental issues as whether law enforcement responsibilities belonged preeminently to the states or to local governments. They were further divided on whether the states, if they participated in the program, had the needed capacity and experience in comprehensive law-enforcement planning. State-local officials were even further apart on whether the states could be entrusted to disperse federal funds in some equitable manner among their local subdivisions. In the absence of any consensus on these issues, the government interest groups and their allies vied for control over the dispersement of law-enforcement funds. Group competition was heightened by mutual expectations that federal efforts in the law-enforcement area would be expanded considerably in future years. Whatever patterns in federal-state-local government relations were established initially would more than likely prevail thereafter.

Crime as a national political issue first emerged in the 1964 presidential election campaign. Widespread rioting in major cities and FBI crime reports indicating an extraordinary rise in crime expanded the public's awareness of and concern over this problem. By 1968 national polls for the first time indicated that the issue of crime ranked as the most important domestic concern.[1] As crime became more salient as a political issue, the Republicans generally exploited it, blaming the Democrats for inattentiveness and inactivity. More than one observer of this situation, in fact, would comment that the Democratic administration's apparent weakness on law and order was quickly becoming another China of the 1940s, where Democrats incurred a generation of recriminations over the alleged mishandling of the problem.

Soon after his 1964 reelection, President Johnson promised congressional leaders that he would take affirmative action in the anticrime field. In 1965 he established by executive order the President's Commission on Law Enforcement and Administration of Justice under Nicholas Katzenbach, the then Attorney General. This Commission was charged with responsibility for conducting extensive investigations into the causes of crime and for making recommendations for congressional action. In the meantime, the President asked Congress to defer action of its own until the Commission's recommendations were formulated into a comprehensive strategy for legislation.

In light of aroused public sentiment over the crime issue and the scope of the problem, a consensus emerged within the administration and Congress that broad national action would be required even though it was considered the near exclusive jurisdiction of state and local governments. The federal government could no longer remain only partially involved in anticrime efforts, leaving state and local governments to deal with the situation. Instead, a new role for federal assistance and involvement had to be defined. Much of the Commission's final report, therefore, addressed itself to this new role, which included a strategy for aiding state and local governments through financial inducements for comprehensive planning and innovative programs.

---

[1] Richard N. Scammon and Ben J. Wattenberg, *The Real Majority*, Coward-McCann, New York, 1970, p. 17.

THE OMNIBUS CRIME CONTROL AND
SAFE STREETS ACT OF 1968

The President first announced the major anticrime program in his State of the Union Message in January 1967.[2] Adopting most of the findings and recommendations of the Crime Commission, he incorporated them into a special message sent to Congress which spelled out a national program for action. His message contained specific proposals for vastly expanded federal assistance to local law enforcement and criminal justice agencies. The Commission concentrated its focus on the cities, for, as the final report stated, "that is where crime is most prevalent, most feared, and most difficult to control."[3] The President, accordingly, developed the anticrime program around a direct federal-local assistance strategy, with large cities as the principal recipient of proposed demonstration projects and funds for training, education, construction, and general innovation. Entitled the Safe Streets and Crime Control Act—a name calculated to be politically appealing to the Congress—the new program, according to the President, would be modeled along the lines of earlier demonstration efforts in the anticrime field initiated by the Office of Law Enforcement Assistance, an agency in the Justice Department created in 1965 to administer modest project grants.

Major credit for structuring the administration's program can be attributed, of course, to the Crime Commission, but responsibility for its final draft resided in the Department of Justice. The White House had imposed seemingly incompatible instructions upon Justice, however. On the one hand it was to come up with a program that would expedite the transfer of federal funds into racially torn cities like Los Angeles, Detroit, Newark, and elsewhere for riot-control training and equipment. Yet on the other hand, it was asked to devise national legislation sufficiently devoid of a "big-city" orientation as not to alarm suburban and rural interests in the Congress. As a consequence of these conflicting instructions, the final product reflected acknowledgely rather poor draftsmanship and considerable ambiguity. The administration's bill, for example, failed to include an exact title-by-title breakdown on how the first year's $50 million was to be spent or explanation as to why minimum eligibility was to be restricted to individual or combined jurisdictions of more than 50,000 population. Justice was further confused as to what comprehensive planning meant or how it might go about reviewing applications for grant assistance from virtually hundreds of local communities.

[2] See *Crime and Justice in America*, 2d ed., Congressional Quarterly Service, Washington, D.C., 1968, p. 30.

[3] Commission on Law Enforcement and the Administration of Justice, Report of the Commission, *The Challenge of Crime in A Free Society*, Government Printing Office, 1967, p. 279.

Justice's draft of the crime bill, modified somewhat by White House staffers, was thus sent to Congress by the President in February 1967. As proposed, the President's legislation invited substantial amendment by Congress, which the administration nevertheless wished to avoid.

The Administration apparently anticipated early enactment of its anticrime program, which the President had proclaimed as an integral part of his overall Great Society effort. Chairman of the House Judiciary Committee Emanuel Celler (D-N.Y.) endorsed the complete program, indicating that outside of minor clarifying amendments, the bill would probably be reported out of full committee before the summer began. The Senate, however, constituted a more implacable problem for the White House. The Senate Judiciary Committee, the institutional stronghold of Southern Democrats and conservative Republic forces, was viewed as the major hurdle which the legislation had to pass. Several committee members were extremely apprehensive about voting greater federal involvement in law enforcement at the local level. John L. McClellan, Chairman of the Judiciary Subcommittee on Criminal Laws and Procedures to which the administration's bill was assigned, introduced the legislation by "administration request" and without his personal endorsement. This was a clear sign that trouble lay ahead.

It soon became apparent to Justice and the White House that McClellan, who prided himself on being the Senate's fiercest crimebuster, would not allow the opportunity to pass for using this legislation and subsequent hearings as a means to gain full committee and congressional consideration for his own anticrime measures. Hence administration attention focused on the Senate, rather than the House, where McClellan and several colleagues embarked on an extensive campaign to overturn Supreme Court decisions concerning defendants' constitutional rights in criminal actions and to attack personally Ramsey Clark, the Attorney General.

During the spring of 1967, House Judiciary Subcommittee Number Five, also chaired by the full committee chairman Celler, began twelve days of hearings on the administration's bill. In stark contrast to its Senate counterpart, Celler's committee dealt exclusively with the substance of the proposed legislation. Considerable support for the bill came both from the USCM-NLC, led by Mayors Lindsay and Briley, and NACO. Each endorsed the program but expressed reservations about jurisdictional stipulations and the fiscal contributions required from participating local governments. NACO specifically requested that the county be designated the minimal unit eligible for planning grants instead of the 50,000 population limit, which Justice admitted was an arbitrary cutoff line.[4]

---

[4] *Anti-Crime Program*, Hearings before Subcommittee No. 5, House Judiciary Committee, 90th Cong., 1st Sess, 1967, pp. 321–323, 435–442, 499–505.

On the other hand, governors and state attorneys general were conspicuously absent from initial testimony, their prospective positions being taken up by several Republican members on the subcommittee. Ramsey Clark, the administration's principal witness, when questioned about the position of state attorneys general regarding the legislation, countered by stating that they "have no great involvement in the process of administrative justice." When queried further about the governors' involvement, Attorney General Clark indicated strong objection to their participation, noting that "when you look at state government and look at their involvement in local law enforcement, you will see that it is almost nil."[5] The Attorney General's appraisal was essentially correct. By law and tradition governors' involvement in law enforcement had been minimal—limited, as it were, to state police, judicial appointments, and intervention locally in civil disorders or natural calamities. Yet governors since 1965 especially had begun taking a more active role in this area, as the 1965 Law Enforcement Assistance Act provided small grants to each state to form a governor's committee or commission on law enforcement. Thus one of the principal aims of the House hearings was to build a major case on behalf of the proposed federal-local program devoid of state participation or control. This goal seemed to have been accomplished by Celler and his proadministration allies during the hearings.

Nonetheless, the issue of state participation arose during full Judiciary Committee review. Several Republican members such as Cahill (N.J.), MacGregor (Minn.), Mathias (Md.), McClory (Ill.), and Railsback (Ill.) expressed strong reservations about specific provisions in the legislation—for planning, research, and demonstration grants—being so heavily oriented toward a federal-local basis. They objected to bypassing state participation and gubernatorial involvement. As far as these members were concerned, recalling the Attorney General's testimony, the administration had written off the states and instead was using the anticrime measure as a back-door method of financing police training in large riot-torn cities.

Congressman Richard Poff (R-Va.), second-ranking minority member of the committee, took up the case for state involvement. He personally wrote each of the governors, requesting their thoughts and comments about the proposed legislation compared to a state-run anticrime effort financed through bloc grants.[6] In light of efforts by Poff and his Republican colleagues, Chairman Celler adopted several clarifying amendments to the bill to placate committee members and to ward off a floor fight on the state issue. One such amendment cut the governor in on local grant applications for anticrime monies, essentially a review and evaluation role.

[5] Ibid., p. 65.

[6] Ibid., pp. 1425–1443.

Thus the Judiciary Committee's report on the President's bill reflected Celler's efforts to build a consensus among committee members and out-side groups. It stated that the objectives of the legislation had been sup-ported by NACO, the USCM-NLC, and numerous law-enforcement groups as well as "organizations and civic groups in every state."[7]

House Reversal

"Never has the committee chairman been so thoroughly reversed on the floor," was how one observer summed up what happened to the House's senior member and esteemed Judiciary chairman when the committee's bill was virtually rewritten under heated debate. Between July 17 when the Judiciary Committee reported out the anticrime bill and August 8 when the House amended the legislation, a series of events occurred which led to the overturning of Celler and the administration's program.

Having established its Washington lobbying operation in early 1967, the staff of the NGC set as its first priority greater state involvement in the President's anticrime program. In July, NGC staff man Jim Martin met with Congressman William Cahill (R-N.J.) and Tom Railsback (R-Ill.) of the Judiciary Committee to explore the possibilities of turning around the anticrime bill from a federal-local program to a federal-state one. The meeting proved fruitful. It laid the basis for future collaboration between the governors' organization and a group of congressmen sym-pathetic to the NGC position.[8] While minority insurgents on the Judiciary Committee were hopeful that something might be accomplished through floor amendments to the bill, they were dubious about undertaking such a venture without the prior approval of their elected party leaders. Ranking committee Republican William McCulloch (Ohio) fully supported the Administration's version and was not a likely prospect for changing his views. To move against McCulloch without Minority Leader Gerald Ford's blessing, for example, was viewed by Cahill as a futile strategy, possibly further fragmenting the ranks of an already divided opposition party.

Thus Cahill convened a meeting on July 31 of fellow Republicans on the Judiciary Committee, without McCulloch but including Ford, for the purpose of finding out whether sufficient consensus existed for an or-ganized attack upon the anticrime bill. Cahill and Railsback each put forward for the group's approval amendments which would channel crime funds through the states under gubernatorial supervision. Those

---

[7] *Crime and Justice*, p. 18.

[8] James Martin, personal interview at the Washington Office of the National Governors' Conference, January 3, 1969.

present at this secret meeting agreed that the fight should be undertaken provided that a single amendment and formula for dispersing the funds could be developed. Since House floor debate on the anticrime legislation was to begin two days later, Ford gave Cahill and Railsback one day in which to prepare their amendment.[9] The revolt was under way.

Working through the night, Cahill's and Railsback's staffs, after rejecting several highly complicated formulas for distributing grant monies, settled upon a simple one. Federal funds would be distributed on the basis of $100,000 for each state for developing a workable program, while the remaining funds would be apportioned on the basis of each state's population. Circulating the draft of the amendment to Republican members of the Judiciary Committee, the NGC staff, and other prospective allies, Cahill informed Ford that a consensus had been attained.

Surprise was the Republicans' most valuable asset. Neither the Democratic leadership nor the administration anticipated a lengthy floor fight over the bill or serious revision. Ford notified House Speaker McCormack that the Republicans contemplated offering several amendments to the bill, which might have tipped off administration lobbyists that something was brewing. It did not, however. Justice officials who were leading the administration's lobbying efforts had little experience in House floor fights over money bills and moreover did not have a well-developed congressional liaison system, as existed in many departments and agencies for anticipating such uprisings. Thus the administration and its allies were caught completely off guard by what transpired.

Meanwhile, Martin and Charles Byrley, the director of the governors' Washington office, wired all the governors informing them of the importance of the impending House vote, and exhorted them to contact their state delegations in support of greater state involvement in the anticrime program. NGC President John Volpe (R-Mass.) led the governors' fight by organizing them nationally and, with the assistance of his state's Attorney General Elliott Richardson, mobilized state attorneys general and principal state law enforcement officials as well.[10]

The scenario evolved just as the governors had hoped it would. They were provided a perfect opportunity to organize against a Great Society measure which bypassed state governments and their chief executives. Some governors spared no resentment in charging that Attorney General Clark had demeaned their law enforcement role, treating them in his congressional testimony more as chief traffic cops than chief law enforcers. With the exception of two loyal administration supporters, Gov-

[9] U.S. House Office Building, Staff of Congressmen Tom Railsback and William Cahill, private interviews, Washington D.C., February 4, 1969.

[10] Taken from National Governors' Conference Washington files on the crime bill, including letters, telegrams, and other communications from the governors concerning the Cahill amendment.

ernors Richard Hughes (D-N.J.) and Otto Kerner (D-Ill.), unanimous support poured in from the state chief executives on behalf of the amendment to substitute a state-run bloc grant program for the administration's federal-local one. The governors were further aided in their cause by NACO. Under strong pressure from members who were aroused by the implicit big-city orientation in the legislation, that organization threw its support to the states' position.

The House spent two days debating the anticrime bill prior to voting on specific amendments. Celler reaffirmed the findings of his committee, namely that the states had little previous experience, expertise, or past record in the law enforcement area to handle the scope of responsibilities called for in the legislation. He was countered by arguments from Democrats and Republicans alike who opposed further federal intervention in local government and warned against the prospects of a federalized police force as the legislation's consequence. Debate revealed little new except that Celler had rather weak support, deserted as he was by many liberal allies who either abstained from participation or absented themselves on voting.

On August 8 Congressman Cahill offered the long-awaited amendments to the anticrime bill—amendments which would substantially change around the entire legislation. He proposed that each state establish a planning agency—under the authority of the state's chief executive—which would be charged with the responsibility for developing a comprehensive statewide plan for (1) the distribution of funds to local and state agencies; (2) the definition, development, and correlation of plans and projects for the improvement of state and local administration of criminal justice; and (3) the establishment of priorities for such improvements. The amendments further provided that $100,000 be made available to each state and the remaining 75 percent be allocated to the states according to population, with at least 50 percent of this money to be given by the states to the cities. If the states failed to establish a planning agency in three months or submit plans in six, the Attorney General could distribute that state's funds to local governments in the state upon submission of proper applications.

The amendments left unaltered the Law Enforcement Assistance Administration (LEAA) under the administration's bill, but it measurably enhanced the governors' power over the entire anticrime program. All applications would have to be evaluated and approved by the state chief executive, and the governor was also given authority to establish the state's anticrime agency and designate appointments to it. Thus the governors were given nearly life and death authority over the program. Cahill's specific amendments dealing with allocation of funds and state planning carried the House by a 188 to 86 teller vote and a 356 to 147 roll call. The magnitude of support for the Cahill amendments and others which restructured the total program surprised Cahill and supporters as much as Celler. The House then proceeded to vote passage on the rewritten legislation by a 378 to 23 margin. Few legislators, as it turned out, wanted to be on record as opposing law and order, even though the program did not meet their satisfaction.

The breakdown on the vote proved highly revealing of the voting coalitions on the legislation. It also suggested what might likely occur in future situations where comparable federal-state-local questions might be involved. Only four Republicans including McCulloch voted against the bill on final passage. With Cahill and MacGregor leading the Republican opposition, both viewed in the moderate to liberal camps within their party, many Republicans of similar persuasion voted with them on teller, roll call, and final passage votes. Most amazing both to the Republicans and the administration, however, was the defection of scores of Southern Democrats who, perhaps fearing greater federal control over local police and possible forced integration of local police agencies, supported Cahill. The voting, in fact, produced the most significant revival of the old Republican-Southern Democratic coalition experienced during the 90th Congress. In effect, Republicans and Southern Democrats had joined forces to take most controls over the administration of funds from federal officials, substituting the machinery of sending federal anticrime funds in bloc grants to state governments, which, in turn, would apportion them to local governments and agencies.

Celler and administration supporters vowed to renew the fight over Titles I and II in the Senate. If unsuccessful there, they were confident that a Democratic-dominated conference committee with McCulloch's backing would be able to negotiate a more acceptable compromise in the House-Senate conference. The battle thus moved to the Senate.

The Senate Decides

The House and Senate hearings overlapped one another. However, the Senate completed its hearings before the House Judiciary Committee had reported a bill and one month before the House's rewriting of the entire legislation during floor debate. Consequently, it devoted little time to the issue of state rather than federal-local involvement. Attorney General Clark reaffirmed the stand he had taken in the House hearings—that law enforcement preeminently is a local responsibility and state or gubernatorial involvement in the program would have harmful consequences.

The adroit McClellan, a former county prosecutor in rural Arkansas, had little time for the administration's proposal to fight crime. He considered the program to be inadequate from the outset, repeatedly contending that rising crime rates were in part attributable to recent Supreme

Court decisions in the area of criminal actions. He was determined to use his committee position and support from those members aligned with his position to bargain with committee liberals and the administration over specific provisions in the bill.[11]

Specifically, McClellan included in the scope of his hearings—and as amendments to the administration's bill—related measures which dealt with the admissibility of evidence in voluntary confessions which modified the Supreme Court's "Miranda decision," and another proposal which dealt with wiretapping. In late October 1967, McClellan's subcommittee, over strong minority objections, reported out S. 917 in three substantive titles: (1) a version of the Administration's original anticrime bill but one which removed control of the grant program from the Attorney General's office; (2) a sweeping amendment overturning Supreme Court decisions on matters dealing with defendants' rights and limiting court review in this area; and (3) a provision both to control illicit wiretapping yet permit widespread use of wiretapping by federal agents and local police under court order.[12] No further Senate action was taken on the legislation during the year.

In early 1968 the President declared in his State of the Union Message that "there is no more urgent business before the Congress than to pass the Safe Streets Act this year that I proposed last year."[13] A divided Senate Judiciary Committee thus reconvened in March to take up the legislation reported to it by the McClellan subcommittee. While the five-month impasse between House reversal and the Senate's resumption of legislative review had given the administration ample time to begin recouping its setbacks, it also provided the NGC invaluable time to redouble lobbying efforts on behalf of the states' position. The crime bill totally consumed the NGC's lobbying efforts. It had become a test case as far as governors were concerned. If the governors could turn this grant program around—and the House's action led them to believe that they could, then other grant-in-aid programs might also be fair game for restructuring into federal-state programs or consolidation into bloc grants. The argument seemed highly plausible at the time.

The NGC staff decided upon working both sides of the aisle, picking up sympathetic Democrats, especially Southerners, wherever possible to do so and otherwise concentrating upon key Republican leaders. Since the Republican National Committee had adopted a party policy supportive of bloc grants and grant consolidation, the governors' Washington staff

[11] Richard Harris, "Annals of Legislation: The Turning Point," *The New Yorker*, December 14, 1968, pp. 68–178.

[12] See *Controlling Crime through More Effective Law Enforcement*, Hearings before the Subcommittee on Criminal Laws and Procedures, Senate Judiciary Committee, 90 Cong., 1st Sess., 1967.

[13] *Congressional Quarterly*, **26**:2, January 19, 1968.

received assistance from the Senate Republican Policy Committee and key Republican legislators. Minority Leader Everett Dirksen and Roman Hruska, both members of the Judiciary Committee, became the principal supporters of the governors' cause and applied pressure upon fellow Republican Senators to follow their lead.

To convince Chairman McClellan that his subcommittee and the full Judiciary Committee should rewrite the administration's bill, substituting language comparable to that written into the House bill, the NGC produced letters from governors and state attorneys general supportive of the House action. McClellan remained skeptical about the states' capacity to implement the provisions in the anticrime bill and thus wrote the governors himself concerning the bill. Forty-nine governors responded to McClellan's request, indicating unanimous support for state involvement and that their states were willing and prepared to implement the program if called upon to do so.[14] These letters found their way into the hands of the NGC and their Senate allies, later to be used during Senate floor debate.

Nevertheless, in spite of the massive outpouring of support for a federal-state program from state officials, the Arkansas Senator, as later revealed, was playing his own game with the administration. He apparently promised the White House that he would not support the bloc grant approach added to the House version if they would not lobby too vigorously against his confession and wiretap amendments tacked on to the administration's bill on the Senate side.[15] While the administration officials reportedly looked to Celler and House conferees for expunging or softening McClellan's anticourt amendments, they initially considered the protection of the federal-local components to be their foremost objective. However, these negotiations did not deter Republican Senators from taking up the bloc grant cause.

Roman Hruska, the principal committee proponent of the bloc grant approach, having been stopped by McClellan from amending the legislation in subcommittee, requested a vote on it in full committee. The measure lost by a close 8 to 7 margin. It was thus expected that Hruska would offer this substitute amendment once again during Senate floor debate on the final bill. To further complicate matters, the Senate Judiciary Committee reported out its version of an anticrime bill on April 29, 1968. It contained not only the administration's original legislation, slightly modified (Title I), the court review and confessions provision (Title II), and a wiretapping amendment (Title III), but also a gun-control provision

[14] National Governors' Conference Washington files on crime bill, correspondence from governors.

[15] Richard Harris, "Annals of Legislation," p. 136. Harris's version was confirmed through my interviews.

(Title IV) that was added to the other measures following the assassination of Dr. Martin Luther King.

Senate floor debate on the anticrime bill began on May 1, with Senator McClellan as floor manager fully in control of the general proceedings. The manner in which separate titles were debated, amended, and voted upon had a direct bearing on the outcome of the administration's grant program. McClellan took up Titles II through IV first. He kept Title I, the essence of the administration's anticrime bill, to the end as a hostage which would reduce White House opposition to Titles II and III. The administration was held captive by McClellan and allies while they engaged in an unmerciful attack upon the Supreme Court, its rulings, and the Attorney General for his alleged emphasis upon defending civil liberties rather than fighting crime.

Justice, the White House, and Senate liberals were completely divided as to counter strategies, organization, and leadership. Titles II through IV, which included confessions, wiretaps, and gun control, produced a complicated spectrum of coalitions among Senate liberals devoid of any clear consensus on any one amendment. The gun-control provision, long advocated by the administration, had further confused the entire situation. No single issue in the memory of several senators had generated such a torrent of constituency mail, both pro and con. Civil liberties, the defense of the Supreme Court, and the rights of defendants in criminal proceedings were one thing. But the gun issue, cutting across liberal and conservative lines, was another. This issue had mobilized the gun lobby in states where liberal senators were up for reelection. Moreover, Justice and the White House officials were themselves split between those who wanted to preserve Title I at all costs and those who considered Titles II and III a dangerous threat to civil liberties. To give in on civil liberties was considered by some an unacceptable trade-off in exchange for preserving the federal-local anticrime program.

Adding to Justice officials' troubles in lobbying for the administration's legislation was the problem of conducting a reasonably accurate head count of its potential allies. 1968 was a presidential election year. The president had stepped down as a candidate of his party, three senators were busily pursuing the Democratic nomination for the Presidency, while fourteen more, identified with the liberal wing of the Democratic party, were campaigning for reelection. Presidential primaries in Nebraska, Oregon, and later California induced such extensive absenteeism among fifteen or so Democrats that no one could be sure as to how voting on any of the four titles and numerous amendments would turn out. As the Deputy Attorney General for Congressional Relations summed up Justice's problem, "With so many liberals out of town campaigning, we estimated that votes on any one of the titles would need a 3 to 2 liberal majority to carry in our favor."[16] Moreover, Justice felt that the White House had sold it out by dealing personally with McClellan on Title I. Barefoot Sanders, who headed up White House Congressional Liaison, reportedly admitted to Justice officials that since the Title I battle would be lost, efforts should be made to curb the more odious provisions in Titles II and III, holding the line on limited gun-control provisions in Title IV. The administration and its allies were disorganized, all expecting the worst.

With some success Senate liberals chipped away at McClellan's amendments, breaking down Title II (confessions), removing the curb on the Supreme Court's jurisdiction, and watering down Title III (wiretaps). The prohibition on the interstate mail-order sale of long guns was enacted. A stronger amendment banning the interstate sale of hand guns and requiring licensing of gun owners, later added by the administration following the assassination of Senator Robert Kennedy in early June, went down to resounding defeat.

After three weeks of often heated and passionate debate, much of it desultory, an endless string of amendments and votes, the Senate turned to Title I, the substantive portion of the administration's original bill which had been proposed fifteen months earlier. Since Roman Hruska had carried major portions of the debate among opponents to stronger gun-control legislation and proponents of the anticourt curb, he turned leadership on the bloc grant amendment over to Minority Leader Dirksen. Nonetheless, Hruska had done the spadework for the amendment, coordinating his activities with House Republicans, the Senate Republican Policy Committee, and the National Governors' Conference (NGC). It was he who had lobbied fellow Republican senators with Dirksen's assistance to take a party stand on behalf of a state approach to Title I. Their combined efforts proved so successful that not a single Republican defected on the two key votes on behalf of bloc grants.[17]

On May 23 Dirksen took the Senate floor to offer the NGC-sponsored amendment to transfer 85 percent of the law-enforcement grants in bloc grants to the states as a substitute for the administration's direct grant-in-aid program to local communities. To soften the effects of this provision, the Dirksen amendment further provided that at least 75 percent of these funds, in turn, would be channeled by the states to local communities under a duly approved statewide anticrime plan. The Senate Minority Leader, backed by Senators Ervin, Stennis, Thurmond, and Hansen, argued that the states could distribute the funds more efficiently than

[16] Tom Finley, personal interview at the U.S. Justice Department, Washington, D.C., January 7, 1969.

[17] Richard Velde, personal interview with in the office of Senator Roman Hruska, Washington, D.C., January 30, 1969.

the federal government and that, without the procedure, "We could in-advertently federalize all of law enforcement in America."[18]

Opponents of the Dirksen amendment included Democrats Tydings, Muskie, and Brewster. Led by Muskie, they emphasized that law enforce-ment is primarily a function of local government, the principal justifica-tion for a federal-local program, and that assistance is needed where crime problems are most acute—in the cities. But the governors had done their homework. They had prepared an elaborate briefing book on the states and law enforcement—including letters, telegrams, and state-ments from each of the states' attorneys general, governors, and state law-enforcement officials—to be used for floor debate by their allies. These documents were introduced in floor debate on what each of the state's efforts were in the law enforcement area and why these officials advocated a state-run and administered anticrime program. Proponents of the administration's federal-local program found it increasingly difficult to take issue with the overwhelming support for the Dirksen amendment offered by fellow state officials in the law-enforcement field.

The key vote, a motion by Senator Tydings to table the Dirksen amend-ment, was rejected by a 30 to 48 vote with all Republicans voting against. By substantially the same margin, a slightly modified Dirksen amendment was then passed by a 48 to 29 vote, including unanimous Republican support as well as half of the Southern Democrat contingency. The absence or abstention of fifteen Northern Democrats, presumably opposed to the Dirksen amendment, constituted the difference in what otherwise might have been a close vote. True to his word, Senator McClellan voted against Dirksen, but with little impact upon fellow Southern Democrats. That same day the Senate took up the entire bill, including Title I as revised, passing it by a 72 to 4 margin.

Once again, House-Senate liberals and the administration looked to a more favorable outcome in House-Senate conferences over the major differences which existed between the House and Senate versions. Two weeks later, on June 5, the House convened to consider the Senate-passed Omnibus Crime and Safe Streets Act. But outside events were to sub-stantially affect the House's already disintegrative climate. Early on the morning of the fifth, Senator Robert Kennedy, campaigning for the Presidency, lay mortally wounded in a Los Angeles hospital. Kennedy's assassination "made absolutely certain what had been virtually certain before it happened," observed Richard Harris, "that the crime bill passed by the Senate would be ratified by the House unchanged."[19]

A bipartisan movement within the House, encouraged by Republican

---

[18] *Crime and Justice*, p. 42.

[19] Richard Harris, "Annals of Legislation," p. 172.

leadership and the House Rules Committee, decided upon bypassing the usual conference between the House and Senate Judiciary Committees. Thus the House rejected by a 60 to 318 vote a motion by Chairman Celler to send the bill to conference. On June 6 the House adopted a resolution providing for the acceptance of the Senate bill by an overwhelming 369 to 77 vote. On June 19, the last day remaining for a Presidential pocket veto, President Johnson signed the bill into law, saying that it "contains more good than bad."[20] Thus, the governors had achieved their most impressive legislative triumph to date.

THE JUVENILE DELINQUENCY PREVENTION AND CONTROL ACT OF 1968

As a companion measure to the Safe Streets legislation, President Johnson sent to Congress on February 8, 1967, a special message on "America's Children and Youth." This message containing the administration's proposal for the Juvenile Delinquency Prevention Act of 1967 was viewed as the second and lesser part of the President's blueprint for a federal action program to combat the nation's rising crime rate. The proposed 1967 act authorized the Secretary of HEW to make federal grants to assist states and communities in planning juvenile delinquency programs. It further provided technical assistance support for local agency services in diagnostic and rehabilitative treatment for juvenile offenders, funds for construction of detention and treatment facilities, and support through project grants for preventive services.

The major controversy that arose over the three-year, $150-million program concerned the method by which federal grants would be allocated. The administration's bill authorized the federal government to make grants directly to localities or to private nonprofit agencies according to specifications outlined in the legislation. House Republican leadership—the newly energized NGC and its state allies—sparked by the House's action in rewriting the administration's Safe Streets proposal, once again coalesced to successfully turn around the proposed legislation. Seven weeks following its first success on the Safe Streets bill, an almost identical coalition of House Republicans and Southern Democrats assembled and rewrote on the House floor the administration's proposal substituting a system of bloc grants to states for juvenile delinquency control to be distributed on the basis of population. Once again the mayors, administration lobbyists, and liberals turned to the Senate for remedy, but this time with greater success than on the Safe Streets legislation.

This case suggests one more example of how the governors and state

[20] *Congressional Quarterly*, **26**:1550, June 21, 1968. See also *Public Law* 90-351.

allies operated to change around an established federal-local program, to redistribute funds and place authority over a program in the hands of state agencies and officials. The mayors and governors, predictably, were at loggerheads over the federal-state-local issue, participants in a major internal struggle for power in the Congress between administration supporters and its opponents. The mayors and their allies were operating in a hostile environment punctuated by reassertion of Republican leadership and its efforts to reshape administration programs.

After years of legislative struggle over whether or not the federal government should get involved in the juvenile delinquency field, Congress in 1961 enacted the Juvenile Delinquency and Youth Offenses Control Act. This rather modest program—as gauged by scope and funds—had been a key part of the New Frontier program, an area of personal interest to the Kennedy family and Robert Kennedy, then Attorney General. Under the leadership of the President's Committee on Juvenile Delinquency and Youth Crime, the $10-million-a-year program provided federal support for research and demonstration projects designed to test a number of specific approaches dealing with juvenile delinquency. Established on a year-to-year experimental basis in 1961, the program was extended both in 1964 and in 1966, with expiration set for June 30, 1967.[21]

Following six years of experience with the program, Congress, especially the House, was little satisfied with its accomplishments. Besides apparent lack of demonstrable results from the program, individual congressmen were particularly aggrieved by what they considered to be political considerations that had entered into the awarding of juvenile delinquency grants to specific cities and their mayors. Relations between HEW, which administered the program, and its overseeing committee, the Special Education Subcommittee of the House Education and Labor Committee, had progressively deteriorated. Congresswoman Edith Green, subcommittee Chairman, not only badgered administration officials over results but disagreed with them substantively over the program's structure and operation. Where the program had a limited scope and was administered on a project basis, she advocated a broader, more comprehensive approach through a state-run program financed on a grant-in-aid basis. These differences proved irreconcilable.

In 1967 jurisdiction over the program was transferred from Mrs. Green's purview to that of the General Education Subcommittee headed by Roman Pucinski. Many observers felt that a new juvenile delinquency program designed out of the remnants of the former one would have easier going in the House, once removed from Mrs. Green's constant recriminations and placed under a large-city legislator like Pucinski (D-Chicago). Further-

[21] See John E. Moore, "Controlling Delinquency: Executive, Congress, and Juvenile, 1961–1964," in Frederic Cleaveland (ed.), Congress and Urban Problems, Brookings Institution, Washington, D.C., 1969, pp. 110–172.

more, the committee's apparent hostility toward the program had assumed secondary importance as compared to its immediate interest in restructuring the administration's poverty program, which was also coming up for renewal.

The President Calls for a New Program

Increased public concern over crime had caused the President to ask Congress for a much enlarged federal role in local crime control. The Safe Streets legislation with its emphasis upon upgrading local law enforcement agencies comprised one component of this new federal activity, while a more comprehensive attack on juvenile delinquency constituted another. The President's Commission on Law Enforcement and the Administration of Justice devoted an entire chapter of its report to discussing problems of youth crime and making recommendations for broader prevention and rehabilitation methods to strengthen the juvenile justice system. The report stated:[22]

> *America's best hope for reducing crime is to reduce juvenile delinquency and youth crime. In 1965 a majority of all arrests for major crimes against property were of people under 21; as were a substantial minority of arrests for crimes against the person. . . . A substantial change in any one of these figures would make a substantial change in the total figures for the Nation.*

Considering the magnitude of youth crime and the emphasis placed upon greater national action by the Crime Commission, HEW recommended that the administration request from Congress an entirely new juvenile delinquency act rather than further amending the existing one. The final version of the new program, spelled out in the President's message to Congress entitled "America's Youth and Children," reflected the work of HEW, outside groups, consultants, and White House staff. Where the 1961 program has been limited to demonstration programs and the training of juvenile delinquency workers, the administration's 1967 proposal provided matching grant funds for a wider variety of projects in the fields of corrections, rehabilitation, preventive services, and research. States and localities, depending upon the specified provisions in the act, were required to match part of the federal grants from a 50 to 10 percent scale. Instead of the $10-million annual authorization under which the program had operated, the administration sought $25 million for the first year, $50 million for the second, and $75 million for the third.

[22] Commission on Law Enforcement and the Administration of Justice, *The Challenge of Crime in a Free Society*, p. 55.

Reversal Again

As in the case of the Safe Streets Program, the House acted first. It completed legislative hearings in May 1967, reported a revised bill from full committee in September, and passed the entire program by late September. The Senate, in contrast, failed to act altogether on the bill during the first session of the 90th Congress.

Pucinski's General Education Subcommittee first took up the administration's juvenile delinquency bill in a slightly modified form, reflecting HEW's emphasis upon youth participation in programs and greater state involvement as emphasized by the National Council on Crime and Delinquency. But Pucinski's subcommittee was badly divided on the legislation, typical of larger splits in the full committee.[23] These divisions ran along partisan, ideological, substantive, and personal lines. Members disagreed on the state versus local issue as well as whether preventive programs should be given more money than rehabilitative ones. Furthermore Chairman Pucinski had apparently antagonized certain liberal committee members as a consequence of his vehement opposition to youth participation in the design and implementation of local programs. Furthermore, old tensions between HEW, its Bureau of Individual and Family Services (which administered the program), and committee members surfaced, reflected in acrimonious exchanges during the hearings.[24]

The United States Conference of Mayors (USCM), long one of the principal support groups for the juvenile delinquency program, testified favorably on the legislation, emphasizing that juvenile delinquency was a local city problem, not a state one, and that the entire program should be run on a federal-local basis without state involvement. The National Governors' Conference recommended that each state "establish necessary machinery to coordinate the planning, leadership, and services of the state agencies which contribute to the prevention, control, and treatment of juvenile delinquency."[25] The state position was further underscored by representatives from state agencies and organizations in the child welfare, penology, and correction fields.

Subcommittee differences carried over to the full Education and Labor Committee. Compromising with organized state forces, the committee deleted provisions allowing communities to apply for planning funds directly. A clean bill severely emasculating the original legislation was

[23] See Richard F. Fenno, "The House of Representatives and Federal Aid to Education," in Robert Peabody and Nelson Polsby (eds.), New Perspectives on the House of Representatives, Rand McNally, Chicago, 1963, chap. 8.

[24] Juvenile Delinquency Prevention Act of 1967, Hearings before the General Education Subcommittee, House Committee on Education and Labor, 90th Cong., 1st Sess., 1967, pp. 13–81.

[25] Ibid., pp. 285–287; 580. See also "Recommendations of the National Governors' Conference on Juvenile Delinquency," State Government, Autumn 1967, pp. 229–244.

reintroduced by Pucinski and cleared by a unanimous vote of the full committee. However, several committee members lacked any real enthusiasm for the final product, due in part to Pucinski's heavy handling and management of the legislation. This was later reflected when the House voted to completely rewrite the legislation on the House floor and committee members did not support their chairman.

Similar to the anticrime legislation and its fate on the House floor, the administration, Democratic leadership, and committee spokesmen for the bill were completely surprised by Republican efforts to turn the legislation around, substituting bloc grants through the states for a primarily federal-local grant-in-aid program. Ralph Huitt, Assistant HEW Secretary for Legislation, after conferring with Pucinski and Democratic House leaders, reported to the White House that the legislation would have smooth sailing on the House floor. Head counts revealed no wide-scale defections or imminent roadblocks. But HEW officials were not altogether attentive to what was developing, preoccupied as they were with their own internal reorganization, pending Social Security amendments, and the forthcoming battle over the poverty program. The juvenile delinquency program was regarded as a rather insignificant program insofar as actual funds were concerned.[26]

On September 26 the House assembled for what developed to be a heated debate on the administration's bill. What emerged was a rerun of House action taken on the anticrime bill on August 8. House Republican leaders, Republican members of the Judiciary Committee who had successfully staged the passage of the states' amendment to the anticrime bill, together with the House Republican Policy Committee, combined forces at the last minute to draft a substitute amendment to the juvenile delinquency bill modeled on the Cahill one. During floor debate Tom Railsback, a member of the Judiciary Committee, proposed the amendment replacing direct grants to local agencies with bloc grants to the states. This amendment was further modified to authorize multicounty agencies to receive funds, a strategy to make the substitute more acceptable to the National Association of Counties (NACO) and rural congressmen. It passed by a roll call vote of 234 to 139, with a coalition of Republicans and Southern Democrats again in the majority. Thus the House, after six hours of heated debate and over the protests of Pucinski and Educational and Labor Chairman Carl D. Perkins, rewrote the administration's bill to provide for bloc grants to the states allocated on the basis of population.[27]

---

[26] Ralph K. Huitt, personal interview at the Brookings Institution, Washington, D.C., July 10, 1969.

[27] *Crime and Justice.* pp. 58–59.

The Senate Finds a Formula

The battle then shifted to the Senate, where the administration, HEW, the mayors, and allied organizations from the social work and correctional field sought redress. Six months later, the Senate Labor and Public Welfare Committee and its Subcommittee on Employment, Manpower, and Poverty took up the administration's bill. More favorable action seemed likely in the more liberal and cohesive Senate subcommittee, which was viewed as being more favorably inclined toward supporting federal-local policies than its House counterpart. Moreover, supporters of the administration's original bill were optimistic that a House-Senate conference on the legislation, dominated by committee liberals, would mitigate the impact of the acknowledgedly poorly drafted House substitute.

Mindful of their errors on the House side, HEW officials Lisle Carter (Assistant Secretary for Individual and Family Services), Virginia Burns (Carter's assistant), and Sam Halpern (Deputy Assistant Secretary for Legislation) took command of guiding the juvenile delinquency program through the Senate. They conducted numerous sessions with Senators and staff men on the Senate Manpower Subcommittee to develop legislation which would withstand House support for a state-oriented program.[28] Members of the Senate subcommittee were in general agreement over a substantive portion of the legislation, including provisions deleted on the House side: restoration of research and planning funds, recognition of OEO agencies as eligible recipients of juvenile delinquency funds, emphasis on prevention rather than correction, and greater coordination of all programs dealing with juveniles at the local level.

Considerable disagreement existed, however, over the issue of state involvement. Subcommittee Chairman Senator Joseph Clark (D-Pa.), the former mayor of Philadelphia, was naturally inclined toward a federal-city program exclusively. Clark's sympathies were staunchly supported by the Kennedy brothers, Robert and Edward, who also were subcommittee members. The subcommittee's two ranking minority members, Javits (N.Y.) and Prouty (Vt.), advocated some state involvement, but not to the extent embodied in the House's bloc-grant approach. Senator George Murphy (R-Cal.), on the other hand, a member of the Senate Republican Policy Committee and aligned with the governors' cause, supported the House's state approach completely. Murphy's insistence on the House's bloc-grant approach, and the threat that if this position did not prevail in committee he would take it to the Senate floor, led Javits to work with Clark in developing a modified state approach.

Meanwhile the NGC Washington office, almost exclusively preoccupied

[28] Virginia Burns, personal interview at the Department of Health, Education, and Welfare, Washington, D.C., February 5, 1969.

with the Safe Streets legislation then tied up in Senate Judiciary Committee, devoted what little time remained before Senate action on the bill to
inform committee members and their staff of the progress states were
making in the juvenile delinquency area. NGC staff sponsored several
luncheons for the staff of Senate members on the Clark Subcommittee for
the purposes of arguing the governors' case. As a result of these meetings
and the Senate vote in favor of bloc grants on the Safe Streets Act taken
on May 23, NGC remained confident of success. Besides Murphy, they
could count on Dirksen, Hruska, and Southern Democrats for support.

The key actors in working out a position acceptable to a majority on the
Clark subcommittee and the full committee were Clark, Javits, and Prouty.
Robert Patricelli, Javits's staff man on the committee, was given the assignment by his senator to develop a formula for state-local involvement.
Meeting continuously with HEW officials, Patricelli came up with one
modeled on the Senate's version of Title III of the Elementary–Secondary
Education Act, whereby states were given a minor role in innovative educational programs but were permitted a major role where they decided to
buy into the program.

Specifically the Javits provision, adopted by the committee, the full
Senate, and later the House-Senate conferees, allowed the federal government to make grants directly to localities—both public and private nonprofit agencies—whether or not a state plan for juvenile delinquency had
been approved by the HEW Secretary. But if a state submitted a statewide
plan and it was approved, grants could also be given in bloc form to them
where they were willing to pay half of the required local matching share
of the grant. In short, the Javits proposal permitted the channeling of
funds and control over the program to go to the states where they were
willing to provide acceptable plans and appropriate funds. This formula
contained the flexibility desired by Javits, Prouty, and Clark. It carved out
for the states a potential major role in the program, but it made participation contingent upon development of statewide plans and the willingness
to pay for their support. Javits and Clark agreed that only the more progressive states with the capacity to engage in the program would probably
take advantage of the trade-off between state financial support in exchange
for state control. Elsewhere the program would be conducted on a federal-
local basis. Moreover, proponents of state control would be muted when
confronted with the argument that if the states really wanted participation,
all they would have to do is to demonstrate it.

Prouty's acquiescence to the Javits proposal was seen as crucial both in
committee and later during Senate floor debate. Prouty was viewed by
fellow senators as a moderate and a representative from a small, nonurban
state, and his sponsorship assuaged the fear of some senators that the bill
might distribute benefits exclusively to large cities. Thus the legislation
came to be known as the Clark-Javits-Prouty bill, indicating its bipartisan

support. In the full committee's report on the legislation, Javits observed that the bill represented a major breakthrough "in dealing with the problem of the proper balance between federal, state, and local responsibilities." Murphy, in writing a minority objection, urged that all funds be channeled through the states in order that a "coordinated program encompassing the needs of a state and communities within it could be established."[29] On June 28 the Senate Labor and Public Welfare Committee reported out the legislation. The stage was set for a floor fight on the state-local issue.

Ten days elapsed between the reporting on the legislation and the floor fight. In an attempt to neutralize or balance the campaign being waged by the governors' organization, HEW, using officials in the Children's Bureau, contacted prominent businessmen, judges, mayors, and other allies to wire or call their senators on behalf of the "Javits-Clark-Prouty" bill. The USCM was prepared this time as well, making sure Senate liberals were informed as to the impending vote and helping HEW with head counts. When the appropriate time arrived, Murphy produced his amendment, virtually the same as the one used in the House reversal, to allocate funds to the states in bloc grants apportioned on the basis of population. However, the amendment was defeated by a narrow 34 to 38 margin, three Southern Democrats and eight Republican senators voting together with twenty-seven Northern Democrats on the winning side. The legislation next went to conference.

House-Senate conferees assembled one week following the Senate's action to reconcile differences between the two versions of the legislation. House Chairman Perkins selected a majority membership from the House side among those already favorably inclined toward the Senate's bill, while the principal Senate conferees were Clark, Javits, and Prouty. The conferees accepted the Senate version with only minor changes, with Javits and Prouty allowing state bloc-grant advocates like Representatives Goodell and Quie one important concession. The House provision for bloc grants for preventive and rehabilitative services was kept intact, but it allowed the Secretary of HEW to make grants for these programs directly to local agencies until the states had their comprehensive plans approved and had contributed one-half of the matching share required by the law. HEW also would be allowed to fund local agencies directly for planning and for the operation of training and research programs.

In short, the Javits formula had been slightly modified—as a strategy to permit some flexibility for compromise with the minority conferees' position of total state involvement. Instead of allowing the HEW Secretary to make grants directly to state and local agencies, whether or not a state plan had been approved and matching funds had been contributed for a

[29] U.S. Congress, Senate, Committee on Labor and Public Welfare, *The Juvenile Delinquency Prevention and Control Act of 1968*, S. Rept. 1332, 90th Cong., 2d Sess., 1968, pp. 20–23.

local agency's participation, the compromise provided that funds would go through the states once plans had been approved and a state had bought into the local agency's program. Javits's fallback position proved acceptable to all concerned. The governors and their allies had achieved a minor concession from the original administration program.[30]

Both chambers approved without debate the conference's bill, including the Senate's provision for the original three-year, $150-million authorizations. The President signed the bill into law (PL 90–445) shortly thereafter.

The Outcome

The legislative battles over the Juvenile Delinquency and Control Act of 1968 reflect more the internal struggles of partisan legislative groupings, their strategies and tactics as well as the political characteristics of the congressional committees involved, than they do outside political pressures and group activities. The 1966 midterm elections greatly altered the composition of Congress, especially activities by the previously disorganized Republican party. Republicans had increased their margin in the House by forty-seven seats, from 32 percent of all House seats to 43 percent.

From the onset of the 90th Congress, House Republican leaders—in conjunction with the Republican Policy Committee and a handful of more activist senior members—embarked on a legislative strategy aimed at reversing established or proposed grant-in-aid programs, substituting bloc grants through the states for federal-local programs.[31] This constituted a new strategy for the minority party from its opposition role, which was pursued with moderate success in the early 1960s but which failed in the 89th Congress. Instead of opposing administration programs as the Republicans typically did, they now sought to sufficiently amend them as to assist their constituencies and downplay their opposition stance.

The first attempt at reversing an administration program occurred in May 1967, when GOP legislators led by Al Quie (R-Minn.), supported by Edith Green, tried to convert some grant programs in the Elementary–Secondary Education Act into a bloc grant to state governments, reversing the previous federal-local school district channel for dispersing funds. Neither the governors nor the mayors were parties to this initial struggle,

[30] See U.S. Congress, House, *Juvenile Delinquency Prevention and Control Act of 1968.* H. Rept. 1724, 90th Cong., 2nd Sess., 1968. Also see *Congressional Quarterly*, **26**:2041–2049, August 2, 1968.

[31] See Charles O. Jones, "The Minority Party and Policymaking in the House of Representatives," *American Political Science Review*, **62**:481–493, June 1968.

which failed for lack of Southern Democrat support, but resulted in state educational agencies' gaining greater control over ESEA Title III funds.

The second attempt proved more successful, however, when in August 1967 a unified Republican party, aligned with Southern Democrats, emerged to rewrite the President's anticrime bill. They substituted a bloc grant through the states in place of a direct federal-local grant-in-aid program. In September 1967, the same House coalition reassembled to gain floor acceptance of a bloc grant amendment to the juvenile delinquency program. Thus both the anticrime and juvenile delinquency bills were caught in a rebellious legislative climate characterized by strong Republican unity, growing Southern Democrat defections from their party leadership, and a general decline nationally and within Congress in Presidential support. The governors were the beneficiaries of internal infighting within the House. They served as catalysts and supporters, more partisans to outcomes favorable to their position than key instrumentalities in changing votes. The mayors, on the other hand, who had benefited from the windfall of the 89th Congress's programs, found themselves on the defensive in the 90th Congress, seeking to consolidate and to preserve previous gains.

Finally, the outcomes from the crime control and juvenile delinquency programs offer an interesting contrast. In the former the governors were the immediate winners, but such an apparent victory had certain consequences, to be sure. Many in Congress were willing to experiment with a multimillion-dollar program under state control merely to see what the states and their chief executives were able to accomplish. Congress would be watching, as would the mayors, to see how the states used the modified bloc grant in comprehensive planning and how they reallocated funds to local units of government. The program would serve as a benchmark, albeit an expensive one, not only for gauging the governors' rhetoric but also for assessing future disputes of this type. The juvenile delinquency program, on the other hand, also put the governors and states in a precarious position. They had demanded complete control over the program, but instead Congress had provided them an opportunity to buy into it in exchange for greater authority.

THE BATTLE CONTINUES

The bloc-grant program had been a victory for the states and their governors. The governors hailed its adoption as the opening of a new era in intergovernmental relations. Having congratulated themselves on the first triumph of their new Washington lobbying operation, the governors soon awakened to the fact that they were now fiscally and programmatically responsible for crime fighting and statewide law-enforcement planning. The USCM-NLC immediately sought to discredit the bloc grant and Congress's misplaced trust in gubernatorial action. They wished to prove that the bloc grant had failed to achieve meaningful results so that the experiment would be terminated as quickly as possible, lest it be extended, as the Nixon administration hoped, to other programs.

Each of the government interest groups had a considerable stake in Congress's thorough review of the legislation and the Law Enforcement Assistance Agency's administration of the program. Grant consolidation and general and special revenue-sharing programs were in the offing; presumably these would be affected by the patterns established and the results of the crime control program. Indeed, President Nixon tauted the LEAA program as a model for special revenue sharing with the states on a broad range of activities. Partisan stakes were considerable as well, insofar as the Republican party now had a plan and mechanism for overhauling federal programs and structures established by the Democrats over the preceding thirty years. The bloc grant controversy kindled enormous intergovernmental competition. It also precipitated a good deal of conflict between Congress and the executive over future control of domestic programs and policies. At the forefront of the debate was the issue of whether the federal government or the states have the primary responsibility for ensuring that the goals of a national program were achieved and discovering how the tensions of the federal partnership could best be resolved.[32] These age-old issues had again been thrust on the government agenda, only this time with renewed fervor.

The governors met the federal planning and funding requirements established under the crime legislation, which included a state planning agency under the governor and a statewide comprehensive law-enforcement plan for allocating action grants to state and local programs and agencies. State agencies were required to distribute 40 percent of the planning funds and 75 percent of the action funds to local units, with the remainder going to the state. All fifty states gained funds and LEAA approval for their plans, so direct grants to local governments occurred only through LEAA's 15 percent discretionary funding allowed under the act.

In early 1969, the League opened the attack upon LEAA and the program, stating that "the act as presently administered will fail to achieve Congress's primary goal of controlling crime in the streets of urban high crime areas."[33] This was accompanied by a constant barrage of mayor-led

[32] B. Douglas Harmon, "The Bloc Grant: Readings from a Fiscal Experiment," *Public Administration Review*, **30**:141–152, Spring 1970.

[33] National League of Cities, *Analysis of State Administration of Planning Funds under the Omnibus Crime Control and Safe Streets Act of 1968*, NLC, Washington, D.C., March 1968, p. 1.

criticism of LEAA directed at congressional and public audiences concerning the diluted city representation on most state planning agencies. These charges were documented by the mayors' allies, the Urban Coalition and Urban America, who had completed extensive research on the subject.[34]

In spite of being a new agency administering a new program, LEAA had no honeymoon from congressional review. Every grant, guideline, and pronouncement flowing from the agency was subjected to extensive monitoring by the government groups and Congress. Overseeing LEAA's operations, in fact, became a full-time activity for the government interest groups. The NGC doubled its Washington staff between 1968 and 1970, assigning several persons to assisting LEAA and the states during the planning grant and approval period. The mayors deployed three full-time staff men to monitoring LEAA activities for purposes of reporting to Congress. LEAA was caught in a highly partisan entanglement both internally within the agency in its divided control and externally between the groups and partisans in Congress. The agency tried unsuccessfully to placate the mayors by allocating much of its discretionary funding to the largest cities. Such actions only provoked protests from the governors that LEAA was circumventing congressional intent and undermining statewide planning. LEAA operated under a congressionally mandated troika arrangement whereby only two of its three administrators could be from the same political party. Charles Rogovin, chief administrator and only Democrat, resigned after fifteen months in office, citing the impossible administrative arrangements and political pressures as the basis for his departure.[35]

The House Judiciary Committee assumed the initiative in reviewing LEAA's operations by conducting hearings on amendments to the program. Chairman Celler obviously wished to gain control over the legislation which had eluded him in 1967. The Brooklyn Democrat was most favorably disposed toward the mayors' demands for direct federal funding to cities and imposition of more adequate statutory safeguards to govern the redistribution of federal funds between the states and their localities. The mayors sought to exploit the basic conflict inherent in the legislation between a policy of fighting urban crime and a grant system dominated by state governments. The governors closed ranks against mounting opposition. The NGC Committee on Law Enforcement, Justice, and Public Safety led by New Jersey Governor William Cahill, the original bloc grant author, and Illinois's Richard Ogilvie, appealed to Republican members of the

[34] The Urban Coalition and Urban America, Inc., *Law and Disorder: State Planning Under the Safe Streets Act,* Washington, D.C., June 1969; *Law and Disorder II: State Planning and Programming under Title I of the Omnibus Crime Control and Safe Streets Act of 1968,* Washington, D.C., April 1970.

[35] *National Journal,* 4:181–192, January 29, 1972.

Celler Subcommittee during the 1970 hearings to defend the existing program against major substantive revision.[36]

To convince the Judiciary committees of the compelling need for restructuring the crime control program, the mayors relied on the personal experiences of several major urban chief executives concerning problems in dealing with their states and governors. The USCM-NLC also relied upon extensive research on the program and its administration. An NLC survey of thirty-one states' planning activities documented the inadequacy of statewide planning agencies and the maldistribution of state allocations to urban areas as opposed to rural-suburban ones. A more extensive survey entitled *Street Crime and the Safe Streets Act—What Is the Impact?* charged the states with giving inadequate attention to urban crime problems, with failing to improve the criminal justice system, and with providing insufficient coordination to statewide programs.[37] The mayors' contentions provided substantial ammunition to congressional critics of LEAA, placing the governors largely on the defensive throughout the course of the hearings.

Once completing the House hearings, Celler and the mayors collaborated on a strategy for amending the crime bill, relying upon the "buy in" provision used in the 1968 Juvenile Delinquency Act. In place of the existing formula whereby LEAA provided 60 percent of the pass-through costs and local government the rest, states would henceforth be required to pay one-fourth the nonfederal funding as a contribution to local costs lest they lose control over the granting process from states to localities. Celler's proposal contained a compromise between those who wanted to eliminate or substantially reduce the bloc grant and those who wanted it kept intact. These amendments were passed by the House with little discussion by a vote of 342 to 2.

In contrast to the House, where the mayors' studies provided much of the data for congressional debate, the Senate hearings gave careful consideration to a study completed in June 1970 by the Advisory Commission on Intergovernmental Relations concerning the Safe Streets Act.[38] The Advisory Commission on Intergovernmental Relations (ACIR) endorsed continuation of bloc grants, state flexibility in priority setting, and gubernatorial control over state criminal justice planning. It recommended, however, that states contribute to local governments' costs through buying

[36] *Law Enforcement Assistance Amendments,* Hearings before Subcommittee #5, House Judiciary Committee, 91st Cong., 2d Sess., 1970, pp. 86–104, 288–236.

[37] National League of Cities and U.S. Conference of Mayors, *Street Crime and Safe Streets Act—What Is the Impact?"* Washington, D.C., February 1970.

[38] The Advisory Commission on Intergovernmental Relations, *Making the Safe Streets Act Work: An Intergovernmental Challenge,* Government Printing Office, June 1970; *Federal Assistance to Law Enforcement,* Hearings before the Subcommittee on Criminal Laws and Procedures, Senate Judiciary Committee, 91st Cong., 2d. Sess., 1970, p. 413–474.

into local programs, much like the provision adopted by the House. The governors and state attorneys general opposed this measure and through their Senate Judiciary Committee allies—McClellan, Hruska, and Thurmond—defeated the adoption of the recommendation in committee. Nonetheless, the Senate sought to placate the mayors by raising the federal matching ratios from 60-40 federal-local contributions to 70-30 both on bloc and discretionary grants. The Senate version also required that beginning in FY 1973 the states make available to localities a percentage of the bloc grant in accordance with that community's overall state-local proportion of law-enforcement expenditures. By doing this, the Senate accepted an equalization formula for state apportionment of funds, which the mayors advocated, based on the local unit's law-enforcement expenditures as a proportion of the total state and local law-enforcement expenditure within the state.

House-Senate Judiciary Conferees reconciled the major differences between the two bills—buy-in and equalization provisions—by incorporating portions of each in a final version. States gained greater flexibility in planning grants, but with the provision that major cities and counties within a state receive adequate funds to develop their own comprehensive plans. The federal share of law-enforcement funds was increased from 60 to 75 percent and future approval of state plans now required that adequate assistance be given to areas characterized both by high crime incidence and high law-enforcement activity. The former constituted a gain for the states; the latter was an assurance to large cities of a more equitable reallocation of state funds.

Conferees also approved a flexible pass-through formula geared to a locality's portion of total state-local law-enforcement expenditures. The House buy-in concept was retained. At least one-fourth of the nonfederal funding required for federally assisted local law-enforcement programs had to be contributed by the state on an aggregate basis beginning in FY 1973. LEAA discretionary grants were increased to 75 percent and the agency's administration was changed, vesting greater power in one administrator instead of being divided among three.[39] NACO also gained acceptance of its demands, that counties be given greater inclusion in the program and that federal grants be allowed for construction of correctional facilities—a heavy county burden.

For the mayors, half a loaf seemed better than none. State discretion in reallocating federal pass-through funds had been clarified by guidelines guaranteeing a more equitable reapportionment to the cities. The mayors fell short of their goal of restructuring the entire program on a federal-local basis, but they could now use mandatory state assistance as a device

---

[39] U.S. Congress, House, *Omnibus Crime Control Act of 1970*, H. Rept. 91-1768, 91st Cong., 2d Sess., 1970.

for breaking loose from state control where commensurate payments were not made. The governors, on the other hand, had retained the bloc grant, gained a greater federal contribution to the program, and increased somewhat their flexibility in administering the program.

No sooner had the amendments to the Law Enforcement Assistance Program become law than President Nixon proposed further restructuring by changing the bloc-grant allocation into a special revenue-sharing design. The President's Law Enforcement Revenue Sharing Act would eliminate categorization and merge into a single special revenue-sharing payment all bloc-grant authorizations and special action grants. The governors welcomed the elimination of matching requirements and much of LEAA's review and amending power, while NACO and the mayors generally opposed relaxation of federal oversight responsibility. In 1973, Congress extended the program for three years, with less cost and more flexibility for the states. The states' matching share was reduced from 25 to 10 percent, with programs divided into six separate bloc grants and categorical programs including juvenile justice and treatment for narcotic addicts and alcoholics. In rejecting the President's special revenue-sharing concept, Congress placated the governors by increasing federal contributions and allowing the states flexibility among programs. It had, however, begun the earmarking process of dividing the program into separate categories and specific allocations.

Where law enforcement and criminal justice assistance had become a major area of federal involvement in state-local affairs from 1968 on, the 1968 Juvenile Delinquency Prevention Act failed to stimulate much activity either on the federal level or by states and localities. Appropriations for law-enforcement funding rose from $64 million in FY 1969 to nearly $1 billion by FY 1973. In contrast, the $100-million authorization of bloc grants to states and localities for juvenile delinquency prevention and rehabilitation programs never materialized. Instead, HEW requested only $49 million total over the three-year period for the program, Congress appropriated $30 million, and something like $15 million in federal funds were actually spent. Much of Congress, the Nixon administration, governors, and mayors gave little attention to the program and its administration after 1968.

Under HEW reorganizations the Office of Juvenile Delinquency and Youth Development was renamed the Office of Youth Development and Delinquency Prevention (YDDPA), and it went well into 1970 without a director. Once guidelines for implementing the 1968 act were issued, state and local governments found them to be so cumbersome and inundated with a maze of administrative requirements that few actually participated in the program. YDDPA lacked not only congressional support, a strong constituency, and funds but also competed with some sixteen federal agencies and forty federal programs affecting youth. LEAA, in effect, became the major grant dispensing agency for juvenile delinquency funds, which led briefly to an unsuccessful campaign by the governors to bring YDDPA under the Justice Department's structure.

After a one-year extension in the program, Congress decided in 1972 on returning to the direct-grant approach with eligibility extended to state and local governments as well as private agencies. The amendments to the program required that funds be concentrated in areas with high youth crime, youth unemployment, and many school dropouts. Thus, as in the crime control program, congressional standards provided for greater equalization in allocation, protecting urban areas against maldistribution. The mayors continued in calling for a direct federal-local program exclusively, while the NGC advocated that the President develop within his office a new Special Action Office to develop a state partnership coordinating the efforts of all government levels in the juvenile delinquency prevention area. Insofar as so little federal money was made available for the program, the governors-mayors controversy surrounding the bloc-grant and state control issues all but evaporated. Both organizations had moved on to areas of greater concern where stakes assumed more sizable proportions.

6

THE GOVERNMENT GROUPS IN
THE POLICY-MAKING PROCESS

The preceding eight cases indicate the government interest groups' investment of time and resources essentially during the 1965 through 1969 period.[1] No doubt the procurement of more urban renewal funds and the passage of Model Cities might rank as the higher accomplishments to many mayors, while to many governors revenue sharing and federal assumption of greater public assistance costs might seem the more important measures pursued and gained. Nonetheless, the eight are representative of the groups' immediate rather than long-term agenda during the particular time frame of the study. Each of the cases can be traced from the beginning to where legislation passed, programs were undertaken, and new administrative procedures were begun. The cases are updated through the early 1970s, thereby providing a more longitudinal perspective from which to assess the relationship among them as well as to further probe intergroup competition and cooperation at later developmental stages.

In reviewing these cases as to their meaning, focus is upon group patterns—the functions and role each group performs. It is essential to inquire as to what these cases tell us about these government interest groups: their activities, policy involvement, and effectiveness. Attention is also given to the institutional and political constraints within which they operate. To what extent do the groups affect other actors and public policies and, reciprocally, how much do the latter affect them? How effectively do the groups use resources, strategies, and specific tactics in pursuing their goals? By disaggregating the various cases into component parts, one may better discern the roles, functions, and activities of these organi-

[1] For the groups' long-term agenda, see the American County Platform, the NLC's National Municipal Policy, and the policy resolutions passed by the NGC, COSGO, and USCM at their annual meeting.

zations and their members. Finally, this chapter goes beyond the immediate cases to probe the rich variety of tactics and strategies employed by the government groups in influencing government decisions.

GENERAL ROLES

The government groups confront the usual panoply of external constraints found in the constitutional and political setting of the American federal system. They contend with separation of powers, broad national legislative and appropriative powers, noncentralized governments, interest groups and political parties with their often local bias, and news media focused upon Washington as the center of all things political. They deal with an active court system whose policies have vastly influenced existing relations among government levels. Also, state and local executives, like their federal counterparts, are buffeted by many of the same pressures and forces in their external environment—forces which have significant consequences for government programs and expenditure patterns. Elections, changes in government, and conditions of the national economy affect those inside government as well as those outside, making each susceptible to forces that neither may readily control.

For the government interest groups, their general activities are directed at securing substantial increases in amounts of federal aid made available for distribution by general-purpose governments. Translated into group policy, this means the reduction of federal categorical grants within broad flexible areas (bloc grants, special and general revenue sharing) to be returned to states and localities on a regular, incremental basis with minimum restrictions as to use and maximum discretionary control by elected officials, especially chief executives. These objectives are the cause, quite obviously, of considerable friction between chief executives and the alliances between Congress, the bureaucracy, and interest groups. Federal executive agencies and bureaus as well as their state-local counterparts view the government interest groups' objective essentially as threats to their jurisdiction over "their" programs. Congressional committees and subcommittees tend to respond with much the same hostility toward loss of influence and control. Most of the program-oriented interest groups surrounding an intergovernmental program also react negatively to these proposed changes. Hence, competition and conflict among these actors is built into their relations.

Each government interest group pursues independently the cultivation of direct federal relations in funding and programmatic support. However, no single government group is self-sufficient in its influence to make decisions or require decisions of others. Every major federal policy involving the groups is consequently the product of mutual accommodation among them. What one group wants is typically desired or held by another, and what all the groups advocate in common is usually what segments of Congress and the bureaucracy have claim upon as well.

In this environment the groups' influence-oriented activities lead them to assume various roles in bargaining for improved position in the intergovernmental decision process. These roles—initiator, facilitator, and obstructor—are not mutually exclusive and often overlap with one another as the groups' strategies and tactics undergo adjustment. Roles are based essentially on expectations of behavior, internally generated and externally imposed. These roles are outgrowths of the groups' institutional and constitutional positions: state and local officials rather than federal; elected, not appointed; generalists as opposed to specialists; and governed by federal-state-local statutes rather than federal exclusively. They also emerge from interorganizational needs, past group experiences, and their relations with other actors in a wide variety of policy areas. Previous outcomes—gains and losses—shape these expectations and strategical choices.

The government interest groups may be the source of new policies and programs. However, diverse constituencies and membership cleavages typically impede them from performing this initiator role, though exceptions are frequent. Membership participation is sustained largely as a consequence of the groups' size and the immediate advantages that accrue from dealing with their federal constituency on this basis. Members pursue immediate payoffs from their activities, leaving to other groups the concern for long-term strategy and future planning. Members have tangible stakes in most policy outcomes, which moderates their activities to an extent and often makes them cautious in their behavior. They are highly protective of previous gains, seeking to expand upon these achievements rather than leap to new programs or policies where outcomes and consequences may be unclear.[2] The groups seek stability in the policy arenas in which they interact, balancing their autonomy as political actors on the one hand with the necessity to form alliances with other claimants on the other. To maintain group consensus, they move deliberately and incrementally, which often prevents them from responding decisively to disruptions in the policy arenas in which they operate.

The groups represent state and local governments as an interest which, in aggregate, means the incorporation of nationwide cleavages and factions within their organizations. Narrow, precise claims, therefore, are often more difficult to generate than broader, more encompassing ones. From a systems perspective the groups provide general demands upon federal actors and institutions. Their initiator and advocacy roles may be diffuse rather than specific. They are protective of the autonomy, fiscal viability,

[2] See Theodore J. Lowi, *The End of Liberalism*, Norton, New York, 1969.

and integrity of the particular level of government they speak for. They are defenders of the interests and prerogatives of political executives. Federal policy makers, on the other hand, perform certain conversion functions by translating group demands into tangible policies and programs. They, too, assume various roles as mediators of group conflict, arbitrators of their differences, brokers for their demands, proponents and opponents of their claims.

It was general group demands concerning the operation of federal grant programs that provided much of the impetus behind A-85 and the Intergovernmental Cooperation Act of 1968. The problems created by federal grant programs were widely recognized by federal officials. Reforming the system never quite made the President's or Congress's agenda prior to escalating group complaints in 1966 about the administration, structure, and implementation of intergovernmental programs. A-85 involved presidential response to some of these problems, while the Intergovernmental Cooperation Act represented joint activity by the groups, congressional committees, and the executive in dealing with administrative reforms.

These two cases suggest another aspect of the groups' advocacy roles. They were united by the common goal, that of greater chief executive control over federal grant programs. The mayors were disturbed by being shut out of drafting the Model Cities legislation, while the governors rebelled against the downgrading of state governments and their chief executives in a score of domestic programs. The bypassing of these governments' elected officials produced general demands upon the White House, Congress, and executive agencies for inclusion. State and local chief executives hoped to gain access to legislative clearance of major programs affecting their interests in advance of Presidential transmission to Congress. A-85 and the Intergovernmental Cooperation Act, however, sanctioned postlegislative interference by the groups in influencing the standards, guidelines, and day-to-day operations governing grant administration. Thus even where the groups operate with complete unanimity on policy, they are likely to achieve only partial success. These modest victories may be cumulative, as further developments stemming from A-85, A-95, and the councils of government (COGs) indicate.

The government interest groups are stimulated into action by public officials as much as they, in turn, stimulate them. The impact of their lobbying effort is generally to reinforce public officials' attitudes and behavior more than to change it.[3] Typically the groups function as facilitators, constantly adapting their agenda and actions in response to stimuli from a well-established network of actors. They seek common grounds

---

[3] See Raymond A. Bauer, Ithiel de Sola Pool, and Lewis A. Dexter, *American Business and Public Policy*, Atherton, New York, 1963; and Lewis A. Dexter, "The Representative and His District," in Robert Peabody and Nelson W. Polsby (eds.), *New Perspectives on the House of Representatives*, Rand McNally, Chicago, 1963, pp. 2–29.

for resolution of outstanding differences between them and actors whose assistance they require. The National Association of Counties (NACO) and the National League of Cities (NLC) redirected their activities to the highway program in late 1967, for example, when they expected that the American Association of State Highway Officials' (AASHO's) preliminary report on the future highway program might become a working blueprint for the Federal Highway Administration and the House Public Works Committees. The mayors' most notable legislative achievements in housing are largely attributable to their ability to join with large coalitions which have organized in support of omnibus programs. The United States Conference of Mayors-National League of Cities (USCM-NLC) assisted Congress in drafting strong air and water pollution programs, and later in ensuring that federal funds were available to aid state and local governments in meeting federal standards.

As facilitators, the groups may exploit existing congressional cleavages to their own advantage. House members and the Republican leadership were ripe for overthrow of the President's federal-local anticrime program. Republican leaders sought allies, which they found not only in Southern Democrats but also in the National Governors Conference (NGC), state attorneys general, and state law enforcement personnel. NACO assumed leadership in the congressional battle over industrial development bonds. It was elevated to a conspicuous position by Treasury and its allies when they needed local government support to split the ranks of the mayors and governors who opposed IDB tax removal. NACO, on the other hand, joined with highway safety advocates behind stronger highway safety legislation in 1966 in exchange for their support of a greater administrative role for the counties in administering highway safety programs. Several additional examples could be offered to describe how the groups function as accommodators, brokers, and reconcilers among groups inside and outside government.

In a highly complex lobbying network, the relation between lobbyists and policy makers frequently is a transactional one. Who is doing what to whom is often blurred. Each may be influencing the other. Take, for example, the case of Senator Edmund Muskie, whose performance as an intermediary among the groups and between them and Congress offers support to this interactional relationship. Muskie achieved a notable reputation in Congress for his specialization and hard work in the intergovernmental area. The Senator maneuvered himself into the vortex of urban and intergovernmental legislation through his committee positions. He progressed to the chairmanship both of the Intergovernmental Relations Subcommittee, and the Air and Water Pollution Subcommittee of the Senate Public Works Committee. As the original Senate sponsor of the legislation creating the Advisory Commission on Intergovernmental Relations (ACIR), Muskie became an advocate of its recommendations and studies. Moreover, as former governor and legislator with special urban expertise, Muskie undertook an active interest in the problems of state and local chief executives. He insisted that Congress hear from these officials, for "it is they," he argued, "who are on the firing line, and who have the ultimate burden of making our federal system work."[4]

Thus a strong relationship developed between Senator Muskie and the government interest groups built upon respect, confidence, and mutuality of interests. They called upon him for assistance as much as he prevailed upon them for support. Muskie's Intergovernmental Relations Subcommittee became one of the principal congressional outlets used by the groups to gain Presidential response to grant-in-aid reform. Muskie and the groups worked together to obtain A-85 and the Intergovernmental Cooperation Act. Serving as an intermediary among the groups. Muskie helped mold a consensus around the Cooperation Act and the COGs-areawide planning program, later translated into a mandate for congressional action. Building upon these earlier accomplishments, Muskie and the groups later gained congressional acceptance of two complementary measures to the Cooperation Act in the 91st Congress. The Intergovernmental Personnel Act (PL 91-468) constituted another milestone in collaborative groups' efforts in gaining national recognition, for the first time, for the need to strengthen core management at the subnational level by upgrading personnel and improving personnel administration. The Uniform Relocation and Land Acquisition Policies Act (PL 91-646) comprised several provisions, supported essentially by the mayors, which were deleted from the original Intergovernmental Cooperation Act.

Groups' roles, as previously argued, are often structured on a routine basis, largely by outside forces. The legislative pace of Congress also affects group roles and the planning of strategies and tactics. While the groups seek to structure the political environment in which they operate to their immediate advantage, more typically they must respond to the workings of Congress and the executive. The groups' carefully articulated national policies, adopted at their annual meetings, may turn out to be a "shopping list" rather than a concrete agenda for daily action. Each group monitors perhaps twenty or so specific legislative items in an average session, but it gives top priority to substantially less. On programs coming up for renewal or congressional review, the groups may have ample time to plan lobbying activities. On the other hand, where the pace of legislation quickens or the congressional agenda is abruptly changed, the groups may have inadequate lead time to respond or to build a unified group position.

During the prolific 89th Congress, with its major programs in poverty, rent supplements, Model Cities, education, and the like, congressional

[4] *Creative Federalism,* Hearings before the Subcommittee on Intergovernmental Relations, Senate Government Operations Committee, 89th Cong., 2nd Sess., pt. 1, p. 3.

committees looked to the government groups for detailed responses. The groups had considerable difficulty reacting to a host of new and controversial items of domestic legislation, which fostered organizational disruptions and often indecisiveness. Organizational leaders and staff may find themselves supportive of new legislation, but commitment of the entire association to policies which have not been fully discussed is another matter. In contrast, the 92nd Congress was distinguished by Presidential vetoes over major domestic spending programs passed by Congress. In light of the Nixon administration's budgetary stringency and retrenchment in many domestic areas, Congress called upon the government groups to respond in defending these programs and selecting priorities among them.

The mayors' restraint from an all-out attack on the initial OEO legislation stemmed in a large measure from their own divided membership. Several prominent large-city mayors — Lee, Cavanagh, and Houlihan — had served as consultants to the Office of Economic Opportunities (OEO) task force and had actively participated in the Ford Foundation's "Grey Areas" program, the precursor to the federal antipoverty effort. A dozen governors and mayors also had testified favorably before congressional committees in gaining its passage, which neutralized opposition to the program from within their own ranks. The 1966 Model Cities program, with its new towns provisions, supported strongly by the League and opposed by the USCM, sparked divisions within the mayors' ranks, as did the rent supplements program in 1965. The Republican-sponsored bloc grant amendment to the Elementary and Secondary Education Act of 1967, which would have replaced categorical grants directly to localities with bloc grants to be administered by the states, placed governors on both sides of the amendment. State and local executives were divided on the issue of removing tax exemptions from industrial aid bonds, eventually opposing removal more out of fear of the precedent it would set than the issue itself. In the 92nd and 93rd Congresses, in contrast, the groups often reverted to protectionist strategies, anticipating the Nixon administration's budget cuts and planning their defensive moves accordingly. The agenda of one Congress was heavily oriented toward new programs and increased federal expenditures, that of another geared toward program elimination and budget cutting.

What this suggests is how the groups take their cues from Congress and the administration regarding immediate priorities and agenda. Whether acting as facilitators or initiators, they must first build internal consensus for action, which often raises insuperable problems for group leaders. Strong opposition may develop, lead time for response may be lacking, and alternative positions may be wanting. Administration officials are keenly aware of the groups' consensus-building difficulties and thus may seek to coopt or neutralize the groups for short-term partisan advantages. The Nixon White House staff, for example, frequently played upon group cleavages, disrupting consensus-building operations within the groups, among them, and between them and agency-congressional actors. Indeed, several of the Nixon programs set mayors against governors and pitted county officials against mayors. One major indicator of the rising importance of the government groups from the White House's perspective is the number of prominent administration officials that frequent the groups' annual gatherings. These officials seek to lobby the groups, neutralize opposition, and play upon partisan cleavages when it is necessary to do so.

Obstructionist or veto roles can be more characteristic of group responses, particularly where the costs, benefits, and possible consequences of policies are not easily discernible. Group leaders generally avoid rendering opinions on new programs or policies in advance of concrete cases or actual legislative proposals. They may specify general guidelines and conditions which would be acceptable to members, but they cautiously await final details, lest the group be recorded supportive of programs that prove unacceptable in the flesh. New legislative proposals are carefully screened with an eye toward details governing implementation, administration, authorizations, and expectations concerning a program's likely funding. Governors and mayors ask the all-important questions of whether this new program will mean less, the same, or more funds for their governments than existing programs. Will it be complementary to, supportive of, or a substitute for existing programs? How long will it take to get going, what are the start-up costs and how will they be paid for? What will the transition from one program or policy to another involve? Who are the intended and unintended beneficiaries of the program and how does this relate to other programs in the area? Will its passage preclude consideration of other pending programs the groups might feel more strongly about? Can existing legislation be amended to incorporate the principal concepts or benefits of the proposed program?

The questions the government interest groups and their members ask are not categorically different from those that the congressmen consider. However, they do differ in priorities, emphases, and concerns. Legislators generally give greater attention to the politics of "program passage," while state-local executives are far more preoccupied with the politics of taxes and administration. Legislators may value highly the public credit accrued from sponsoring new programs or the benefits attained from new constituencies. They can blame poor administration or inadequate funding when the programs they sponsor fall or go astray. Chief executives, on the other hand, typically concern themselves with revenue acquisition, service delivery, and program administration. Thus the basic differences in views, responsibilities, and electoral needs may lead not only to conflict among them but also to the assumption of contrasting roles.

Considering the innumerable veto points in the policy-making process, distinctive advantages are often gained by those who seek to prevent rather than initiate action. Every major policy change, whether legislative or administrative, entails the fear of costs for some participants as well as the hope of gain for proponents. The legislative process is so structured that defenders of the status quo can block, frustrate, and delay changes more easily than advocates of new proposals can marshal sufficient resources to overcome these pitfalls. The government groups are rarely recorded in opposition to new proposals initially, instead witholding support in the expectation that congressional leaders, committee members, or executive officials will bargain with them to gain their support. Such negotiations may occur within an executive agency in the prelegislative stage. They may begin just after the introduction of legislation and prior to congressional hearings, as occurred in the case of the 1968 Highway Act. Usually, however, the center of bargaining exchanges and accommodation emerges in congressional committees and subcommittees, as in the cases of Model Cities, Juvenile Delinquency, Mass Transit programs, and the Safe Streets amendments of 1970. When demands are not accommodated at this juncture, the groups may resort to the floor stage, where debates and amendments can assist them in attaining their objectives. The governors, for example, were successful at this stage in the crime bill and—to an extent—the poverty program as well.

The areawide planning agencies proposed by Muskie suggest another variation of the groups' veto roles. The mayors' initial opposition led successfully to several different versions, including elected official control and exemption from review of housing programs. The poverty program generated greater opposition from the groups than any other case examined. In retrospect, most observers feel that the program would have been adopted by Congress in 1964 whether or not the groups had closed ranks against it. By 1966, however, the balance of support in Congress had shifted considerably. Governors and county officials had an attentive audience for their complaints, while the mayors' turnabout in support for the programs perhaps spelled the difference in preventing OEO from being dismantled earlier than it was.

Several other examples of group veto are notable. Between 1965 and 1968, the Council of State Governments (COSGO) successfully stopped tax reform legislation for establishing uniform limitations of the states' power to tax small out-of-state firms doing business within their borders. COSGO argued that such legislation would usurp states' power in interstate matters, and that the states could be best left to resolve the situation through interstate compacts. The NGC together with the Reserve Officers Association got Congress to block Secretary McNamara's proposed merger of the Army National Guard with the Army Reserve in 1964. President Johnson's agreement with the governors to consult them on programs and policies affecting their interests allegedly prevented Secretary of Labor

Wirtz from proceeding with his announced reorganization of manpower programs in 1968. The governors blocked Wirtz's plan because it downgraded state employment offices and administrators.[5] The five government groups, joined by labor and civil rights organizations, pressured Congress to reverse itself by postponing indefinitely a provision in the Social Security amendments of 1967 which placed a freeze on the level of federal participation in AFDC (assistance to families with dependent children).

In the case of general revenue sharing, a supportive coalition of the government groups took several years to form as a consequence of the veto posture one or more exerted in early negotiations. The formulas for distributing federal revenue sharing among states and local governments were constantly being redrawn by the White House and Congress as each sought to reward particular constituencies. In the meantime the groups were hopelessly divided as to which bill offered the greatest potential for building consensus among them. President Nixon first proposed that $500 million be divided roughly 70-30 between states and local government, while Congressmen Mills responded with a version that allocated funds only to local governments. The President countered with a version that divided payments equally between the states and local governments and eventually settled for Congress's alternative, which essentially allocated one-third to the states, with the remainder going to counties and municipalities. It was the latter version that brought the mayors and county officials together.

The government groups also played a lead role in blocking special revenue sharing and executive reorganization plans during President Nixon's first term. NACO's failure to support the proposed Department of Community Development amounted to one more nail in the coffin of this presidential reorganization request. As much as administration architects labored between 1970 and 1973 to bring the government groups into support of a community development revenue-sharing plan, no specific plan could possibly meet the objections of the governors, mayors, and county officials alike. The counties and mayors were at virtual loggerheads over the control of funds between large urban counties and inner core cities. In each of these cases, major domestic programs had to run a gauntlet of veto groups that was often fatal, particularly where one government group or another had sufficient support to carry out its negation roles successfully.

Being on the losing side of a battle can have its advantages. Some defeats matter less than others, especially where future struggles over an issue are likely to arise. The mayors and governors, for example, were not particularly concerned about the unfavorable outcome on the industrial

[5] See Stanley H. Ruttenberg, *Manpower Challenge in the 1970's,* John Hopkins Press, Baltimore, 1970, chap. 7.

bonds issue. They were geared for the forthcoming fight, the attempt by Treasury to end altogether the tax-exempt status on state and local bonds. This developed one year later during Congress's review of the Nixon administration's tax reform legislation. On this occasion the groups rallied together to successfully gain congressional removal of any abridgement to the status of tax-exempt bonds in conference and ended the matter at least temporarily.

What these examples indicate, in part, is how the government interest groups withhold support or maintain an opposition posture to enhance their bargaining leverage in final outcomes. The line between a facilitator and obstructionist role is often obscured by the fact that the groups may move from one role to another as the situation dictates. A negative stance may be a delaying tactic to allow the situation to clarify, for alternatives and compromises to emerge, or for consensus to form. Such a stance also may be the last extreme where viable options fail to materialize and compromise disintegrates. Once again, no single group is self-sufficient or powerful enough to require decisions of others unilaterally. All cases where the groups were successful in opposition, in fact, involved a coalition of groups and supportive congressional allies.

Fiscal incentives may be the strongest and most compelling justification for policy changes. The governors' reversal on the national highway program in the 1950s from a state-run and financed program to a federal one is no more remarkable than the mayors' turnabout on the poverty program. The governors were relieved of the greater costs in highway financing and thus readily shifted positions with the enticement of federal financing. The mayors were able to cope both with the poverty program and Model Cities, becoming the principal support group of the former and major clientele of the latter. The mayors also reversed themselves on the earmarking of OEO appropriations in the changeover from the Johnson to Nixon administrations. The case against earmarking was predicated on the advantages to cities and their mayors where OEO administrators had flexibility in apportioning funds among various programs. However, under the Nixon administration, Congress's failure to earmark OEO funds into separate categories would likely have led to even further executive impoundment, and hence the mayors reversed their earlier position against earmarking.

The President, Congress, and federal agencies frequently use such fiscal inducements to gain group support. The USCM, for example, was far more enthusiastic about President Johnson's proposed Model Cities legislation in 1966, once the administration agreed to substantial increases in urban renewal authorizations lest this new program threaten to cut into the renewal program's allocations. Once President Nixon proposed to raise the base figure for revenue sharing from $1 billion during the first year to $5 billion, the government groups were prepared

to subordinate their outstanding differences in building a strong supportive alliance on the program's behalf.

Thus, in reviewing the groups' record, one finds that their roles are
somewhat flexible, susceptible to change, and undergo constant adjustment to new situations. Organization policy provides a bargaining stance,
while accommodation to the shifting political arena occurs from program
initiation to implementation. It is next important to inquire how the
organization and structure of Congress and the executive affect group
activities, strategies, and tactics.

SPATIAL CONCERNS AND VESTED INTERESTS

The age-old administrative problem—area and function as competing
bases of organization and governance—confronts the groups in their
Washington lobbying. The scope of immediate concerns to the government
interest groups is influenced by geopolitical boundaries. Policies and
problems tend to be defined largely within the context of a spatial setting
determined by city, county, and state lines. But since Congress and its
committee structure are organized along functional and not geographic
lines, the government interest groups confront a chronic and overriding
problem. That is, they seek the imposition of spatial concerns on functionally oriented and structured institutions. Not only are committee work
groups organized along such functional patterns as agriculture, armed
services, public works, education, and the like, but most congressional
members' perceptions of public policy tend to coincide with established
boundaries between functional programs and committee jurisdictions.
Many of the bills to which Congress devotes a large proportion of its time
fall easily into what Fred Cleaveland terms "issue contexts." These he
defines as the way members of Congress perceive a policy proposal that
comes before them, how they consciously or unconsciously classify it for
study, and what group of policies they believe it is related to.[6] Such issue
contexts strongly influence legislative outcomes because their structure
helps determine the approach for analysis, statutory review, and revision,
as well as the advice and expertise that enjoys privileged access.

The similarities between the functional organization of Congress and
that of the executive reinforce the interdependence and mutual interests
which bring together agency officials, congressional committee members,
and interest group leaders. They are all concerned with the same area of
government activities and programs. The legislative committee-executive
agency structure, and attendant policies which link them, often defines,

---

[6] Frederic N. Cleaveland (ed.), *Congress and Urban Problems*, Brookings Institution,
Washington, D.C., 1969, pp. 359–360.

once a bill is introduced and assigned to a committee, the frame of reference guiding policy makers' view of that policy and the arena of action for interest group activity.[7] Therefore the great majority of bills introduced in Congress fall traditionally into readily identifiable and predictable issue contexts. The entire process can be quite predictable in terms of previous experience, interested parties, sources of support and opposition, agency relations with overseeing committees, steps in passage or defeat, and eventual results. New committee-subcommittee chairmen, party alignments, executive reorganization, and other changes may alter this process. So too, media focus, public investigations, and cataclysmic events may move policy concerns into broader, more inclusive arenas of decision making. But such events and actor realignment are the exception rather than the rule. Their impact may be immediate, but their long-term effect is likely to lead to incremental policy adjustments. Thus the functional organization of Congress and its ties with executive agencies and interest groups are crucial not only to understanding group behavior but also to an explanation of the groups' activities.

As previously noted, most government interest groups' policies tend to be worded in a spatial context. They call for a greater role or participation of one level of government as opposed to another—for the expansion of certain programs and benefits. However, as a matter of practice, general group policies are amended to conform to what is realistically attainable in the legislative process. Spatial issues may, deliberately, not even be raised so as not to arouse vested functional interests. Groups have the alternative either to adapt their objectives to the limits fixed by institutional structures and competing claimants or to seek to mold the environment toward acceptance of their objectives.[8] The groups do both, yet they invest greater efforts in the former within the permissible limits of previous policy commitments. Initially the mayors cooperated with the highway lobby interests rather than fighting them. By doing so, the mayors were able to gain highway lobby support for using Highway Trust Funds for "highway related" purposes like fringe parking areas, special bus lanes, and traffic control. They also gained their help in lobbying for separate mass transit appropriations and operating subsidies for mass transit systems. From the mayors' perspective they gained their short-run objectives, while the highway lobby felt that the more funds Congress directly appropriated for mass transit the less pressure there would be for breaking open the HTF for mass transit uses.

The governors, of course, have historical and structural advantages over the other groups. The Senate already is organized on the basis of

---

[7] Ibid., p. 359.

[8] See V. O. Key, *Politics, Parties, and Pressure Groups,* 5th ed., Crowell Co., New York, 1964, p. 130.

equal state representation and, in spite of the natural rivalry which flares between governors and senators, a substantial basis exists for accommodating federal programs to state interests. As Matthews observed of the Senate, most lobbyists believe that the best argument for most senators most of the time is in terms of advantage to the senator's state. Quoting a powerful Washington lobbyist, "A Senator won't go along with us because of friendship, or persuasiveness. . . . The real argument is that the bill will do something worthwhile for his state."[9]

Thus the primary advantage the governors have over local government interest groups stems from the historical tendency for allocative programs to be channeled through the states. For the major part of the nation's history, this has been the case. The federal government dealt with the states from the perspective of structure, potential federal influence and leverage, accountability, and tradition. The states were thereby used wherever necessary to deal with their corporate creations—local governments. This had been the case at least with nearly all categorical grant programs including agriculture, welfare, unemployment, higher education, mental health, highways, and conservation.

Because Congress and executive agencies are organized primarily along functional lines, they have a certain bias in doing business with the states. Mayors and their urban allies often most compensate for this by accommodating their strategies to the positions of other actors, previous programs, and the arenas in which they seek benefits. Moreover, the search for political constituencies is frustrated by the complexity of overlapping jurisdictions at local levels. These entail congressional districts, counties, and special district lines which crisscross city maps and state boundaries and rarely correspond to metropolitan problems. Policy for urban areas often emerges indirectly as a result of pursuing other objectives. Public housing programs began, for example, primarily as an employment palliative and stimulant for the building trades, while federal aid to airport construction was adopted to promote civil aviation. Both are considered urban program with benefits distributed primarily to urban residents.

The government groups also seek geographic inclusion in programs regardless of their original scope and intended beneficiaries. Group admission often requires skillful bargaining and negotiation. Federal investment programs designed to meet specific problems of the inner city are invariably broadened by congressional amendment to include rural areas, while programs targeted to specific rural needs are enlarged to include metropolitan areas. Schultze terms this process "functional logrolling" to point out how trade-offs emerge on a strictly functional basis among urban and rural interests to broaden a program's benefits

[9] Donald R. Matthews, *U.S. Senators and Their World*, Random House, New York, 1960, p. 182.

and expand its constituency.[10] Trade-offs rarely occur across functional lines, though increased rural, suburban, and urban cleavages within Congress may change this. Such characteristic trade-offs also suggest the difficulty in enacting programs, especially those of a public investment nature, that are targeted to a specific geographically limited problem.

Case studies involving the highway program, poverty legislation, anti-crime and juvenile delinquency bills amply support Schultze's observation. Several other cases may be drawn upon as well. Model Cities, for example, was designed initially to concentrate funds on a complete face-lifting for a few selected cities. Two years following passage, 147 cities were participating in the program, with benefits spread among the maximum number of congressional districts by the time actual federal funds began being dispersed. Grants were made in forty-nine states and to cities of all sizes, including several below the 10,000 population level. The water and sewer grants program, which was intended to assist suburban communities primarily in planning and developing their growth, represents another such case. By the time this popular program traversed Congress, virtually all sizes of communities were made eligible for funding, with three separate programs developed to ensure their participation. Thus the government interest groups share with the President the problem of dealing with a policy-making process which involves agencies and congressional committees, their constituency orientation as well as functional structures.

Moreover, the government groups generally compete at a disadvantage with more well-established claimants which tend to be more cohesive and possess greater expertise in special areas of public policy. Guilds and functional support groups, organized at all levels, operate with maximum visibility, and usually with maximum effectiveness. They help shape public policy by assisting government agencies and bureaus in developing support groups. Depending on an agency's need for these groups, it may allow these groups considerable freedom in negotiating arrangements with other guilds and allies that benefit directly or indirectly from the agency's programs. Indeed, governors and mayors discover not only the enormous problems they have in gaining admission to policy systems dominated by guild groups but also the fact that they must often rely upon them as interpreters and implementers of public policy. Guild leaders can be found leading and misleading political executives in their relations with higher government levels.

State-local executives have been known to rely on guild leaders for dealing with Washington and may even follow their lead in lobbying. Such dependency has led many an outside observer to wonder exactly who is

---

[10] Charles L. Schultze, *The Politics and Economics of Public Spending,* Brookings Institution, Washington, D.C., 1968, p. 134.

leading whom. The governors, for example, almost blindly followed state highway officials in advocating more funds for highways—winning the applause of rural and suburban constituents—without much concern for the program's overall impact. The mayors tended to depend upon their housing experts, the National Association of Housing and Redevelopment Officials, for shaping much of their housing policy. The USCM initially echoed NAHRO's opposition to President Johnson's rent supplements program in 1965 which produced a tremendous uproar among many of the mayors' allies inside and outside of Congress. "How could the mayors follow the public housers in opposing this new program," some asked, "when it offered an opportunity to expand housing specifically and provided a strategy for dealing with urban density generally?" Once again, numerous cases could be cited illustrating the dependency of the government groups upon guilds, which was far more characteristic of group behavior prior to 1968 than after.

RESOURCES, STRATEGIES, AND TACTICS

Central to the achievement of group purposes are strategies and tactics. One must first describe how the government interest groups pursue their objectives, a question of strategy, and then what specific actions they take in fulfilling a strategy, notably tactics. Strategies are the links between goal attainment and perceptions of group leaders and the political arenas that impose restraints as well as create opportunities for them. Policy consists of relatively long-range purposes and objectives. Goals are short-range and immediate. Strategies and tactics, of course, relate to group resources and such factors as scale of lobbying, intensity of effort, allies, and coalition building, which necessarily leads into a description of the activities, resources, and other skills of the groups and their leaders.[11]

Lobbying, by definition, involves communications, whether direct or indirect, Washington-based or constituency-generated. Studies of lobbying generally indicate that information and its uses are viewed as the most important exchangeable commodity by legislators and lobbyists alike.[12] Among the many functions interest groups perform in the American political system—such as structuring alternatives and choices, serving as buffers, providing access and functional representation—the channeling

[11] Aaron Wildavsky, The Politics of the Budgetary Process, Little Brown, Boston, 1964, pp. 63–64.

[12] See Lester W. Milbrath, The Washington Lobbyist, Rand McNally, Chicago, 1963, chap. 11; Raymond A. Bauer, Ithiel de la Sola Pool, and Lewis A. Dexter, American Business and Public Policy, chap. 32; and Margaret A. Hunt and Andrew Scott, Congress and Lobbies, University of North Carolina Press, Chapel Hill, N.C., 1966, chap. 2.

of information ranks highest. "Information is often power," note Bauer and associates, "while facts are [lobbyists'] stock in trade."[13] Whether dealing with legislators, agency officials, or the White House, these groups are a constant source regarding attitudes and needs of often significant subsets of an official's constituency. They provide facts and information about programs and feedback on their consequences, which aid policy makers in achieving their goals and performing their own roles successfully.

Thus the ubiquitous task encompassing all group functions entails the acquisition, translation, and dissemination of information. The gathering of information may occur on at least three levels: (1) through interaction with policy makers in federal officialdom; (2) through a Washington network of other groups, allies, and the media; and (3) through rank and file members, local allies, or constituents. *Feedback* refers to the total information process—involving actors on all government levels, federal officialdom, group demands and actions—to data which are fed back to the organization and compared with desired performance or goals. In a systems orientation, information and feedback are constantly circulated through innumerable channels between and among the government groups, policy makers, and group clients. The government groups operate at the vortex of a steady stream of information up through the federal system, within the Washington community, and back down from leaders to members.

The strategies and tactics of the groups tend to be shaped by decisions governing the means, methods, and timing for making information available to allies—executive and legislative officials. As Milbrath aptly notes, "the essential task of lobbying groups is to figure out how they can handle communications most effectively to get through to decision-makers."[14] Communications are not without intent, for groups seek to reinforce, change, or neutralize perceptions that policy makers may have of a situation. The groups use many varieties of strategies and tactics. Several of the more typical ones are of particular importance, however, in understanding how they operate.

Use Access and Get the Matter on the Agenda

The intermediate objective of all political interest groups bent on maximizing their influence is to develop and improve access. Considering the many points of entry that groups enjoy, almost all are held to be able to gain access at some stage or level in the policy process. Yet some groups

---

[13] Raymond A. Bauer, Ithiel de la Sola Pool, and Lewis A. Dexter, *American Business and Public Policy*, pp. 346–347.

[14] Lester W. Milbrath, *The Washington Lobbyist*, pp. 210–211.

assuredly gain access more easily than others. For a number of reasons the government interest groups find access to Congress, the White House, and most executive agencies readily facilitated. This is a function of the groups' prestige, national membership and orientation, and the "door opening" power of one or more members. Group demands generally tend to be accommodated to the extent that they are viewed as being legitimate ones by policy makers.[15] One of the principal resources that the government interest groups take advantage of is a certain legitimacy in standing. Since they represent the interests of state and local governments and are elected government officials, their legitimacy as actors is generally enhanced in the short run over other lobbying groups that are often private in composition and protective of narrow, specialized interests. Though the general public, segments of the media, and others may accord the government groups considerable legitimacy, this high status does not necessarily carry over to federal policy makers who may see them differently. Nevertheless even these federal officials are attentive to their demands largely because of the status accorded them by others.

Effective access is no assurance of success. An attentive audience is not synonymous with influence over decision making. Access should be seen as a gradual and distinctly cumulative process. It relates to the development of expertise, confidence attributed to the reliability of their information, and the political needs of policy makers. The lobbying tasks of the groups, once gaining access, are defined in terms of trying to convince and persuade federal officials that what state and local executives desire is what they, the officials, also want or should want as well. On an aggregate basis it means persuading the White House and executive officials that broader constituencies will be affected by particular decisions or actions which are in their interests to consider.

Revenue sharing is a particularly good example of the latter. Nelson Rockefeller, the leading state-local advocate of the measure, helped convince White House advisers that President Nixon and the GOP had to make revenue sharing their first domestic priority. Regardless of how the issue went in Congress, the New York Governor argued, the GOP would have a major campaign advantage to take to the voters in 1972. If revenue sharing failed to pass, the Republicans could blame the Democratic Congress. If it passed, the President and the party would take a lion's share of the political credit, something positive to show the electorate. Rockefeller's campaign to get revenue sharing on the President's agenda won out in the inner White House battles between late 1970 and early 1971.

Also, Rockefeller had become the senior statesman for the governors. Elected to a fourth term in 1970, the New York Governor had compiled an illustrious career of government service at the federal and state levels.

---

[15] V. O. Key, *Politics, Parties, and Pressure Groups*, chap. 6.

He played a strong supportive role in developing the President's domestic program. It was Rockefeller who argued the case for grant reform, phased federal assumption of welfare costs, and revenue sharing before the President and his Urban Affairs Council in February 1969. The governor came to the White House armed with a domestic legislative program and an immediate agenda for the new Republican administration. The *Washington Post* editorialized on Rockefeller's role: "Whether the matter at hand is a presidential program or a party platform . . . Rockefeller's role seems to be that of the forcer of issues, the man sets forth a capacious list of musts which he believes Mr. Nixon can ignore only at his own and the nation's—or Party's peril."[16]

The job of persuasion is one of adjusting group objectives to achieve a certain harmony of values between the groups and the policy makers they are attempting to influence. As executives, group members often feel the pinch of service demands, taxpayer revolts, and voter discontent more quickly than federal officials. Their stakes and constituencies may differ from those of the people they seek to lobby. Nonetheless the obvious differences may be blurred to the extent that the demands upon these officials have electoral implications for federal officialdom.

The all-important problem of group leaders is to figure ways to make the often preferential access they enjoy most productive. The direct approach, the personal presentation of a case, is widely considered to be the most effective tactic for communication.[17] Consequently, the best lobbyists from the groups' vantage are individual members. Permanent organizational staff and elected leaders may engage in direct lobbying themselves from time to time, but primarily insofar as they are opening access, making contacts, and directing tactics of members. As NACO's Hillenbrand remarked, "It doesn't do any good for some NACO lobbyist to call on a representative. Generally he's not one damn bit interested in someone like me. But his local elected county official is a different matter. He'll listen to him."[18]

Government interest groups build upon their high degrees of access by maintaining direct contact between them, their clients, and Washington officials. All the groups make an effort to know the majority and minority counsels of every major legislative committee and subcommittee. These people become vital information sources for anticipating and responding to congressional action: members' positions, committee scheduling, voting patterns, past experiences, and anticipated results. The mayors have their own special relations with members and staff of the Banking and Currency Committees, key congressional activists, heads of city congressional

[16] *Washington Post,* February 15, 1969, p. 18.

[17] Lester W. Milbrath, *The Washington Lobbyist,* chap. 1.

[18] *National Journal,* **3**:1138, May 29, 1971.

delegations, and others. The mayors' groups have taken the lead in cultivating those congressmen and senators who champion their bills, assist them in committees, on floor debates, and in legislative passage. The governors, after years of filial reliance on former governors in the Senate, have nurtured a broader group of allies concerned with state problems and with encouraging state leadership in national programs, particularly in the wake of President Nixon's New Federalism.

Similarly, the groups seek to maximize the use of their formal and informal liaison with the White House, cabinet, and agency officials through several channels, some recently instituted under the Johnson and Nixon administrations. The NGC and USCM-NLC executive committees, for example, meet separately with the President annually, following the State of the Union and Budgetary Messages, to review prospective legislation for the forthcoming congressional session. They also use such sessions to air specific problems of state and local governments. The Johnson White House efforts, aimed at strengthening communications between the groups, their clients, and the White House office, have been continued in the Nixon administration through other institutional forms such as the Office of Management and Budget, the Urban Affairs Council, the Domestic Council, and the Vice President's assignment in intergovernmental relations. The NGC's "Mid-Year Meetings on Federal-State Relations," and the USCM-NLC's "Congressional-City Conferences," and federal aid coordinators' sessions conducted by all groups, provide annual forums between the groups and federal officialdom for channeling grievances and exchanging information.

Each of the groups have their own individual intercessors at the White House. NACO found Vice President Agnew, a former NACO director and county executive, and John Ehrlichman, assistant to the President and executive director of the Domestic Council, often receptive to their demands. The NGC uses its ties to former governors in the Nixon cabinet and GOP party allies as a means for gaining a hearing. Besides Richard Lugar and other large-city mayors, the USCM-NLC have departmental advocates for their demands in Floyd Hyde, former mayor of Fresno, who became Assistant Secretary of HUD, and former Seattle Mayor James D. Braman, the assistant secretary of the Department of Transportation (DOT). But the groups use their White House access sparingly. They have discovered that the President and White House aides have higher priorities or, for other reasons, feel that they should not intervene. Lobbying the White House typically is preceded, accompanied, and followed by lobbying efforts directed at departments and agencies. Greater centralization of decision making at the White House, particularly during the first Nixon administration, made agencies less of an immediate resource than they otherwise might have been. Since the groups deal regularly with departments and agencies, they begin most lobbying initiatives there. Agencies often are the forcers of issues, the administrators of federal guidelines and regulations, and a potential helper when key programmatic decisions affect their constituencies. Hyde and Romney at HUD defended Model Cities throughout Mr. Nixon's first term, seeking to accommodate basic changes in the program's philosophy, goals, and orientation to the mayors' interests.

To the extent that all the groups work energetically and continuously at the task of extracting dollars from the federal Treasury, their general appeals for assistance are directed at the President and Office of Management and Budget. Periodic meetings between the President and group leaders only reinforce these objectives as applied to specific programs and pending decisions. But where the White House is the ultimate target of influence strategies, the groups may focus upon Congress, federal agencies, other interest groups, and the media as a means of persuading the White House of the political support for their demands.

Individual incursions by governors or mayors also may serve both the purpose of the chief executive and the group. When high-ranking administration officials or key congressional leaders meet with a governor or mayor, the groups seek to elevate matters of collective concern to the agenda. Big-city mayors who journey to Washington with some frequency call upon the USCM-NLC to prepare an agenda and arrange appointments. The mayors' organizations typically brief the visiting chief executive on his particular concern, relating it to problems of fellow mayors, so that he might take up the broader question with agency or congressional officials. Whether visiting a congressman or an agency, the mayors increasingly come to Washington with their homework done, while backup support by the USCM-NLC adds to their effectiveness as lobbyists. A tactic used to enhance group access is for a staff member of the association to accompany a mayor or governor on his rounds to ensure that the federal official might identify the staff man with that particular state-local chief executive for purposes of future contacts. The staff man also serves as a check upon administrative officials to ensure consistency with what has been told others.

Whether it is visits by individual chief executives or group meetings with agency, White House, or congressional leaders, the organizations pursue the common objective: "Get the matter on the agenda, impress upon federal officials the need for immediate action, or let them know of your concern and that of your constituents for the continuation or expansion of a certain program."

In addition to annual meetings where the President, his emissaries, and congressional leaders are welcomed guests, each group conducts one or more organizational session in Washington where the serious business of implementing group policies is pursued. At times the groups may coordinate these meetings, as in the case of NACO and the mayors or, in spring 1971, when the groups jointly lobbied for revenue sharing. Complementing these full organization sessions, each has periodic gatherings in Washington of its officers, standing committee leaders, or ad hoc lobbying arms where the focus typically is on a particular bill, issue, or problem. The USCM's Legislative Action Committee complements the organization's executive committee by implementing previously agreed upon lobbying strategies. NACO's counterpart to the mayors' lobbying arm, the Council of Elected County Executives, does much the same thing.

The government groups also may rely on partisan subgroups to carry out strategies and tactics. In late 1970, for example, a delegation from the Republican Governors' Association personally delivered to the White House a resolution stating that "nothing less than a federal revenue sharing of at least $10 billion annually" would prevent "an impending collapse of confidence in state and local government, particularly in urban areas."[19] One month later President Nixon announced his support for a $5 billion annual revenue-sharing program. Similarly, several Democratic mayors who publicly endorsed the President's new plan came to Washington in early 1971, where they criticized Capitol Hill Democrats for opposing the President's revenue sharing proposal more out of a partisan reflex action than on the legislation's merits. Once Democratic leaders in Congress were confronted by a situation where their opposition to revenue sharing had split party leaders on the federal and state-local levels, their receptivity to the legislation changed dramatically.[20] Three months after the mayors' rebuke of party officials, revenue sharing hearings began under Wilbur Mills' sponsorship, eventually leading to passage.

Build Coalitions—Form Alliances

One observer of Washington lobbying states that "lobbying can be understood only as the reflection of interests shared by shifting coalitions made up of members of Congress, outside pressures, and executive agencies."[21] Coalition and alliance building is a way of life for the government interest groups, especially on matters of important legislation or funding. Few lobbying associations, after all, including the government groups, have the staff, expertise, personnel, or funds to mount either a Congresswide campaign or significant grass roots effort. Preceding case studies only underscore the fact that no single group is likely to be entirely successful in gaining its immediate objectives without the assistance of numerous allies and probably the aid of other government groups.

[19] Resolution adopted at the Republican Governors' Association Annual Meeting, Sun Valley, Idaho, December 14, 1970.

[20] National Journal, 3:719–724, April 3, 1971.

[21] The Washington Lobbyist, 2nd ed., Congressional Quarterly, Inc., Washington, D.C., 1971, p. 52.

The government interest groups individually do not possess sufficient resources to compete successfully in most congressional battles when aligned against larger, more powerful vote-getting groups. They are generalists with a wide scope of activities and interests, needful of allies inside and outside government to accomplish objectives. They do not have the members, resources, and potential sanctions of organized labor, the narrow policy specialization of the American Medical Association, or even the special-interest focus of the National Rifle Association.

For years large-city mayors viewed urban renewal as their principal federal-local program. In focusing much of its lobbying activities on the housing-renewal areas, the USCM works most closely with two main support groups, the National Association of Housing and Redevelopment Officials (NAHRO) and the National Housing Conference (NHC). NAHRO is a voluntary association of state and local housing officials which serves as a clearinghouse for information on low-cost housing and slum clearance. The NHC is a peak association of more than 40 national groups constituted for purposes of promoting the interest of public housing. Since the 1930s NAHRO and the USCM have had a symbiotic relationship with the mayors who were more concerned about urban renewal than public housing.[22] This triumvirate joins the mayors' political resources with NAHRO's expertise and NHC's support groups in a cohesive alliance for protecting, promoting, and expanding public housing and urban renewal programs. They compromise the core group of the mayors' housing allies but are joined by satellite actors whose assistance is needed in lobbying for federal housing programs.

The federal government's involvement in housing programs since the 1930s has been accompanied by a proliferating network of actors who have substantial stakes in policy decisions. The mayors are a key component of this housing subsystem, using their leverage and bargaining resources to achieve many of their goals—such as continuous increases in federal contributions to urban renewal, more flexible use of funds for commercial redevelopment, enlarged capital grants and loans, broader and more encompassing housing programs like Model Cities, new towns, and rent supplements. The mayors have proved to be somewhat flexible in moving from program to program, concentrating their resources either in Congress or the executive as housing leadership changed. Once urban renewal and public housing had fallen on bad times during the Nixon administration, the mayors first pushed to preserve Model Cities and then to expand it under broader community development programs. They went back and forth from HUD to the congressional Banking and Currency

---

[22] See Suzanne Farkas, *Urban Lobbying*, New York University Press, New York, 1971, chap. 2.

Committees in building consensus around housing policies for the cities. With HUD's obvious difficulties in gaining White House acceptance for its housing policies, Congress snatched the housing initiative from HUD in the early 1970s. When the White House declared a moratorium on federally subsidized housing in early 1973, the mayors moved with full force to get their congressional allies to force decisions favorable to their interests.

However, where urban lobbying might have been considered parochial, both in terms of issues and allies, it has changed dramatically, best typified by the USCM-NLC consolidation. In addition to organized labor, civil rights organizations, ideological support groups like the Americans for Democratic Action, and a spate of municipal officials' organizations, the mayors have built their own support groups and formed their own coalitions. These efforts are aimed at expanding their constituencies. Following wide-scale urban rioting, the mayors helped create the Urban Coalition in 1967 for the purposes of affecting "a certain sense of immediate urgency about the need for positive and progressive action for our cities."[23] The Coalition—with leaders from business, labor, religious, and civil rights organizations—teamed up with other groups like Urban America, the National Alliance of Businessmen, the Lawyers Committee on Civil Rights, and other professional associations. Together they comprised a broad-based coalition to lobby in 1967–1968 for restoration of appropriations for OEO's Head Start and Summer Job Programs, rent supplements, Model Cities, open housing, and other programs. Several spin-offs from this alliance were brought into being in the late 1960s and early 1970s, like John Gardner's Common Cause and comparable groups which often assist the mayors in their lobbying endeavors.

The mayors' groups also formed ad hoc alliances in which they played down their lead role for fear of antagonizing opponents as well as maintaining internal group cohesion. The USCM, for example, formed the Urban Alliance in June 1966, at the White House's request, to lobby on behalf of the administration's Model Cities program. This coalition—composed of some sixty organizations from labor, business, civil rights, and HUD's traditional allies (planners, builders, and money providers)—proved so successful in aiding congressional passage of Model Cities that it was reassembled the following year to lobby for appropriations.

Similarly, the USCM-NLC organized and helped finance the Urban Passenger Transportation Association in the early 1960s to lobby for the passage and funding of the Urban Mass Transit Act of 1961. This was an umbrella-type of alliance under which the mayors, major commuter

---

[23] Statement adopted at the Emergency Convocation of Urban leaders creating the Urban Coalition, Washington, D.C., August 24, 1967.

railroads, the transit industry, and railway unions obtained funding for the mass transit program.[24] However, this was a rather narrow lobby composed of management and unions and the mayors from those cities which were suffering from collapsing commuter transportation service (New York, Philadelphia, Chicago, and Boston). But with burgeoning financial difficulties of public and private transit agencies nationally and growing environmental concern over pollution and highway construction, the transit lobby grew by leaps and bounds, including citizen groups, conservationists, planners, and the media. The mayors directed this new coalition not at its obvious central city allies but instead toward suburban interests to convince Congress and the public that subways and mass transit programs would benefit suburbanites as much as inner-city dwellers.

Revenue sharing constitutes a special example of coalition building among the government groups and a wide spectrum of allies. It was not until late 1970 that USCM's Gunther proclaimed that the "six big pigs" (the five government interests groups and the ICMA) had decided to work jointly to get a revenue-sharing program through Congress. Once united, the government groups reached out for support from businessmen, academics, church groups, and prominent citizens to form a bipartisan coalition to lobby Congress for action.

Following President Nixon's FY 1974 Budget Message in which he proposed to terminate more than a hundred federal programs, the government groups became a key component of the vast interest group system which formed numerous coalitions to fight the White House's move. The mayors participated, for example, in the Coalition on Human Needs and Budget Priorities, which brought together church groups, labor, and various citizen organizations to dramatize the sweeping impact that proposed budget cuts would have in each state and each congressional district.

Virtually dozens of examples of comparable coalitions formed by the NGC, NACO, and the Council of State Governments (COSGO) could be cited. These latter groups more often than not, however, form alliances with various clientele organizations' and guild groups. The governors may work with state school superintendents and administrators in education, AASHO in highways, state employment administrators in manpower, state health officials in health care and pollution, and the Chamber of Commerce in industry and economic development. NACO has its county affiliates in welfare, education, recreation, parks, highways, and the like, which are helpful to it in gaining county inclusion in intergovernmental programs. Thus, shifting coalitions are indeed characteristic of contemporary lobbying, which the government groups participate in fully.

[24] See Royce Hanson, "Congress Copes with Mass Transit, 1960–1964," in *Congress and Urban Problems*, pp. 311–349.

Nourish Your Allies

It should not be surprising that congressmen hear most often from those who agree with them and, conversely, lobbying groups tend to communicate with and service most extensively those legislators already known to be friendly toward them.[25] The same generally holds for relations between the groups and executive agencies and bureaus. Each of the government groups begins with potential allies in Congress. Anywhere from ten to twenty former governors have served in the Senate continously since 1945, while scores of former mayors and county officials familiar with the government interest groups can be found in the House. Reciprocally, several congressmen have left federal service to become mayors and governors. Former group leaders predictably are greater allies than mere former members. Senators Carlsen, Jordon, Mundt, and Fannin were NGC leaders. Senator Caleb Boggs was a past COSGO president and NGC chairman, while Senators Hartke, Clark, Douglas, and Humphrey were former city officials. Vice President Agnew, Senator Cook, and several House members had been active in NACO when serving as county officials. However, potential allies may not be actual allies, for as Frank Bane observed of former governors elevated to the Senate, "They quickly become 'federalized,' leaving behind them their sympathies for state chief executives."[26]

In addition to city and state congressional delegations, each of the groups has its committee and subcommittee allies of whom they take special care by feeding information, research, drafting legislation, or merely acting as an intermediary between the elected official and key groups in their constituency. Similarly, much effort in building this friendly relationship requires that governors, mayors, or county officials take every opportunity to make the congressman or senator look good back home. This resource should not be underestimated. What many mayors and county officials try to accomplish with legislators from their home district is to interject themselves into the communications process on legislation which relates to their city or county specifically. For a mayor, this means trying to become the person that the legislator looks to in interpreting various legislative proposals dealing with urban affairs. Thus it is incumbent on the lobbying mayor to put the situation into terms that the legislator can understand and make him see how it affects the particular city both may represent.[27]

With large-city mayors' proprietary interest in housing and urban

[25] See Lewis A. Dexter, "The Representative and His District," in Robert Peabody and Nelson W. Polsby (eds.), New Perspectives on the House of Representatives, pp. 2–29.

[26] Frank Bane, private interview held at the U.S. Office of Emergency Preparedness, Washington, D.C., December 2, 1968.

[27] See Nation's Cities, May, 1971, pp. 8–16.

renewal, the Banking and Currency Committees have been their primary focus of activities. The staff and members of these committees—including such figures as Douglas, Williams, Barrett, Raines, Dwyer, Reuss, Ashley, Moorehead, Muskie, Sparkman, and others—have built a trusting and confidential relationship with the USCM and its staff. Former committee staff man Lawrence Henderson, and Albert Rains (D-Ala.), past Housing Subcommittee chairman, both served as consultants to the USCM on housing legislation upon leaving congressional service, further tieing the mayors to the committees.

Each of the groups strengthened its staff throughout the 1968–1973 period, hiring legislative assistants from Capitol Hill and high-ranking departmental personnel from the executive and elsewhere in government. The government groups, in fact, resemble older, more established national lobbies which typically recruit from these places. They have become active participants in the Washington "musical chairs" game, where policy experts and "in and outers" move easily from congressional staffs, to executive positions, to interest groups or law firms, and then back again. By using practitioner talent, the groups enhance their expertise, expand access, and promote their own interests by providing talent for future administrations. Also by including both Democrats and Republicans on their staffs, the groups increase their bipartisan orientation and broaden their ties to a diverse clientele.

A major aim of the government groups, like that of many interest groups, is to induce Congress to create agencies in their own image to the greatest possible degree. This is typically reflected in the groups' lobbying activities whether they are responding to the creation of new federal agencies or to the reorganization of older ones. Similarly, as program constituents and agency support groups, they seek to remold agency structure and behavior internally to make the agencies more conducive to their particular needs.

Federal agencies have been increasingly accommodating to the groups, exchanging information with them and recognizing the value of their expertise and potential as a support group. Strength in a constituency is no less an asset to an agency and its programs than to an elected politician. Whether seeking to coopt the groups and their members, build amicable relations, or neutralize their opposition, agencies find the government interest groups to be a direct pipeline to their clients for dispersing information, gaining feedback on programs, and in anticipating problems or meeting needs. HUD needs the mayors, for example, in defending urban renewal, sustaining Model Cities, and preventing White House budget cutters from terminating housing subsidy programs. DOT requires the assistance both of governors and county officials in expanding mass transit programs. HEW must deal with the NGC and NACO on a host of human resource programs. Indeed, the fortunes of department heads can, in the eyes of the White House, rise and fall depending on the degree to which they keep the government groups' constituency supportive of the President's programs. This may be evidenced by how assiduously these executives officials court the groups and their members at their midyear and annual meetings.

Exploit Cleavages

Whether seeking to benefit from differences within or between the legislative and the executive branches, the groups often exploit these cleavages when significant advantages may accrue toward achieving their goals. When Democrats controlled the Presidency, the mayors and allies generally benefited from access, programmatic support, and a close working relationship with Democratic congressional leadership and White House liaison on matters within their fields of interest. Under the same conditions, governors often looked to Republican congressional leadership, Southern senior leaders in the Democratic party, and allies like the Republican National Committee seeking an alternative to Democratic programs favoring federal-local relations. On the other hand, under a Republican President, governors have found the White House more receptive to their demands, while the mayors turned to Congress for program support and fiscal aid to the cities. An incumbent Democratic President imposes limitations upon Democratic mayors, as does a Republican one upon GOP governors, curtailing somewhat public criticism of their party's chief leader which might prove embarrassing.

However, the groups seek support within both parties, developing or otherwise joining coalitions which may further their goals. Historical tendencies and past alliances notwithstanding, the groups are not wed to either party exclusively, nor can they afford to be. The NGC has gained support from Republican leadership, the Republican Policy Committees, the Wednesday Club, Southern Democrats, state delegations, and supporters of state-run programs like Congresswoman Edith Green. The mayors, on the other hand, work largely with liberal Democrats and Republicans like Javits, Kennedy, Mondale, Williams, Brooke, Matthias, Percy, and, in particular, the Democratic Study Group (DSG) in the House. The DSG, an informal work group of some 160 members predominantly from the North and West, continues to play a strong supportive role of the mayors on transportation, housing, welfare legislation, and on urban appropriations. DSG leaders like Frank Thompson, Henry Reuss, Charles Boland, Tom Ashley, and John Blatnik are ranking or near ranking members on several major committees involving urban interests. Where the mayors looked to Congress during the Eisenhower Presidency for protecting and expanding urban programs, they have reverted, as it were, to this earlier strategy again during the Nixon administration to maintain and expand funding levels attained under the previous Democratic administrations.

The governors were among the beneficiaries of President Johnson's abdication in 1968. They worked hand in hand with Republican leaders in turning around the President's crime bill to a state-run program. They also assisted their congressional allies in raising the bloc-grant issue in the education, poverty, and juvenile delinquency programs. The mayors lined up with the White House on the Model Cities program, assisting in passage and funding, and, under the Nixon administration, protecting HUD and Model Cities from dismemberment by eager enthusiasts close to the President.

With housing leadership between 1969 and 1972 essentially divided between Romney at HUD, the President's Domestic Council and budget advisers, and congressional committees, the mayors played one off against the other to achieve the most favorable outcome possible. In the omnibus Housing and Urban Development Act of 1970, the mayors worked closely with HUD and the Housing Subcommittee of the House Banking and Currency Committee in developing a $2.8-billion multiyear authorization bill. Fearful of the long-term costs and program rigidity that might emerge from this bill, the White House at the last minute tried to disrupt the HUD, committee, and interest group negotiations by calling for a $695-million one-year extension of existing authorizations. The House Banking and Currency Committee not only rejected the administration's alternative but wrote its own version. In December 1970, the 91st Congress passed a massive $2.9 billion housing program over the administration's strong objections. This case illustrates how the USCM-NLC attempt to touch all the bases, working with each of the major housing actors separately. The mayors made peace with HUD, sought White House approval for HUD's recommended housing package, and then reverted to Congress to gain the best possible arrangement against White House opposition.[28]

The mayors and county officials lobbied Congress successfully for substantial increases in the 1970 HUD appropriations bill. The Senate added $700 million to the President's urban renewal request, while the House increased the water and sewers appropriation by $350 million. The President thereupon vetoed the appropriation, citing these two increases as his justification. A compromise bill appropriating $17.7 billion, still $900 million above the President's original request, was eventually agreed to. The mayors and county officials, working with their congressional allies, achieved in part their goals of increasing appropriations for these two separate programs which each favored.

A number of cases could be cited where the government groups have

---

[28] See *National Journal*, **3**:59–67, January 9, 1971.

turned the cleavages within Congress, among committees, and between branches of government to their advantage. The internal fragmentation among executive and legislative actors over fiscal and programmatic choices provides ample opportunities for intergroup negotiations as well as negotiations with those they seek to influence. Furthermore, the sequence of the legislative process—proposal, passage, funding, and implementation—ensures that losses can be remedied and decisions appealed, allowing even greater advantages for groups to exploit the governmental process.

Gear Strategies to the Legislative Climate

The groups seek to avoid arrogance, presumptive thinking, and such sins of venality as implying that they know what state and local needs are better than federal policy makers do. After all, most congressmen and senators think they know more about a particular bill or constituency than a governor or mayor and can show their seniority in many cases to substantiate this. So the groups generally try to impress upon the legislator that his constituents are supportive of the policies the groups advocate. Whether through a congressional hearing or personal contact, the groups call upon a member who is deemed the optimum conveyor of information to the target of their influence strategy. Group leaders choose the official who best suits their strategy and can gain maximum mileage from a contact, whether through personal influence with an individual policy maker or, in the case of a larger audience, through greatest media exposure.

Selection of congressional witnesses is often made for tactical reasons. It may reflect audiences appealed to, targets of influence, expertise required, or special political relationships, if any, between the witness and key members of a congressional committee. Therefore the groups often match witnesses with committee members. New Jersey's Richard Hughes testified on behalf of the NGC on housing legislation, in large part due to his state's strong representation on the House and Senate Banking and Currency Committees, which oversee housing legislation. Hughes's successor, William Cahill, a former congressman and author of the 1967 bloc-grant amendment on the crime bill, represented the NGC in 1970 in defense of the state-run program. James Tate, the mayor of Philadelphia, often presented the USCM-NLC position on housing legislation before the Housing Subcommittee because its chairman, Congressman William Barrett, is also from Philadelphia. To appeal the punitive welfare amendments added to the Social Security Act of 1967 by the Senate Finance Committee, NACO relied upon testimony from a county executive from Chairman Russell Long's home town to make its case. Nelson Rockefeller was the governors' most effective spokesman on revenue sharing from all accounts, in part due to the fact that his state, New York, had the highest state-local per capita tax burden in the nation.

An audience broader than a congressional committee may be a group's target. New York City's John Lindsay has been extremely effective in gaining press coverage for his congressional testimony in appealing for welfare reform, summer job funds for the cities, and on drug rehabilitation programs. The USCM-NLC relies on Lindsay and other photogenic mayors where grass roots lobbying and national attention is needed to move Congress. Chicago's Richard Daley tends to be most effective on low-key lobbying efforts. It was Daley, for instance, whom the USCM used in dealing with David Kennedy, the new Secretary of the Treasury and a fellow Chicagoan, in 1969 on the issue of retaining tax exemption on municipal bonds. As head of the USCM's Transportation Committee, Daley organized much of the behind-the-scenes lobbying for mass transit funding, subsidies, and breaking open the Highway Trust Fund for local discretionary use. Richard Lugar, the Republican Mayor of Indianapolis and 1971 NLC president, took advantage of preferential White House access to help sustain the Model Cities program when prospects for retention seemed bleak. Finally, the groups not only go through considerable effort in matching witnesses to committees but also pair witnesses off against one another. To refute John Lindsay's testimony before the Celler Subcommittee on how New York State was shortchanging the city in its redistribution of federal anticrime funds, the NGC countered with testimony from Nelson Rockefeller, who challenged Lindsay's assertions.[29]

Each of these tactics is vitally important to group strategies and the conveyance of information. Each official has a role to play with individual strengths and weaknesses the organizations seek to tap. A well-timed and executed appeal by a governor, mayor, or county official may keep a bill alive, an amendment intact, an appropriation higher than it might have been. It may even get a bill out of committee or keep an objectionable one dormant. Members vitally affect group fortunes. This fact places a premium upon leadership skills: knowledge of the legislative process and maximization of the intervention strengths of individual members.

This is not to suggest, however, that appeals by a mayor, governor, or county official to a legislative or executive actor automatically produce results. Group officials and members alike attest to the fact that legislative interference on behalf of state-local executives has changed. The complexity of the federal system and the preoccupation of major policy makers with more immediate demands make individual appeals less successful, in most cases, than perhaps they were in the past. This situation

[29] *Law Enforcement Assistance Amendments,* Hearings before the House Judiciary Committee, Subcommittee No. 5, 91st Cong., 2nd Sess., 1970, pp. 293–323, 104–133.

requires all the more that lobbying be conducted in a routinized, concerted, and well-executed manner rather than on a hit-and-miss basis as once was the case.

The mayors, however, have an added problem in gearing their strategies to Congress. They assiduously avoid having major legislation they support being considered a "big-city bill," with benefits thought to favor large cities exclusively. Such legislation not only might open splits between the USCM and NLC, but also would reduce the size of any prospective coalition the large-city mayors could assemble in support of the legislation. Congress is still composed of many members from rural communities and small towns, especially several senior leaders who have nonurban constituencies. Advocates of urban legislation necessarily enlarge a program's coverage to account for this by including metropolitan communities, small towns, and rural areas. Broadening eligibility is essential for attracting the support of legislators and groups who represent small and medium-sized constituencies. As the Brookings study *Congress and Urban Problems* points out, principal sponsors of urban legislation in airports, mass transit, pollution, juvenile delinquency, and food stamps defined these programs in such a manner as to "allay the opposition of and attract support from those representing non-metropolitan constituencies."[30] Even established programs that large-city mayors perhaps have the greatest vested interest in preserving and expanding, like urban renewal, have as a matter of course become middle-sized and small-town programs. In fact, more than half of the cities with urban renewal projects have been found to contain populations of less than 25,000.

The same problems confront the mayors and their allies in obtaining appropriations for urban programs. Since 1965 the mayors' groups have shifted greater attention to gaining maximum funds for existing programs rather than the enacting of new ones. Once again, the mayors and their allies had to convince legislators of the prospective benefits for their constituents and avoid having legislation labeled a "big-city bill." According to USCM's Gunther, "in lobbying for urban legislation our organization thinks in terms of possible appropriations, which means community eligibility of 5,000 in population—a level necessary not only for program passage, but funding."

The mayors' calculations concerning eligibility and benefits are predicated on a general strategy aimed often at selling "urban" programs to as large a following as possible, whether it be housing, transportation, manpower training, or solid waste treatment. In particular policy areas, this may mean gearing specific strategies to key senior leaders. The chairman of the House Education and Labor Committee and the chairman of the House Appropriations Subcommittee on Independent Offices which

---

[30] Frederic N. Cleaveland (ed.), *Congress and Urban Problems*, p. 363.

oversees HUD's funds, for example, are both from communities of less than 5,000 population. Not a single member, in fact, of this all-important House Appropriations Subcommittee between 1966 and 1970 had a city in his district above 200,000, most representing small communities. "To sell urban programs," continues Gunther, "we must appeal to Chairmen like Evins, Perkins, and others in terms of their own constituencies."[31]

Indeed, with the increasing metropolitization of the nation, the groups have become more attentive to the suburban "swing" constituency in Congress. Large-city mayors have dropped much of their former hostility to federal programs with a metropolitan orientation rather than specific inner-city concentration, not only as a clear recognition of their declining power but also because inner-city problems are spilling over to suburban communities. The USCM opposed "new towns" funding in 1966, only to support it actively in the 1970 housing legislation. To retain its alliance with the NLC and broaden its constituency, the mayors see potential benefits obtainable from greater federal focus upon metropolitan approaches to national problems. Similarly governors and mayors compete for influence over administration of metropolitanwide programs, while NACO asserts its own territorial prerogatives where county governments are involved.

In gearing one's strategy to the prevailing congressional climate, the groups often try to anticipate congressional reaction. Congress, for example, is no less perplexed than HUD about the fact that housing subsidy programs seem to have had little demonstrable impact on larger-city problems. Urban renewal, public housing, and low-income home ownership programs have come under attack from a host of clients and critics. Instead of staunchly defending these programs, the mayors worked with HUD and various congressional committees in developing more comprehensive strategies aimed at overhauling existing programs and tailoring them to each city's needs. In some cases the mayors were out in front of Congress in seeking reform as long as such changes meant no diminution of aggregate funds presently directed for inner-city programs. Thus the success of groups' leaders is often dependent upon their "strategic sensitivity," the ability to recognize and to anticipate the expectations of committee members and to relate these to their own actions.

Count Heads and Money

Both the USCM and the NLC are head counting, tabulating committee-, subcommittee-, and Congress-wide voting on matters in which they have a stake. Each of the groups has developed a whip-cracking system for

---

[31] John Gunther, private interview held at the Offices of the U.S. Conference of Mayors, Washington, D.C., January 8, 1969.

mobilizing members, allied groups, and state and local constituents on behalf of its positions. State and city congressional delegations and, in emerging form, suburban delegations as well, can play an essential role in congressional bargaining. Though such delegations differ in cohesiveness, interaction, and party alignment, they nonetheless compromise a potential force in legislative outcomes. They often function as an informal work group, cue-giving mechanism, and bargaining entity. The cohesiveness of urban delegations from New Jersey, Chicago, and Philadelphia is well known, but less so in the case of state delegations. Several governors, especially those from Texas, California, North Carolina, Massachusetts, Pennsylvania, and Ohio, work closely with their congressional representatives and staffs on matters of mutual concern. City delegations were substantially involved in the passage of the Model Cities program in 1966, as were several state delegations on behalf of the NGC-sponsored bloc grant adopted in the 1968 Safe Streets Act. Delegations or portions of delegations are frequently key targets of groups strategies, especially when legislation emerges from committees and is scheduled for floor voting.

Polling of legislators by the NGC and mayors' groups before an important vote also can prove helpful in alerting the organizations and their allies to wavering or undecided legislators. Last-minute calls by a mayor, governor, or key constituent may prove the difference in turning around or otherwise neutralizing an undecided or opposition vote. The mayors, in fact, perform a vital function for Democratic administrations and congressional leaders. They help keep urban congressmen in Washington on major votes. This constitutes a sizable task, given the propensity for absenteeism by many northeastern urban legislators who belong, by common denigrative reference, to the "Tuesday through Thursday Club." NACO also performs this function—limited, however, to mobilizing last-minute contacts by larger counties, mostly in the South and West where county structures and officials tend to be strongest.

President Nixon's extensive use of executive impoundment of previously mandated or congressionally appropriated funds as a means to impose expenditure control produced torrents of criticism from governors, mayors, and county officials. The groups turned first to Congress for redress and, gaining little immediate satisfaction there, brought suit in federal district courts over release of federal funds. Beginning with highway trust funds in 1970 and extending to impoundments for welfare, social services, and water pollution control, states and local governments found the courts increasingly sympathetic to their cause. The courts thus were employed as a key supportive actor for group demands in gaining release of funds and bolstering Congress's determination to curb Presidential impoundment.

Each of the groups now pays increasing attention to congressional authorizations and appropriations: the politics of money. Where the sixties were characterized by the politics of program passage, the seventies ushered in the politics of adequately funding existing programs. The gap between congressional authorizations and actual appropriations widened, exacerbated further by Presidential impoundments. Governors and mayors found Great Society rhetoric and large authorizations devastated by appropriations where, in many cases, less than half the full authorization amount would be appropriated by the Congress. With executive impoundment, even less would be actually spent. The governors began extensive lobbying for increased funding for education, health care, and manpower programs, joining often with the mayors in fighting against federal cutbacks in welfare, medicaid, and social service programs. One of the important considerations leading to consolidation between the mayors' groups, in fact, was the added resources the NLC brought to urban lobbying. Through its small-city membership and state league affiliates, the NLC aids the USCM by reaching into the bailiwicks of rural and suburban legislators on behalf of legislation both support.

Each of the organizations keeps running tabulations on agency and program expenditures, pending grant applications for federal funds, and federal impoundments. "Backlogging" is a supportive tactic used by the groups to provide congressional committees with lists and complaints regarding the backlog of unfunded grant applications. Backlogging may support the groups' claim as to the popularity of a program, or it may be used to demonstrate to a congressman or senator how much federal funds are being denied his district or state. In its successful effort to gain increased congressional appropriations for HUD's water and sewers program, NACO obtained from HUD a computer printout on grant backlogs indicating that there existed $2.5 billion in rejected or pending applications for participation in the program. NACO further broke these figures down by state and congressional district to be used for congressional hearings and floor amendments. Congress not only appropriated $200 million more for the program than the President had requested in 1970 but also passed the Emergency Community Facilities Act of 1970, which provided an additional $1.15 billion for water and sewers and related programs.[32] NACO has since become the repository for pending grant applications for this popular program, which it periodically feeds to congressional supporters. The mayors do much the same thing for urban renewal funds, while the governors keep tabulations on federal allocations for the Clean Waters Program.

Federal funds also may be the incentive that brings the groups together. The Nixon administration's success in obtaining the government interest

<hr/>

[32] See *Housing and Urban Development Legislation 1971,* Hearings before the House Banking and Currency Committee, Subcommittee on Housing, 92nd Cong., 1st. Sess., 1971, pt. 2, pp. 558–562.

groups' support for federal revenue sharing in 1971 was largely contingent upon increasing the program's baseline figure from $500 million to $5 billion annually. Once the President announced his support for the larger figure, the groups had a sufficient reason to work together for the program's enactment. On the other hand, the groups' support for general revenue sharing was contingent upon it not being a substitute for existing grant programs. When it became evident that the President's FY 1973 and FY 1974 budgets would, if successfully passed, reduce and eliminate scores of federal programs, the groups reverted to defense of existing categorical grants and their full authorization levels. Instead of supporting the President's FY 1972 budget, which called for six special revenue-sharing programs with states and localities, the USCM's Legislative Action Council released its own detailed analysis of the budget, which indicated that less, not more, federal funds would be spent on cities. The mayors then decided to examine each special revenue-sharing program on its merits rather than endorsing the six. Where it may not be politically feasible to gain greater federal funds, the groups may opt for reducing federally required matching contributions. In some cases this may be even more desirable to the groups than moderate increases in appropriations for a program. Mass transit funding, for example, was changed in 1970 from two-thirds federal and one-third local to 80 percent federal and 20 percent local. Under the 1970 Federal Highway Act the federal share of the noninterstate component was raised from 50 to 70 percent; in amendments to the Safe Streets Act, the federal share of law enforcement grants was increased from 60 to 75 percent. In each of these cases, mayors, governors, and county officials welcomed lower state-local matching requirements, which reduce the pressures on expenditures for their own funds to support an intergovernmental program.

Research—Counterresearch

Not only the conveyor of information but also the substance of the information is important to successful lobbying. The government interest groups are a constant source of information about members' attitudes, government programs and policies, and clients needs. The outlet for this research and information has its strategic importance as well. Congressional hearings, for example, enable the groups to convey information often not otherwise available to committees and members from the executive or other groups. Whether it is research, surveys, or personal experiences by state and local executives, such information often finds an outlet through general and specialized media. It aids in establishing a committee record, and this is often supportive of a particular program, policy, or amendment which is read by legislators, their staff, and agency people.

It may also be used as background material for congressional debate, appropriations review, and conference committee deliberation.

The mayors have conducted research on the long-term fiscal needs of the cities, their tax bases, need in transportation, housing pollution control, health care facilities, and the like. In urban renewal and housing, the mayors often have more complete data than HUD for the Banking and Currency Committees on work in progress, pending applications, projected needs, and proportion of federal subsidies going to nonurban as opposed to inner-core cities. Such research and detailed analyses of programs have gained increasing respect from congressional committees and executive agencies alike. In 1966, for example, the Conference conducted an Urban Renewal Survey jointly with NAHRO and the League which revealed that some 363 cities could effectively utilize over $5.4 billion in federal grants for planning and executing urban renewal projects during the FY 1967 through FY 1969.[33] These results were presented to the Urban Renewal Administration in HUD and before the Banking and Currency Committees; they were targeted to convince executive and legislative policy makers that the $2.2-billion urban renewal authorizations made for the three-year period were woefully inadequate and nowhere near commensurate with actual needs.

Much of the groups' research is generated to oppose, contradict, or otherwise modify research and statements made by the executive. This counterresearch has its strategic uses as well. The NGC and COSGO, for example, gathered survey information in 1969 on water pollution control costs to counter the Nixon administration's claim that an $800-million appropriation was not required for the federal water pollution program.[34] The NLC-USCM's study, *Clean Water for the 1970s,* aided congressional allies in the same case to boost water pollution treatment appropriations from $214 million, as requested by the administration, to slightly less than $1 billion for FY 1970. To repudiate charges made by mayors and the Johnson administration that governors were unwilling to develop state planning programs under the pending Crime Control and Safe Streets Act of 1968, the NGC generated letters and detailed state studies indicating plans underway and the governors' enthusiasm for having state control over the program. To support claims made before Congress that federal funds going to cities were bypassing general-purpose governments, a HUD-mayors study of Oakland found that over a five-year period less than 15 percent of all federal dollars going into that city went to the general-purpose government. The Oakland study provided substantial credibility to

[33] *Housing Legislation of 1967,* Hearings before the Senate Committee on Banking and Currency, Subcommittee on Housing and Urban Affairs, 90th Cong., 1st Sess., 1967, pt. 1.

[34] *Current American Government,* Congressional Quarterly, Inc., Washington, D.C., 1970, p. 123.

the mayors' demands for greater mayoral control over federal-local programs and funds, especially the Model Cities program. This study of the, operation of federal grant programs, replicated by OMB in other cities, firmed up the Nixon administration's determination to use Model Cities as a device for improving local government management and led to its planned variations experiment in 1971.

Information is frequently conveyed by an individual governor, mayor, or county official to his elected federal counterpart personally. Thus, in 1967, the mayors' lobby needed the support of Gordon Allott of Colorado, the ranking Republican member of the Senate Appropriations Subcommittee on Independent Offices, to gain funding for the embattled Model Cities program. To impress upon Allott the support that the program had in his own state and largest city, Denver Mayor Tom Currigan testified before the subcommittee at the USCM-NLC's request. Currigan indicated how the Denver program received strong popular backing through an open referendum and gained support from the city's media and business interests. The strategy of providing local information to select legislators apparently paid off in this case as it has in others. Allott supported funding for Model Cities. The mayors, for example, in appealing to congressmen for support of the 1970 Public Employment Act, fed them constant information concerning rising unemployment rates in their cities. NACO's information on pending grant applications for federal water and sewer assistance undermined the administration's position that only slight increments in appropriations were needed to update grant backlogs in this program. The NGC's own estimate of increased state and local borrowing costs under the proposed modification of federal tax exemption on state-local bonds contributed to the defeat of this tax amendment in the 91st Congress. These examples underscore the strategic role of information in lobbying.

Perhaps the classic case of how a governor persuaded a congressman he should not do something involved Nelson Rockefeller's negotiations with Wilbur Mills on revenue sharing. At one point Mills expressed considerable interest in an alternative to President Nixon's revenue-sharing bill, namely a three-year direct federal aid scheme for aiding cities and rural communities and bypassing states altogether. Rockefeller came to Washington to dissuade Mills from pursuing this plan, even though the mayors supported it. On a plane trip back to New York with the Arkansas Democrat, Rockefeller argued convincingly that this idea, if implemented, would have two consequences: the cities would become permanent wards of the federal government, and the states would react by reducing their aid to cities in the amount of the new federal assistance. Hence, the cities would be no better off than before and perhaps worse off once the federal government terminated the program. Upon consulting with his urban colleagues on Ways and Means, Mills was apparently convinced of the soundness of the Rockefeller argument, because he abandoned the idea shortly thereafter.[35]

Research is also used to counter the claims made by a competing group. Facing several highly unfavorable studies by the USCM-NLC concerning state ineptitude under the Omnibus Crime Control and Safe Streets Act, the NGC provided the Senate Judiciary Committee with its own research on a state-by-state breakdown of law enforcement programs and their allocation of federal funds to large cities. Federal agencies contract with the groups to conduct research on programs in which they are involved. The USCM-NLC, for example, surveyed mayors for OEO, regarding whether OEO programs should be incorporated under Model Cities in cities where both programs existed. Research may be targeted at client members. With foundation support, NACO's New County project consists of research on county governments, using this research information as a modernizing force in reforming county governments. Much of COSGO's research activities also are directed at state clients rather than federal ones.

The research and analytical capabilities of the groups have grown significantly over the past five years. The mayors, in particular, are able to detail the beneficiaries of programs: number of cities, funds spent, jobs provided, housing built, and pending recipients. This research is relied upon by the mayors' allies, Congress and its committees, and often the home-town media where the actual programs are operating. The groups have discovered that their research has multiple uses: counterresearch, intergroup competition, monitoring and servicing for congressional and agency clients, and even for internal consumption by state and local governments. In a very real sense the groups have become competitors with research conducted by federal agencies, while in another they have become collaborators with committee staff, agency personnel, and others in legislative drafting, developing, and revising existing federal programs.

Grass Roots Efforts

The most carefully staged direct lobbying is not as likely to be successful except on small or narrow issues unless it is accompanied by significant grass roots efforts. The groups gauge their strategies to the importance of the issue at hand: its visibility, amount of opposition, and limitations of resources. When stakes are high, payoffs attainable, and timing propitious, the groups may go all out on a grass roots appeal. Predictably, most of their lobbying efforts already involve stimulation at the local

---

[35] *General Revenue Sharing,* Hearings before the House Ways and Means Committee, 92nd Cong., 1st Sess., 1971, pt. 5, p. 804. Also, interview with Mary Kresky, special assistant to Governor Rockefeller, at the Governor's New York City Office, June 7, 1973.

level insofar as contact and communications are carried on nearly exclusively by members with their federal counterparts rather than by organization staff. Governors and mayors regularly refer claimants to Washington, whether or not requested to do so, as a matter of deflecting pressures on themselves. But encouragement of organized excursions by nongovernmental groups to federal officials to inform or educate them on the problems and needs of subnational governments often assumes the form of group strategy. To further legitimize their own demands, the mayors, for example, may request assistance from civic and church groups, labor, commercial banking and business groups, and other important segments of a legislator's constituency to write, wire, pass resolutions, and otherwise aid their cause. The governors often do the same.

The resources available to large-city mayors perhaps are obvious. But those of small-city mayors are equally significant. As one major subcommittee chairman from the South informed a mayors' gathering in 1965, "If a congressman comes from an organized district, the most important people to him are the hometown mayors."[36] By dividing the labor between the USCM and NLC in contacting mayors and local allies, the mayors' lobby is able to reach a substantial number of legislators. The mayors' campaign on behalf of the Model Cities program received White House acclaim as one of the most successful grass roots efforts yet undertaken by a lobbying organization. NACO's persistence in its activities aimed at restructuring the poverty program is also notable. The governors, on the other hand, have been less deft thus far in this type of lobbying, but they are finding statewide interests an effective ally in dealing with Washington.

The tactful design and execution of grass roots lobbying place considerable responsibility on the government groups' executive directors. Pritchard, Gunther, Byrley, Hillenbrand, and their staffs usually plan strategies, identify targets, and devise tactics for contacting officials. Members still provide the best information on contacts ånd therefore are brought into lobbying activities at all stages. To the extent that the groups generate a local-level campaign and use their membership, they maintain a bipartisan stance, abstain from threats, and seek to disguise or play down their role as stimulator. The purpose of a grass roots campaign, whether elitist, group-oriented, or directed at shaping local opinion, is largely educational. Whatever the specific type of grass roots campaign may be, the overall goal of communications—getting certain messages most effectively through to decision makers—remains the same.

Each of the groups relies on multiple methods for getting feedback and information from members. These may include personal contact, letters,

---

[36] "Address by Congressman Albert Rains," United States Conference of Mayors, *Proceedings of the Thirty-third Annual Meeting,* Washington, D.C., 1966, p. 23.

telephone calls, questionnaires, conventions, meetings, newsletters, reports, and other publications. On major legislation, for instance, the NGC Washington office may contact all governors or their staffs, explaining a certain bill or upcoming vote in Congress, requesting action or response in writing, and detailing the implications or anticipated consequences of the action for their state. The mayors do the same, but they also request advice from their members as to strategy or tactics. The USCM has a general strategy it relies on, distributing to its five hundred members a detailed position paper four or five times a year on all legislation and appropriations of direct importance to mayors and their cities pending before Congress. These materials are sent to the mayors prior to congressional recesses (Easter, Memorial Day, etc.), enabling the mayor to personally discuss these matters with a congressman who is presumably back home campaigning or handling constituent problems. On specific bills, the USCM-NLC generally works through individual members and state leagues, requesting that mayors get in touch with legislators or an entire city delegation, as the case may be, alerting them to the importance of a particular vote.

In addition to the affiliated organizations which each of the groups may mobilize, they have other contacts such as budget officers, federal aid coordinators, and housing experts who can serve as the go-betweens in getting a mayor's, governor's, or county official's attention. City and state legislators, bankers, prominent businessmen, and others may also enter, directly or indirectly, into the communications-feedback process generated by the groups for building support or stimulating action. Each of the groups also may rely on a network of Washington allies who, because of coalition politics and overlapping membership in organizations, join with elected chief executives in mobilizing local support behind a bill or program.

The passage of general revenue sharing is the most successful grass roots lobbying effort undertaken thus far by the groups collectively. Once the government groups united behind the President's $5-billion proposal, they turned to grass roots lobbying to move the recalcitrant Democratic-controlled Congress. Under Nelson Rockefeller's leadership, the groups formed a National Citizens Committee for Revenue Sharing, a bipartisan organization composed of businessmen, academics, church groups, and others with some thirty-three state affiliates. This Washington-based committee helped orchestrate a national campaign to raise the saliency of the revenue-sharing issue. In spring 1971, delegations of mayors, governors, and county officials swarmed over Capitol Hill demanding congressional passage of this program. These efforts were aided by regional and local briefings for state-local officials conducted by President Nixon, his cabinet, and advisers, who built local support groups to pressure Congress. The Democratic leadership and Chairman Mills eventually capitulated to this outpouring of favorable support. The Ways and Means Committee's hearings on revenue sharing began in June 1971, and a bill was passed fifteen months later.

Another example of grass roots impact involves the case of an individual congressman—John C. Kluczynski of Chicago. As chairman of the House Subcommittee on Roads, which oversees the federal highway building programs, Kluczynski was a notorious defender of the Highway Trust Fund, keeping it intact from raids by mass transit supporters. Fellow Chicagoan and political ally Mayor Richard Daley not only was chairman of the USCM's Transportation Committee but also a leading advocate for using HTF monies for mass transit systems. Daley found embarrassing the opposition of his own congressional district's congressman to a policy with which he was closely identified. Daley quietly supported the city's newspaper stories in 1972–1973 on the financially ailing Chicago Transit Authority, its stalled capital construction expansion, and the importance of the HTF issue to the city's transit program. Kluczynski soon got the message and became a passionate convert to using HTF diversion for urban mass transit systems.

Whether one group wins or loses a round in Congress, the political struggle over a bill or policy continues predictably into the next congressional session. It is carried on in the courts and executive agencies or on the state level. A group or coalition that achieves its immediate goals in one arena usually becomes ever more protective of consolidating those gains to win in another. This requires of the groups, among other things, vigilance, persistence, and flexible response. The enactment and funding of the Model Cities program between 1966 and 1967 marked just the beginning for the mayors. From that point on they devoted considerable time and lobbying efforts in dealing with HUD, the Nixon White House, and Congress: servicing and expanding the program, preventing state incursions, and frustrating moves to merge the program with urban renewal, fighting off White House budget cutters and Presidential impoundment as well as efforts to divert its funds to other programs.

Similarly the NGC, after successfully gaining a bloc-grant anticrime program channeled through the states, had the major job of assisting states to develop viable programs. The NGC Washington office spent considerable time in assisting LEAA draw up guidelines and gain full state participation. The mayors, on the other hand, set as one of their priorities in the 91st and 92nd Congresses the overhaul of the bloc grant and reallocation of federal crime prevention funds directly to the cities. The mayors reported to their congressional allies that federal funds were being inequitably distributed by state agencies and that cities were getting insufficient funds to do much good. The clash between the governors and mayors in 1970 over the amendments to the Safe Streets Act led to a compromise between the existing law and the mayors' demands. The pass through of federal funds from states to large cities was more closely regulated and states were required to buy into local programs as the price for controlling grant disbursements. On the other hand, the bloc-grant approach remained essentially intact.

The cases of Model Cities and the LEAA programs are indicative of the oversight and monitoring operations run by the groups on those programs and agencies where their stakes are the largest. Federal departments, agencies, and bureaus recognize the groups' capacity to generate information on programs and to conduct research. They are utilizing the groups as a contractual source of information on a routine basis. COSGO, for example, has become the repository for many of the federal government's technical assistance programs to the states. Through funds provided by a variety of agencies and departments, it offers consulting services, basic research, and training assistance to state governments. The USCM-NLC have contracts with OEO, DOT, HUD, Labor, and other agencies involving basic research and technical service operations. They even run government-sponsored service delivery programs on their own. NACO and the USCM-NLC also administer a number of technical service and clearinghouse operations on Model Cities, COGs, labor relations, and community relations. Much of the research conducted by the groups, as it turns out, is aimed at monitoring programs in which their members are participating. Frequently this research is supportive of a particular program or aids the agency in gaining congressional authority for something both the agency and government group want in common. In short, the political game goes on and, as the groups realize, much is attainable in working through federal agencies and bureaus rather than Congress predominantly.

Summary

Disaggregation of the eight cases by policy areas, strategies, and tactics provides a deeper understanding of how the government groups operate. It suggests how they seek to exploit the multiple cracks and access points in the American federal system to attain their goals. Nondisciplined parties, routinized legislative interference, and extensive intergovernmental consultation among the groups and federal officialdom permit them considerable flexibility in choices of strategies and tactics, as previous analysis indicates. On the other hand, group activities are constrained—limited by the basic structure of the federal system, separation of powers, and the functional organization of Congress and the executive, as well as by existing policy arenas. To be effective, the groups must continuously adjust spatial concerns not only to these structures and functional organizations but also to outside social, economic, and political forces.

The principal activity of the government groups involves lobbying.

Nearly all relationships between lobbying groups and government, directly and indirectly, take place through means of communication. The groups communicate to their members what is happening or is likely to happen in government. They, in turn, communicate to government policy makers what is happening or likely to happen to their clients as a consequence of government action or inaction. Communication with government, as this chapter suggests, takes myriad forms and occurs through innumerable channels. The groups assume various roles, constantly aspiring to enhance their position, competing with other would-be influencers, and seeking new alliances and coalitions to augment their claims.

Several general roles of the groups have been analyzed, providing an overview to group behavior in the context of the political setting in which they operate. The rich variety of strategies and tactics employed by the groups points to the patterned behavior of lobbying organizations engaged in conventional practices of influencing government. Cases and examples covered indicate the degrees of success the groups have enjoyed over more than a decade of activity. Each group seeks to aggregate power in several policy fields and all, together, seek to enlarge their influence upon federal politics and administration.

These Washington lobbies are organized to get results, which means that they pursue their objectives wherever their attainment is most likely to occur. They rely on methods deemed appropriate for success within the limits of their resources and organizational policies and the general expectations of those with whom they interact. Their activities and growth reflect the further nationalization of American politics and the increasing shift of interest-group attention from Congress to the executive.

The cases also bolster the claim that group struggle inside government is not appreciably different from that outside. Both constitute organized instrumentalities of power. Both possess a sense of group identity and register claims through multiple access points. "The forms of private government differ from the forms of public government," observes Latham, "principally in that public governments possess the characteristic of officiality."[37] The chief distinction between public and private lobbying groups is "officiality," which means essentially legitimacy in standing. The legitimacy of governors, mayors, and county officials within the general-purpose governments over which they preside is unquestionable. But as individual or collective claimants before the federal government, they have no real formal standing as federal political actors. The legitimacy bestowed at one government level carries over to the superior level, but not without a certain political devaluation in transference. Nonetheless, this legitimacy remains the essential resource which members seek to capitalize upon.

---

[37] Earl Latham, "The Group Basis of Politics: Notes For A Theory," *American Political Science Review,* **46**:391, June 1952.

Finally, in a behavioral sense, the activities of the government groups and private groups differ little. The strategies and tactics employed by NACO, NGC, COSGO, USCM, and NLC are much the same as those used by private lobbies composed on nongovernmental officials. Indeed ongoing alliances between the government groups and others is sufficiently common and widespread as to blur many of the distinctions which may arise.

7

THE NIXON ADMINISTRATION
AND NEW FEDERALISM

Like pieces fitting into a mosaic, President Nixon's domestic policy gradually assumed form during his first term in office. The White House developed ambitious plans geared to changing the balance of power in American federalism by shifting money and authority from Washington to state and local governments. This was to be achieved through a wide range of legislative proposals and strategies for administrative action. The President proclaimed the goal of this plan to be a "New American Revolution" whereby power will be returned to the people, and governments at all levels will be "refreshed, renewed, and made more truly responsive."[1]

Reorganization became his immediate objective at the executive level. The President's Advisory Committee on Executive Reorganization, known as the Ash Commission, evolved recommendations approved by Congress to establish a Domestic Council and to transform the Bureau of the Budget (BOB) into the Office of Management and Budget (OMB). Gradual growth of White House staff and subordination of BOB to White House aides and task force operations in the policy area were further formalized by Mr. Nixon through this reorganization. The President explained this new division of labor between the Council and OMB by saying simply that the former "will primarily be concerned with what we do" and the latter "will primarily be concerned with how we do it and how well we do it."[2]

One of the President's first objectives, therefore, was putting his own house in order. Mindful that the GOP administration inherited a bureaucratic machinery largely wedded to Democratic programs and tied to a Democratic majority and committee structure in Congress, the Presi-

[1] Budget Message of President Richard M. Nixon to Congress, January 29, 1971. See *National Journal*, **3**:280, February 7, 1971.

[2] Reorganization Message of President Richard M. Nixon to Congress, March 12, 1970. See *Congressional Quarterly*, **28**:825–826, March 20, 1970.

dent attempted to centralize power in the White House and within his own staff. Centralizing policy functions and legislative clearance under the Domestic Council, strengthening OMB budget oversight, and infiltrating departments and agencies with persons loyal to the White House comprised part of a strategy aimed at interdicting patterns of collaboration between agencies, the bureaucracy, and Congress on domestic programs.

Another strategy involved even more comprehensive reorganization of the executive, reducing eleven federal departments to eight by dismantling seven cabinet-level departments and reassembling them as four super-departments. The functions and responsibilities of these seven were to be reassigned to four new departments: Human Resources, to deal with needs of individuals and families; Community Development, to focus on government activity at the local level in both urban and rural areas; Natural Resources, to plan for the judicious use of the nation's physical resources; and Economic Development, to deal with jobs, business, and the economic well-being of the country.[3] The essence of the plan, also derived from the Ash Commission, was to organize federal activities according to function and goal rather than program, forcing constituent groups to deal with new departments that were often in competition with related interests within that same department.[4]

DECENTRALIZING CONTROL

The President also proposed in early 1971 six special revenue-sharing programs which constituted a programmatic interface to the new departments. He called for the phasing out of more than a hundred federal grant-in-aid programs and the transferring of these funds into six broad categories: urban development, rural development, education, transportation, job training, and law enforcement. While each of the special revenue-sharing proposals differed and passed through several revisions, common elements could be found in all: (1) elimination of state or local matching requirements in most cases as well as built-in guarantees that no state or community now sharing in categorical aid programs would receive less funds in the transition to broad-purpose revenue-sharing programs; (2) state and local elected officials would be given maximum flexibility in using these funds to meet their specific needs and priorities within the broad categories by eliminating or drastically reducing administrative requirements, planning, and reporting specifications; and (3) state and local elected officials would be strengthened at the expense of functional spe-

[3] See *Papers Relating to the President's Departmental Reorganization Program: A Revised Compilation*, Government Printing Office, 1972.

[4] State of the Union Message by President Richard M. Nixon, January 22, 1971. See *National Journal*, **3**:244, January 31, 1971.

cialists at all government levels through the decentralization of decision making and the consolidation of grant programs.[5]

In early 1971, administration architects of special revenue sharing attempted to broaden its constituency and to make it more politically attractive to state-local officials by linking these proposals to general revenue sharing—the unrestricted return of federal funds to state and local units. Through one pipeline would flow general revenue-sharing funds beginning at $5 billion the first year and increasing gradually to a $30-billion total over a five-year period, while the other pipeline would carry $11.4 billion the first year for special revenue-sharing funds. Together, general and special revenue sharing would provide these governments with a $16-billion initial investment, of which more than $6 billion would be new money over and above what states and localities were then receiving.

In pursuing the goal of decentralizing federal programs and power to nonfederal elected officials, President Nixon tested the limits of administrative authority by going as far as the White House could through executive action under the Federal Assistance Review (FAR) program. Congressional intent would be stretched, procedures circumvented, and grant regulations eased, all without enabling legislation. OMB and the Domestic Council developed detailed plans for executive action: federal field structure reorganization, joint funding programs, uniformity in federal grant program requirements, and simplifying the grant-in-aid applications process.[6]

The Department of Housing and Urban Development (HUD) engaged in the most sweeping experiments in grant consolidation and decentralization of decision making. For more than two years a tug of war between HUD and the White House over Model Cities' future threatened the program's continuation. In brief, Model Cities was virtually overhauled from its initial thrust under the Johnson administration. Its size was expanded to nearly 150 cities, its scope enlarged from a neighborhood basis to an entire city, its goals transformed from a service delivery orientation to a process of management, and its operating philosophy converted from the cornerstone of Great Society urban programs to a laboratory for testing the Nixon administration's special revenue-sharing concept. Thus, Model Cities survived as a major vehicle in implementing President Nixon's New Federalism by moving much decision making from the federal to the local level under elected official control and by consolidating various categorical grants into bloc grants.

Launched in mid-1971, twenty existing Model Cities were selected to participate in a demonstration program called "planned variations" which

[5] See Advisory Commission on Intergovernmental Relations, Special Revenue Sharing: An Analysis of the Administration's Grant Consolidation Proposals, Government Printing Office, 1970.

[6] See National Journal, 4:1908–1944, December 16, 1972.

had been designed to test some of the concepts of urban community development revenue sharing. In light of OMB studies which concluded that many mayors had little knowledge of and control over federal programs operating in their jurisdictions, planned variations offered participating mayors new powers over the administration and expenditure of federal funds. Sixteen of the twenty cities were given nearly $80 million in supplementary funds to implement planned variations on a citywide basis, while in all twenty cities mayors were afforded chief executive review and comment (CERC) authority regarding applications for federal assistance affecting their communities. Thus the scope of the experimental program was to be citywide, with the gradual devolution of power to local chief executives its essential component. Planned variations also enabled mayors to obtain waivers of federal regulations governing other categorical grant programs used in conjunction with Model Cities. Federal departments and agencies were requested to honor CERC by reducing their administrative grant requirements attached to funds flowing into participating cities. The Domestic Council assumed the responsibility for monitoring planned variations due to its interagency scope, while HUD became the lead department insofar as it provided the bulk of the programs and funds.

Complementing planned variations, the White House developed another strategy for meshing categorical grant programs into locally designed plans for total community development termed "annual arrangements." This device also was conceived to circumvent the categorical grant system and to strengthen mayors' management powers. The annual arrangements process enabled some one hundred client cities to be recipients of one annual lump-sum funding from major HUD programs such as urban renewal, Model Cities, public housing, open space, and water, sewer, and other physical development projects under a prearranged contractual basis between the participating city and HUD. HUD officials negotiated directly with a city's mayor in developing a comprehensive citywide development strategy to which all city agencies were required to conform. Cities participating in annual arrangements were assigned a total subsidy ceiling prior to negotiations. HUD then funded up to that ceiling regardless of how many grant applications were received or funds requested by that city. In short, annual arrangements, a precursor to the administration's special revenue sharing proposal for community development and its "hold harmless" doctrine, would fund cities annually on a predetermined basis, bringing a variety of often discrete programs and agencies under greater mayoral control.[7]

The Nixon administration developed comparable experimental programs within HEW both on the state and local levels. Using the A-95 process to

[7] For a review of President Nixon's administrative reforms, see *The First Biennial Report on National Growth Policy*, Hearings before the House Banking and Currency Committee, Subcommittee on Housing, 92nd Cong., 2nd Sess., 1972, pp. 1–75.

strengthen state areawide planning and program coordination, governors gained their own review and comment powers regarding the impact of federally assisted programs on state programs and planning. Individual governors could, upon request, receive grant waivers and relaxation of federal guidelines when seeking to integrate various intergovernmental programs. The Nixon administration proposed, in 1972, the Allied Services Act, designed to consolidate nearly half of all HEW grant programs. Again, the aim was to allow state and local governments greater planning discretion for modernizing the delivery of social services into consolidated programs. Like HUD's planned variations, HEW experimented with co-ordinating programs in medium-sized cities, once again focusing on new instruments in and concepts for integrating social services without actually merging these service programs into special revenue sharing.

Besides those experiments previously referred to, clearly among the most important, the White House consolidated federal field structure organization into ten federal regions, established Federal Regional Councils, and empowered the councils with new coordinating authority. FRCs aided mayors in using the CERC process and, under the Integrated Grant Administration program, experimented with packaging categorical grants on the regional level rather than in Washington.

THE SEARCH FOR CONSTITUENCIES

By the early seventies, President Nixon had moved beyond the rhetoric of New Federalism to an operating philosophy. Touted as the GOP alternative to the centralization that began with at least the New Deal, the administration had initiated what one White House aide described as "a positive Republican alternative to running things out of Washington through the categorical grant-in-aid system."[8] In a pragmatic, realistic alternative to largely Democratic-sponsored programs, the President had developed a total scheme for overhauling the federal administration. Utilizing executive tools of veto, reorganization, impoundment and freezes of congressionally appropriated funds, President Nixon had taken the Congress by surprise and seemed well on his way in 1971–1972 to succeeding on many fronts.

The principal beneficiaries and supporters of the Nixon administration's New Federalism policies were to be state and local chief executives: governors, mayors, county officials, and city managers. The President's determination to overhaul the federal categorical grant system produced their enthusiastic response, while his unmitigated support for a $5-billion revenue-sharing plan in early 1971 generated a chief executive alliance with the White House. The fact that many states, large cities, and local

[8] *National Journal,* **4**:1909, December 16, 1972.

governments were financially strapped, particularly as a consequence of the 1969–1970 economic slowdown, only added further cohesion to the alliance. This coalition had its instability, cleavages, and obvious partisan differences, but it proved increasingly useful during this 1971–1972 period.

The Nixon strategy manifested itself with the linking of reorganization of general and special revenue-sharing plans as outlined in the President's State of the Union Address on January 22, 1971. The President's New Federalism plan moved far beyond its initial state orientation. The stunning GOP defeat at the gubernatorial level in the 1970 elections freed the President from his outstanding commitments to Republican governors concerning a greatly enhanced state role in federal domestic programs. From at least 1970 on, the White House staff and Domestic Council concentrated much of their domestic efforts on working with the mayors and county officials. The USCM and NLC supported the Nixon reforms and goals: revenue sharing; program consolidation within broad, flexible areas; setting of program goals at the state and local government rather than federal level; reduction of federal application and review procedures; abolition of local matching requirements; funding of general-purpose local governments rather than special purpose governments and semiautonomous agencies; and establishment of more stable and equitable funding procedures.

The Nixon grand design incorporated plans for the most sweeping overhaul of the federal system by any administration to date. It included a whole new realignment of political power among congressional committees, interest groups, and federal agencies. If implemented, it would likely have amounted to a comprehensive restructuring of both the national government and the framework of intergovernmental relations. However, the President's intention to make maximum use of executive authority in implementing this plan confronted a major obstacle, namely Congress. The sharing of powers between branches meant that the President's capacity to act remained limited. These reforms, to be durable, required congressional assent. Congress failed to take the President's massive reorganization plans very seriously.[9] The proposed shifting and fusing of scores of agencies, bureaus, and offices in seven departments sparked the instantaneous opposition of interest groups, committee chairmen, and agencies alike. The Department of Community Development, one of the four new departments proposed by President Nixon in 1971 and the one thought to have the best chance of acceptance, failed. This proposal would have taken the Federal Highway Administration and Urban Mass Transportation from the Transportation Department and the Farmers' Home Administration and Rural Electrification Administration

[9] See *Congressional Quarterly*, **28**:279–281, January 29, 1971.

from the Agriculture Department, merging them into the new Community Development Department together with units from other departments. This reorganization proposal, like others, had little support or acquiescence from other executive agencies; met strong opposition from relevant interest groups, especially rural agricultural clients; and succumbed to attack by no fewer than seven chairmen of important House committees and subcommittees.[10] Reorganization had little or no constituency, not even the public at large. The administration's attempt in 1972–1973 to implement the President's reorganization plan without congressional approval proved to be ineffectual and likely ended further reorganization efforts by the President during his second term.

Special revenue sharing and major grant consolidation also constituted a direct assault on Congress by the executive—on Congress's role in determining priorities and its constitutional prerogatives of oversight and legislative interference into program administration. Such a scheme involved not only a large-scale transfer of power from Congress to the White House but also a shift of power to governors and mayors. The obvious cleavages between governors and senators, local elected officials and congressmen, alone constituted sufficient political justification for strong congressional opposition to special revenue sharing. Beyond congressional unwillingness to help actual or potential rivals, the Nixon programs would have scrambled all the grant system circuits which connect members of Congress, interest groups, and the bureaucracy creating new constituencies for these bloc-grant programs. A sampling of just a few of those interests threatened by special revenue sharing suggests the global nature of the Nixon scheme. Education revenue sharing would have consolidated thirty-three categorical grants into five bloc grants, antagonizing virtually hundreds of educational groups, guilds, and their congressional sponsors. Transportation revenue sharing combined twenty-three categorical grants, opening up the Highway Trust Fund to governors and mayors and cutting across several congressional committees. It produced an outcry from the highway users' federation and scores of transportation groups aligned with their own special grant program. The urban community revenue sharing brought opposition from the mayor's allies: the builders, urban renewal people, and others. Rural Development revenue sharing threatened the vested interests of committees, interest groups, and clientele of programs administered by the Agriculture and Commerce Departments as well as by the Appalachian Regional Commission.[11]

Other efforts at grant consolidation failed also. The proposed Intergovernmental Cooperation Act of 1972 passed the Senate but lapsed in

[10] See Executive Reorganization Hearings, Senate Committee on Governmental Operations, 92nd Cong., 1st Sess., 1971, parts 1–4. Also *Congressional Quarterly*, June 4, 1971, pp. 1211–1213.

[11] See *National Journal*, reprint no. 11 on *Governmental Reorganization*, Spring 1972.

the House. One of the key amendments in this act would have given the President authority to merge categorical grants in functionally related areas if neither house of Congress vetoed the plan. In the 91st Congress, grant consolidation proposals for comprehensive headstart child development, water and sewer facilities, library services, and education programs were not passed and indeed rarely progressed to the hearing stage. After more than two years of committee effort, the Senate passed in 1972 the omnibus Housing and Urban Development Act, which among other things would have consolidated nearly fifty categorical programs into eight and would have authorized a new bloc-grant program to local governments for community development efforts. It, too, failed in the House at the session's end.

Thus, as President Nixon's second term began, his administration's efforts to introduce a flexible combination of federal financial assistance to states and localities consisting of categorical grants-in-aid, general functional bloc grants, and general revenue sharing had not fully materialized. Indeed, with the exception of revenue sharing, the President had made like progress whatsoever. Traditional approaches to grant reform had furnished only marginal success. The President had helped prevent further growth of categorical grants in the 93rd Congress due to revenue sharing's enactment and extensive presidential vetoes. Yet the drastic overhauling and streamlining of the categorical aid system did not follow. Nonetheless, the federal grant system to states and localities by types of aid did undergo moderate changes between 1963 and 1973, as indicated by Table 7.

Only two major bloc-grant programs would be found in operation in 1973, those provided by the Partnership for Health Act of 1968 (PL 89-749) and the Omnibus Crime Control and Safe Streets Act of 1968 (PL 90-351). Each of these seemed to be falling short of expectations. The former consolidated sixteen previously separate categorical programs, giving

T-7   Federal Grants-in-Aid to State and Local Governments by Type (in billions of dollars)

Type of Grant	FY 1963	FY 1968	FY 1973 (est.)
Categorical	8.6	18.6	37.7
Block	0	0	.5
Revenue sharing	0	0	6.8
Total	8.6	18.6	45.0

Source: Budget of the United States, Fiscal Years 1963, 1968, 1974.

greater discretion to states and their governors in developing plans for the delivery of services. However, Congress failed to follow up on this approach, categorizing related measures, while state and local health agencies coalesced around the program impeding much elected chief executive leadership over its direction. Under the latter bloc grant, law-enforcement operations had been frustrated by organizational problems both at the federal and state level, while many states were laggard in developing a comprehensive law-enforcement assistance system. The record of these two bloc-grant programs, according to the Advisory Commission on Intergovernmental Relations (ACIR) in 1973, "can only be described as mixed and uneven in light of the basic objectives of the bloc–grant strategy."[12] The tendency to categorize or recategorize is still strong even after consolidation has been achieved, while subnational chief executives find curbing the parochialism of their program professionals a difficult task.

In spite of the fact that grant consolidation, special revenue sharing, and executive reorganization had been blocked by Congress, the Nixon administration with the strong support of the government interest groups had general revenue sharing to show for its efforts. Revenue sharing had met considerable opposition from Congress, interest groups, and the bureaucracy. Once it had emerged from the Ways and Means Committee and the government interest groups rallied around its enactment, the opposition largely shifted its tactics. By fighting revenue sharing and mobilizing all possible arguments against it, the battle was in part being waged against special revenue sharing. General revenue sharing, after all, was new money, which did not yet detract from ongoing categorical systems. Its passage, many predicted, would lead to the breakup of the government group coalition, diffusing the momentum behind the President's programs. In the meantime, defenders of the categorical system rallied around the cause of existing federal grants-in-aid.

Mr. Nixon's commitment to decentralizing federal programs and elevating elected state-local officials over the guilds and categorical grant constituencies generated deep hostility in federal agencies, driving them even closer to their congressional allies. Moreover, the expansion of the White House staff and the short-lived policy authority of the Domestic Council also had the consequence of promoting agency ties with their congressional supporters. Thus organized resistance to Mr. Nixon's reforms arose from career executives in the federal bureaucracy who were supported by public and private interest groups, and congressional committees. Opposition alliances emerged and coalesced on all fronts. Defenders of the categorical grant systems raised with new vigor the justifications of federal grant programs, their continuation and expansion: assertion of

---

[12] Advisory Commission on Intergovernmental Relations, *Fourteenth Annual Report,* Washington, D.C., January 1973, pp. 12–14.

national priorities; state-local government inactivity, incompetence, venality, and paucity in management talent; that minorities, the poor and others would be deprived of assistance in state-local redistribution; and that subordinate governments were less efficient and competent than the federal government in the domestic area.[13] Many of these same arguments would carry over to the 93rd Congress, where a certain upsurge in sentiment developed that federal revenue sharing should be reviewed in its earliest stages of operation. Lingering questions and potential problems arose concerning revenue sharing's continuation in its existing form—its distribution, equity in reallocation, subsequent uses, and its relationship to bloc and categorical grants.

GOVERNMENT GROUPS REACT

While it is premature to evaluate President Nixon's New Federalism policies so shortly following his reelection to a second term in office, certain conclusions can be drawn regarding the fate of Presidential programs and the reaction to them by the government interest groups thus far. These are tentative but nonetheless grounded in events and trends stemming from the period of 1970 to 1973.

Three explanations are offered regarding why the government groups and their members failed to fully embrace Mr. Nixon's specific legislative proposals for implementing his New Federalism plan. According to the first, the President's plans comprised a general theory regarding the devolution of power, which, beyond administrative efforts, failed to specify which powers and functions should be more fully shared with which government levels. The uncertainty as to details and even flexibility in proposals, when once offered, set in motion a fierce competition among governors, mayors, and county officials which, short of revenue sharing, provided a major impediment to congressional action. Another explanation, that of money and shifting partisan alignment, holds that once President Nixon's strategies of returning major programs to state and local governments became linked to controlling federal expenditures, subnational chief executives' enthusiasm suddenly evaporated. In the absence of Presidential assurances that special revenue sharing would not lead to reductions in other forms of state-local aid, these officials pursued the least risky strategy—that of continuation and expansion of the existing categorical grant system mixed with expectations that Congress might approve some grant consolidation.

The third, explanation, largely academic insofar as it never fully mate-

---

[13] National Journal, 4:1921, December 16, 1972. Also see American Enterprise Institute, General Revenue Sharing Proposals Washington, D.C., June 1971, pp. 24–30.

rialized, is that subnational executives really did not want the major priority-setting choices and programmatic responsibilities embodied in the President's New Federalism plan. To the extent that general and special revenue-sharing programs constituted a laissez faire arrangement—a bouncing back of major responsibilities to states and local governments, even with added resources—the groups and their members opposed it. They encouraged the Nixon efforts of returning power, funds, and decision making to state and locally elected officials, but at the same time they rejected any movements toward reassembling a form of federal bureaucracy on their own levels.[14] The added problem, of course, for many subnational chief executives, was that federal efforts to enhance the role of elected executive generalists over the role of the "vertical autocracy"— the functional specialists, guilds, and middle-management programs administrators on all government levels—could not fully compensate for basic structural, statutory, and political weaknesses of their offices. Federal intervention even under the most advantageous of circumstances could not make chief executives or decision makers out of men and offices where such authority did not exist in the first place.

One can conclude, according to the first theory, that New Federalism's apparent decline is attributable to cleavages among the government interest groups. On the whole, it is plausible to maintain that it was not these groups that stymied the President's programs but an alliance of major national policy makers—labor, media, career civil servants, congressional committees, the guilds, and categorical grant supporters. These actors were for the most part unsympathetic and indeed even hostile to the idea that previously shared functions and responsibilities should be remanded in bulk to state and local governments and placed under the direct control of elected officials. The actions and behavior of these actors as well as basic research on their attitudes generally bear this out.[15] However, as the intended beneficiary and prospective support group for the Nixon programs, the government interest groups' maneuvering, indecisiveness, and at times outright opposition contributed immeasurably to congressional inactivity and its own opposition to the Nixon programs.

Governors, mayors, and county officials failed to reconcile their differences. They responded favorably to the Nixon programs in theory, ap-

[14] Edward C. Banfield, "Revenue Sharing in Theory and Practice," *The Public Interest*, **23**:42–44, Spring 1971.

[15] See Allen H. Barton, "The Limits of Consensus among American Leaders," Bureau of Applied Social Research, Columbia University, July 1972 (mimeographed). By asking a broad-scale representative elite of the American leadership structure the question, "Should most government social programs, such as housing, job training, and health, be controlled by local government and not by federal agencies?" Barton found strongest disagreement from labor, media, interest groups, and federal career civil servants. Both Democratic and Republican party leaders on the state and local government level agreed with the above more strongly than either party's congressional members.

plauded the objectives, and championed their overall purposes. But the gap between rhetoric and practice became evident when the groups and their members confronted actual legislative proposals in which one government level might be the principal beneficiary over the other. The New Federalists tried to convince the government groups that symmetry of structures and sharing were not their goals and that federal patterns had not really evolved that way. Instead, power should seek its own level, with the "sorting out" process in sharing patterns—which level of government does what for whom—largely a function of individual intrastate negotiations. Nonetheless, when confronted with such issues of funding formulas in special revenue sharing legislation or in alternative bloc grant programs favored by Congress, the groups characteristically splintered. In housing, for example, both the NGC and NACO demanded greater roles—a demand that the mayors resisted. NACO opposed the initial community-development revenue sharing and the bloc-grants version of the proposal contained in the Housing and Urban Development Act of 1972 because of the preferential status given to central cities as opposed to urban counties. NACO also stood to lose much control over one of its favorite programs by inclusion of the water and sewers program in the urban bloc grant. The governors singled out this revenue-sharing proposal as indicating that the Nixon administration was giving the mayors too strong a role in running programs in which the state should at least be a partner. When HUD countered in 1973 with its Better Communities Act by including urban counties and the states as grant recipients, the mayors objected.

The governors and mayors also disagreed over transportation revenue sharing. The NGC insisted that the program flow through the states, with the governors authorized to transfer funds and set statewide priorities. The mayors, on the other hand, wanted federal funds for mass transit operation and subsidies channeled directly to the cities for their use, not on a metropolitanwide basis or through the states. So, too in law enforcement, manpower training, allied services, and in other areas, each of the government groups sought preferential treatment for its government level and direct federal response to meet its individual needs. The Nixon administration, in its haste to get special revenue-sharing programs before the 92nd Congress, failed to adequately consult with the groups and their leaders, build a consensus among them on provisions, and gain their support prior to congressional action. The National Association of Counties (NACO), National Governors' Conference (NGC), and United States Conference of Mayors—National League of Cities (USCM-NLC) were, in most cases, peremptorily excluded from the drafting of the very measures of which they were to be the major beneficiaries. Consequently, each of the groups tended to go off in separate directions working with its own professionals, support groups, and congressional allies in redesigning the administration's proposals for its own benefit. Each special revenue-sharing proposal had a much narrower constituency than general revenue sharing, which resulted in the picking apart of specifics by functionalists and categorical grant advocates during congressional deliberation.

The enactment of revenue sharing led to a brief period of good feeling among the government groups, only to lapse into renewed competition. Governor Dan Evans, head of the National Governors' Conference for 1973–1974, attempted in late 1973 to build upon the success of the revenue-sharing coalition. The result was that the officers of the government groups formed a Coalition of State, City, and County Officials aimed at increasing the collective influence of nonfederal elected officials over programs operating in their jurisdictions. In December 1973, the coalition was seeking agreement on such issues as congressional budget reform and energy and environment policy as well as more divisive policies in welfare reform, housing, transportation, and land use. Once again, the test for this lobbying coalition will likely be on allocation politics, group and specific benefits. This will probably be all the more the case since fundamental policy differences exist between Congress and the White House on all these issues. Thus, the post-revenue-sharing era of government group relations began on a note of discord and passed to a rather fledgling stage of reconciliation with future relations still unclear.

Money and Support

Another explanation why the President's bold proposals, geared—as the administration thought—to the needs and demands of subnational chief executives, failed to evoke their strong and unswerving support is simply money. Fiscal inducements to support special revenue sharing were not nearly as great as those in general revenue sharing. The former held the prospect of less overall funds relative to the aggregate growth of categorical grants available to states and localities, while the latter provided billions in new funds. Revenue sharing meant that no one level lost something it already had; every general-purpose government gained. Special revenue sharing, on the other hand, held out the prospect that some government levels or perhaps all might lose funds—if not at first, then in future years. President Nixon offered in 1971 to add $1 billion in new monies to the $10.4 billion in funds derived from the consolidation of categorical grants. Looking beyond the first two years of these programs, as governors and mayors did, the aggregation of dozens of federal grant programs into lump sums could make expenditure control by Congress, the executive, or both presumably an easier task to achieve. In short, the government interest groups might be committing themselves to a "no-win" proposition where future and dependable federal aid increases might slow to a trickle. Some governors expressed their skepticism concerning special revenue sharing,

,g to it as a "shell game" whose initial attractiveness would lose
,mour once chief executives faced the prospect of less, not more funds
,g to states and local governments relative to previous growth patterns
,ederal assistance.

In early 1971, the USCM released its own detailed analysis of the President's six special revenue-sharing programs, making exactly this point. Overall budget implications in the FY 1972–1973 budget reflected cutbacks and redirections of urban programs, which led the Conference to caution its members that "more important than the concept of bloc grants or grant consolidation is the question of whether these vital programs will be adequately funded—and whether the level of funding will grow to keep pace with the rising demands."[16] The government interest groups thus remained adamant about the money issue, taking each special revenue-sharing proposal at its face value rather than rallying around the concept and philosophy of all six as the administration had hoped.

The Nixon administration invested greater time and resources on its community development revenue-sharing plan than on others. This program aimed at terminating much grantsmanship, where the amount of federal funds available and conditions governing acquisition were ever changing, by allocating urban development funds for a two-year period to each city on a predetermined formula basis. Cities and their mayors under this Nixon scheme would be able to plan for the first time on a specific basis of how much federal money they would receive annually according to formula allocations which weighted population, poverty, housing overcrowding, and previous activity in HUD programs. To assuage those mayors who felt they had accrued certain advantages in grantsmanship, HUD developed a so-called "hold harmless" stipulation in its proposed legislation. This type of grandfather clause provided that the amount a city was to get by formulas would not be less than the annual average over the past five years from HUD programs.

Even though mayors had long demanded that federal funds be allocated to cities on a bloc-grant basis, predictable as to amounts with annual substantial increments, many objected to a predetermined formula mechanism for distributing federal funds indiscriminately to cities regardless of their past activities and initiatives. HUD sought to convince the mayors that such a program would work to their benefit: expanding their constituency insofar as all cities above 50,000 population inside a Standard Metropolitan Statistical Area (SMSA) would be recipients, and that the size of this constituency would be a strong deterrent against cutbacks and presidential impoundments. It also sought to convince large cities that small and medium-sized cities, for the most part, were already getting more federal funds on a per capita basis than they deserved on the basis of

[16] *National Journal*, **3**:734, April 3, 1971.

need. [17] Responding to this plan, USCM's Gunther stated, "we cannot begin to support any proposal which would hold cities with a high level of participation at their present level of funding until all the others caught up." The "hold harmless" provision created a major conflict between the administration and mayors' lobby over what came to be called the "favored client" question. NLC's Healy stated the problem more succinctly: "The cities that need the money are the ones who have been going after it; it's as simple as that."[18]

The money issue—that New Federalism meant reductions rather than increases in overall federal aid flowing to state and local governments— fully surfaced in early 1973. With a landslide Presidential victory behind him, Mr. Nixon turned his attention to federal expenditure control. This issue had divided Congress late in the 92nd Congress when the President requested a budget ceiling of $250 billion for FY 1973, which, after being rejected, was imposed in part through Presidential impoundment. In the 93rd Congress, however, this issue had created a major constitutional crisis between the two branches of government. Announcing that his highest priority was to avoid inflation and a tax increase, the President moved on a broad front to eliminate more than a hundred categorical programs, to impose a freeze on federal housing subsidies, and to shut out future applications for a variety of grant programs like water and sewer aid and open space grants. He also persisted in impounding funds previously appropriated by Congress for expenditure.

For the President, it was a question of economic management. Federal domestic expenditures had grown more than 300 percent between FY 1960 and FY 1973, and coupled to reductions in federal income and excise tax rates, this growth had reduced the flexibility of the federal government to control future expenditure rates. The federal government's fiscal problems had added a new dimension to the rising public debate over national priorities in that economic growth was no longer automatically producing an annual growth in federal revenues that substantially exceeded expected increase in civilian expenditures. [19] Thus as the Nixon administration entered its fifth year of budget deficits and the nation experienced a strong economic recovery from the recession of 1969–1970, the President attempted to place a lid on government spending. Presidential advisers warned Congress of profligate government spending as detrimental to curbing inflation and potentially contributing to another recession in the mid-seventies. Temporarily, the Democratic-controlled Congress found itself on the defensive, with the Republican President determined to blame it either for future inflation or increased federal taxes.

[17] Ibid., **4**:895, May 27, 1972.

[18] Ibid., **3**:736, April 3, 1971.

[19] See Charles L. Schultze et al., *Setting National Priorities the 1973 Budget*, The Brookings Institution, Washington, D.C., 1972, p. 449.

The government interest groups and Congress took immediate note of the President's FY 1974 budget and self-imposed expenditure ceiling of $268.7 billion.[20] They warned their members in early January that they should be prepared for significant reductions in federal expenditures on a host of categorical grant programs. For governors and mayors, the cutbacks meant that if dozens of federal programs were to be continued, state and local governments would have to fund them. The White House confirmed the groups' worst suspicions when it repeatedly indicated that the antipoverty program, public service employment, library assistance, and a host of social service programs specified for phase out or reductions could be continued if states and localities wanted to use their new general revenue-sharing funds to do so. After all, administration spokesmen would argue that in light of a robust economy, more than forty states and hundreds of local governments were experiencing budget surpluses while others were engaging in tax reductions and speeding up capital construction programs. At the same time, the federal government still anticipated a multibillion-dollar deficit again in FY 1974—or, at best, a balanced budget.

This is precisely what the governors and mayors had feared. As USCM's John Gunther said in late 1972, "We know that he [Nixon] will prime the pump in times of recession, but we don't know what he will do during an economic boom. What the mayors fear is more of the feast-and-famine cycle which they have been on in the past."[21] Many states and localities survived the recession by significant increases in sales and income taxes which left them with stronger, more progressive tax structures as a result. One major consequence of reliance on these taxes for revenues, however, is that much larger fluctuations would be experienced in response to national cyclical movements in the economy. State and local governments generally keep their expenditures in line with expected receipts, which makes economic fluctuations enormously painful.[22]

For many, revenue sharing amounted to a booster against such a development. In urban states and large cities where these new federal revenues still constituted something between 2 to 4 percent of their overall revenues, this was not the case, however. Thus for many subnational executives with strong memories of their governments' tax shortfalls over the past years, the fear of future economic cycles and impact far outweighed the prospect of special revenue sharing which might lead to reductions in federal aid flowing into their jurisdictions. These elected officials' caution in approaching New Federalism in the absence of any federal grant policy

[20] Office of Management and Budget, *The United States Budget in Brief, Fiscal Year 1974,* Government Printing Office, 1973, pp. 3–4.

[21] *Wall Street Journal,* August 11, 1972, p. 4.

[22] See Joseph A. Peckman, *Fiscal Federalism for the 1970s,* Brookings Institution reprint, Washington, D.C., 1971.

to serve as a countercyclical supplement or statutory increases in federal aid during periods of economic slowdown and attendant dropoff in tax receipts is therefore understandable.

In reviewing federal grants to state and local governments since 1960, interesting expenditure patterns emerge. Between 1961 and 1969, federal assistance to subnational governments increased at an average annual rate of 12.6 percent, while between 1970 and 1973, President Nixon's first term, this rate of increase, including revenue-sharing funds, averaged nearly 22 percent per year. Federal aid to states and localities as a portion of total federal outlays increased in aggregate only 3.4 percent between 1961 and 1969, but it expanded by 7 percent total between 1970 and 1973, or from 11 percent to 18 percent. Human resource outlays including social security increases were growing at an average rate of 15 percent from 1970 to 1974—considerably faster than other spending.[23] Similarly, between 1961 and 1969, the percentage allocation of federal expenditures for domestic purposes increased only 2 percent, from 42 to 44 percent. By 1974 estimates, the allocation for domestic purposes had increased to 62 percent of total federal expenditures, an 18 percent total rise. Federal aid to states and localities since 1960 had climbed 539 percent, while state and local expenditures from their own funds also had increased significantly by roughly 270 percent above 1960 levels but still at one-half the overall increase of federal aid during the period. Table 8 indicates these expenditure patterns since 1960.

There could be little question that revenue sharing, from the President's vantage, had absorbed much, if not most, of the projected budget increments for categorical grant programs. Predictably, some of these programs would expand, but to pay for these increases and future budgetary gaps created by revenue-sharing outlays, dozens of programs had to be terminated and reduced. Revenue sharing's passage had closed off, at least for the short term, presidential options. The White House had a certain degree of flexibility in bargaining with Congress and the government groups by increasing special revenue-sharing funds as a trade-off in gaining grant consolidation and some elimination of grant programs. Once revenue sharing had been passed, however, this budgetary flexibility was reduced —short of a tremendous increase in federal tax receipts through economic expansion. In short, the government groups would not accept a zero growth rate in federal aid as projected in the Nixon FY 1974 budget, in spite of the windfall of revenue sharing the previous year. Federal aid to states and localities had risen by 25 percent from FY 1972 to FY 1973, a postwar high for any single annual increment.

Indeed, revenue sharing involved a highly precarious strategy by White House architects and proponents insofar as its implications were unclear.

[23] *Budget in Brief, Fiscal 1974*, p. 29.

T-8   Recent Trends in Federal Aid to States and Localities, 1960–1974 (est.) (in

	1960	1961	1962	1963	1964	1965
Federal grants to state-local governments	$7,040	7,112	7,893	8,634	10,141	10,904
Increase/decrease since preceding year (%)	—	+1	+11	+9	+17	+8
Increase since 1960 (%)	—	+1	+12	+22	+44	+55
Portion of total federal outlays to state-local governments (%)	7.6	7.3	7.4	7.8	8.6	9.2

Source: Congressional Quarterly Weekly Report, August 14, 1970, p. 2069; *Special Analyses, The Budget for Fiscal Year 1974*, Table N-5, p. 217.

Some viewed it in highly partisan terms: the unwinding of major Democratic programs, forging new constituencies at the state-local level, and a major vehicle for gaining the adoption of the President's remaining agenda with Congress. Even with Presidential impoundment and expenditure control pressures, these White House advisers felt it was unlikely that the mayors and other members of the New Federalism coalition would withdraw their support when confronted by budget cuts in a broad range of social programs. Moreover, impoundment and selected grant termination could force the groups and their allies into submission. Any delays in acting upon the President's special revenue-sharing programs would be costly. Therefore, the carrot and stick strategy, if maintained, could turn opposition into support. Even if many mayors and local officials did abandon the coalition, the administration might gain politically by putting the blame on big-city mayors when funds were not available to continue programs cut back by the White House. In short, revenue sharing could serve as a device for splitting up the old Democratic coalition, turning minority groups and grant constituencies against mayors who failed to use their revenue sharing funds to support local programs.

On the other hand, others saw revenue sharing as a precursor to special revenue sharing—not only a strategy for decentralizing federal programs and priority setting but also a modernizing force in Congress itself. By consolidating federal grant programs on a broad scale, Congress might gain greater control over expenditures, working with the executive in changing the total appropriations process through fixed budgetary ceilings and greater legislative centralization over disparate spending entities. Revenue sharing, in effect, seemed to many a major step in government reform. Its consequences, however, proved contrary to what the administration expected.

The FY 1974 budget, with its cuts in domestic social programs, con-

millions of dollars; by fiscal years)

1966	1967	1968	1969	1970	1971	1972	1973	1974 (est.)
12,960	15,240	18,599	20,255	$23,954	29,844	35,940	45,008	44,825
+19	+18	+22	+9	+18	+24	+20	+25	0
+84	+116	+164	+188	+240	+324	+415	+539	+537
9.7	9.6	10.4	11.0	12.2	14.1	15.5	18.0	16.7

tributed to the decline of the New Federalism coalition, uniting the governors, mayors, and county officials, temporarily at least, against the Nixon administration. These officials, critical of presidential impound-ment and extensive budget cutting, focused their attacks on the White House, demanding that the President make good on his promise that New Federalism would not result in sharp reductions in federal subsidies and fiscal support for states and local governments. The mayors charged that they had made plans in good faith to use revenue sharing for needed local improvements, reduce or prevent rises in property and other taxes, only to discover that this money might have to be used to pay for federal programs reduced or abolished by the administration. The governors, mostly Democrats, too, cited the administration's "bad faith," that revenue sharing was passed under the explicit condition that it would be a net addi-tion or supplement to funds already going to states and localities, not a replacement for categorical assistance. Even Republican governors and mayors could not be silenced, complaining that the transition between revenue sharing and categorical grant cutoffs was too swift and indeed jeopardized any forthcoming support for the administration's special revenue-sharing plans.[24]

Much of the groups' reactions to the Nixon policies first emerged in early 1973 before Senator Edmund Muskie's Intergovernmental Relations Subcommittee, whose hearings focused on New Federalism. These hear-ings provided a major forum for publicly airing the rising discontent of state and local government officials at the President's FY 1974 budget.[25] The government groups and their members argued that the President's tax prevention plan in effect constituted an inequitable tax shifting, plac-ing heavier burdens on the already overburdened state and local tax sys-

---

[24] *Wall Street Journal,* June 13, 1973, p. 20, and *National Journal,* **5**:360, March 10, 1973, p. 360; **5**:935–943, June 30, 1973.

[25] Ibid., **5**:531–534, April 14, 1973.

tems, typically far more regressive on the whole than the federal income tax. Some mayors even challenged the President to confront the inevitable, claiming that a federal tax increase was long overdue, that without it sufficient funds would not exist on a broad scale to support existing federal commitments in the domestic area.

At their June 1973 conventions, the governors and the mayors separately acknowledged their defections from the New Federalism coalition. Projected cuts in federal spending for domestic programs produced a major reaction by the governors against special revenue sharing, one which the administration had hardly anticipated. The two-year courtship between the administration and large-city mayors seemed all but ended on the spending issue. Their romance, openly flourishing in 1971–1972, had turned into a jilted courtship, where the urban suitors were referring to revenue sharing as a "cruel hoax" and the White House's strategy as a "doublecross."[26]

The money issue, in effect, sparked an abrupt turnabout in the relations between the Nixon administration and the government interest groups, forging a new coalition between the governors and mayors against the White House's domestic spending policies. The governors, mayors, and county officials remained steadfast in their desire to gain greater control over federal programs, but they exhibited far greater concern over how much money they would get from Washington in the months ahead. States and localities would probably use much of their first year's revenue-sharing money to reduce or avoid increases in taxes. The prospects thereafter, in light of rising inflation, the leveling off of or decreases in federal aid, and greater demands for public services, clearly pointed to further substantial tax increases. Thus, the governors and local officials turned their attention to Congress for the purpose of working with congressional committees, the federal bureaucracy, and interest group supporters of the categorical system to revise domestic programs on their terms, not the White House's. The government groups did not rush to Congress to push for continuation of existing categorical grant programs. By joining forces with the categorical grant supporters around funding of these programs, they saw new opportunities for bargaining and negotiating with grant constituencies over program consolidation, bloc grants, and multiyear appropriations.

By midsummer 1973, after several unsuccessful attempts by this emerging coalition to override Presidential vetoes of categorical grant programs scheduled for extinction, the balance of power in the federal budget battle shifted abruptly from the White House to Congress. Prior to June 1973, President Nixon was winning the struggle over appropriations and expenditure control, with Congress failing to override vetoes as well as confront-

[26] Ibid., 5:1099–1108, July 28, 1973.

ing head on the constitutional issues of impoundment and elimination of federal programs by executive directive. However, the President's apparent dominance over Congress was dealt a shattering blow by deepening implications of his personal involvement in the famed Watergate incident and its later coverup efforts. With the commencement of the Senate hearings investigating Watergate in late May 1973, the President's influence upon Congress weakened rapidly. With each new round of charges against the President and his advisers, the Democratic Congress increased in its resolve to restore and expand major social programs that the President had sought to eliminate. By late 1973, dozens of big expenditure authorization measures adding billions to the FY 1974 budget had been cleared and signed into law. Congress gained an upper hand, with New Federalism an immediate casualty and the categorical grant system much intact.

In a sense, funding battles and the Watergate scandals had mutually reinforcing consequences insofar as the groups were concerned. The former justified breaking with the White House, while the latter reflected the recognition of a politically incapacitated President. As further events unfolded in 1973, shifting alliances became more apparent. Incentives for collaboration with the White House—more federal funds and more power to state-local executives—evaporated in light of budget cuts and sweeping Presidential impoundments. Congress virtually ignored Mr. Nixon's request to enact special revenue sharing on the scale that he had proposed. Also on the decline, however, were actual or would-be Presidential sanctions used to gain group cooperation. Congress began overriding Presidential vetoes, the courts held Presidential impoundment to be unconstitutional, and the White House hold upon the congressional agenda dissipated. The Domestic Council had become a shadow of its former self. Vice President Agnew's resignation and that of several cabinet officers had the effect of remanding greater responsibility for domestic programs and intergovernmental relations to the Office of Management and Budget, and especially to agencies and bureaus. Moreover the Democrats increased their electoral control over state governorships in the 1973 elections, while several large-city Democratic mayors, penitent for supporting Republican Nixon in the 1972 elections, renewed their allegiances to the party and to the Democratic controlled Congress.

Decentralization's Consequences

A third interpretation, related to the first two, posits that most governors, mayors, and county officials, though supportive of a complete overhaul of the federal aid system to states and localities, were generally unreceptive to its consequences. By seriously disrupting the functional status quo and directly challenging the operations of various bureaucratic fiefdoms organized around narrow-purpose programs, New Federalism zealots sought to create a new power base among subnational executive generalists. These state-local elected officials, so the strategy went, would assist the administration in restructuring the categorical system and curbing the power of functional autocracies, and by doing this they would be strengthening themselves.

However, these same officials experienced their initial taste of New Federalism under conditions of Presidential impoundment, cutbacks in federal categorical funding, and elimination of federal programs. They were less than delighted by the results. The governors, for example, confronted a host of federally aided claimants who channeled their demands upon statehouses in such areas as education, housing, public service jobs, library assistance, highway building, and pollution control. The mayors experienced comparable problems under federal social service ceilings, termination of Office of Economic Opportunity (OEO) projects, freeze on housing programs, reduction in summer youth funds, and cutbacks in other social service programs. The President's decision to cut back or eliminate these programs, coupled to the addition of new federal revenue-sharing monies available at the state-local level, resulted in the establishment of much larger pressure-group activity—previously lodged at the federal level—on the state and local government levels. The arena of claimants and lobbying activities had proliferated immeasurably as federal agencies and the administration deflected pressures upon them by sending claimants back to governors, mayors, and county officials. Public employee unions demanded more men, pay, and equipment; functionalists, the guilds, and grant program constituencies redoubled their efforts to get states and cities to back up the actual loss or impending reduction in federal funds. As one mayor quipped of this situation, "Revenue sharing was far better before we actually got the money, because then we could at least spend, borrow, or plan against it."

Several examples may be cited as evidence of the groups' willingness to follow New Federalism only so far. In the Omnibus Crime Control and Safe Streets Act of 1968, Congress approved a bloc-grant approach in assisting state and local crime reduction efforts rather than following the categorical aid approach which maximized the authority of federal agencies and congressional oversight. Following certain amendments to the act in 1970, the President proposed that the bloc grants be eliminated and replaced by special revenue sharing which, among other things, would restrict the Law Enforcement Assistance Administration's (LEAA's) role in reviewing, commenting and making recommendations on statewide plans. Specific programmatic, administrative, fiscal, and accountability guideposts set up in the bloc-grant would be replaced by a comprehensive plan including statewide priorities and indicating steps for coordinating law-enforcement activities, improving facilities, etc. In short, a real difference existed between special revenue sharing and the bloc-grant program in terms of federal oversight and programmatic and fiscal accountability.[27] The mayors opposed this weakening of federal oversight and accountability by states to federal agencies much, in a sense, as governors opposed the administration's special transportation revenue sharing, which left discretion over use of federal funds to metropolitan areas rather than the states.

The distinction between bloc grants and special revenue sharing emerged most conspiciously in the administration's Better Communities Act of 1973, a follow-up to the 1972 Community Development revenue-sharing plan which failed to pass the 92nd Congress. At the heart of this legislative controversy between the administration and mayors are the issues of federal oversight and funds. The HUD proposal eliminates grant applications, instead requesting that cities merely file a statement of development objectives and proposed uses. The USCM and much of Congress wants applications as a backstop against abuses and assurance that funds are being used to meet national housing goals, slum clearance, and improvement of community facilities. Congress seems willing to accept a more streamlined grant application process, but—like many mayors—has deep reservations about community development funds being poured into cities on a "no strings attached" basis. Large-city mayors also fear dissipation of scarce federal funds by automatic federal funding to all cities, including wealthy counties and suburbs, on a formula basis. To accentuate its basic differences with the administration over the Better Communities Act, the USCM overwhelmingly approved at its June convention a resolution supporting the grant application process whereby each city must specify its needs and objectives for meeting national goals; for making a community's past funding level a factor in the distribution formula; for a hold harmless provision assuring a community that it would not receive less in each of the next five years than it got in FY 1973; and for a provision for multiyear appropriations under the program. In spite of HUD's admonition to the mayors that their opposition to President Nixon's domestic programs might jeopardize New Federalism and prolong the housing subsidy freeze, large-city mayors seemed determined to work with their Democratic allies in Congress in fashioning a bloc-grant program to their mutual specifications.[28] This will likely include the grant application process, federal strings, and procedures to allow grant maneuvering by those mayors and cities which have demonstrated commitment to federal programs in the past.

By 1973, the temporary chief executive alliance between the White House and state-local chief executives had undergone significant disinte-

[27] Advisory Commission on Intergovernmental Relations, *Special Revenue Sharing Analysis*, pp. 32–36.

[28] See *The New York Times*, June 18, 1973, p. 11, and June 21, 1973, p. 21.

gration. The Nixon programs had challenged the total system of congressional organization, categorical grants, and bureaucratic-functionalist interest group ties; by doing so, it had perhaps made Congress more conscious of federal expenditure problems and the needs of subnational chief executives. But in the tradition of American politics, coalitions shifted. Congress and executive agencies responded to the Presidential challenge in the name of strengthening state and local chief executives by bringing these officials into their camp. The decentralization movement had peaked and seemed to be succumbing once again to cyclical pressures for some moderate centralization. For the government interest groups, President Nixon's New Federalism had in many cases gone too far, too fast, and demanded too much from state and local chief executives. It also had provided too few incentives and guarantees to the groups and their members in moving away from the existing system with all its liabilities to a new one where outcomes were unclear.

Less than two decades before, a committee of high appointed federal executives and governors, under a personal mandate from President Eisenhower, set about eagerly to alter the direction of the federal system by designating programs in which the federal government particpated that might be remanded to the states exclusively with revenues to support the programs. The Kestnbaum Commission's efforts to "unwind" the system of relationships dating from the New Deal and earlier proved monumentally unsuccessful. According to the late Morton Grodzins, it was not so much that federal agencies opposed the ordered devolution of functions to the states but that the governors themselves would not accept them.[29]

Much has changed since. Modernization of state and local governments is occurring on a broad front, but it is not yet commensurate with the new roles and responsibilities envisaged by the Nixon administration in implementing New Federalism. Certainly one of the most conspicious shortcomings of some Great Society architects was their assumption that managerial, administrative, and technical skills and personnel would be found in and outside government to enable state and local governments to carry out their portion of a new partnership. Similarly, New Federalism sponsors assumed that state and local chief executives had the capacity and desire to assume the enormous responsibilities called for in the Nixon programs.

One who studies political executives cannot fail to be impressed by the extent to which they still remain creatures of the past and the degree to which they are denied legal, political, or economic means for taking action. As USCM's Gunther noted derisively of the governors' national

---

[29] Morton Grodzins, in Daniel J. Elazar (ed.), *The American System,* Rand McNally, Chicago, 1966, chap. 12.

lobby, "HEW in all its power, funds, and programs, cannot make stronger governors out of daisies." What Gunther and other commentators on chief executives assert is that if a state does not allow its governor to be a strong chief executive, federal assistance at best can improve only marginally the resources to bolster the office and the incumbent. The same holds for local governments and the thousands of cities and counties operating under a commission or weak mayor form of governments. These officials perhaps viewed New Federalism as an outside pressure for government modernization, but some also saw it as adding a host of new and insuperable problems that they could not hope to cope with in their present situation.

Finally, New Federalism amounted to a philosophy of government that was overly concerned with the devolution of power without specifications as to what goes where or who is responsible ultimately for assuming leadership and for dealing with problems national in scope. For many chief executives, the President's plans increasingly smacked of a kind of "dual federalism" theory, seeking to separate much national responsibility for major domestic policies and goals from that of state and local responsibilities, leaving to the latter many of the choices and commitments previously made at the national level. In spite of subnational executives' frustrations in dealing with their federal constituency, most of these officials acknowledge the interdependence among governments and the sharing of responsibilities for solving complex social problems. As a major shareholder and resource allocator, the federal government could not easily assume a lesser role in the partnership. What is more, subnational chief executives were not about to let this happen and indeed took steps to prevent it.

Thus all three explanations of why New Federalism faltered as a domestic strategy suggest ways in which the government groups emerged during the Nixon Presidency at the forefront of interest group-congressional activity involving the disposition of the administration's programs. They had become full participants on a broad front in the bureaucratic, congressional, executive, and media discussion of the nation's domestic programs and policies.

"Restoring the balance in the federal system" had become a rallying cry for the government groups during Mr. Nixon's first term. Slowly and at times imperceptibly, this balance began returning: a balance, as Grodzins observed, "between national dominance, where the national interest is primary, and local discretion, where local options are more important than national ones."[30] This balance had moved in the direction of greater state-local government discretion not, perhaps, as much as the Nixon administration wanted but—by several indicators—as much as the Congress and the government interest groups wanted.

[30] Ibid., p. 381.

States and localities achieved considerable relief through revenue sharing and federal takeover of certain welfare programs. Much progress had been made in simplifying and decentralizing grant programs by administrative reform. Congress offered some grant consolidation as an alternative to special revenue sharing, so further changes were likely. Also, strong pressures were building within Congress for committee reorganization and reform of the total revenue and expenditure process. Even more sweeping changes had been set in motion at the state and local level which seem destined to profoundly affect government interest group behavior.

8

CHIEF EXECUTIVES
NEED EACH OTHER

★ ★ ★

It will be recalled that, at the outset of this study, the relations between the government interest groups and their federal constituency were traced from the period of the 1930s through the early 1970s. These relations have been divided into three periods. During the first phase of group relations with Washington, large-city mayors could be found at the forefront of intergovernmental activities. The governors, with the exception of their brief wartime aggressiveness, did not welcome federal intervention, while big-city mayors were no less determined to block state incursion at their city boundaries. The Depression and President Roosevelt's New Deal recovery programs generated a brief interlude of unprecedented unity among large-city mayors. However, as the national economic crisis subsided and Fiorello LaGuardia's hold on the Conference slipped, the mayors retreated to the politics of their own bailiwicks, interrupted only periodically by their staunch defense of public housing and urban renewal programs. Generally speaking, nothing of very great significance occurred in Washington between 1945 and 1964 insofar as these subnational chief executives were concerned.

In the second phase of group relations, between 1964 and 1968, the groups reacted internally to vast changes which occurred in American society and on the national government level. The federal government shifted its relationship to subnational governments in a massive way from an assistor role in the development of programs to initiator of hundreds of detailed new programs geared to narrow sectors of the population and involving substantial federal intervention in state-local governance. The narrow specialization of each government level in separate programmatic relationships with federal officialdom became scrambled, casting the groups into open warfare over participation in and control over these intergovernmental programs and funds.

The second phase entailed a shaking-out period for the groups as they strengthened their operations in order to play a more vital role in federal policy making. Mayors fought mayors, small cities organized against large ones. The National League of Cities-United States Conference of Mayors (NLC-USCM) vigorously competed against one another and also were joined by a host of new urban actors like Urban America and the Urban Coalition, seeking rewards and recognition as urban spokesmen. The National Governor's Conferences' revival stemmed largely from what state chief executives perceived as preferential treatment accorded the mayors and cities under Great Society programs and Washington's apparent resolve to write off the states in dealing with the cities. More partisan governors saw the poverty program and Model Cities, which bypassed the states altogether, as a direct pipeline from the federal Treasury to large-city mayors, a ploy by the Democratic administration to reward its allies and constituencies. Breaking out from under the Council of State Governments' umbrella, the governors opened their Washington lobbying in part to become an ideological buffer for interdicting the Washington–big-city alliance. The National Association of Counties (NACO) also came to life in this period. NACO responded both to rising suburban population and influence, establishing itself as an alternative to state-municipal jurisdictions by bargaining with the mayors, governors, and federal officialdom for inclusion in federal programs.

The third phase constitutes a maturing period for the groups: consolidation of the USCM-NLC's operations, the establishment of a strong governors' lobby, and the reorganization of NACO on a more urban basis. During this period, the groups enlarged their staffs, developed research and service capabilities, and bolstered their lobbying activities. The competitive relations among the groups characteristic of the previous phase intensified on many fronts. However, greater cooperation among the groups also occurred on federal revenue sharing, overhauling the categorical grant system, and on the strengthening of the role of state-local executives. Indeed, during this phase the groups emerged on center stage of Washington, lobbying at the forefront of executive-legislative battles over President Nixon's domestic policies and his New Federalism plan for restructuring intergovernmental relations.

GROUP EFFECTIVENESS

Beyond a historical narrative and analysis of intragroup dynamics, individual case studies spanning the second and third phases in the groups' Washington relations have been employed to ascertain not only the extent to which these officials affect public policy, but also how these groups implement their influence strategies. Several cases also have been disaggregated for probing group effectiveness over a wide range of issues and in different policy arenas. On the basis of the preceding cases and analysis, certain conclusions may be drawn concerning the operation of government interest groups in the federal system.

Case studies amply support the proposition that these subnational officials, directly and indirectly, have an impact upon federal decision making. Relying on various qualitative assessments as proxies for more quantitative indexes, one can conclude that the influence of the groups as intergovernmental actors has expanded and that their contribution to the decision-making climate has grown considerably over the years. Indeed, the eight cases illuminate the extent to which the groups marshaling various resources are able to affect public policies at all stages of development. The revenue-sharing case demonstrates how the government groups working together and with White House sponsorship overcame enormous congressional, bureaucratic, and interest group resistance in what is their most significant accomplishment to date.

In the absence of readily identifiable methods for evaluating group influence, political scientists as a rule have been content with a general statement of factors which appear, in one way or another, to affect the potential or actual influence of groups. They include their size and national distribution as well as the groups' prestige and cohesiveness, leadership skills, and capacity to rally public support.[1] Also important are such resources as money and technical expertise. Yet these characteristics of would-be or actual influence groups are not altogether satisfactory in viewing the government interest groups in light of their composition and range of policy concerns.

As Robert Dahl points out regarding assessments of group influence, "There is at present no single best way of solving the problems of comparability when different actors have different levels of influence in several different issue-areas."[2] The differences between participating in a decision, influencing a decision, and being affected by the consequences of a decision are subtle issues to which answers are often highly qualitative, descriptive, and even impressionistic. Case studies further underscore the problem of objectively assessing the effectiveness of any actor or groups of actors.

Certain disparities in perceptions arose among the groups—as represented by their leaders and those whom they felt they had influenced—over the former's contribution to and participation in decisions. Moreover, the case studies emphasize that the government interest groups do not rank high in possessing those resources more characteristically ascribed to

[1] See William J. Keefe and Morris S. Ogul, *The American Legislative Process*, Prentice-Hall, Englewood Cliffs, N.J., 1968, pp. 378–379.

[2] Robert A. Dahl, *Modern Political Analysis*, Prentice-Hall, Englewood Cliffs, N.J., 1965, p. 16.

influential group actors. They lack the funds, cohesion, sanctions, and vote-getting capacity commonly associated with influential groups.

Nevertheless, some tentative judgments are possible. Group effectiveness tends to be proportional to the number and strength of other would-be or actual influential actors. It is also related to the degree to which what the groups want is supported by the President or large segments of Congress. The groups' capacity to influence other actors to behave in a way they otherwise would not have acted remains rather limited. Two major resources the groups effectively utilize are their membership and information. It is the leverage and access that one or more members may exploit as high-ranking public officials that aid the groups in pursuing their goals successfully. The recognition that these officials are the principal political executives of state and local government provides them with a certain respectability for their claims.

Public official status, therefore, constitutes one of groups' more important resources. It provides them with a legitimacy as political actors that can carry over to their demands. This legitimacy as political actors may be traded upon in political currency. Group members' demands can be made openly through the media or in testimony before Congress. That is not to equate formal position or reputation with actual influence. Rather, it is to suggest that these groups and their members perform multiple roles and functions which enhance their political intervention at the federal level. These roles sufficiently overlap one another as to be interchangeable. The legitimacy of one carries over to the others.

The government interest groups have attained visibility and representative status for state-local governments at the national level. In a more formal sense, these accomplishments have been achieved through task force and commission membership, under federal statutes and through executive orders. On an informal level, the groups serve as consultants and advisers to agencies, congressional committees, and the executive. Major domestic programs are increasingly cleared through the groups and their members. Their liaison role within the intergovernmental system has been strengthened as they have been accorded representative status as bargaining agents for state and local governments.

Much of the groups' effectiveness, in fact, is an outgrowth of their information and feedback functions. They provide federal officialdom with information and research upon operational problems, management concerns, and defects in federal programs from their distinctive vantage. Policy specialization and expertise enable them to participate broadly in drafting and amending legislation, prelegislative clearance, and post legislative rule making.

Thus the government interest groups have won certain recognized support and prominence in the Washington community. Many of their gains stem from recent aggressiveness in activities—"their growing insistence and clout," as the Advisory Committee on Intergovernmental Relations (ACIR) observed in 1970.[3] They have matured as interest groups in defining goals and purposes, overcoming earlier isolated activities to work extensively through broad coalitions. Their activities and policies are national in scope. In addition, the groups have passed through various stages of internal transformation consonant with the growth and expansion of the federal system in becoming vital components of the intergovernmental policy-making process.

One measure of group effectiveness is the capacity to influence legislative behavior. Another, equally important, involves the ability to penetrate executive officialdom. After expending considerable efforts in the former, the groups in the late sixties concentrated much more on the latter. Several reasons may account for this, both internal and external to the groups themselves. A change of administration, a slowdown in legislative activity, and a period punctuated by reorganization, consolidation, and decentralization provide one plausible explanation. Another is the widespread recognition among the groups and in federal officialdom that the structure and administration of federal grant programs needed reform. But a third, related to the others, suggests that internal developments within the groups—their expanded activities and services, development of expertise, and information capabilities—yielded necessary resources for them to play a more formidable role vis-a-vis the executive than previously possible. By the early seventies, the groups' access to the executive—including the Office of Management and Budget (OMB)—had improved, though opinions differ on this score. Federal agencies have found the groups to be a significant ally, frequently a buffer between them and the President, or between them and Congress. Alliances have formed, partnerships have been created, and greater interdependency has been stimulated between the groups and many agencies. These relationships have been further solidified where agencies have contracted with the groups for research, have asked them to deliver services to clients, and have even delegated to them program administration.

Nonetheless, as important as the groups' contribution to federal policies may be, it would be erroneous to conclude that they are powerful entities as contrasted to more cohesive and narrowly oriented pressure groups. They are vocal, persistent, skillful, and at times fully participate in federal policy decisions. "They have come a long way in the past five years," observed Senator Muskie in 1970. "The PIGS (government interest groups) are much more sophisticated and knowledgeable about the legislative process than they once were, and now know how to get things accomplished."[4]

[3] Advisory Commission on Intergovernmental Relations, *Eleventh Annual Report*, Washington, D.C., 1970, p. 8.

[4] Senator Edmund Muskie, personal interview, Old Senate Office Building, Washington, D.C., August 1970.

Such a response is indicative of the rising esteem held for the groups by important segments of the legislative and executive communities. Congressmen and executive officialdom alike find the groups filling much of their need for information and pressure. They also acknowledge that the groups perform vital functions necessary for aiding them in performing their own roles more effectively.

On the other hand, group lobbying activities where broad national policy questions are at stake still may be said to have a limited impact. The passage of revenue sharing would rank as a significant exception to this generalization, however. Their impact is restrained particularly where substantial consensus and bargaining is required among a wide variety of actors, officials, and institutions. Their vote-getting capacity is not considerable if weighed against efforts to move a sizable number of legislators. Their importance lies more in the capacity to support and reinforce behavior. Nonetheless, this assessment does not diminish the importance of their growth, maturation, and recent effectiveness as political actors operating at the federal level. The groups, individually, have recorded several successful lobbying efforts where targets have been restricted to a handful of key legislators—namely, committee-subcommittee chairmen and ranking committee members.

Events of the past decade emphasize the pervasiveness of centralizing forces at the national level. In light of often weak state and local governments which are unwilling or unable to support their share of the partnership, federal policy makers have been inclined toward using new instrumentalities for intervening in state-local activities. Centralizing pressures seem all the more compelling given federal fiscal resources, nationwide problems, and the inherent tendency for federal officialdom to preserve and protect power, once gained, in its own hands. Nonetheless, substantial national pressures still exist for decentralization—the protection of the prerogatives and traditions of states and localities. These pressures are more active than they appear as the system cyclically swings from the centralization of the Johnson era to the decentralization of the Nixon period thus far. Like so much else in the pragmatic evolution of American federalism, disturbances in the political relationships among governments bring with them countervailing forces seeking adjustment to and accommodation of changes.[5] The emergence of the government interest groups representing the territorial integrity of subnational governments and the political positions of chief executives constitute one such set of forces. This broadened system of state and local government representation in Washington, built upon an older one, is a consequence of vast changes throughout the

[5] See Daniel J. Elazar, "The Shaping of Intergovernmental Relations in the Twentieth Century," in Robert Crew, Jr. (ed.), State Politics, Wadsworth, Belmont, Calif., 1968, pp. 53–68; and Morton Grodzins, in Daniel J. Elazar (ed.), The American System, Rand McNally, Chicago, 1966, chap. 2.

federal system. It is, in sum, a predictable outgrowth of the general-purpose units pursuing their own political interests and those of the geopolitical areas they represent.

AN ERA OF CHIEF EXECUTIVES

The nation's family of political executives invites comparison to the American President. They, like him, were founded in the colonial fear of chief executives; they grew from the stepping-stones of legislatures to figureheads and progressed to political leaders. They, like him, have been buffeted by and transformed through those forces of the twentieth century which have enlarged the office's powers and influence. They, like him, find themselves at the center of overlapping constituencies and audiences: bureaucracy, legislatures, partisans and supporters, citizens at large, and leaders of other governments. They, like him, must struggle to convert insubstantial powers into strength, often relying on informal powers of persuasion, bargaining, and coalition building.

Such comparisons are not always apt or revealing, however. Historical forces have had differential impacts on and consequences for chief executives. Few doubt, though, that chief executives on all government levels bear certain resemblances to each other, and any one of them has influenced the development of all.[6] To begin with, where the President is the mainspring of the American political system today, so governors, mayors, and county executives are the central political figures on state and local government levels. Their overall responsibilities and functions tend to be more congruent than not. They are singularly accountable for everything that occurs within their corporate jurisdictional boundaries during their terms of office, whether or not they possess the authority, powers, resources, or capacity to do anything about it.

Reassessing the office of the Presidency against new domestic and international conditions at the century's turn, Woodrow Wilson argued that the President of the United States would never again be the political figurehead he once was. New roles and responsibilities had been added to previous ones, while the occupant and the office assumed greater visibility and powers.[7] Similarly, events and trends underlying the transformation of the federal system—including the emergence of critical urban problems, the minority quest for equal opportunities, dissolution of once-powerful party organizations, massive federal involvement in subnational governments, and a more managed economy—have elevated political executives

[6] Louis W. Koenig, *The Chief Executive*, rev. ed., Harcourt, Brace, New York, 1968, p. 392.

[7] Woodrow Wilson, *Constitutional Government in the United States*, Columbia University Press, New York, 1908, pp. 74–81.

to conspicious positions of leadership. This is increasingly the situation whether or not these executives are prepared or allowed to perform leadership roles. Governors, mayors, and county executives, therefore, are undergoing the same kinds of transformation, at differential rates, that previously overtook the Presidency earlier in the century.[8]

Moreover, as chief executives, their roles parallel those of the President—as chief administrator, chief legislator, chief policy maker, and chief party leader—in domestic matters. Though important variations spring from differences in constituencies and responsibilities, these state-local executives are, in fact, diminutive Presidents characterized by less prestige, authority, and resources at their disposal. The President's domestic roles have expanded tremendously, particularly following the 1964 period, when Congress enacted a record number of new programs. So too, governors, mayors, and county officials are being compelled to take programmatic leadership. Most of these executives are assuming greater responsibilities not only as chief administrators, chief budget officers, and chief legislators but also as chief social service officers, chief health officers, chief law enforcers, and chief educators. These titles, as Williams notes, "are only symbolic of [their] expanding roles, which now are seen more in programmatic than administrative terms."[9] This is the case more for governors than local executives. Mayors and county officials too are being required to assume policy roles and engage in programmatic choices, but with added indeterminacy of state, regional, and national politics.

Roles tend to be shaped by historical and contemporary factors including constituencies, crises, constitutional and statutory provisions, tradition, and the legacy of past officeholders. These officials' perception of their roles suggests that officeholding status confers and is responsible for the assumption of many interrelated roles organized within institutional confines. Roles tend to be defined in an interactive process between officeholders and other actors and involve sets of complementary expectations between them and those with whom they interact. Recent observations on the Presidency, for example, have clustered executive roles in such a manner as to underscore the duality of the office's responsibilities. The "two Presidencies" interpretation holds that the President is largely consumed by matters of foreign affairs, national security, and defense which often drive out domestic concerns including legislation, administration, and party roles.[10] The President's preoccupation with defense and foreign

---

[8] See Duane Lockard, *The Politics of State and Local Governments*, Macmillan, New York, 1963, p. 395; and Joseph A. Schlesinger, "The Governors' Place in American Politics," *Public Administration Review*, 30:3, January 1970.

[9] J. Oliver Williams, "Changing Perspectives on the American Governor," in Tad Beyle and J. Oliver Williams (eds.), *The American Governor in Behavioral Perspective*, Harper and Row, New York, 1972, pp. 3 and 4.

[10] Aaron Wildavsky, The Two Presidencies", in Aaron Wildavsky (ed.), *The Presidency*, Little, Brown, Boston, 1970, pp. 130–162.

affairs and the institutionalized operations of the permanent government (the bureaucracy) in domestic matters have analogies to other members of the nation's family of political executives: governors, mayors, and county officials.

They well may be the most important participants in the subnational politics of the federal system, but they too have major relations with other governments outside their geopolitical boundaries. The President's constitutional powers and actions in foreign affairs are peculiarly suited to modern conditions, perhaps a reflection of legislative and bureaucratic domination of the domestic political arena. Mayors and governors find their relations with Washington and state capitals assuming greater significance, but unlike the President's often awesome powers and resources in the foreign sphere, they discover available resources for success in their foreign relations greatly lacking. Indeed, the uncertainties of outcome in their relations with higher levels of government have increased in proportion to their importance.

This condition of chief executives, in both intergovernmental and intragovernmental arenas, has led some observers to contend that they have obvious difficulties ahead. A real crisis in leadership prevails, asserts Seidman, which "has contributed as much as anything else to the loss of confidence in our general institutions."[11] That state and local executives are saddled with new roles and responsibilities, to a great extent imposed from outside their jurisdictions, tells us little about the future probability of success in coping with these burdens. The Watergate affair will likely affect chief executive behavior as well as that of other elected officials in American politics. It already has had an impact upon the institution of the Presidency, and it may well leave its imprint upon governorships and mayoralties for years to come.

Herbert Kaufman has argued that three dominant values can be traced through the development of this nation's political institutions: representativeness, politically neutral competence, and executive leadership. One value tends to succeed another in relative importance at any time.[12] The quest for representativeness, for example, centered on legislative bodies in the nineteenth century in the form of direct election of senators, proportional representation, and legislative dominance of executives. In the following century, it assumed the form of administrative representatives on regulatory commissions, clientele domination of services, and the like. Politically neutral competence in officialdom was manifested in the form of the short ballot, nonpartisanship, at-large elections, the city manager movement, and—in the bureaucracy—through civil service re-

[11] Harold Seidman, *Politics, Position, and Power,* Oxford, New York, 1970, p. 162.

[12] Herbert Kaufman, "Administrative Decentralization and Political Power," paper delivered at the Sixty-fourth Annual Meeting of the American Political Association, Chicago, September 3, 1968.

form, the merit system, independent boards, and commissions. As government units proliferated and fragmented, the movement for stronger chief executives set in through strengthening of chief executive powers, longer tenure in office, budgetary control, the strong-mayor form of government, and greater centralization of power. The movement toward a strong chief executive, in fact, has been on the ascendant for the greater part of this century.

These values are more than an abstraction. They are found in different segments of the population among many diverse groups who may agitate for structural changes to improve their positions and influence. Hence the values tend to run in cyclical fashion, strongly influencing government structures and leaving behind them their often indelible imprint. Countertrends develop when one value tends to be overly maximized at the expense of others and a new coalition of actors assembles to rectify the imbalance.

One finds in the seventies thus far eroding support of the bureaucracy and a drive for administrative and political decentralization. The decentralization movement has been elevated to neopopulist fervor by some politicians, the effects of which can be found on all government levels and in nearly all sectors of political life.[13] Subnational chief executives, for example, who once championed measures aimed at insulating bureaucracies from partisan politics (often in benign expectation that such measures might yield them benefits), have found outcomes often to the contrary. The dissolution of state-urban machines and the passing of political power to bureaucracies, which, in most cases, remain unaccountable and unresponsive to elected officials, have thrust many a chief executive into the decentralization movement in the hope of thereby strengthening their own offices.

Government interest group lobbying in Washington points to one facet of the movement for stronger chief executives. Mayors and governors sought recognition by federal officialdom for their common plight, demanding control over federal programs carried on within their jurisdictions and a diminished role for functional specialists at all government levels. Yet in spite of President Johnson's recorded efforts in aiding the groups to combat the centrifugal forces fed by Great Society programs, he tended to be more preoccupied with completing the New Deal agenda than with successful administration of intergovernmental programs. The latter tasks — by political necessity and choice — have been left to his successor.

President Nixon has enthusiastically embraced the causes of stronger chief executives in his New Federalism. His programs and proposals for executive reorganization, revenue sharing, grant consolidation, and strengthening executive management are geared to the overlapping inter-

---

[13] See Alan Altshuler, *Community Control,* Pegasus, New York, 1970.

ests and needs of these officials. He has made it emphatically clear to the governors, as Vice President Agnew did to local officials, that elected officials must be given total responsibility for the administration of their affairs and that the bypassing of state and local governments must end.[14] Thus, with fragmented congressional support and a largely unsympathetic bureaucracy, the President has found it strategically advantageous thus far, notes Kaufman, "to build closer ties with governors and large-city mayors than was ever the case before."[15] The congruence of Presidential, gubernatorial, and mayoral interests, well under way by the late sixties, has intensified since under an administration often more responsive to executive than congressional needs.

One of the principal aftermaths of the Great Society is that Presidents for some time to come will have to be concerned with intergovernmental affairs. The establishment of new departments and agencies, several hundred additional grant-in-aid programs, and the attendant difficulties of meshing together the fragmented activities of Washington, states, and localities, public and private instrumentalities, are legacies of the Johnson era. President Nixon and no doubt his successors will continue being drawn into the intergovernmental thicket for the same reasons that Presidents became involved in interdepartmental matters: that is, no single department has full jurisdiction and the President cannot rely on the departments for effective program delivery.[16] Additional reasons compel presidential involvement as well. Presidential responsibility for managing the economy and presiding over expenditure control require his attention to the rapid rise in domestic spending, particularly the growth of categorical grant programs. Reliance on the White House staff, the Domestic Council, and the Office of Management and Budget provides some presidential leverage in interdicting relations between federal agencies, congressional committees, and subnational jurisdictions. But these instruments and resources are not commensurate with the task which, to be even marginally successful, necessitates strong pressure and personal involvement by the President.

On the other hand, presidential intercession in the intergovernmental thicket also means dealing with a highly partisan constituency. Governors, mayors, and county officials make appeals directly to the President for his intervention into the bureaucracy on their behalf. Where President Johnson relied on "flying feds" to play executive troubleshooting roles and the Vice President to handle other grievances by state-local chief executives, Mr. Nixon has forged his own instruments to accomplish these tasks. The Johnson machinery has been replaced by the Domestic Council, Fed-

[14] See *Nation's Cities*, February 1972, p. 44.

[15] Herbert Kaufman, "Administrative Decentralization and Political Power," p. 11.

[16] See Allen Schick, "The Budget Bureau That Was: Thoughts on the Rise, Decline, and Future of A Presidential Agency," Brookings Institution Report, Washington, D.C., 1971.

eral Regional Councils, A-95 agencies, and other bodies for airing demands and opening interagency negotiation on matters affecting governors and mayors. It is unlikely that these instrumentalities will become institutionalized any more than the Johnson apparatus did. Future Presidents will by necessity prove flexible, adaptive, and experimental in dealing with intergovernmental negotiations.

Nonetheless, the fact that chief executives at all government levels require the assistance of each other more than ever before stands as another conclusion of this research. This need increases as governments become more interdependent and more power becomes disbursed throughout the system. The centrifugal forces of domestic politics may well require balance by the centrifugal force of strong presidential leadership, as Grodzins asserts.[17] It also requires strong effective spokesmen for state-local governments and their leadership. For national chief executives—with whom the government groups and their members tend to have greater overlapping needs—the groups are both their bane and their boon. The incessant demands for federal funds can be an annoyance, even politically embarrassing. Yet chief executives' reciprocal needs may also comprise a vast potential resource for Presidents as well, a leverage upon Congress and the bureaucracy for gaining acceptance of programs and agenda. President Nixon has recognized this, and future Presidents also are likely to rally subnational chief executives as a constituency to work with the executive in dealing with Congress. The Office of Management and Budget has increasingly turned its attention to aiding the President in his dealings with intergovernmental problems and in so doing has become at times an ally of the government interest groups.[18] OMB has found the groups to be a buffer, a new force in dealing with agencies, functionalists, and professional guilds which tend to dominate intergovernmental relations from a programmatic perspective. OMB's single client and constituency may well be the President himself, but, by way of Presidential encouragement to expand this mandate, it has also become what will probably be one of the more significant friends that the government interest groups have both in Washington and on their own government levels.

STATE GOVERNMENT REVIVAL

Surely the growth and emergence of government interest groups in Washington rank high among major developments in intergovernmental relations during the sixties. By the early 1970s, far-reaching changes, largely

[17] Morton Grodzins, in *The American System*, pp. 389–390.

[18] See "Summary of Recent Activities to Promote Improved Intergovernmental Relations," Office of Executive Management, U.S. Bureau of the Budget, Washington, D.C., June 1968, (mimeographed); and Office of Management and Budget Circulars No. A-95, July 24, 1969; No. A-95 Revised, February 9, 1971; March 8, 1972; No. A-98, June 5, 1970; and No. A-102.

federally induced, were also unfolding at the state-local level. These developments may be even more significant in the years ahead than what already has happened in Washington by way of charting the direction and movement in intergovernmental policy as well as relations between governors, mayors, and county officials.

The states have had a bad press, perhaps deservedly so, as state officials became the whipping boys of commentators who deplored their inactivity, corruption, and ineffectiveness. Where one generation of political scientists exhibited deep concern over the demise of state government—the "hollow shell theory"—the next applauded it in seeking greater social progress through the Washington-city hall axis.[19] But writing off and bypassing states in dealing with cities and local problems, as occurred in the Johnson years, misconstrued both the nature of these problems as well as the finite resources of the national government to cope with them.

Cities, counties, townships, and boroughs alike are legal creatures of the states. State governments hold vast power over these instrumentalities, almost life and death, including the authority to restructure them geographically, administratively, and politically. They possess the range of choices, options, and alternatives for dealing with their subdivisions often not available or otherwise exercisable by the federal government. Even under conditions of further federal reach into domestic matters, many areas will still lie beyond effective federal intervention. States have not only considerable financial resources and legal powers but also the capacity to confront urban problems on a statewide basis.

National recognition of urban problems has come rather late in our country's history, and indeed some would argue that federal policies in highways, housing, and industrial development exacerbated these problems.[20] The civil disorders of the sixties shocked many states and their governors into reviewing their tax structures, school systems, zoning laws, planning and development controls, and endless state laws which contributed to the urban malaise. The combination of restricted annexation and unrestricted incorporation, the uncontrolled mushrooming of special districts, the limitations upon municipal taxing and borrowing powers, and the abdication of all important police powers of zoning, land use, and building regulation into the hands of thousands of fragmented and competing local governments are but a few of the effects of decades of state governments' nonfeasance and malfeasance concerning urban affairs.[21] Thus,

[19] See Leonard D. White, *The States and the Nation*, Louisiana State University Press, Baton Rouge, La., 1953; and Roscoe C. Martin, *The Cities and the Federal System*, Atherton, New York; 1965.

[20] See Advisory Commission on Intergovernmental Relations, *Urban America and the Federal System*, Government Printing Office, 1969, chap. 2.

[21] See William G. Colman, "Making Our Federal System Work: A Challenge For the 70's," speech before the American Bar Association Section of Local Government Law, Dallas, Texas, August 12, 1969, pp. 3–4.

following rather feeble response at first, most urban governors are now involved in restructuring and redefining the states' role and responsibility for their local subdivisions.

Moreover, subnational chief executives and state legislatures have been compelled to respond to increasingly greater federal control over state political systems. Areawide planning and coordinating devices have been generated by federal programs for bypassing general-purpose governments at the local level with the same determined zeal that encouraged bypassing state government earlier. Special districts have grown on the state-local level at an astonishing rate, increasing by 16 percent between 1962 and 1967 alone. By 1972 an estimated 25,000 special districts existed, essentially single-purpose in structure, and about 70 percent of these overlapped with general-purpose local governments.[22] These special districts comprise more than one-third of all local governments in metropolitan areas. New federal programs continue to encourage new and more functionally contained metropolitan planning bodies in law enforcement, health, manpower, economic development, and pollution control, with prospects for others in education, land use, housing, and environmental control.

Forces spurring this proliferation are substantial. Special districts, for example, provide federal leverage for bypassing restrictive tax and debt limits imposed by states on their subdivisions, often reduce fiscal disparities among jurisdictions, and make state-local governments confront new problems. Many federal policymakers view these new instruments as vital tools for planning and coordination in selected problem areas which go beyond geopolitical boundaries of cities, counties, or even states. All federal departments engaged in domestic activities have had, in the past, regional and substate planning or service delivery boundaries that were rarely symmetrical or contiguous with one another. Even newer departments like HUD have entered the competition fostering, as it has, new metropolitan constituencies in water and sewer programs, councils of government, and in its efforts to reshape housing programs.

Thus federal intervention in state-local politics through planning, coordination, and problem-solving instrumentalities is creating both a nightmare and unparalleled opportunities for action by state-local officials. The consequences of federal activity are painfully visible. They have further splintered local governments and created new government bodies often unrelated to or overlapping general-purpose governments. These new units also tend to be unresponsive to control by elected officials and the general public. As mandated by federal stipulations, several require consumer representation and special elections, which, among other things, become fair game for the more powerful guilds who seek representation on, if not control over, their activities.

[22] Advisory Commission on Intergovernmental Relations, *Fourteenth Annual Report*, Washington, D.C., January 1973, p. 26.

State-local executives are well attuned to the fact that special districts and federally inspired planning bodies bolster, in many cases, federal power at their expense. Large-city mayors, once opposed to federal planning interference in local affairs, now welcome it, but on their terms. Unhappy experiences from these proliferating instrumentalities have caused the NLC, for example, to actively promote COG or A-95 agencies.[23] The USCM also has come around to support for A-95 agencies, but under greater elected official control—especially with mayoral representation. In late 1972, the government interest groups began work on developing recommendations for clarifying the functions and consolidating the role of "umbrella multijurisdictional organizations" operating at the substate level which would lay a basis for federal policy.

However, ambivalence tends to be characteristic of much of federal officialdom's attitude concerning this problem. Some federal officials feel that Washington has no business influencing the evolution of these instrumentalities at the substate level. Another view is that the federal government must do more by encouraging joint state-local action wherever it is possible to do so. OMB and the President's Domestic Council have sided with the latter view by seeking to curb previously uncontrolled federal intervention. With more than four hundred A-95 agencies of various types and powers functioning at the substate and regional level in 1972, OMB has recorded significant progress in getting certain functionally oriented programs to operate coterminously with A-95 areas. Also with state and gubernatorial roles in designating substate planning districts enhanced as a consequence of OMB directives, gains have been made in achieving conformity between state-established districts and federally sponsored areawide bodies. These efforts are likely to be strengthened further through some form of a national land-use policy, proposed by President Nixon and before the 93rd Congress. This would provide states with strong inducements to assume control over land-use planning and regulation for states areas of critical environmental concern such as watersheds, coastal zones, and scenic, historical, and recreational areas.

Activities on the state-local level to combat, in some cases, federal influence and respond more positively in others are clearly underway. If the 1969 to 1972 state legislative sessions are benchmarks for evaluating these activities, then it may be concluded that states have awakened from their long slumber. Many of these sessions were dominated by environmental issues which have given rise to greater state involvement in land use, housing, substate regional structure, and planning and have produced new state agencies to deal with multijurisdictional problems. Where states once delegated nearly all responsibilities in land use regulation to their subdivisions, they are now seeking to reclaim these powers and authority.

[23] See *Nation's Cities*, November 1971, p. 6.

Court pressure and citizen demand for property tax relief are forcing states to assume greater responsibility for traditional property taxes and school financing. States also are moving in overhauling their tax structures, playing a greater role in local and statewide public union negotiations, and developing service delivery systems.

Where concern of the environment helped shake states and their legislatures, massive energy shortages in the early 1970s have further compelled them to assume a greater legal and administrative role in all facets of local governance. The problems of environment and energy, amply reflected in changing public attitudes, are forcing a stronger public role in the use and the treatment of land as a resource rather than strictly as a commodity for private gain in the market place. The shape of urban growth and development is likely to be significantly altered as a consequence of active state involvement. This suggests, at least for the near future, that no unified urban policy or growth strategy imposed by the federal government will soon emerge. Rather, many different policies will develop as individual states, probably with strong federal encouragement, sort out their particular needs and develop their own intervention strategies.

One conclusion drawn from these trends and activities is that Creative Federalism required governors and mayors to be concerned about what was going on in Washington. President Nixon's New Federalism and the counterbalancing forces of the federal system stimulated by Creative Federalism have forced these officials to confront one another in their own political systems. Energy and environmental issues have furthered this trend. Federal programs and policies are redirecting subnational governments to respond actively to the threat of greater federal influence or incur the consequences. Moreover, it can be asserted that by almost any inventory of state defects and shortcomings as they relate to urban-metro problems, the states have demonstrated a new responsiveness—much of it uneven, belated, and not yet commensurate with the complexity of the problems confronted—but nonetheless significant.[24]

Using several structural indicators of these changes over the past twelve years, one finds major developments in state modernization. Table 9 tabulates these changes, most of which have occurred in the period of 1966 to 1972. One-third of the states raised taxes in 1972, after legislatures in three-fourths of the states had increased taxes previously in the 1970–1971 session. Virtually dozens had constitutional conventions or experienced major structural changes in their operations both at the state level and in dealings with their subdivisions. Indeed, income taxes finally surpassed sales taxes in FY 1973 as the biggest source of state tax dollars.

[24] See Advisory Commission on Intergovernmental Relations, *Eleventh Annual Report*, Washington, D.C., January 1970, pp. 20–32; and Ibid, *Fourteenth Annual Report*, pp. 22–27, 44–56. See also Ira Sharkansky, *The Maligned States*, McGraw-Hill, New York; 1972.

T–9 Key Indicators of State Modernization

	Number of States	
	1960	1972
Governor able to succeed himself	31	43
Governors with 4-year term	32	46
States with annual legislative sessions	19	36
States with Washington liaison office	1	27
States with a personal income tax	29	40
States with income and broad-based sales tax	22	36
States with transportation departments	2	16
States with departments of urban/local affairs	2	32

Source: ACIR

By way of prognosis, there are some indications to suggest that the more significant developments emerging in intergovernmental relations as gauged by lobbying activities of subnational chief executives may not emanate solely from Washington during the decade ahead. Instead, they may well reside at the state level in the working between state capitals, city halls, and other local governments. The battle lines between governors and mayors may have been drawn both in rhetoric and action in Washington during the sixties. However, the ultimate resolution of their differences in the seventies tends to fall largely within state political systems. Thus governors and mayors need each other for success in the Washington community, but they need each other even more for success on the state level.

The resources most mayors possess in dealing with their respective state capitals are typically not very impressive. As much as they may distrust state government, they cannot ignore it. Not only mayors and cities but also most other participants in city politics are more dependent upon state legislatures and governors for financial aid and use the state route to achieve their goals. Mayors may choose to bolster their state influence through alliance with one another as well as with county officials or even suburban legislators. On the other hand, mayors probably have more to gain in the short run from courting the favor of executive officials elected on a statewide basis rather than from such legislative coalitions.

Mayors and governors historically have each had their own constituencies, their own special interests in programs, and the resources to be largely self-reliant of one another. Mayors have not been a particular threat to governors in modern times, as few have ascended to statehouses. Sayre's Law regarding New York City mayors perhaps has wider application: "What they must do to get elected and re-elected are the very things that prevent them from ever moving on to higher office."[25] However, this arrangement of separation between mayors and governors worked, according to Kolesar, "only as long as the big cities were on the upward slope of their economic growth curves."[26] Once service demands and expenditures began exceeding tax bases and the often counterproductive effects of federal-state policies took hold, many large cities were in trouble. Shrinking or static tax bases generated a vicious spiral of rising tax rates, service decline, and emigration of taxpayers and industry.

Governors, on the other hand, cannot afford politically to completely write off mayors and large cities. Such a strategy may have been politically advantageous, but this is no longer the case in most urbanized states. The fact that cities, even in the case of Republican governors, may give only a minority of their votes to the gubernatorial winners does not free candidates or incumbents who have suburban or rural support to disregard their cities. Moderate and liberal Republican governors in the Northeast and Midwest who won elections in these states between 1966 and 1970 generally did so not only as a consequence of the emerging strength of suburban votes but also because they gained substantial support in large cities themselves. In most populous states, Reichley notes, "The primary means employed by Republicans to build their urban constituencies have been to campaign on platforms that promise more state aid to cities, and later, if elected, actually to devote a good deal of effort to meeting city needs."[27]

A seeming paradox that occurs periodically in New York State politics, with analogies to other unimetropolitan states, is that Republican governors tend to work harder for New York City and Democratic governors do more for upstate—both leaning over backward to gain support outside their natural constituencies. Republican governors seeking enactment of progressive legislation often find urban Democratic legislators a more compatible coalition to work with than an intransigent block of conservative outstaters. Similarly, Republican governors often win normally conservative Republicans to the support of progressive programs, while Democratic chief executives find that rural legislators stiffen their backs in a reflex action to programs viewed as favoring large cities. Governors Romney, Scranton, Rockefeller, Ogilvie, Volpe, Sargent, and Cahill are significant examples of state chief executives who received Republican legislative

[25] This quote comes from the late Wallace S. Sayre, Chairman of the Political Science Department, Columbia University.

[26] John H. Kolesar, "The Governors and the Urban Areas," in *The American Governor in Perspective*, p. 241.

[27] A. James Reichly, "The Political Containment of Cities," in Alan K. Campbell (ed.), *The States and the Urban Crisis*, Prentice-Hall, Englewood Cliffs, N.J.; 1970, p. 187.

approval for substantial city-oriented measures and, in several cases, a state income tax as well.

This is not to suggest that the Republican governor-urban Democratic coalition is the wave of the future, though it might be in some cases. It is to argue that anticity moves by large-state governors can be politically detrimental to their interests, while such a stance is often helpful with outstate and suburban legislators with their constituencies. Thus, for the short run at least, mayors must deal with governors, maximizing their often overlapping political needs, administrative requirements, and chief executive bonds rather than engaging in interminable squabbles which drive them apart.

Mayors are not without resources to keep pressure on an urban state governor concerning commitments and responsibilities to urban constituents. Even New York City's Lindsay, who had few legislative allies in Albany during his two terms as New York City Mayor, formed coalitions with other New York State mayors and urban county executives to pressure the state legislature for returning greater state aid to cities and urban counties. In effect, this alliance of a metro-urban type served as a frontal attack on the governor and GOP-controlled legislature, making it extremely difficult to pick apart New York City's needs and demands from the rest.

Such intrastate coalitions of mayors, county officials, and city managers are becoming ever more typical of alliance building and state lobbying activity. In Connecticut, local representatives from the state's thirty largest cities have organized to lobby both at the state level and in Washington. New Jersey's seven largest cities and mayors have also organized to work at the state level and with the state's congressional delegation in Washington on federal housing programs. The NLC, with several well-organized state leagues of cities in the West and South, finds the USCM-NLC joint lobbying operations at the federal level widely replicated on the state level. California and its communities have perhaps the most highly developed public official lobbying system. More than one-tenth of all lobbyists registered before the state legislature in 1972 represented government units, either individually or collectively: cities, counties, public education organizations, law-enforcement agencies, and a miscellany of special districts, redevelopment agencies, and authorities.[28] The city of Los Angeles's lobbying team, for example, includes representatives of the board of supervisors, the city council, the district attorney, the mayor, the police chief, the school board, the metropolitan water district, a rapid transit district, and others. In addition to strong statewide representation from the League of California Cities and the County Supervisors' Association, the state's five largest cities, nine largest counties, and a host of smaller cities and counties have individual lobbyists representing their governments on a full-time basis at the state capital in Sacramento.

[28] California Journal, 9:292–296, October 1972.

One finds intergovernmental lobbying at the federal level by elected officials and their surrogates replicated extensively at the state level, especially within the more urban states. Much of the same competition that one finds between state-local officials and their federal representatives is replicated on the state level in the rivalry between local government officeholders and state officials. Small-town mayors, selectmen, city councilmen, and county officials are usually the biggest threat state legislators face in election challenges. Consequently, state tax politics—burdens of taxation and distribution of revenues—provides often durable cleavages between local officials and state representatives. Local officials lobby the state for increased statewide taxes to meet local deficiencies, while state officials often view local government problems in terms of each municipality's or county's property taxes. The stakes that these individual units have in state government are frequently too great to be left entirely to elected legislative representatives or even locally elected officials. With similarities to the federal level, chief executives of local governments are also belated entrants in a collective sense into state lobbying systems; their full impact, in most cases, only now is beginning to be felt.

Other overlapping interests compel greater unity among chief executives: the common need for revenues and control over their bureaucracy. While these officials may be preoccupied with revenue-raising and disagree bitterly over state budgets and allocation of state funds, each eschews initiation of major tax increases, whether state-generated or locally inspired. They are forced to work together on statewide bond issues, the raising of debt limits, property taxes, and sales or income taxes which provide considerable latitude for bargaining and cooperation where their mutual survival is at stake. Furthermore, the mayors' conspicious need to control expanded and increasingly autonomous bureaucracies with their public unions has confronted state chief executives with similar problems. The rise in bureaucratic intransigence and influence has made governors and mayors alike sensitive to each other's plight. Once again, greater collaboration has been spawned out of mutual necessity and the understanding of one another's problems.

In viewing the future direction of intergovernmental lobbying and even intergovernmental relations, the trends operating against large cities both in dealing with their federal constituency and state government need to be mentioned. Loss of voting power to the suburbs certainly ranks among the highest. Migration to suburbs increased by more than 25 percent in the 1960s, so that by 1970, for the first time, more Americans were found living in the suburbs of big cities than in the cities themselves. This trend seems to be durable and will probably not lead to any appreciable reverse migration back to large cities but rather to movements from suburb to suburb. Visions of a highly urbanized nation to the contrary, the number of persons residing in cities of over 500,000 population has declined in each of the past six decades; in fact, three fourths of the nations' Standard Metropolitan Statistical Areas (SMSAs), even when central cities and suburbs are combined, contain fewer than 500,000 people.[29] Indications of urban growth trends over the next decade or two can be inferred from the 1970 census. The 56 urban centers with population over 250,000 contain some 20.8 percent of the U.S. population, while the 840 urban areas with populations of 25,000 to 250,000 contain 24 percent, the latter being the areas of greatest increase, particularly among cities in the range of 50,000–100,000 population.

Regionally, the population of the country and its economic activity continue to shift South and West. Major cities east of the Mississippi River peaked in their populations between 1940 and 1950, and most have declined since, some at more than 10 percent per decade. Newer cities in the Southwest and West continue to expand. Their strength, economically and politically, is growing: that of older cities — often dominated by manufacturing activity — is declining.

Most new employment opportunities are being created in the outer rings of cities and metropolitan areas, a trend likely to continue indefinitely into the future. Older central business districts are losing their monopoly of accessibility to suburban markets. Industry seeking cheaper space for expansion and access to new markets has vacated large central cities for these reasons as well as taxes, linkages to regional markets and suppliers, and employee amenities.[30] Even the changeover in the national economy — manufacturing toward services; blue-collar to white-collar; centralized markets to decentralized ones — has had severe consequences in most cases for older, large cities, breeding unemployment for the uneducated and unskilled and myriad related social problems. For many large cities, their basic problem seems to be that the core-city has lost its "economic value"; for these cities vast amounts of federal and state aid may stabilize the situation, but they are not likely to turn it around.[31]

These changes have already had an impact on political institutions and party politics. The balance of power in the House of Representatives and in most urbanized states resides with suburban legislators, who — with assistance from rural compatriots — are in key positions to advance or block claims made by central cities or even coalitions of cities.[32] The new suburban influence has been hailed by Chief Executive Ralph Caso of New York's Nassau County as signifying the capacity "to maintain the subur-

[29] Daniel J. Elazar, "Are We a Nation of Cities?" *The Public Interest,* 4:42–58, Summer 1966.

[30] See Thomas N. Stanback, *The Metropolitan Economy,* Columbia University Press, New York, 1970.

[31] See George Sternlieb, "The City as Sandbox," *The Public Interest,* 25:14–21, Fall 1971.

[32] Gerald L. Pomper, "Census '70: Power to the Suburbs," *Washington Monthly,* 5:20–24, May 1970.

ban way of life."[33] Reapportionment and suburban growth point to further shifts in traditional party alliances clearly under way in the late 1960s. Black migration to urban centers and a parallel exodus of middle-class whites to the suburbs are transforming the urban electorate. Ample evidence supports the gradual but conspicious falling away of white city dwellers from the Democratic party, best exemplified by the fact that Richard Nixon outpolled his Democratic opponents among big-city whites in both of the last two presidential elections.[34] Even the President's electoral constituency, once thought to be skewed slightly in favor of large cities due to the electoral college's sensitivity to the "swing vote" exercised by large cities and populous states, has changed. Only two of the nation's twelve largest cities in 1970 contained more population than their suburban fringes, which means that one major link between cities and national politics has been partially severed.

Such trends lead to the conclusion that large cities do not presently or will not likely have the political resources necessary to dictate the means in Congress or at the state level by which urban problems are to be met or resolved. The dream of the mayors and their sympathizers in the 1950s and early 1960s that cities might someday be able to impose their will on federal and state officials will not bear the test of political reality.[35] This does not imply complete impotence by mayors and large cities, for they still have resources with which to bargain and negotiate. It does illuminate, however, the rising political weakness and vulnerability of large cities to forces beyond their control. Even the most deft and concerted lobbying activity by them is not likely to redress this growing imbalance in political influence without a significant expansion in coalitions and alliances, including suburban and metropolitan interests. What the mayors have in their favor is that suburbs, smaller cities, and older communities alike are experiencing on a smaller scale many of the same problems besetting the large central cities—namely, a static or shrinking tax base, problems in services and municipal unions, pollution, welfare, housing, education, and others.

Thus governors and large-city mayors are reaching out to suburban communities and voters as the source of alliances and political leverage. At the national level, the same groping for metropolitan interests affects both the President in his political constituency and Congress, which increasingly reflects this diverse and heterogeneous electorate.

These findings and trends revert back to the theme of governors needing

---

[33] Ralph G. Caso, "Counties: New Suburban Power and Influence," report done for the National Association of Counties by the Nassau County Executive, New York, July 19, 1971, p. 12 (mimeographed).

[34] See, Everrett C. Ladd, Jr., et al., "A New Political Realignment?" *The Public Interest*, **23**:46–63, Spring 1971.

[35] A. James Reichly, *The Political Containment of Cities*, p. 178.

mayors as much as mayors need governors. As governors seek to cope with rising urban demands and gain admission to urban systems, so mayors have begun putting aside home-rule rhetoric to reach out into adjoining metropolitan areas. Each has come to recognize the need for dealing with cities on a metropolitan scale and each acknowledges that central to the solution of the nation's greatest urban problems is improved government machinery in metropolitan areas. In light of expanding A-95, COG, and special district units in urban areas, it seems all but certain that some form of metro governance will emerge. The issue is no longer whether there will be metropolitan government but rather what form it will assume — ranging from a clustering of unintegrated, semiautonomous districts to a highly integrated, coordinated single unit. The federal government can speed this movement through incentives and sanctions. However, the shape each assumes will be determined, predictably, by states and their subdivisions.

Thus the resolution of urban problems demands a broadening of interests if it is to be successful. It will require majoritarian interests and demands unrestricted by geography, class, or ethnic limitations, including metropolitan interests in consumerism and service-oriented areas.[36] Leadership of such interests and coalitions necessitates even greater collaboration among subnational chief executives to achieve a broader distribution of benefits. No single conclusion emerges more fully than the fact that states and local governments — governors, mayors, and county officials alike — have a broad spectrum of overlapping needs from which to bargain, reconcile differences, and more successfully articulate demands. Their dependencies are increasing.

CONCLUDING COMMENTS

The contributions made by the government interest groups past and present to policy making at the federal level and the development of federalism seem endless. Their achievements and prospective accomplishments have been traced from the groups' formative years through the 1970s. Their growth has been an evolutionary one. It has been punctuated by several successive stages in their relations with Washington as well as with each other.

Acknowledgedly, these groups represent the interests of general-purpose governments as defined by city halls, county courthouses, state capitals, and chief executives from these units. Nonetheless, it can be asserted that such interests are often more encompassing and broader than those represented by special interest groups, functionalists, or even individual con-

---

[36] See Robert C. Wood, *The Necessary Majority: Middle America and the Urban Crisis,* Columbia University Press, New York, 1972; and Frederic N. Cleaveland, "Congress and Urban Problems: Legislating for Urban Areas," *Journal of Politics,* 2:303–304, May 1966.

gressmen whose purview is often limited by committee assignments and less identifiable constituencies. In a true Madisonian sense, the government interest groups and their members provide another form of political representation at the national level, one founded not on functional lines or shifting congressional boundaries but on representation of interests based essentially on geopolitical units—states, counties, and municipalities.

These groups constitute a kind of "third house" of elected representatives at the national level as well as an institutional interface between the President and Congress. They are, however, private, voluntary associations comprising essentially chief executives of state-local governments with no formal toehold in the executive or legislative branches. They have no elected federal mandate, no formal constitutional position, and rather meager standing at the federal level. But as outsiders they may be found in often strategic positions to exploit the rampant cleavages within the federal establishment. These subnational elected officials are able to maintain their influence through their positions within state-local political systems—positions with which to bargain and negotiate with federal officialdom. They indeed have become a significant counterbalance in the federal system to the rising influence of the national government, which pervades all of American life.

The government groups also constitute an ongoing force confronting Congress and the executive with gnawing questions concerning program effectiveness, domestic priorities, balkanization of governments, accountability among elected officials, tax politics, and control over bureaucracy on all government levels. The representation function of Congress, personified by the march of an endless number of narrow federal programs geared to small sectors of the population, frequently subverts its governing activities in terms of legislative implementation, administrative oversight, revenue raising, and taxation. Governors, mayors, and county officials seek to impress upon Congress the importance of being concerned about broader, more inclusive aggregates of the population than the narrow, often limited interest group representation system with which many congressmen must deal on their particular committees.

Group members are professional politicians—not amateurs, often party leaders and key figures in subnational politics. Their skills and knowledge of the political process are considerable, while their capacity to maximize and enhance the access often tendered them ranks among their greatest assets. Besides articulating the needs of their constituents as well as their own, they offer considerable support to federally elected officials. They provide formidable linkages between constituents and elected officials, not to mention the bureaucracy. Through constant supply of information and lobbying pressures, the groups assist Congress and the President in performing their representative roles more effectively.

These subnational chief executives are caught, as it were, between the flow of demands upward through the federal system and the reverse flow downward of federal funds and policies. They constitute an early warning system, a platform for the expression of aggregate demands by constituents, and a weathervane for the shifting mood of the electorate. They may afford a scape goat for errant policies or a buffer between constituents and federal policy makers. Nonetheless, the legitimacy of these groups and the demands they make in Washington are not easily dismissed or ignored. They have come to operate in a multicentered group system of alliances, often playing down the key roles they perform in molding and directing interest group coalitions. Their involvement has increased, the scope of their activities has broadened, and the resources necessary to accomplish their goals have expanded appreciably.

Moreover, the government interest groups and their members contribute to the range of values, tensions, movement, and strength found in the American federal system. The friction of government acting upon government, officials upon officials, and institutions upon institutions for the forwarding of state and local interests only adds to the vitality of all governments. This seems to be the case in spite of conspicious tensions found in intergovernmental relations. Where some observers of the system call for the development of a "consistent set of principles and governing doctrine," the lowering of tensions and conflict, and the clarification of responsibilities among government levels, the evolution of American federalism suggests that none of these will probably emerge. "Like so much else in American government and politics," notes Leach, "federalism is an exercise in pragmatism."[37] No consistent or rigid set of governing principles will likely emerge given the countless political forces operating against any such development.

While greater collaboration among the groups and their members may emerge in the years ahead, the characteristic veto power, bargaining, and conflictual forces inherent in federalism will not easily vanish. One observer of the system has aptly noted that the basic political fact of federalism is that it "creates separate, self-sustaining centers of power, privilege, and profit which may be sought and defended as desirable in themselves as a means of leverage upon elements in the political structure above and below."[38] Federalism builds into our political system veto politics: a certain conservative bias which tends to expand geometrically as access points on all government levels increase and new constituencies are created. The government interest groups constitute such a veto instrumentality, but also one which has proved to have a significant capacity for joint action as well.

Martha Derthick concludes from her study of federal assistance pro-

[37] Richard H. Leach, "Federalism: Continuing Predicament," *Public Administration Review*, 31:223, March 1971.

[38] David B. Truman, "Federalism and the Party System," in Aaron Wildavsky (ed.), *American Federalism in Perspective*, Little, Brown, Boston, 1967, p. 92.

grams that "for the federal government to impose value choices on state governments, it must arrive at such choices itself."[39] If the past provides any clues to future trends, it suggests that no broad-based or durable consensus on such values will develop. In practice, the federal government's powers to impose definite and enforceable choices on states, their subdivisions, and other executors of public policy are severely limited, as are the states' on their subdivisions. Even where higher government levels have direct powers over the program or agency of lower-level ones, officials on both sides tend to agree that such powers are generally exercised through a process of competition and conflict, negotiation and compromise, maneuver and strategy.

The government interest groups contribute to this diversity in the federal system not only in their capacity to check one another through well-developed coalitions and forceful articulation of demands but also in their combining with one another against narrow and parochial interests. They add further to the viability of the overall system through the legitimacy they confer on the often negotiated outcomes among government levels.

[39] Martha Derthick, *The Influence of Federal Grants*, Harvard University Press, Cambridge, Mass., 1970, p. 209.

APPENDIX

PERSONS INTERVIEWED
AND POSITIONS HELD AT TIME

Alexander, Don	Staff, NLC
Bane, Frank	Former COSGO Director; Executive Secretary NGC; Director, ACIR
Baker, Don	Legal Counsel, U.S. Office of Economic Opportunity
Beckman, Norman	Assistant Secretary for Intergovernmental Relations, U.S. Department of Housing and Urban Development
Beck, Lowell	Executive Director, Urban Coalition Action Council
Bell, George	Staff, COSGO
Bookbinder, Hyman	Assistant Director of National Councils and Organizations, U.S. Office of Economic Opportunity
Bresler, Charles	National Relations Officer, State of Maryland
Brussat, Bill	Office of Management and Organization, OMB
Burrows, Ken	Staff, House Banking and Currency Committee
Burns, Virginia	Deputy Assistant Secretary for Individual and Family Services, Department of Health, Education, and Welfare
Byrley, Charles	Director, Office of Federal-State Relations, NGC
Cannon, Jim	Aide to Governor Nelson Rockefeller
Canty, Donald	Staff, Urban America
Caso, Ralph	County Executive, Nassau County, New York
Colman, William	Executive Director, ACIR
Crawford, Bob	Assistant Director for Governmental Relations, U.S. Office of Economic Opportunity
Crihfield, Brevard	Executive Director, COSGO
Culbertson, Sam	Legislative Assistant, Senator George Murphy

Danaceau, Paul	Staff, Subcommittee on Executive Reorganization, Senate Government Operations Committee
Dirks, Harley	Staff, Senate Appropriations Committee
Dorsch, Jim	Legislative Assistant, Senator Abraham Ribicoff
Finley, Tom	Assistant Attorney General for Congressional Relations, Justice
Gallagher, Hugh	Director of Public Affairs, Office of Emergency Planning
Garvey, John	Staff, NLC
Gaul, Bill	Staff, House Committee on Education and Labor
Gibbons, Wayne	Director, Federal-State Relations, State of Texas
Goldberg, Delphis	Counsel, Subcommittee on Intergovernmental Relations, House Government Operations Committee
Graves, Tom	Assistant to the Assistant Director, Office of Management and Organization, OMB
Graves, W. B.	Senior Research Analyst, Legislative Reference Service, Library of Congress
Gunther, John	Executive Director, USCM
Hartigan, Neil	Past Corporation Counsel, City of Chicago
Harkins, Peter	Staff, NLC
Hartman, Richard	Director, National Service to Regional Councils, Washington, D.C.
Hardeman, D. B.	Former Staff Assistant to Speaker Sam Rayburn, U.S. House of Representatives
Healy, Pat	Executive Director, NLC
Henderson, Elmer	Staff, Subcommittee on Executive Reorganization, House Government Operations Committee
Huitt, Ralph	Assistant Secretary for Legislation, U.S. Department of Health, Education, and Welfare
Ireland, Casey	Minority Counsel, House Banking and Currency Committee
Jackson, John	Federal Coordinator, Commonwealth of Massachusetts
Johnson, Jim	Staff, NGC
Josten, Bob	Staff, NLC
Kresky, Mary	Aide to Governor Nelson Rockefeller
Kirst, Michael	Staff, Subcommittee on Employment, Manpower, and Poverty, Senate Labor and Public Welfare Committee
Martin, Jim	Staff, NGC; former staff, NACO
McGrath, Kyran	Chief Washington Office, State of Illinois
McClean, Ken	Staff, Senate Banking and Currency Committee

McDaniel, Paul	Office of Legal Counsel, Treasury Department
Merryman, Jack	Staff, NACO
Meyer, Barry	Counsel, Senate Public Works Committee
Mields, Hugh	Past staff, USCM; City consultant, Washington, D.C.
Muskie, Edmund	U.S. Senator, Maine
Naftalin, Arthur	Mayor of Minneapolis
Nicoll, Don	Administrative Assistant, Senator Edmund Muskie
Patricelli, Bob	Minority Counsel, Senate Labor and Public Welfare Committee
Peterson, Neal	Assistant to Vice President Hubert Humphrey
Pritchard, Al	Assistant Director, NLC
Quie, Al	Congressman, Minnesota
Radcliffe, Charley	Special Education Counsel, House Education and Labor Committee
Richter, Al	Staff, ACIR
Robinson, Bill	Office of Budget Review, OMB
Sanders, H. B.	Assistant to the President for Congressional Liaison
Schnoor, Howard	Assistant Chief Officer, Office of Management and Organization, OMB
Seidman, Harold	Assistant Director, Office of Management and Organization, OMB
Shannon, John	Assistant Director, ACIR
Shoemaker, Alvin	Legislative Representative, Investment Bankers Association
Skolar, Dan	Deputy Director of Law Enforcement Assistance Agency, Justice Department
Smith, Charles	Staff Director, Subcommittee on Intergovernmental Relations, Senate Government Operations Committee
Stanfield, Rochelle	Staff, NGC
Steiner, Gil	Director of Government Studies, The Brookings Institution
Sundquist, James	Senior Research Associate, The Brookings Institution
Turner, E. Win	Counsel, Subcommittee on Intergovernmental Relations, Senate Committee on Government Operations
Velde, Richard	Legislative Assistant, Senator Roman Hruska
Walker, Dave	Assistant Director, ACIR
Wallerstein, David	Former USCM staff; Director, NLC-USCM Man-in-Washington Service; City consultant for Los Angeles and others
Ward, C. D.	Counsel, NACO

Warren, Aubrey   Staff, Subcommittee on Roads, House Public Works Committee

Wood, Robert C.   Secretary, U.S. Department of Housing and Urban Development

Zalenko, Ben   Staff, House Judiciary Committee

BIBLIOGRAPHY

BOOKS

American Municipal Association: *Proceedings of the Thirty-eighth Annual Congress of Cities,* Washington, D.C., 1962.

Baker, Gordon: *Rural versus Urban Political Power,* Random House, New York, 1955.

Banfield, Edward C.: *The Unheavenly City,* Little, Brown, Boston, 1970.

Banfield, Edward C., and James Q. Wilson: *City Politics,* Vintage, New York, 1963.

Bauer, Raymond, Ithiel de la Sola Pool, and Lewis A. Dexter: *American Business and Public Policy,* Atherton, New York, 1964.

Beyle, Thad and J. Oliver Williams (eds.): *The American Governor in Behavioral Perspective,* Harper and Row, New York, 1972.

Brooks, Glenn: *When Governors Convene,* Johns Hopkins Press, Baltimore, 1961.

Brownlow, Louis: *A Passion for Anonymity,* University of Chicago Press, Chicago, 1958.

Bryant, Farris: *Nine Months of Progress in Federal-State Relations,* Report to the President, Washington, D.C., August 1967.

Caso, Ralph G.: *Counties, New Suburban Power and Influence,* Report to the National Association of Counties, Washington, D.C., July 1971.

Cater, Douglass: *Power in Washington,* Vintage, New York, 1965.

Charlton, Billy L.: "A Study of State-Local Governmental Liaison Activities in Washington, D.C.," unpublished master's thesis, American University, Washington, D.C., 1967.

Cleaveland, Frederic N. (ed.): *Congress and Urban Problems,* Brookings, Washington, D.C., 1969.

Congressional Quarterly: *Congress and the Nation, 1945–1964,* Washington, D.C., 1965.

———: *Congress and the Nation, 1965–1968,* Washington, D.C., 1969.

———: *The Washington Lobby,* Washington, D.C., 1971.

———: *Crime and Justice in America,* Washington, D.C., 1968.

Committee for Economic Development: *Reshaping Government in Metropolitan Areas,* New York, 1970.

Connery, Robert H., and Richard Leach: *The Federal Government and Metropolitan Areas,* Harvard Press, Cambridge, Mass., 1961.

Council of State Governments: *The Book of the States,* Chicago, 1950–1970 (published biennially).

———: "National Governors' Conference, 1908–1966," Chicago, May 11, 1966 (mimeographed).

Dahl, Robert A.: *A Modern Political Analysis,* Prentice-Hall, Englewood Cliffs, N.J., 1965.

Davidson, Roger: "Creative Federalism and the War on Poverty." A paper presented at the Sixty-second Meeting of the American Political Science Association, New York City, September 6–10, 1966.

Davis, David W., and James W. Sundquist: *Making Federalism Work,* Brookings, Washington, D.C., 1969.

Derthick, Martha: *The Influence of Federal Grants,* Harvard University Press, Cambridge, Mass., 1970.

Dexter, Lewis A.: *How Organizations Are Represented in Washington,* Bobbs-Merrill, Indianapolis, 1969.

Dixon, Robert G.: *Democratic Representation,* Oxford, New York, 1968.

Donovan, John: *The Politics of Poverty,* Pegasus, New York, 1967.

Duncombe, Robert S.: *County Government in America,* National Association of Counties, Washington, D.C., 1966.

Dye, Thomas R.: *Politics in States and Communities,* Prentice-Hall, Englewood Cliffs, N.J., 1969.

Easton, David: *A Systems Analysis of Political Life,* Wiley, New York, 1965.

Elazar, Daniel J.: *American Federalism: A View from the States,* New York, Crowell, Collier, 1966.

———, R. Bruce Carroll, A. Lester Levine, and Douglas St. Angelo (eds.): *Cooperation and Conflict,* Peacock, Itasca, Ill., 1969.

———: *The American Partnership,* University of Chicago Press, Chicago, 1962.

———: "The Shaping of Intergovernmental Relations in the Twentieth Century," in Robert E. Crew, Jr. (ed.), *State Politics,* Wadsworth, Belmont, Calif., 1968.

Farkas, Suzanne: *Urban Lobbying,* New York University Press, New York, 1971.

Flynn, Edward J.: *You're the Boss,* Viking, New York, 1947.

Freeman, J. Leiper: *The Political Process,* Random House, New York, 1965.

Graves, W. Brooke: *American Intergovernmental Relations,* Scribners', New York, 1964.

Greenstone, J. David: "Party Pressure on Organized Labor in Three Cities," in M. Kent Jennings and Harmon Ziegler (eds.), *The Electoral Process,* Prentice-Hall, Englewood Cliffs, N.J., 1966.

Grodzins, Morton: in Daniel J. Elazar (ed.). *The American Federal System,* Rand McNally, Chicago, 1966.

Herring, E. Pendleton: *Group Representation Before Congress,* J. Hopkins Baltimore Press, 1929.

Hess, Stephen and David Broder: *The Republican Establishment,* Harper and Row, New York, 1967.

Humphrey, Hubert H.: *The Vice President and Local Government,* Report to the President, Washington, D.C., August 1968.

Kaufman, Herbert: "Bureaucrats and the Organized Civil Servants," in Robert H. Connery and Demetrios Caraley (eds.), *Governing New York City.* Academy of Political Science, New York, 1969.

——: "Administrative Decentralization and Political Power," paper presented at the Sixty-fourth meeting of the American Political Science Association, Chicago, September 3, 1968.

Keefe, William J., and Morris Ogul: *The American Legislative Process,* 2nd ed., Prentice-Hall, Englewood Cliffs, N.J., 1968.

Key, V. O.: *American State Politics,* Knopf, New York, 1966.

——: *Politics, Parties, and Pressure Groups,* 5th ed., Crowell, New York, 1964.

Koenig, Louis W.: *The Chief Executive,* rev. ed., Harcourt, Brace, New York, 1968.

Kolesar, John: "The Governors and Urban Areas," in Thad Beyle and J. Oliver Williams (eds.), *The American Governor in Behavioral Perspective,* Harper and Row, New York, 1972.

Lipson, Leslie: *The American Governor: From Figurehead to Leader,* University of Chicago Press, Chicago, 1939.

Lockard, Duane: *The Politics of State and Local Government,* Macmillan, New York, 1963.

Lowe, Jeanne R.: *The Near Side of Federalism,* Ford Foundation, New York, 1972.

Lowi, Theodore: *The End of Liberalism,* Norton, New York, 1969.

MacMahon, Arthur (ed.): *Federalism: Mature and Emergent,* Macmillan, New York, 1955.

Mansfield, Harvey C.: "Intergovernmental Relations," in James W. Fesler (ed.), *50 States and Their Governments,* Knopf, New York, 1967.

Martin, Roscoe C.: *The Cities and the Federal System,* Atherton, New York, 1965.

Matthews, Donald R.: *U.S. Senators and Their World,* Vintage, New York, 1960.

Milbrath, Lester: *The Washington Lobbyist,* Rand McNally, Chicago, 1963.

Mogulof, Melvin: *Federal Regional Councils,* Urban Institute, Washington, D.C., 1970.

——: *Governing Metropolitan Areas,* Urban Institute, Washington, D.C., 1971.

Moore, John E.: "Controlling Delinquency: Executive, Congress and Juvenile, 1961–1964," in Frederic N. Cleaveland (ed.), *Congress and Urban Problems,* Brookings, Washington, D.C., 1969.

Moynihan, Daniel P.: *Maximum Feasible Misunderstanding,* Free Press, New York, 1969.

National Association of Counties: *Urban County Congress of the National Association of Counties,* Washington, D.C., 1959.

———: *The Second Urban County Congress of the National Association of Counties,* Washington, D.C., 1963.

———: *The American County Platform,* Washington, D.C., 1967.

National Governors' Conference: *The Modern State in the Federal System,* Chicago, 1968.

———: Official Papers: Special Interim Meeting, White Sulpher Springs, W. Va., December 16–17, 1967, Chicago, 1968.

National League of Cities: "The National League of Cities and the United States Conference of Mayors," background paper on the relations between the two groups, Washington, D.C., 1967 (mimeographed).

———: *Proceedings of the Forty-second Annual Congress of Cities,* Washington, D.C., 1966.

———: *Proceedings of the Forty-third Annual Congress of Cities,* Washington, D.C., 1967.

———: *Proceedings of the Forty-fourth Annual Congress of Cities,* Washington, D.C., 1968.

———: *Proceedings of the Forty-fifth Annual Congress of Cities,* Washington, D.C., 1969.

———: *Proceedings of the Forty-sixth Annual Congress of Cities,* Washington, D.C., 1970.

———: *Analysis of State Administration of Planning Funds under the Omnibus Crime Control and Safe Streets Act of 1968,* Washington, D.C., 1969.

——— and the United States Conference of Mayors: *Street Crime and Safe Streets— What Is the Impact?,* Washington, D.C., 1971.

Office of the Vice President: *The Vice President's Handbook for Local Officials,* Government Printing Office, 1968.

Peabody, Robert L., and Nelson Polsby (eds.): *New Perspectives on the House of Representatives,* Rand McNally, Chicago, 1963.

Ransone, Coleman B., Jr.: *The Office of Governor in the United States,* University of Alabama Press, University, Ala., 1956.

Reichly, A. James: "The Political Containment of Cities," in Alan K. Campbell (ed.), *The States and the Urban Crisis,* Prentice-Hall, Englewood Cliffs, N.J., 1970.

Ripley, Randall: *Power in the Senate,* St. Martin's Press, New York, 1969.

Ruchelman, Leondard I. (ed.): *Big City Mayors,* University of Indiana Press, Bloomington, Ind., 1969.

Sanford, Terry: *Storm Over the States,* McGraw-Hill, New York, 1967.

Sayre, Wallace S., and Herbert Kaufman: *Governing New York City,* Norton, New York, 1965.

Schlesinger, Joseph A.: *How They Became Governor,* Michigan State University Press, East Lansing, Mich., 1957.

Schultze, Charles L.: *The Politics and Economics of Public Spending,* Brookings, Washington, D.C., 1968.

Segal, Morley, and A. Lee Fritschler: "Policy-making in the Intergovernmental System," paper presented at the Sixty-sixth Annual Meeting of the American Political Science Association, Los Angeles, September 8, 1970.

Sharkansky, Ira: *The Maligned States,* McGraw-Hill, New York, 1972.

Stanback, Thomas N.: *The Metropolitan Economy,* Columbia University Press, New York, 1970.

Stanfield, Rochelle: "Intergovernmental Relations: The Role and Program of the Council of State Governments," Internal working document prepared for the National Governors' Conference, Washington, D.C., 1968 (mimeographed).

Sundquist, James L.: *Politics and Policy,* Brookings, Washington, D.C., 1968.

Talbot, Allan R.: *The Mayor's Game,* Praeger, New York, 1970.

Tolchin, Martin and Susan: *To the Victor,* Random House, New York, 1971.

Truman, David B.: *The Governmental Process,* Knopf, New York, 1951.

———: *The Congressional Party,* Wiley, New York, 1959.

Udell, Jerry: "The Governors' Ambassadors," unpublished master's thesis, American University, Washington, D.C., 1966.

United States Conference of Mayors: *Proceedings of the Thirty-second Annual Meeting,* Washington, D.C., 1965.

———: *Proceedings of the Thirty-third Annual Meeting,* Washington, D.C., 1966.

———: *Proceedings of the Thirty-fourth Annual Meeting,* Washington, D.C., 1967.

———: *Proceedings of the Thirty-fifth Annual Meeting,* Washington, D.C., 1968.

———: *Proceedings of the Thirty-sixth Annual Meeting,* Washington, D.C., 1969.

———: *Proceedings of the Thirty-seventh Annual Meeting,* Washington, D.C., 1970.

———: *The Mayor and Federal Aid,* Washington, D.C., 1968.

Weidenbaum, Murray: *The Modern Public Sector,* Basic Books, New York, 1969.

White, Leonard D.: *The States and the Nation,* Louisiana State University Press, Baton Rouge, La., 1953.

Weintraub, Robert A.: *Options for Meeting the Revenue Needs of the City Government,* Report by TEMPO, Santa Barbara, Calif., January 1967.

Wildavsky, Aaron: *The Politics of the Budgetary Process,* Little, Brown, Boston, 1964.

———: "The Two Presidencies," in Aaron Wildavsky (ed.), *The Presidency,* Little, Brown, Boston, 1970.

Wilson, Woodrow: *Constitutional Government in the United States,* Columbia University Press, New York, 1908.

Wright, Deil S.: *Federal Grants-in-Aid: Perspectives and Alternatives,* American Enterprise Institute, Washington, D.C., 1968.

———: "Governors, Grants, and the Intergovernmental System," in Thad Beyle and J. Oliver Williams (eds.), *The American Governor in Behavioral Perspective,* Harper and Row, New York, 1972.

Wood, Robert C.: *1400 Governments*, Harvard University Press, Cambridge, Mass., 1961.

———: *The Necessary Majority*, Columbia University Press, New York, 1972.

ARTICLES

Anton, Thomas: "Roles and Symbols in the Determination of State Expenditures," *Midwest Journal of Political Science*, 11:27–43, February 1967.

"A Tax Incentive That's Coming under Fire," *U.S. News and World Report*, June 12, 1967, pp. 94–95.

Bailey, Stephen K.: "Co-ordinating the Great Society," *Reporter Magazine*, March 24, 1966, pp. 39–41.

Banfield, Edward C.: "Revenue Sharing in Theory and Practice," *Public Interest*, 23: 38–46, Spring 1971.

Berryhill, John: "AASHO Fires Opening Salvo and the Post 1975 Highway Battle Begins," *Nation's Cities*, September 1967, pp. 15–18.

Crihfield, Brevard: "Future Operations of the Council of State Governments," *State Government*, 40:16–20, Winter 1967.

Congressional Quarterly Weekly Reports, 25(December 15, 1967):254; 26(January 19, 1968):2; 26(May 24, 1968):1198–1200; 26(June 21, 1968):1550; 26(July 19, 1968):1796–1800; 26(August 2, 1968):2041–2049; 27(January 31, 1969):202; 36(September 5, 1969):1642–1643; 28(March 20, 1970):825–826; 28(April 17, 1970):1018; 39(January 29, 1971):213–225; 39(June 11, 1971):1272–1274.

Cottin, Jonathan: "Washington Pressures: National Governors' Conference," *National Journal*, 21:454–459, February 28, 1970.

Elazar, Daniel J.: "Are We A Nation of Cities?" *Public Interest*, 4:42–58, Summer 1966.

———: "Urban Problems and the Federal Government," *Political Science Quarterly*, 82:520–525, December 1967.

"Expanded NLC/USCM Services for America's Cities," *Nation's Cities*, June 1969, pp. 19–45.

Farkas, Suzanne: "The Federal Role in Urban Decentralization," *American Behavioral Scientist*, 15:15–35, September–October 1971.

"Financing Our Urban Needs," *Nation's Cities*, March 1969, pp. 19–50.

"Five Former Governors Appraise the Governors' Conference," *State Government*, 31:168–172, Summer, 1958.

Gilbert, Charles E.: "Of Marble Games and Stately Mansions," *Public Administration Review*, 29:87–94, January/February 1969.

Gitell, Marilyn: "Metropolitan Mayors: Dead End," *Public Administration Review*, 23:18–24 January/February 1963.

Green, Edith: "Who Should Administer the War on Poverty?" *American County Government*, January 1968, pp. 8–10.

Grodzins, Morton: "American Political Parties and the American System," *Western Political Science Quarterly,* 38:984, December 1960.

Harmon, B. Douglas: "The Bloc Grant: Readings From a Fiscal Experiment," *Public Administration Review,* 30:141–152, Spring 1970.

Harris, Joseph: "The Governors' Conference: Retrospect and Prospect," *State Government,* 31:190–196, Summer 1958.

Harris, Richard: "Annals of Legislation: The Turning Point," *New Yorker Magazine,* December 14, 1968, pp. 68–178.

Hartman, Richard: "Regional Review?" *American County Government,* June 1968, pp. 56–59.

Healy, Patrick: "Editorial," *Nation's Cities,* November 1971, p. 6.

Hillenbrand, Bernard F.: "COGS: An Idea Whose Time Has Come," *American County Government,* June 1967, pp. 5–7.

————: "The County as a Regional Government," *American County Government,* September 1966, pp. 6–66.

————: "The Snake Pit of Revenue Bonds," *American County Government,* July 1967, pp. 8–9.

Knecht, Robert W.: "Land Use Planning at the Crossroads," *Nation's Cities,* June 1971, pp. 30–33.

Ladd, Everett, Jr., Charles Hadley, and Lauriston King: "A New Political Realignment?" *Public Interest,* 23:46–63, Spring 1971.

Latham, Earl: "The Group Basis of Politics: Notes for a Theory," *American Political Science Review,* 46:3, June 1952.

Leach, Richard H.: "Federalism: The Continuing Predicament," *Public Administration Review,* 31:222–224, March 1971.

Martin, James L.: "Let's Reorganize the War on Poverty," *American County Government,* February 1967, pp. 11–12.

"National Governors' Conference": *State Government,* 33(Summer 1960):154–187; 35(Autumn 1962):222–260; 37(Summer 1964):143–174; 38(Autumn 1965): 219–243; 39(Summer 1966):181–186; 40(Winter 1967):15–23; 41(Winter 1968):17–30.

National Journal, 2(June 6, 1970):1193–1206; 2(September 19, 1970):1840–1841; 2(November 21, 1970):2550–2553; 3(January 9, 1971):59–67; 2(January 31, 1971):244; 3(April 3, 1971):704–736; 3(April 10, 1971):761–784; 3(May 29, 1971):1138; 3(September 11, 1971):1969–1975; 4(January 29, 1972):181–192; 4(February 12, 1972):264–275; 4(March 4, 1972):395; 4(March 18, 1972): 484–492; 4(May 27, 1972):895; 4(July 15, 1972):1143–1144; 4(October 7, 1972):1564–1566; 4(December 16, 1972):1908–1944; 5(March 10, 1973):360; 5(April 14, 1973):531–534; 5(June 30, 1973):935–943; 5(July 28, 1973):1099–1108.

"National Municipal Policy for 1972," *Nation's Cities,* February 1972, pp. 8–9.

"The NLC: To Safeguard and Improve City Government," *Nation's Cities,* March 1972, pp. 17–34.

Nolan, Martin: "Muskie of Maine," *Reporter Magazine,* July 13, 1967, pp. 44–46.

Pechman, Joseph: "The Rich, the Poor, and the Taxes They Pay," *Public Interest,* 17:36–41, Fall 1969.

Pomper, Gerald L.: "Census '70: Power to the Suburbs," *Washington Monthly,* 2: 20–24, May 1970.

Powledge, Fred: "The Flight from City Hall," *Harper's Magazine,* November 1969, pp. 69–86.

Pritchard, Allan E.: "The National Municipal Policy," *Nation's Cities,* November 1968, pp. 14–20.

Ransone, Coleman B., Jr.: "Scholarly Revolt in Dullsville: New Approaches to the Study of State Government," *Public Administration Review,* 26:343–352, December 1966.

"Recommendations of the National Governors' Conference on Juvenile Delinquency," *State Government,* 40:16–20, Winter 1967.

"Revenue Sharing: Who'd Get What," *U.S. News and World Report,* July 2, 1972, pp. 46–47.

Schlesinger, Joseph A.: "The Governor's Place in American Politics," *Public Administration Review,* 30:2–10, January/February 1970.

Schick, Allan: "The Budget Bureau That Was: Thoughts on the Rise, Decline, and Future of a Presidential Agency," *Brookings Reprints* (1971).

Stenberg, Carl W. and David B. Walker: "Federalism and the Academic Community: A Brief Survey," *P.S.,* 2:155–167, Spring 1969.

Sternlieb, George: "The City as Sandbox," *Public Interest,* 25:14–21, Fall 1971.

Ways, Max: "Creative Federalism and the Great Society," *Fortune Magazine,* January 1966, pp. 121–228.

Wilson, James Q.: "The War on Cities," *Public Interest,* 3:31, Spring 1966.

———: "The Mayors vs. the Cities," *Public Interest,* 16:25–40, Summer 1969.

Wilson, Pete: "Nixon's Urban Record," *City,* Fall 1972, pp. 7–8.

Wright, Deil S.: "The Advisory Commission on Intergovernmental Relations," *Public Administration Review,* 25:196–198, September 1965.

———: "Executive Leadership in State Administration," *Midwest Journal of Political Science,* 11:1–26, February 1967.

———: "The States and Intergovernmental Relations," *Publius,* 1:7–76, Winter 1972.

NEWSPAPERS

The New York Times, November 4; December 16, 1966; July 2, 1967; December 7, 10, 21, 1969; January 4, October 10, 1970; January 27, March 28, July 16, August 14, December 1, 1971; June 18, 21, 1973.

The Wall Street Journal, September 1, October 10, 1967; June 13, 28, 1972; June 13, 1973.

The Washington Post, February 15, September 2, 1969.

GOVERNMENT DOCUMENTS

Advisory Commission on Intergovernmental Relations, *Eighth Annual Report,* Washington, D.C., 1967, p. 4.

——— : *Ninth Annual Report,* Washington, D.C., 1968.

——— : *Tenth Annual Report,* Washington, D.C., 1969, p. 8.

——— : *Eleventh Annual Report,* Washington, D.C., 1970, pp. 2, 3, 6, 8, 20–32.

——— : *Twelfth Annual Report,* Washington, D.C., 1971, pp. 1–5.

——— : *Thirteenth Annual Report,* Washington, D.C., 1972, p. 55.

——— : *Fourteenth Annual Report,* Washington, D.C., 1973. p. 26.

——— : *A State Response to Urban Problems,* Washington, D.C., 1970.

——— : "Annual Report on Operations Under Bureau of Budget Circular A-85," Washington, D.C., December 1969.

——— : *County Reform,* Washington, D.C., 1971, p.1.

——— : *Fiscal Balance in the American Federal System,* vol. 1., Washington, D.C., 1967, pp. 55, 87–99; 115, 151–155.

——— : *Profile of County Government,* Washington, D.C., 1972, p.1.

——— : *Making the Safe Streets Act Work,* Washington, D.C., 1970.

——— : *Special Revenue Sharing Analysis,* Washington, D.C., 1970, pp. 22–37.

——— : *The Gap between Federal Aid Authorizations and Appropriations, Fiscal Years 1966-1970,* Washington, D.C., 1970, p. 1.

——— : *Urban America and the Federal System,* Washington, D.C., 1969.

Anti-Crime Program, Hearings before Subcommittee No. 5, House Judiciary Committee, 90th Cong., 1st Sess., 1967, pp. 65; 321–323; 435–442; 499–505; 1425–1443.

After 1975 Highway Program of AASHO, Hearings before the Subcommittee on Roads, House Public Works Committee, 90th Cong., 2nd Sess., 1968.

Commission on Law Enforcement and the Administration of Justice: Report of the Commission, *The Challenge of Crime in a Free Society,* Government Printing Office, 1967, pp. 55, 279.

Congressional Record, 112, 89th Cong., 2nd Sess., 1966, 6834; 113, 90th Cong., 1st Sess., 1967, S. 16023–16025.

Comptroller General of the United States: *Review of Economic Opportunity Programs,* Washington, D.C., 1969, p. 54.

Controlling Crime through More Effective Law Enforcement, Hearings before the Subcommittee on Criminal Laws and Procedures, Senate Judiciary Committee, 90th Cong., 1st Sess., 1967.

Creative Federalism, Hearings before the Subcommittee on Intergovernmental Relations, Senate Government Operations Committee, 89th Cong., 2nd Sess., 1966, pt. 1, pp. 270; 390–397.

Creative Federalism, Hearings before the Subcommittee on Intergovernmental Relations, Senate Government Operations Committee, 90th Cong., 1st Sess., 1967, pt. 2A–2B, pp. 858–859.

Demonstration Cities and Metropolitan Development Act of 1966, H. Rept. 1931, 89th Cong., 2nd Sess., 1966, pp. 133–156.

Economic Opportunity Act of 1964, Hearings before the House Committee on Education and Labor, 88th Cong., 2nd Sess., 1964, Vol. I–II, pp. 22–25; 389–390; 766–767; 780; 825; 903.

Economic Opportunity Amendments of 1967, H. Rept. 866, 90th Cong., 1st Sess., 1967.

Effectiveness of Metropolitan Planning, Study prepared for the Subcommittee on Intergovernmental Relations, Senate Committee on Government Operations, 87th Cong., 2nd Sess., 1962.

Federal Aid Highway Act of 1968, Hearings before the Subcommittee on Roads, House Committee on Public Works, 90th Cong., 2nd Sess., 1968, pp. 26–27.

Federal Aid Highway Act of 1968, Conf. Rept. 1790, 90th Cong., 2nd Sess., 1968.

Federal Assistance to Law Enforcement, Hearings before the Subcommittee on Criminal Laws and Procedures, Senate Judiciary Committee, 91st Cong., 2d. Sess., 1970, pp. 413–474.

Federal Role in Urban Affairs, Hearings before the Subcommittee on Executive Reorganization, Senate Government Operations Committee, 89th Cong., 1st Sess., 1966, pt. 3, p. 636.

Federal Role in Urban Affairs, Hearings before the Subcommittee on Executive Reorganization, Senate Government Operations Committee, 90th Cong., 1st Sess., 1967, pt. 20, pp. 4317–4318.

Federal-State-Local Relations, Hearings before a Subcommittee, House Government Operations Committee, 85th Cong., 2nd Sess., 1958.

The Federal System as Seen by State and Local Officials, A Study prepared by the staff of the Subcommittee on Intergovernmental Relations, Senate Committee on Government Operations, 89th Cong., 1st Sess., 1965, pp. 2, 203–214.

Financing Municipal Facilities, Hearings before the Subcommittee on Economic Progress, Joint Economic Committee, 90th Cong., 1st Sess., 1967, pt. 1.

General Revenue Sharing, Hearings before the House Ways and Means Committee, 92nd Cong., 1st Sess., 1971, pt. 2, pp. 237, 257, 268, 273; pt. 5 pp. 804, 833; pt. 6, pp. 1026–1027.

Impact of Federal Urban Development Programs on Local Government Organization and Planning, Report prepared by the Advisory Commission on Intergovernmental Relations in cooperation with the Subcommittee on Intergovernmental Relations, Senate Committee on Government Operations, 88th Cong., 2nd Sess., 1964, pp. 1–5.

Intergovernmental Cooperation Act of 1967 and Related Legislation, Hearings before the Subcommittee on Intergovernmental Relations, Senate Committee on Government Operations, 90th Cong., 2nd Sess., 1968, pp. 90–100.

Intergovernmental Cooperation, Hearings before a Subcommittee on Government Operations, 90th Cong., 2nd Sess., 1968, pp. 96–103.

Intergovernmental Cooperation Act of 1972, Committee on Government Operations, U.S. Senate, 92nd Cong., 2d Sess., 1972, S. Rept. 92–1109, pp. 2–5.

Intergovernmental Revenue Act of 1971 and Related Legislation, Hearings before the Subcommittee on Intergovernmental Relations, Senate Committee on Government Operations, 92nd Cong., 1st Sess., 1971, pp. 213–230.

Juvenile Delinquency Prevention Act of 1967, Hearings before the General Education Subcommittee, House Committee on Education and Labor, 90th Cong., 1st Sess., 1967, pp. 13–81; 285–287; and 490–491.

Juvenile Delinquency Prevention Act of 1968, S. Rept. 1332, 90th Cong., 2nd Sess., 1968, pp. 20–23.

Law Enforcement Assistance Amendments, Hearings before the House Judiciary Committee, Subcommittee No. 5, 91st Cong., 2nd Sess., 1970, pp. 104–133; 293–323.

Metropolitan America: Challenge to Federalism, Report submitted to the Subcommittee on Intergovernmental Relations by the Advisory Commission on Intergovernmental Relations, House Committee on Government Operations, 89th Cong., 2nd Sess., 1966, p. 9.

National Growth Policy, Hearings before the Subcommittee on Housing, House Banking and Currency Committee, 92nd Cong., 2d Sess., 1972, pp. 1–74.

Omnibus Crime Control Act of 1970, U.S. Congress, House of Representatives, 91st Cong., 2d Sess., 1970 H. Rept. 91–1768.

Preliminary Report of AASHO on Federal Aid Highway Needs After 1972, Hearings before the House Committee on Public Works, 90th Cong., 1st Sess., 1967.

Replies from State and Local Governments to Questionnaire on Intergovernmental Relations, H. Rept. 575, House Committee on Government Operations, 85th Cong., 1st Sess., 1957.

Ten-Year Record of the Advisory Commission on Intergovernmental Relations, Joint Hearings by the Intergovernmental Relations Subcommittees of the House and Senate Government Operations Committees, 92nd Cong., 1st Sess., 1971.

U.S. Bureau of the Budget: "Bureau of the Budget Circulars of Interest to State and Local Governments," Washington, D.C., December 1968.

———: *Special Analyses,* Budget of the United States, Fiscal Year 1970. Government Printing Office, 1969, pp. 201–202, 209.

U.S. Office of Management and Budget: *Special Analyses,* Budget of the United States, Fiscal Year 1973, Government Printing Office, 1972, p. 9.

———: *United States Budget in Brief,* Fiscal Year 1974, Government Printing Office, 1973, pp. 3–4, 8, 29.

U.S. Office of Economic Opportunity: *Community Action Guide,* vol. 1, Government Printing Office, 1965.

U.S. President: "Quality of American Government," Message from President Lyndon B. Johnson to Congress, H. Doc. 90, 90th Cong., 1st Sess., March 20, 1967.

INDEX